The Other Side of Western Civilization:
Readings in Everyday Life

Volume II

under the general editorship of John Morton Blum

Yale University

The Other Side of Western Civilization

Readings in Everyday Life

Volume II: The Sixteenth Century to the Present

Edited by Peter N. Stearns

Rutgers University

HARCOURT BRACE JOVANOVICH, INC.

New York   Chicago   San Francisco   Atlanta

ISBN: 0-15-567647-4

Library of Congress Catalog Card Number: 72-94550

Printed in the United States of America

PICTURE CREDITS

Cover: Amsterdam, Holland. Bicycles in rush-hour traffic. At right, a monument to the resistance fighters. Fritz Henle, PHOTO RESEARCHERS, INC.

Page 12: (Top) Pinel unshackles the insane at the Salpetriere in Paris. From the painting by Robert T. Fleury. THE BETTMANN ARCHIVE, INC. (Bottom) *The Hartley Colliery Disaster*. Reading the Queen's letter of sympathy. Painting by H. J. Emmerson. THE BETTMANN ARCHIVE, INC.

Page 86: (Top left) *Tu me porteras comme cela tous les soirs* by N. Maurin. THE BETTMANN ARCHIVE, INC. (Top right) Pickpocket steals handbag of woman shopper. Seventeenth-century engraving. THE BETTMANN ARCHIVE, INC. (Bottom) *The Uprising (L'Emeute)* by Daumier. PHILLIPS COLLECTION, WASHINGTON.

Page 154: (Top) *The Village School* by T. Webster. THE BETTMANN ARCHIVE, INC. (Bottom) Factory for silk hats. Ca. 1900. All work done manually by women. THE BETTMANN ARCHIVE, INC.

Page 218: (Top left) Pregnant woman in Wales. Bruce Davidson, MAGNUM PHOTOS, INC. (Bottom left) West German worker. Leonard Freed, MAGNUM PHOTOS, INC. (Right) High school students in West Berlin. Leonard Freed, MAGNUM PHOTOS, INC.

Page 294: London underground. Richard Wood, BLACK STAR.

Preface

This volume focuses on the involvement of the common people of Europe in some of the massive social changes that have occurred over the past three hundred years as Western society became more urban and industrial. Unlike most surveys, its major concern is not with the leaders of society, the prominent people whose names and deeds are well known and whose importance is obvious, but with the masses of ordinary people, the "inarticulate," whose impact on history is not well documented. The intent is to provide some insight into the impact of change on the daily lives of these people, and through this insight to promote a better understanding of the nature of modern society and how it evolved.

In order to make valid judgments about how liberating or oppressive modernization has been, the nature of premodern society must first be analyzed and evaluated. In addition, the origins of social change must be ascertained: was change imposed on the masses by forces beyond their control, or did the people actively participate in the construction of modern society? The opening selections of this book deal with these issues, and because they represent a number of different interpretations, the student may assess for himself the impact of change, the adjustments it promoted, and the resistance it provoked.

Some of the topics dealt with in this volume are relatively familiar: the meaning of political involvement in the modern world, the nature of industrial work, and the plight of the industrial worker. Other subjects covered here, however, are less common: the evolution of the family, the impact of modernization on women, the rise of new attitudes toward madness and deviant social behavior, and the changing nature of sexual relationships. These topics rarely, if ever, receive the attention they deserve in standard works on European history. Though the actions and values of most people were undoubtedly affected by the policies set forth by society's leaders (and a number of essays in this book discuss this connection), the masses of people shaped society through their own actions. Modern civilization may owe as much to the changes in sexual behavior and family life that occurred among young peasants and workers in the eighteenth century as it does to the ideas of enlightened thinkers or the governmental policies established by enlightened despots.

Obviously, this collection focuses on only some of the many facets of the modern history of Europe's people. Even for the topics studied, the selections presented here could be enhanced by additional essays, and the bibliographies provide numerous suggestions for further reading. While not intended to be a collection of debates, the volume presents a number of different viewpoints. The essays included here were chosen with an eye to recent research presented in a stimulating manner and with an awareness of the major conceptual problems involved.

A number of people provided vital assistance in the preparation of this book. I am grateful to those who read and commented on the original plan for this work: J. Kim Munholland, University of Minnesota; James T. Sheehan, Northwestern University; Mack Walker, Cornell University; and especially Edward Shorter, University of Toronto, whose reviews of the manuscript stimulated several constructive revisions. My wife, Nancy, helped in a number of respects. The editorial and production staffs at Harcourt Brace Jovanovich were of great aid. For suggesting readings and for other assistance, I also thank Howard Zehr, Peter Meyers, and Patricia Uttrachi. I am, finally, grateful to the many students, both graduate and undergraduate, at Rutgers University who have helped me apply some of the key problems of modernization to the study and teaching of European social history.

Peter N. Stearns

Contents

* The first page number refers to the headnote, the second to the selection proper.

Topical Table of Contents

The Other Side of Western Civilization:
Readings in Everyday Life

Volume II

Introduction

Most of the people who lived in the past rarely appear in historical studies. It is, of course, true that most of the histories of European civilization concentrate on rather small groups of people—the thinkers, the artists, the political leaders. The importance of the elites is undeniable. In addition, these people have left unusually clear records, so that historians can study them without too much difficulty. But their acts and ideas form only a part of human history. This book focuses on the other, and possibly the more important, part. It deals with groups of people who are rarely heard from in surveys of Western civilization—women and workers, criminals and the insane, ordinary soldiers and peasants. They are a diverse lot, but they have in common the fact that contemporary social elites and later historians usually regarded them as inarticulate. Popular revolutions periodically brought them on the scene of history, but in normal times they were largely ignored.

Most elites in the past, and most historians more recently, have tended to think of ordinary people in rather simple categories. This does not necessarily mean that they were insensitive to them, but it does suggest that they knew rather little about them. Until the nineteenth century most ordinary people in Europe were peasants, a word that immediately suggests a variety of images, for even the most conventional historical surveys say something about peasants. According to the simplest definition, although peasants rebelled occasionally, they normally valued tradition and stability and changed little. But did peasants have a changing history, or were they a mindless constant beneath the surface of great events? In fact, from time to time peasants' families changed, their economic habits and values changed, their definitions of crime and morality changed. Peasant families rose and fell in social standing, often with great rapidity. Many of them moved about; many welcomed new ideas and methods, and some even produced them, although peasants tended to resist novelty. We should not be content with merely occasional references to the millions of people who were peasants in Europe as Western civilization developed. Although we cannot know the details of their individual lives and ideas, we must seek to fill in broader generalizations. We must keep in mind that simply knowing that a peasantry existed means little unless we also know what trends were operating in each major period and area. In some periods peasants regularly practiced infanticide because they could not support the children born to them; in others they were eager to have many children, and not just because of special economic opportunities. Peasant culture was not a constant, yet from its evolution in western Europe came much of modern civilization.

The masses of people in the last two centuries have received more attention, if only because they have impinged more often on the political process. But still, many aspects of their lives are ignored, while others are subjected to judgments by people who are remote from their ordinary existence. Working-class families have decayed, say many conservatives who deplore modern times. Many socialists, seeking to condemn the disruptive effects of capitalism, agree. Few scholars have even tried to look at the actual evolution of family patterns. With rare exceptions, until recently, the history of the masses received attention only when the masses rocked the boat, annoying conservatives and giving heart to radicals. But protest, although important, is too difficult to be normal for people whose lives are demanding in the best of times; so most of the history of people long went untouched.

A great deal of historical research is now being devoted to the history of "inarticulate" people. It is now becoming clear that historians have regarded these people as mute in part because they themselves have not tried to listen. To be sure, it is much more difficult to know what "the workers" thought than it is to outline the philosophy of Descartes. Some speculation, some historical intuition is essential if we are to get at popular ideas, which means that there is considerable room for disagreement. The history of the inarticulate is a rather new field of study. It is rife with debate (and it is exciting for this very reason), but already some points are reasonably well established. Aspects of popular behavior can be measured with some precision, even if the outlook that prompted the behavior is more difficult to determine. The common people had ideas, and they left their own kinds of records. In protest, in crime, in family behavior, and in religious practices we can discern the mentality of the broad masses of people, even those who lived centuries ago. We can know how many people were born and died, how they structured their families, how often they rioted. Now that historians are looking for them, the sources of information about the inarticulate are proving abundant, even overwhelming. They are different kinds of sources from those historians have been accustomed to. Many of them reveal information only about large groups of people rather than about individuals. Yet we cannot pretend that resurrecting a mass of new names for students to learn would prove useful; we need to know about major types of people, not about individuals. But there are individual records as well, to rescue this new kind of history from impersonality. Criminals, workers, and many others have left statements of what their lives were like and what they thought about.

So we can learn about the common people. But why should we want to? E. P. Thompson has argued eloquently that the common people must be rescued from "the enormous condescension of posterity." He means, among other things, that history, even when written by radical historians, has usually had an upper-class bias, regarding the mass of humanity as a silent lump to be shaped or abused by the elites. This is a valid point, which does not mean that one has to be a political radical to appreciate the history of the inarticulate.

In adding a vast new dimension to what we can learn about people, the history of the inarticulate fascinates many students of the past—but not all. Many historians and students of history continue to be most interested in the great men and the great ideas. Some people, however, who were never able to get terribly excited about the "greats" can find a new meaning in history through studying the masses; others who began with a conventional interest in history may decide that the real meaning of history lies in this new approach and the issues it raises.

Reactions of this sort are personal, of course. But whether or not one is really enthusiastic about studying the history of the inarticulate, there are three reasons why students should know something about it. First, the history of the common people provides one measure of the nature and quality of civilization. Did peasants and artisans gain a new outlook during the Italian Renaissance? Did their lives change, and, if so, did the changes follow the same direction as those of the political and intellectual elites? Many thinkers of the Enlightenment urged humanitarianism and a belief in progress. When and to what extent did such beliefs enter the popular mentality? We cannot fully determine the historical importance of great men and great ideas unless we know what impact they had on the bulk of society. Often the process of dissemination is more important than the initial cause.

Furthermore, we must dispel the notion that the masses of people have not themselves been active agents in history, although perhaps they have reacted to outside forces more than they have acted spontaneously. In many of the readings in this volume, this point is implicitly debated. Did the common people adopt more modern attitudes toward work and sex because they were prodded and compelled to do so by forces from above, or did they have, to some extent at least, their own reasons for changing their outlook? There is no question that the common people had an important voice in determining exactly how they adapted to change. They often resisted change as well, and their resistance could have been an important historical force in its own right. When masses of people changed their views about their sexual goals or about how many children to have, they played a direct role in altering the course of history.

These arguments apply to the history of the common people at any place and time. There is a final, more specific reason for studying the common people in modern times. The simple fact is that most of us judge modern society by different criteria from those most historians have used in judging the past. Perhaps we shouldn't, but we do. Many of us think of our own time more in terms of divorce rates and crime rates than in terms of, say, artistic achievements. We think in terms of the quality and nature of life of *most people*, and this means that we need histories of precisely these areas. Has the suicide rate been rising or falling in modern societies? Has child abuse increased or decreased as families have grown smaller and child-rearing changed? Hopefully, someday students of modern history will have as much information on patterns of this sort, and as satisfactory explanations for major changes in these patterns, as they now have with regard to formal political theory and the development of new forms of government.

We return here to the point that historians have ignored many significant developments in the past. What has been studied in most Western civilization surveys is vitally important, but it is incomplete. We are left without genuine historical knowledge of many of the features of our own society that are closest to us, and, hence, in a real sense we cannot assess the direction our society is taking. For example, until recently historians have virtually ignored the history of crime, while piling study upon study of the details of diplomatic interchanges. Historians are empiricists; they learn from observation and therefore need sources; sources from diplomats are more abundant than sources from criminals. So historians tend to study diplomats, although it might be argued that criminals are at least as important in shaping society. (Some might even argue that the different labels exaggerate the differences between the two groups.) But the fact that diplomats are more honored than criminals by historians leads us to assume that their historical importance is greater, until we think about our own times and realize that most of us devote a great deal of attention to crime and its significance for us personally and for our society.

Historians need not pretend that every current opinion reflects an important historical reality, for some who demand that history be "relevant" really mean only that it should reinforce their own views of what should happen from here on. But history *is* relevant. We can't understand crime today if we don't know about crime in the past, for we have no sense of direction or means of comparison. We have no way of knowing if crime is rising, falling, changing in nature, or staying the same. Yet contemporary comments on crime often assume a historical knowledge. Newspaper accounts, for example, talk about rising crime as an inescapable aspect of modern urban society. This is a historical judgment, but in view of how little is generally known about the history of crime, it is an invalid historical judgment. Modern urbanization has not necessarily produced more crime; the situation is more complex.

The readings in this book suggest the directions in which the masses of people in Europe have been heading during the broad process of modernization. They deal with some of the main problems that preoccupy us in trying to evaluate the present, giving at least the beginnings of a historical dimension to such aspects of human behavior as sex and violence in modern times.

The term *modernization* is a broad one. The process began in Europe during the sixteenth and seventeenth centuries. It has included the steady growth of central governments and the development of new state functions. Political modernization includes not only more direct contact between the government and individual citizens, but also a keen sense of loyalty to the state and nation on the part of most citizens. It has been argued that only two forms of government are possible in a truly modern society, democracy, and totalitarianism, because modern people either must have an outlet for their demands or, if they do not have such an outlet, must be actively propagandized and policed. Political modernization, then, involves both the form and function of government and the political attitudes of the citizenry. Economic modernization also involves new values as well as new institutions. Industrialization means factories, new kinds of cities, new economic activities for the state; it also means new motives for work, new kinds of protest, new kinds of family life.

Modernization thus encompasses many of the key developments of recent human history, and since modernization began in western Europe, we can hope to find some of the key causes of the process by studying the evolution of European history. What was there in Western civilization that opened the way to such vast change? We can look for specific developments in the sixteenth and seventeenth centuries, but in all probability the quest should reach into still earlier history. European technology, for example, was the most advanced in the world by the late Middle Ages, although Europe was far from being the most civilized part of the world according to other criteria. It can be suggested that Western man developed a distinctive attitude toward the exploitation of nature and material advance, which was then vastly heightened as outright modernization began.

Modernization in Europe took place in a society with strong traditions. It was to occur in North America as well—in some ways more rapidly— and tradition had a role to play here too; it is nonsense to claim that Americans freed themselves from custom in crossing the Atlantic or moving west. In many ways, European and American modernization was a single process pitted against the same traditions, but the traditions were stronger in Europe. Peasant life, particularly, was firmly entrenched in Europe, whereas a peasantry never developed in North America. The study of European modernization, therefore, is more revealing of the stresses of modernization that have occurred or are likely to occur in other parts of the world, than is a study of a frontier society such as the United States.

Certainly, European modernization has differed in important ways from the process in the United States, in part because of the distinctive leavening of traditional forces. The modern European family is not the same as its American counterpart. Nor is modern European crime. Nor is the modern European welfare state. In these and other instances, similar trends are at work on both continents, but they often take different specific expressions. Despite this, it is worthwhile to compare Europe's modernization with our own. We might learn something about ourselves that a preoccupation with self-examination ironically can cause us to overlook.

A study of the impact of modernization on the common people, whether in Europe or elsewhere, invites some value judgments, and a word must be said about these in advance. The term *modernization* may be a loaded one, suggesting a kind of blanket approval of change, for many people have been conditioned to believe that what is modern is what is good. This is profoundly different from the traditional outlook, which tended to look to the past for standards. We know that formal Christianity saw a golden age in the past (although, significantly, it looked forward to a brighter future as well). Before the onset of modernization, peasants tended to believe that rural society had been better in past ages; artisans looked back to the ideals of the early guilds. Indeed the common people had little historical sense and tended to merge past with present. Since modernization, however, we have become acutely, perhaps exaggeratedly, conscious of how different we are, and often how much better we are than our predecessors. So when we talk of something becoming more modern, we may be too quick to praise or at least to find the development entirely natural and easily understandable. For example, one important aspect of modernization is the development of a belief in the possibility and desirability of material progress, for oneself as well as for society as a whole. Most Americans probably find this a good change, at least when contrasted with the resignation and stagnancy of a more traditional view. A minority—those concerned about the ecological damage that material progress can cause, for instance—would find this aspect of modernization dangerous. But almost everyone would find it natural. It's hard for us to believe that people might think anything else. Economic thought from the early nineteenth century onward has assumed that the goal of "economic man" is to maximize his wealth. Yet, even applied to most people in the nineteenth century, this is not a proper historical view. Interest in material improvement constituted a profound change in the popular mentality. It came slowly and, in fact, has not yet been completed. "Modernization" is probably not a sufficiently neutral word to describe what it must describe, but we have not yet found a better one.

Our focus on the common people may appeal to a different set of values, leading to a condemnation of trends within modern society itself. Debates over the effects of industrialization and urban growth on the lower classes, for example, began a century and a half ago, and they continue today. Historians still argue over whether material conditions improved during the first stage of British industrialization, and the topic is important in the history of any area undergoing the initial stages of an industrial revolution. This is an important question, for conditions in such a formative stage of working-class life may have influenced outlook to such an extent that attitudes and behavior persisted even after the material setting changed. But our concern is broader, for we are trying to assess general outlook and style of life, and not just of workers but of other groups as well. Still, some of the problems of interpretation are similar, for if one dislikes contemporary society, it is easy to emphasize how much people have suffered since its inception; or, if one finds current conditions improving, it is tempting to assume a constant process once traditional society began to break down. In the British standard of living debate, historians favorable to capitalism and convinced of the essential soundness of the modern world generally try to show that conditions were improving even during early industrialization. Leftist historians, who dislike capitalism and commiserate with the workers, invariably look for signs of deterioration. Note that the connection between political judgment and historical judgment is not entirely logical. One could well argue that capitalism has proved a good thing in the long run and that modern life is lovely, even for the workers, while admitting that in the first stage of industrialization conditions deteriorated. Or one could urge the need for fundamental reforms in modern life while admitting that conditions have improved somewhat compared with pre-industrial times. Obviously, ideological commitments can predetermine an approach—and most of us have an ideology, even if it is not neatly labeled. Changes in mood can also change our historical perspective. What American, in the 1970s, after a decade of riot and assassination, can blithely assume our superiority to Europe? Yet twenty years ago it was normal for intelligent historians to focus on Europe's instability and bellicosity. Perspectives change quickly, as do historical trends, which means that it may be impossible to offer a simple characterization of any of the developments affecting the common people during the modernization process. But the most common impulse, among historians who have dealt with the inarticulate, is to find an example to support one's own reaction to modern life, whether that example is valid or invalid.

The readings that follow present a variety of approaches, some commending the liberating aspects of modernization, others stressing the deterioration. Few historians who deal with these vital topics content themselves with simply saying that things have changed, which might be the most objective view. They generally try to assess the quality of that change. Try to study the modern history of women, for example, without asking whether things have been getting better or worse. Many now argue that with modernization and the decline in the family as a productive unit, women's inferior status became more pronounced, for her economic utility was less obvious and her dependence on her husband greater. Others point to better education and the declining birth rate as indications of improvements in women's lot.

Each student of history must make up his own mind about trends. Two preliminary points should be kept in mind. First, most historians who have been drawn to the study of the common people have sympathized with their lot. They tend to dwell on their hardships and to see their subjects as victimized by some outside force—workers by capitalists, women by men, and so on. It is important also to study the ways in which the common people adjusted to their situations and the values they used and changed in doing so. It is important to see the common people as an active force, not just in protest—though this is a significant aspect of their lives—but also in shaping family structure, recreational patterns, and so on. This view is quite consistent with an emphasis on the hardships of life, but it goes beyond a dreary catalogue of exploitation. More generally, any judgment of trends must use some basis of comparison. Too often this basis is not clearly spelled out. If a historian argues that the horizons of middle-class women in Victorian England were becoming more limited, he must describe an antecedent situation in which they were less so.

Overall, most large evaluations of modernization involve an implicit or explicit comparison with premodern life. We have to know where we came from to know where we are going.

In fact, whether one is a historian or not, it is impossible to study modernity without asking "where from?"—which is of course a historical question. Any journalist or politician who claims that values or behavior patterns are changing or that violence is rising or falling or that a situation is unprecedented is making a historical judgment, and it would be well if he made it intelligently. Some of the judgments are short term, of course. It is possible and useful to compare crime rates and patterns of the 1960s with those of the 1920s. But the larger evaluations, those, for example, which are concerned with the nature of industrial life or of urban man, involve or should involve a knowledge of the premodern world. We have no other way to assess the direction of change, and we are far from agreeing on this direction, for our knowledge of facts is limited. So is our ability to cut through biases and slogans. We hear of the loosening of family ties; we therefore assume that premodern families were close knit and jolly—but has the subject really been studied? Only a historical view can tell us the extent to which present problems are recent and human-caused, as opposed to being durable reflections of human nature or at least the nature of Western man. Divorce, for example, is a rather new institution, but does it signify a really new problem in family life or does it represent a new answer to a persistent tension? We must look at the past to find out. We might avoid a lot of nonsense from advocates of the brand new as well as critics of the present if we required every statement of "never before" or "a sign of these troubled times"—unquestionably judgments of present in terms of past—to be backed by solid historical evidence. This book stems from the need to approach key trends in modern life in the only way they can really be understood.

The book does not cover all the major topics in the history of the common people during the centuries of modernization. It would be fascinating to trace, for example, the interaction between people and modern medicine. The profession of medicine was modernized in the nineteenth century: formal medical societies and licensing became increasingly important—though self-professed "quacks" could still be found in London in the 1880s. Traditionally inferior branches of medicine, such as surgery and dentistry, became highly regarded professions. Interestingly, most of this happened before huge advances in medical techniques. But popular attitudes to medicine remain an uncharted territory. We know that traditionally the urban lower classes looked on hospitals as alien institutions to which one would go only to die. When did this attitude change, and to what extent? The question is intimately bound up with the problem of the general belief in progress. When did people start to believe that their own health could improve? A German woman around 1900 expressed the traditional view: "God is the best doctor. If he wishes, I'm healthy. Otherwise not." Correspondingly she, and most workers up to this time, even in industrially advanced England, devoted little or no expenditure to medical care. But we do not know enough about the social history of medicine to venture more than impressions at this point. Even many of the topics dealt with in this book have only been outlined. There is insufficient information on many of them; there is great disagreement on many of them. We are not in total ignorance, though, and the whole issue of modernization is so essential that we cannot constantly beg off on grounds of insufficient information. If we are to understand ourselves and our society, we must venture a genuine historical view of such topics as the evolution of family life or the situation of women. Confusing signals and outright disagreement add spice to our effort to know.

The readings that follow are arranged more or less chronologically, but they can also be grouped into eight topics that cover essential aspects of the formation of a modern outlook in the general population. Readings on rural society discuss the nature of preindustrial life, which was overwhelmingly agrarian, and allow an assessment of the changes in the countryside in more recent times. A section on modern attitudes presents varying interpretations of where we are now. Two large groupings of the inarticulate, women and workers, receive extensive treatment, and the readings on workers discuss the nature of industrial work in general. The family is elaborately studied, for it was and remains a basic institution in the lives of most people, although its nature has changed in a number of respects. The family must be understood if we are to comprehend what values children bring into adulthood. Its strength or weakness helps us measure the extent to which key groups were able to adapt to modernization at various points. Readings on education and popular culture deal both with the formal values taught to the lower classes and with new types of recreation that played a growing role in life outside of school and work. Discussions of crime and related subjects consider changes in forms of individual protest and maladjustment, while readings on protest concern the evolution of the forms and goals of collective action.

The focus is for the most part on western Europe, where the process of modernization began, and where it has gone farthest. The history of modernization in other regions is equally interesting and important, but many of the major issues and trends can be suggested within the more familiar context of Britain, France, and Germany. Even this zone is by no means homogeneous. The process of modernization has important general features in common, but national and regional differences are important in any detailed study. The readings that follow, although not explicitly comparative, allow some assessment of the differences in rates and patterns of change from one country to the next. But the main focus is on developments of wide applicability, even where regional variations would modify the basic generalizations to some extent.

Because historians are just beginning to sketch the history of the common people, we cannot easily pinpoint where decisive breaks occurred. Conventional periodization (1715–63, 1870–1914, and so on) has little relevance, for the lives of most people were not always decisively shaped by the doings of diplomats and politicians. Indeed, we should probably seek a decade or more in which some measurable change occurred—when rapid population growth began or waned, for example—rather than a single year. The chronological organization of this book is meant to be loose and suggestive, but it does provide a necessary framework. The first section, 1550–1750, allows an understanding of the society and the traditions that were to change; but the period itself saw important developments that set the basis for modernization. Between 1750 and 1850 the confrontation between tradition and change was extremely intense. Industrialization began but was not yet dominant, while the attitudes of ordinary people began to take more modern form. Between 1850 and 1914 the nature of industrial society became far clearer. Problems of adaptation remained, but they were more subtle. To many Europeans, this period seemed a golden age, at least in retrospect. However, those who lived through it, outside of the upper classes, may have judged it differently. The period from 1918 to the present opened with the intense dislocation caused by the First World War. The confused nature of European society between the wars is important in its own right and in its contribution to more enduring social trends. But the overriding theme of the twentieth century is the extent to which a new society is taking shape and what kind of society it is. Many observers talk of a postmodern or postindustrial age; we must try to find out what this means in human terms.

The history of the common people is a new kind of history in many ways, but it is not a total departure. It involves a testing of many conventional historical themes to see what impact major ideas and political forms had on the masses. Hence, while the readings that follow do consider some unusual subjects, they can and should be linked to the more obvious developments in modern European history. Rural society was clearly affected by religious doctrine and organization. The spread of popular education involved a deliberate attempt to inculcate attitudes such as nationalism, liberalism, and a belief in science and progress. New forms of protest related to changes in political ideology, most obviously the rise of socialism. The world workers lived in was conditioned by state action and the actions of employers, and these can in turn be assessed in terms of liberalism and other political doctrines. Connections of this sort are not always simple. One cannot assume that liberal ideas about the treatment of workers fully describe the actual ideas of employers, even employers who claimed to be liberal. But the connections are there, and they clearly relate the history of the common people to history in general. Other links can be found as well. We will see how the rise of rationalism changed the definition of madness and, therefore, the attitudes toward the treatment of insanity. Changes in the family or in sexual behavior cannot be understood solely in terms of formal ideas or political activities, but they are not entirely independent either. By the late eighteenth century, people in Europe seemed to have gained a new interest in romantic, or at least sensual, love. Surely this must have helped cause the rise of romanticism, or at least that aspect which stressed human emotions. The historian deepens his understanding of the common themes in political and intellectual history by understanding their relationship with the world of the common people.

Bibliography

A bibliography follows the introduction to each section, to provide further reading on each of the topics covered. There is no general survey of the period from 1600 to the present that satisfactorily covers the subjects included in this volume. For the first part of the period, Fernand Braudel, *Civilisation matérielle et capitalisme (XVe–XVIIIe siècle)* (Paris, 1967), constitutes a major study. Henry Kamen, *The Iron Century: Social Change in Europe 1550–1660* (New York, 1971), stresses development among the lower classes. Important works on industrialization include David Landes, *The Unbound Prometheus: Technological Change and Industrial Development in Western Europe from 1750 to the Present* (New York, 1969), and Alexander Gerschenkron, *Economic Backwardness in Historical Perspective* (Cambridge, Mass., 1962). W. W. Rostow, *The Stages of Economic Growth* (New York, 1960), is a controversial work that suggests an economic periodization possibly related to major stages in the broader modernization process. Cyril Black, *The Dynamics of Modernization: A Study in Comparative History* (New York, 1966), offers a historical sketch of the general process. A major interpretation of basic types of modernization is Barrington Moore, *Social Origins of Dictatorship and Democracy* (Boston, 1966). A more general survey is Peter N. Stearns, *European Society in Upheaval* (New York, 1967).

P A R T 1

Premodern People, 1550-1750

The modern world, young as it is in the span of human history, has broken decisively with the past. Yet we must begin with the past to understand modernity.

Premodern society was never static, and many changes occurred in Europe between 1550 and 1750. Since the end of the Middle Ages, Europe had witnessed important shifts in population levels, social structure, and popular culture. By the sixteenth and seventeenth centuries, some of the changes began to point toward the formation of modern society. Under absolutism, governments became more centralized and efficient. Most of these governments encouraged economic change, if only in the interest of augmenting the tax base for the royal coffers. By the early eighteenth century, several governments were promoting the cultivation of new crops, such as the potato, and establishing new factories, which encouraged the utilization of new machinery.

During the eighteenth century, the tone of intellectual life was dramatically altered. Leading intellectuals vaunted man's power to reason and the possibility of progress. They urged further scientific and technological advances. God and religion receded in importance, and in some cases were directly attacked—the new world of the intellectuals was aggressively secular. This period, called the Enlightenment, marked the beginning of the scientific revolution.

Somewhat apart from both government and intellectuals, a variety of businessmen and landowners, primarily in Britain and Holland, were experimenting with new techniques and new forms of organization. New crops, drainage methods, and farming equipment began to increase agricultural production. Many landowners—and not just those who directed great estates—began to produce primarily for sales to distant markets. In business, the most spectacular innovators were the merchants who organized great trading companies for worldwide commerce. New systems of investing and accounting developed. Manufacturing changed more slowly. By the eighteenth century, manufacturers were rapidly extending the systems of rural manufacture, drawing hundreds of thousands of peasants into a new market system. The manufacturers provided raw materials and sold the finished products. The rural worker set up a loom or a spindle in his home and produced what he was told to produce. Never before had so many people been involved in a capitalistic production system.

Government, intellectuals, entrepreneurs—three obvious and important sources of change, though historians still debate their relative importance and their interconnections, and we are still far from understanding the dynamics of initial modernization. The new entrepreneurs, for example, knew little about scientific discoveries or the growing belief in progress. They increased industrial production by applying new techniques, but most of the techniques were devised by artisans. It is more likely that their success led the industrialists to their belief in science and progress than vice versa. The essays that follow, however, deal with groups that were remote from the most obvious sources of change. The majority of Europe's preindustrial people were rural and were wedded to a belief in a stable society. The rural population was diverse, including landowning peasants, near-landless cottagers, and artisans. But the common people of the countryside, as well as most of their counterparts in the cities, shared a set of values that was fundamentally opposed to change.

Even a brief glimpse at Europe's preindustrial people must raise two vital and related issues. First of all, a judgment about the nature of preindustrial life is essential in order to assess the impact of modernization. If rural life was in fact comfortable and secure, surely the advent of industrialization and urban life must have been profoundly disruptive. If, on the other hand, rural life was marked by persistent tension and frustration, perhaps change was welcome. (We need not, of course, regard the preindustrial lower classes as homogeneous. Certain areas, personality types, or even age groups may have been particularly restless.)

The second question that must be dealt with is the extent to which the common people of Europe, or at least of western Europe, actively contributed to modernization. We might assume that most change came from above—from the governments, intellectuals, and entrepreneurs—and that the common people were forced into new political and economic roles. This approach would presumably be the most compatible with a belief that modernization imposed profound dislocation on most people. But perhaps some change was spontaneous, stemming from the values of the common people themselves. There is evidence that these values were changing, at least by the eighteenth century. The spread of domestic manufacturing, for example, though sponsored in part by urban capitalists, found a quick response in the countryside. Rural workers learned new consumption habits —they adopted more urban styles of dress and bought processed food products such as tea and sugar. This was the first step, perhaps, in a new esteem for material acquisitions that would ultimately prove vital for the industrialization process. Family patterns also changed; many rural workers began to marry at an earlier age.

In other words, the lower classes in preindustrial western Europe may have been ripe for change. Although no one can deny that disruption was involved—bringing not only material hardship, but intense psychic stress—the common people may have been more than passive victims in the modernization process. Indeed, it was from their ranks that some of the key innovators stemmed. The ancestors of most of the dynamic factory owners of the early nineteenth century could be found, a hundred years earlier, among the peasants and artisans. Their rise was unusual, but it may have drawn on an openness to change that was more widely shared and that served to cushion the shock of modernization for those who remained in the lower classes.

So we are trying to determine both the distance Europeans had to travel to become "modern" and the extent to which they launched the process themselves in the seventeenth and eighteenth centuries. Obviously, any discussion of the values of ordinary people is a chancy business, even for the present day. For the premodern period, historians must use very fragmentary records. In a few cases there is good statistical evidence on behavior patterns—size of families, for example—but the question of the motives and values that gave rise to the patterns is open to speculation.

This means that the historian's own preconceptions can take on added importance. There has been a constant tendency to idealize the past. As far back as the beginning of the nineteenth century, many people turned to the preindustrial past as a solace from the evils of the present. Even late into the nineteenth century, workers retained a nostalgia for the countryside, although they seldom acted on it. In the United States, as in Europe, "back to the land" impulses continue to appear, based at least in part on a belief in the purity and simplicity of preindustrial existence. Not surprisingly, many of the historians who try to assess this existence have similar yearnings. Since the peasants and artisans left few direct records of their thoughts, making it impossible ever to be absolutely certain how they viewed their own life, it is all too easy for the nostalgic historian to fill in the gaps with his own projections of what preindustrial life must have been like.

The study of preindustrial society, in America and in Europe, is being actively pursued on a number of fronts. We are beginning to know more. We can already come to some tentative conclusions about why modernization began on the shores of the Atlantic and what impact it had on the people involved.

Bibliography

Studies of preindustrial rural society are somewhat sparse. In addition to the works by Bloch, Laslett, and Goubert, see B. H. Slicher Van Bath, *The Agrarian History of Western Europe A.D. 500–1850* (New York, 1963), and Robert Trow-Smith, *Life from the Land: The Growth of Farming in Western Europe* (New York, 1967), which deal with the traditional rural economy. Traian Stoianovich, *A Study in Balkan Civilization* (New York, 1967), outlines a society unique in some respects, but one perhaps more genuinely "premodern" than the society of western Europe. Early changes in English rural life are discussed in Joan Thirsk, ed., *The Agrarian History of England 1500–1640* (Cambridge, Eng., 1967); Charles Wilson, *England's Apprenticeship* (New York, 1965); and G. R. Mingay, *English Landed Society in the Eighteenth Century* (Toronto, 1963). John Lough, *An Introduction to Seventeenth Century France*, 2nd ed., (New York, 1969), is a valuable survey of French society and politics. Although it deals with the end of the eighteenth century, Charles Tilly, *The Vendée* (New York, 1967), shows the impact of economic change on peasants and the readiness of some to come to grips with it in contrast to the bitter resistance of others—a division that depended on an earlier exposure to a market economy.

There are few historical studies of madness. Michel Foucault, *Madness and Civilization*, trans. by Richard Howard (New York, 1965), offers a sweeping interpretation. George Rosen has published other works on the history of the insane and their treatment in his collection *Madness in Society: Chapters in the Historical Sociology of Mental Illness* (New York, 1968). Changes in attitude toward the insane in America are suggested in David Rothman, *The Discovery of the Asylum: Social Order and Disorder in the New Republic* (Boston, 1971), and Gerald N. Grob, *The State and the Mentally Ill: A History of the Worcester State Hospital in Massachusetts* (Chapel Hill, 1966).

The preindustrial family is beginning to receive considerable attention. A pioneering work, with an important general thesis about the development of the modern family, is Philippe Ariès, *Centuries of Childhood: A Social History of Family Life* (New York, 1962). Two recent histories of French villages provide important information on family structure: Thomas Sheppard, *Lourmarin in the Eighteenth Century: A Study of a French Village* (Baltimore, 1971), and Patrice Higonnet, *Pont-de-Montvert: Social Structure and Politics in a French Village, 1700–1914* (Cambridge, Mass., 1971). Another major work on the period, though with an American focus, is Philip J. Greven, Jr., *Four Generations: Population, Land, and Family in Colonial Andover, Massachusetts* (Ithaca, 1970).

On changes in the nature and rhythm of work, E. P. Thompson, *The Making of the English Working Class* (New York, 1964); W. G. Hoskins, *The Midland Peasant: The Economic and Social History of a Leicestershire Village* (New York, 1957); and three classic studies by J. L. and Barbara Hammond: *The Village Labourer, 1760–1832* (New York, 1970 [Reprint of 1911 edition]), *The Town Labourer, 1760–1832* (New York, 1968 [Reprint of 1917 edition]), and *The Skilled Labourer, 1760–1832* (New York, 1970 [Reprint of 1919 edition]).

French Rural History

MARC BLOCH

Marc Bloch, a French historian and one of the first to undertake a systematic study of past societies, presents an ambiguous picture of the key values and structures of French rural life in the sixteenth and seventeenth centuries. On the one hand there is an emphasis on the tightly knit community. Not only economic and recreational activity, but also protest stemmed from the close links among residents of a single village. Community loyalty was reinforced by religion and other traditional rituals. Yet rural society was changing, largely due to the pressure exerted by outside forces. New laws, new impositions by landlords could not easily be resisted. Institutions crucial to community life, such as the common lands, began to erode, albeit slowly.

But not all change resulted from external pressures. Bloch's study suggests some changes within peasant society itself. Beginning in the later Middle Ages, peasant life became more individuated. The focus shifted from strong extended families—groupings that included three generations and a vast array of collateral relatives—to the single household of parents and children. Ownership and control of noncommon lands shifted accordingly. Peasants in western Europe began to marry later, reducing their birth rates and thereby preserving the family lands against the pressure of too many heirs. Adoption of this birth control procedure, stemming apparently from a keen sense of individual family property, was unusual in peasant societies, where early marriage was generally the accepted norm.

In other words, peasants in western Europe abandoned some key traditions quite early. The rise of market agriculture and capitalistic farming was imposed upon them to a great extent. They used their sense of tradition and community values to protest, although ineffectively. But their own modifications of tradition and community structure, however gradual, left the way open for further change.

The individuals and families who cultivated the same ground and whose houses stood close to one another in the same hamlet or village were not separate individuals and separate families, living side by side. They were neighbours, *voisins*—in Frankish times this was their official title, as it has always been in Gascony—linked by economic and sentimental ties and form-

From Marc Bloch, *French Rural History*, translated by Janet Sondheime (Berkeley: University of California Press, 1970), pp. 167–71, 180–89. Originally published by the University of California Press; reprinted by permission of The Regents of the University of California and Routledge & Kegan Paul Ltd., London.

ing the small society of the "rural community" which was the ancestor of most of the communes—or communal subdivisions—existing in our own day. . . .

The territorial limits of a rural community were those containing the land subject to the various rules of communal husbandry (which dealt with temporary cultivation, grazing on the commons, dates of harvests etc.) and to the performance of collective services for the benefit of the group as a whole; its boundaries were especially clear-cut in unenclosed regions where nucleated settlement was the rule. The *seigneurie* consisted, amongst other things, of the land subject to the payment of rents and services to a single lord, and over which he exercised his rights to aid and his power to coerce. Were the two coterminous? Sometimes, as in the new settlements, they must have been. But this was not always or even most frequently the case. Naturally our information is fullest for more recent periods, when very many of the older *seigneuries* had already been broken up by alienations and, still more frequently, by subinfeudation. But even in Frankish times a *villa* often contained *manses* dispersed over different villages. The same is true of all the countries of Europe where the seigneurial regime was in operation. If it is true that we should regard the Frankish and French lords as the latter-day heirs of the ancient village chieftains, we should add that it was apparently possible for a number of separate authorities to flourish side by side in the same place. This simple topographical observation is in itself sufficient refutation of the idea that the rural community could ever have been completely absorbed by the *seigneurie*. Conscious of its unity, the rural group could react just as vigorously as any urban community to the break-up of a *seigneurie*. For example, the lands and village of Hermonville in Champagne came to be divided among eight or nine sub-fiefs, each with its own court; but from 1320 at latest the inhabitants appointed their own communal officers to enforce agrarian discipline, irrespective of *seigneurie*.

It was above all in dealing with its enemies that the small rural collective not only became more conscious of its own identity but also gradually forced society as a whole to accept it as a viable and living institution.

The principal targets for opposition, which was often accompanied by violence, were the masters. "How many serfs have killed their lords and burned their castles!" exclaims Jacques de Vitry in the thirteenth century. Flemish "slaves" whose plotting was denounced in a capitulary of 821, Norman peasants massacred around the year 1000 by the ducal host, peasants of the Sénonais who in 1315 elected a "king" and "pope" as their commanders, Jacques and Tuchins in the time of the Hundred Years' War, the peasant leagues in Dauphiné massacred at Moirans in 1580, the "Tards Avisés" of Périgord under Henry IV, the Breton *croquants* strung up by "the good Duke" of Chaulnes, the incendiaries of castles and archives in the blazing summer of 1789—all were so many links (and many have been omitted) in a long and tragic chain. Shocked and surprised, Taine described the last act of the drama, the upheavals he witnessed in 1789, as "spontaneous anarchy." But there was nothing novel about this "anarchy." What appeared a newly-minted outrage in the eyes of the ill-instructed philosopher was little more than the recurrence of a traditional phenomenon which had long been endemic. The forms rebellion took (and they were nearly always the same) were also traditional: mystical fantasies; a powerful preoccupation with the primitive egalitarianism of the Gospels, which took hold of humble minds well before the Reformation; lists of grievances in which precise and often far-reaching proposals were mingled with a host of petty complaints and often quite ludicrous suggestions for reform (the Breton *Code päisant* of 1675 called indiscriminately for the abolition of tithes, to be replaced by a fixed stipend for parish priests, for limitations on hunting rights and seigneurial monopolies and for the distribution of tobacco with the blessed bread at Mass, purchased with money raised from taxation, "for the satisfaction of the parishioners"). Finally, at the head of these "stiff-necked" yokels as the old texts describe them, as leaders of this stubborn people who were "unwilling," as Alain Chartier said, "to suffer the subjection of the *seigneurie*," one nearly always finds a few country priests, whose plight was often no better than that of their parishioners but whose minds could better encompass the idea that their miseries were part of a general ill; in a word, men well-fitted to play the time-honoured role of the intellectual by acting as leaven in the long-suffering masses. None of these traits is specifically French; they are common to peasant revolts all over Europe. A social system is characterized not only by its internal structure but also by the reactions it produces; a system based on authority at times may result in the sincere performance of mutual obligations, at others in a brutal outbreak of hostility on both sides. To the historian, whose task is merely to observe and explain the connections between phenomena, agrarian revolt is as natural to the seigneurial regime as strikes, let us say, are to large-scale capitalism.

Almost invariably doomed to defeat and eventual massacre, the great insurrections were altogether too disorganised to achieve any lasting result. The patient, silent struggles stubbornly carried on by rural communities over the years would accomplish more than these flashes in the pan. During the Middle Ages the consolidation of the village as a group and its recognition by the outside world was a constant preoccupation of peasant life. These goals were sometimes achieved by concentrating on the village in its ecclesiastical aspect. The parish, whose territory in some places was co-extensive with that of a single community although in others it might embrace several, had one or other of the local lords as its master; he was in the habit of appointing the priest, either directly or by nomination to the bishop, and of appropriating some part of the dues which should have gone towards the maintenance of church services. But it was precisely because the lord was more concerned to profit from these dues than to employ them for their proper ends that the parishioners were able to take his place and undertake what he neglected, in particular the upkeep of the church. The church was the only really large and solid structure in the village, towering above the huddle of dwellings; might not the House of God serve also as a house for the people? Meetings for the discussion of communal affairs were held in the church—except when men preferred to gather under the shade of the elm tree at the crossroads or among the grass of the cemetery; at times the church was used for the storage of surplus produce, to the great indignation of academic theologians; in time of danger it was the place of refuge, a centre of resistance even. The men of the Middle Ages found it easier than we do to treat sacred things with a familiarity from which reverence was not excluded. Many places started, at latest in the thirteenth century, to elect "parochial church councils" or "fabrics," which had official ecclesiastical sanction; here was yet another opportunity for the inhabitants to meet and debate their common affairs, in short, to become aware of the solidarity of their common interests. . . .

The bond created by collective obligations in the cultivation of the arable was strong; but stronger still was the bond uniting a village group which possessed common lands, no matter what agrarian regime prevailed over the rest of the fields. As Rétif de la Bretonne observed, writing at the end of the eighteenth century: "the little parish of Saci, since it has commons, governs itself like a large family."

The commons had multifarious uses. Waste or woodland supplied livestock with the additional grazing which was normally indispensable, even where there was access to meadows and fallow land. Woodland was also a source of timber and of the many other useful products found in the neighbourhood of trees. Marshland provided peat and rushes; from heathland came brush for bedding, turves, and broom or bracken for mulches. Last but not least, in many regions the commons acted as a reserve of arable, used for temporary cropping. It goes without saying that the use of the commons was subject to regulation; otherwise agrarian life would have come to a standstill, especially in the earlier periods when agriculture offered little scope to individuals working on their own account and few goods could be purchased from the minimal proceeds of small independent holdings. What we have to discover is not whether rules existed but how they were applied at different times and in different regions.

The exploitation of these valuable possessions sometimes led to the formation of a group larger than the village. So we find an extensive tract of heath or forest (such as the forest of Roumare in Normandy), and more frequently still the slopes of a mountain, in the joint occupation of several communities; these might be products of the break-up of a larger grouping, or communities which had originally been independent, but were persuaded by necessity to co-operate with their neighbours over the use of intervening territory. One example is the confederations of the Pyrenees *vallées*, where pasturage was the cementing bond. In most cases, however, commons were exclusive to a single village or hamlet and formed an adjunct to the arable.

In legal terms, the ideal "commons" would be land unencumbered by any property rights other than those of the group, the type of land known to medieval law as "allodial," although in this instance possessed by the inhabitants jointly. Although examples of collective allods exist, they are extremely rare. It is far more usual to find the commons, like the rest of the village lands, subject to a complex tissue of rights claimed by a whole hierarchy of interested parties: the lord, the lord's lord and the body of the peasantry. The exact limits of these rights long remained unclear, far longer in fact than was normally the case with individual holdings. Definition was achieved only as the result of bitterly contested litigation.

This battle over the common lands was to be expected. The commons had always been a cause of dissension between the lord and his subjects. A Frankish legal formula from the ninth century (it was actually written down at the Swabian monastery of St. Gall, but could just as easily have come from Francia) refers to litigation between a religious community and the occupiers over the exploitation of a forest. Over the centuries, encroachment on common land figures as one of the oldest and most constant grounds for agrarian revolt. William of Jumièges says of the Norman peasants who revolted about the year 1000 "they sought to bend the customs concerning ponds, rivers and forests to their own laws." Under the pen of the poet Wace, writing a little later, this becomes a fiery challenge: "In numbers we are many—let the knights then feel our strength—then we can go to the woods as we will—to cut the trees and take our pick—to catch the fish as they swim—to chase the deer through the forests—to do there what we please—in the clearings, waters and trees." The feeling that wild places and water, untouched by human hand, could not lawfully be appropriated by an individual was deep-rooted in man's primitive social conscience. A religious of Chartreuse, writing at the end of the eleventh century, says of a lord who had violated custom by making the monks pay grazing rights: "against all justice, he withheld grass which God ordained the earth to produce for the nourishment of all beasts."

However, so long as unoccupied land was plentiful, the struggle over waste and woodland was not very acute. Nor was there any urgent need to define the legal status of the commons. The lord usually enjoyed the same rights over grazing land and forest as he did over the arable: rights, that is to say, which were superior but not necessarily supreme, since he was himself usually the vassal of another baron and bound by ties of homage on his own account, so that over and above his rights might tower the edifice of a whole feudal hierarchy. Let us concentrate, however, on the immediate lord of the village, the first link in the chain of vassalage. The users of the uncultivated ground, that is to say the villagers, were obliged (either individually or collectively) to pay the lord rent in recognition of his superior right. Can we then say that the commons belonged to him? If we do, we shall be speaking recklessly: for peasant customs—to which the lord himself, in his capacity as producer, also subscribed—were in their own way as powerful as any laws. They had all the authority and protection of tradition; in medieval speech the lands subject to communal use were popularly referred to as the "*coutumes*" or "customs" of the village, a highly revealing expression. A perfect manifestation of this outlook is to be seen in the inventories of the Frankish period, which in listing the appurtenances of a *villa* rarely fail to mention the presence of *communia*. Here indeed is a seeming paradox: why should anyone include "common lands" among the possessions of a private individual who was free to alienate, sell or enfeoff his properties at will? The reason is that the *seigneurie* covered more than the demesne directly exploited by its master. It also embraced territories which were merely under his dominion and from which he could exact charges, that is to say, the lands held in tenure (even where they were hereditary) and the commons: and these last were the subject of collective rights which had to be respected just as scrupulously as the individual seisin of each tenant. The *Customs of Barcelona*, which applied at this period to Roussillon, declare c. 1070 that "the public highways and byways, running water and springs, meadows, pastures, forests, heaths and rocks . . . are not to be held by lords as though they were '*in alodium*'— that is to say without regard to rights other than their own—nor are they to be maintained on their *dominicum* in any other way than that their people may always be able to use them."

Then came the great clearances, which meant that uncultivated land became scarcer; and a new, more acute phase of the conflict began. The lords were not as a rule tempted to encroach on the commons so as to increase their own arable—demesnes were everywhere dwindling; when seigneurial officials ordered the ploughing up of grazing used by the common herd, it was because the ground was wanted for allocation to tenants. The fields thus won brought great gains to their cultivators and to the lords who benefited from their rents; but the community as a whole lost both its rights of usage and the unrestricted opportunity for making assarts. In other instances the lord's invasion of the commons was prompted by the desire to exploit them directly, usually by converting them into grazing reserved exclusively for his own stock: in this period of diminishing demesnes, seigneurial husbandry was concentrated far more on sheep-farming, with its minimal demands on labour, than on tillage. Alternatively, there was the possibility of exploiting a particular commodity produced by the waste. We have an example of this from about the year 1200, reported by the cleric Lambert d'Ardres: "about this time Manasse, the elder son of the count of Guines . . . ordered that the peat be dug out and cut into blocks from a marshy pasture which had formerly been granted to all the inhabitants of the parish of Andres as common land." The lords appear at their most covetous where the common land happened to be planted with trees; for as we have seen, timber was becoming more and more valuable. How did the law stand in all these cases? The truth is that the boundaries of legal definition were so uncertain that even the most scrupulous of men could feel at a loss; more than one nobleman no doubt found himself justifying his usurpation of common land, at least in his own sight, by the thought expressed with such candour in 1442 by the squire of Sénas after he had seized the waste in his Provençal village: "reason shows that there must be a difference between the lord and his subjects." But the peasants did not suffer in silence. Often the dispute was concluded by a "cantonment," a partition between the lord and the villagers. This meant that the lord gained full control over part of the formerly undivided commons, while the community, usually in return for a rent, retained the use, "aisement," of the rest. In many places, therefore, the crisis had the effect of securing official recognition for the rights of the group over at least a part of the ancient communia: and a fair number of our existing townships can trace the origin of their lands back to agreements of this kind.

With the sixteenth century a new and still graver crisis was precipitated. This was the time when the rejuvenated seigneurial class was concentrating all its energy and skill on the reintegration of great estates. Townsmen and prosperous peasants followed their example in accumulating properties. The revolution in legal thought came just at the right moment to support these ambitions. The jurists were now hard at work constructing a clear concept of ownership to replace the tissue of superimposed rights over property. Commons, like other land, had to have a dominus, in the Roman sense. In general the dominus was identified as the lord. This purely theoretical notion was backed up by a hypothesis concerning the origins of the lord's ownership, a theory which has even been advanced, surprising though it may seem, by historians of our own day. It was asserted that at first the commons had belonged to the lords alone; the inhabitants only enjoyed the use of them in virtue of concessions made down the centuries—which is to say that the village must always be younger than its lord! These theorists had naturally no intention of sacrificing whatever rights communities had won for themselves. But, in keeping with a line of jurisprudence which had been developing from the thirteenth century, they were in general only prepared to accept as valid those rights which had been sanctioned by the payment of a fee: "concessions" made out of pure generosity unsupported by any formal deed appeared insubstantial and, what is more, left room to doubt whether there ever had been any "concession" or merely a usurpation on the part of the villagers. This progress towards definition was attended by many hesitations and qualifications. Professors of law, practising lawyers, administrators—all were engaged in unconcerted and not very successful attempts at classifying the mass of communal properties in a manner which took account of the conflicting rights, unequal in force, claimed by the lord and his men. Imbued with this spirit and armed with doctrine, the lords, their legal advisers and even the courts (strongly influenced by respect for rank) felt entitled to adopt a simpler and cruder view. In 1736 the Procurator-General of the Parlement of Rennes adopted the seigneurial thesis in its most unequivocal form: "all the heaths, *galois* and empty and waste spaces in Brittany are within the demesne of the Lords of the Fief." Under a deed dated 20 June 1270 the lord of Couchey (Burgundy) was forbidden to alienate "the commons of the village" without the consent of the inhabitants given in due form; yet notwithstanding this explicit prohibition, from 1386 the Duke's Council, followed at a distance of some three and a half centuries (1733) by the Parlement, held that "the squares, streets, by-ways, footpaths, grazing grounds . . . and other common places" of the village could be treated by the lord as he willed, since they were his. In 1777 the Parlement of Douai refused to register an edict in which there was mention of properties "belonging" to the communities; the phrase should have run: "properties used by the communities."

To sum up, from the sixteenth century the attack on common lands was renewed with unprecedented vigour, as is only too evident from the stream of complaints from villagers, carried up to the Provincial Estates or the Estates General.

The attack took a variety of forms; the first to be noticed is barefaced usurpation. The lords were abusing their authority and judicial powers, as we learn from the deputies of the Third Estate in their address to the Estates of Blois in 1576. "There are those who have made themselves judges in their own cause, who have seized and apprehended the customs, empty places, heaths and commons which are enjoyed by the poor subjects, and who have even taken away the papers by which their good right is shown." Rich proprietors, peasants among them, were quick to take advantage of this favourable conjuncture, whose influence, according to an eighteenth century agronomist, could be seen triumphantly at work all over the country. In 1747 the people of Cros-Bas in Auvergne complained that "Geraud Salat-Patagon, an inhabitant of the said village . . . has taken it on himself, . . . since he is rich and cock of the walk, to shut and enclose the greater part of the commons pertaining to the said village and join them to his fields."

Encroachment was sometimes effected under more specious forms, legally almost above reproach. A prosperous *laboureur* might acquire the lease of part of the commons at too low a price. Or a lord might insist on partition (*cantonment*), a relatively harmless manoeuvre so long as the conditions were not too unfavourable to the community. But many lords demanded as much as a third of the land so divided; this was the right of *triage*, which with legal backing became widespread in post-medieval centuries and in 1669 received pusillanimous recognition from the Crown. Admittedly, in theory *triage* was held to apply only in certain circumstances, notably where the initial alleged concession had been gratuitous. In practice these qualifications, which in any case still left room for numerous claims, were not always scrupulously observed.

Finally, it must be noted that the peasants were often in debt, not only as individuals (we have already seen that loans were raised for the purchase of advantageous parcels by men who were extending their holdings) but also collectively. The debts, which might be heavy, were incurred by expenditure in the common interest, necessitated for example by reconstruction in the wake of war, and above all by the need to meet the pressing demands of royal and seigneurial taxation. How tempting it must have been to discharge this burden by selling all or part of the commons! The lords readily supported such moves, either because they saw themselves as prospective purchasers or else because they hoped, by invoking their right to *triage* as indemnity for the loss of their superior right over the soil, to take a share of the cake at no personal expense. The law and custom of Lorraine was so extreme on this point that it recognised the lord's right to a third of the purchase price obtained by the villagers. Official suspicion was sometimes aroused by these sales, either because the alleged reason appeared dubious—a royal ordinance of 1647 claimed that some persons setting out to "fleece" the villages had saddled them with "fictitious" debts—or else because of the conditions attached to fixing the price. But the pressure of self-interested parties and the deplorable financial situation of many small rural groups (often also victims of mismanagement) combined to make such sales inevitable. Between 1590 and 1662 the village of Champdôtre in Burgundy sold its commons three times over: the first two transactions were cancelled as fraudulent or erroneous; the last—to the purchasers concerned in the second attempt—was final.

The movement naturally encountered some fierce resistance. It is true that even where abuse was most flagrant, the peasants often hesitated to take on a struggle in which the odds were heavily against them. As the intendant of Dijon remarked in 1667 "since all commons have been usurped and are possessed either by the lords of the communities or by persons in authority, the poor peasants will not dream of complaining if they are ill-treated." This opinion is corroborated by Fréminville, the great authority on estate management: "will any villagers dare to incur the disfavour of a powerful lord?" But not all were so easily intimidated. Towards the beginning of the eighteenth century many Breton lords started leasing out heathlands to contractors in timber or for commercial farming. The limits of such appropriations were marked by sizeable earth embankments, thrown up round the portion of land withdrawn from communal use; and these irksome symbolic enclosures were often attacked by armed mobs. The Parlement was ready to take punitive measures, but it was impossible to find witnesses. After several embankments on Plourivo heath had been destroyed in this way, the lord published warning notices "in order to bring the guilty parties to light." But one fine day a gallows appeared on the boundary between the two parishes concerned; at its feet was a pit with the inscription "anyone who surrenders will find himself in here."

The peasants were not alone in their efforts to check the movement.

They had some support from the monarchy and its officials, who cherished rural groups as a source of taxes and soldiers. Starting in 1560 with the Ordinance of Orleans, which deprived lords of their judgment "*en souveraineté*" of suits relating to commons, a whole series of edicts was issued, some of general, some of local application, which prohibited alienations, annulled sales or *triages* concluded after a given date, and initiated enquiries into rights usurped from communities. The Parlements supported the lords in their aggressions; the intendants, their habitual enemies, in the seventeenth century embraced the opposite cause. At the time, this policy was so obviously the right one for any state at all mindful of its interests that it is no surprise to see it in action elsewhere, in the duchy of Lorraine for example. The shift in government sympathies—the concomitant of what amounted to a total reversal of ideas— came towards the middle of the eighteenth century, with the appearance of the "Agricultural Revolution." . . .

Neither the monarchy nor the peasants were very effective in their resistance. The efforts of the monarchy were vitiated by fiscal preoccupations: the declarations of 1677 and 1702 authorise those who have seized common land to keep it, at least for the time being, provided they "restore" (to the king, of course) the profits received over the past thirty years. The peasants were all too often content with fruitless "popular demonstrations." At this period the break-up of common lands for the benefit of the nobility and the wealthy was a European phenomenon. The operating causes were everywhere the same: the trend towards the reintegration of large estates; the increasing emphasis on production as a private undertaking, with an eye always on the market; and the crisis among the rural proletariat, painfully adjusting itself to an economic system based on money and exchange. The communities were no match for these forces; what is more, they were far from possessing that perfect inner coherence with which they are sometimes credited.

Madness in Society

GEORGE ROSEN

A number of scholars, including several historians, have maintained that a decisive change in the definition of madness is one key feature of modernization. George Rosen finds the beginnings of a new outlook in the seventeenth and eighteenth centuries, when more rigorous concepts of rationality led to new and more restrictive notions of what "normal" behavior was. He discusses some of the reasons for the shift and views the results in terms of the treatment of the insane. (He suggests that further changes were to come in the nineteenth century, with the rise of humanitarianism, but these would only modify the "modern" definition of madness, not change its direction.) In contrast to the medieval tolerance of insanity and its integration of the insane into family and community life, modern man insists on defining madness as something apart. The fact that this new definition developed so early points up once more the complexity of the origins of modernization.

The history of madness is a somewhat offbeat subject, with many questions still to be answered. How quickly did the new attitudes toward the insane spread to ordinary people? Rosen, after all, is talking mainly about definitions by formal theorists and institutional leaders. But there is little doubt that the new definition ultimately became widespread and that it constitutes a major feature of the modern mentality.

To some observers, the decline in the tolerance of madness is a major weakness of modern society. This is open to debate. What does seem clear is that the insane themselves have been losers in the modernization process.

In 1785 Jean Colombier, inspector-general of French hospitals and prisons, summed up the situation of the mentally ill in a succinct, devastating statement.

> Thousands of lunatics are locked up in prisons without anyone even thinking of administering the slightest remedy. The half-mad are mingled with those who are totally deranged, those who rage with those who are quiet; some are in chains, while others are free in their prison. Finally, unless nature comes to their aid by curing them, the duration of their misery is

From George Rosen, *Madness in Society* (New York: Harper & Row, 1968), pp. 151–57, 158–61, 162–65. Copyright © George Rosen 1968. Reprinted by permission of Harper & Row, Publishers, Inc., and Routledge and Kegan Paul Ltd., London.

life-long, for unfortunately the illness does not improve but only grows worse.

The validity of this picture is generally supported by other contemporary evidence. Indeed, one historian of psychiatry was led to conclude from such evidence that up to the end of the eighteenth century there were no real hospitals for the care and treatment of the mentally ill, only "places where they were *kept* . . ." Moreover, he attributed the sad lot of the mentally ill to a psychological factor, to the view that they were "step-children of life," a social attitude which survived in the community as an atavistic inheritance from the primitive past.

Yet the situation was not so simple, nor can it be explained solely in terms of an atavistic but potent psychological factor which has operated through the ages. Various sources clearly indicate that not all those who were mentally or emotionally disturbed were treated in the manner described by Colombier. At the very same time there were to be found in Paris, on the street or in cafés, individuals whose peculiarities of dress or behaviour did not attract undue notice. Without much astonishment, Sebastien Mercier encountered a crack-brained maker of projects in a coffee-house, simply remarking that there were others like him who had the public weal at heart "but who unfortunately were addlepated." Diderot's brilliant portrayal of Rameau's nephew presents another social deviant who is a strange mixture of good sense and folly. Delineated with great acuteness and intelligence, he was, according to Diderot, "one of the most bizarre fellows in a country where God has seen to it that there is no lack of them."

Mentally disturbed individuals occur as social personages, as distinctive characters on the social landscape not only in the later eighteenth century but in earlier periods as well. Consciousness of public responsibility for the mentally deranged was limited to the medieval period. Custody of the mentally ill generally rested with their relatives and friends; only those who were considered dangerous or socially disturbing were dealt with by the community. In some places it was customary to receive persons who were acutely disturbed and agitated into general hospitals. Harmless lunatics were permitted to roam the streets and roads; others were whipped out of town.

William Langland described the "lunatick lollers" wandering over the countryside and referred compassionately to their sad state. Another instance in point was depicted by Thomas More in 1533. Writing of a poor lunatic, he stated that he was

> one which after that he had fallen into these frantick heresies, fell soon after into plaine open franzye beside. And all beit that he had therefore bene put up in Bedelem, and afterward by beating and correccion gathered his remembraance to him and beganne to come again to himselfe, being thereupon set at liberty, and walkinge aboute abrode, his old fransies beganne to fall againe in his heade. I was fro dyvers good holy places ad-

vertised, that he used in his wandering about to come into the churche, and there make many mad toies and trifles, to the trouble of good people in the divine service, and especially woulde he be most busye in the time of most silence, while the priest was at the secrets of the masse aboute the levacion . . . whereupon I beinge advertised of these pageauntes, and beinge sent unto and required by very devout relygious folke, to take some other order with him, caused him, as he came wanderinge by my doore, to be taken by the counstables and bounden to a tree in the streets before the whole towne, and ther they stripped [striped] him with roddes therefore till he waxed weary and somewhat lenger. And it appeared well that hys remembraunce was goode ineoughe save that it went about in grazing [wool-gathering!] til it was beaten home. For he coulde then verye wel reherse his fautes himselfe, and speake and treate very well, and promise to doe afterward as well. And verylye God be thanked I heare none harme of him now.

A characteristic group among the vagrants and wandering beggars of Tudor England were the Abram-men or Toms o' Bedlam. They were patients discharged from Bethlem Hospital, sometimes not entirely recovered, who were licensed to beg. As a means of quickly identifying those allowed to solicit alms, they wore a metal plate as a badge on the left arm. The Bedlam beggars were a familiar sight throughout England until well into the later seventeenth century. According to John Aubrey,

Till the breaking out of the Civil Warres, Tom o' Bedlams did travell about the countrey. They had been poore distracted men that had been putt into Bedlam, where, recovering to some sobernesse, they were licentiated to goe a-begging . . . they wore about their necks a great horn of an oxe in a string or bawdric, which, when they came to an house for almes, they did wind, and they did put the drink given to them into their horn, where they did put a stopple.

Some of these beggars were undoubtedly impostors, and by 1675 the license to beg had been revoked. The ubiquitous presence of these vagrant mental patients is fully reflected in the literature of the Elizabethan and early Stuart periods. Illustrative are the close of the third scene in the second act of *King Lear* when Edgar announces his intention of becoming a Bedlam beggar, and the mad songs, "Loving Mad Tom," and "Old Tom of Bedlam."

Social attitudes towards the mentally and emotionally disturbed have clearly not been uniform at all times but have exhibited modulations and nuances. During the medieval period and the Renaissance, forms of unreason were considered fundamental elements in the fabric of the universe and of man. Medieval men believed that there were compelling forces making for righteousness and perfection, not only within the individual but as well in nature. Moreover, there were norms in nature which should not be violated, for their transgression led to vice. The later Middle Ages, particularly from the thirteenth century onwards, placed madness in the hierarchy of the vices. Another view of mental derangement is implied by the passage in the Prologue of *Piers Plowman* where a lunatic speaks up to praise the ideal king, while an angel speaks from heaven. The implication that only madmen and angels can speak the truth is related to the idea of holy madness, the idea that the ultimate of Christian truth is revealed to Christ's fools, to those who throw themselves utterly on God. Actually this view is very old and is based on the *New Testament* (I Corinthians 1: 18ff.).

Numerous students of the waning Middle Ages have commented on the feeling of melancholy and pessimism which marked the period. A sense of impending doom hung over men and women, intensified by a belief that the end of time was approaching and that the last days were at hand. Nor was this apocalyptic sense of anxiety and urgency unjustified. A world was indeed disintegrating, and in its midst a new order, the shape of which could be seen only dimly, was agonizing towards birth. The feudal order was yielding to absolute monarchy and the early nation state. The all-embracing Christian commonwealth, fashioned and guided by the Church of Rome, was wracked by dissension, hatred, and violence. Abuses in the Church brought forth a desire to return it to its pristine state, to a new birth of life. The need for renewal was felt by many, and to perceptive men the troubles of the time were evidence that the age was at hand which would usher in the Last Judgement. The prevalence and spread of heresy, popular mysticism and personal piety in the later fourteenth and fifteenth centuries were hardly an accident. History was moving towards renewal and divine fulfilment, and men looked for signs and interpretations that warned sinners and encouraged the just.

Within this context madness through its linkage with the revelation of religious truth became a means of achieving knowledge. Madness was a primitive force of revelation, revealing the depths of menace, destruction, and evil that lurked beneath the illusory surface of reality. Unreason revealed the unbearable, the things in the world upon which one could not otherwise bear to look. Madness was on the increase, clearly a sign that the end of the world was at hand. But it was also a cause, for human folly had unleashed forces of disorganization and destruction that could end only in ultimate catastrophe. These forces were loose in a world that had succumbed to self-delusion, a world grown callous, hard-hearted, and rotten with selfishness, where people maddened with fear were pressed to the very brink of existence, a world which must therefore inevitably end in frenzied self-destruction. This theme of cosmic madness is a major element in the art and literature of the fifteenth and sixteenth centuries. Grünewald's Temptation of St. Anthony, the Lisbon painting by Bosch on the same subject, as well as his Millennium, provide evidence on this point. Writers as diverse as Pierre Ronsard and Sebastian Brant dealt with madness as a cosmic phenomenon, as a cause of the troubles which seemed to herald the end of the world. Ronsard combined these ideas in his *Discours des misères de ce temps*, denouncing the senseless errors of belief that turned the world upside down so that reason and justice were replaced by violence, hate, and death, and even God was no longer secure in his own dwelling. Similarly, the episode in Brant's *Narrenschiff*, where a furious storm drives the ship off its course and wrecks it, symbolized a world driven mad and its coming catastrophic end.

Irrationality personified in the figure of Folly loomed large in the Renaissance, but there was little discrimination between species of folly. Erasmus speaks of foolish persons and of the insane without clearly differentiating between them. He has Stultitia remark that the latter are the happiest of all; perhaps he was referring to harmless deranged folk, perhaps to mental defectives. In large measure this identification of stupidity with irrationality reflects an attitudinal shift from the idea of madness as a cosmic phenomenon to the view that madness is born in the hearts of men. Sebastian Brant published his highly popular satire, *Das Narrenschiff*, in 1494. In it he pilloried the follies connected with a whole gamut of human activities. Irrational desires and behaviour become objects of ridicule in this context and are exposed to the laughter and scorn of the world. Folly is no longer a vice and a punishment, but only a defect of human nature appropriate for castigation by the moralist. For Erasmus, irrationality is no longer a menace but a necessity to make the wheels of the world go round. In the *Moriae encomium*, which appeared in 1511, Folly wearing a fool's cap and bells points out how prosaic is her rule in the affairs of mankind.

Even religion seems to have some affinity with a certain kind of folly. Did not Paul say, "The foolishness of God is wiser than men"? This touches on the old Christian theme that the world is folly in the eyes of God, a theme that was revived in the sixteenth century and explored by thinkers as different as Calvin and Sebastian Franck. According to Calvin,

> as long as our views are bounded by the earth, perfectly content with our own righteousness, wisdom and strength, we fondly flatter ourselves, and fancy we are little less than demigods. But, if we once elevate our thoughts to God, and consider his nature, and the consummate perfection of his righteousness, wisdom, and strength, to which we ought to be conformed— what before charmed us in ourselves under the false pretext of righteousness, will soon be loathed as the greatest inequity; what strangely deceived us under the title of wisdom, will be despised as extreme folly; and what more the appearance of strength, will be proved to be most wretched impotence.

When compared to the limitless reason of God, human reason is fallacious and irrational. Man can endeavour to reach God by breaking the chains which bind his spirit and thus escaping into the liberty of other-worldliness. However, in so doing he fathoms the depths of unreason and enjoys the highest wisdom. Heavenly bliss is the greatest madness, and is achieved when man transcends the gap between the things of this world and their divine essence, when he reconciles the cruel contradictions which God created.

Thus, in the sixteenth century, from the humanistic as well as from the Christian viewpoint, irrationality is not regarded as having any absolute existence in the world. Folly exists only in relation to some form of reason, whether it be that of God or of man. Indeed, folly itself becomes a form of reason, even though distorted. ". . . Reason has taught me," wrote Montaigne, "that to firmly condemn something as false and impossible is to assume that one knows the bounds and limits of God's will and of the power of our Mother Nature; and that there is no more notable folly than to reduce these things to the measure of our capacity, and self-conceit."

> Men fail to recognize the malady of their mind. It does nothing but pry and seek, and keeps spinning about incessantly, constructing and becoming enmeshed in its own work, like our silkworms, and is suffocated in it. A *mouse in pitch*. It thinks that it sees from afar some apparent gleam of imaginary light and truth; but while it is running to it, so many difficulties, obstacles, and new quests cross its path that they mislead and intoxicate it.

Folly and madness had become integral elements of the world of people and things. It is certainly no coincidence that the literature of the late sixteenth and early seventeenth centuries is so rich in the portrayal of distraught and insane characters. . . . The shift in social attitudes towards mental illness which took place in Europe at this time can be analysed and explained in terms of socioeconomic, philosophical, and moral factors. Furthermore, this attitudinal change is closely linked with the character of the institutions developed and used during the seventeenth and eighteenth centuries for the mentally and emotionally deranged. These institutions must be seen first in relation to the evolution of the hospital. At various periods in history the need to care for the needy and the dependent, the sick and the disabled, has crystallized sufficiently in terms of attitude, theory, and practice so that one may speak of characteristic institutional models. In this sense, the history of the hospital may be seen in terms of certain types that have predominated in given historical periods. While knowledge concerning the healing shrines and the secular healing institutions of antiquity is not complete enough to be generalized, this is not the case for the medieval period. The medieval hospital in all its varied forms was essentially an ecclesiastical institution, not primarily concerned with medical care. This type was eventually replaced in the sixteenth century by another kind of hospital whose goals were not religious but primarily social. That is, the hospital from the sixteenth into the nineteenth century was intended chiefly to help maintain social order while providing for the sick and the needy. To achieve this aim the medieval hospital was to a large extent secularized, placed under governmental control, and its activities were accepted as a community responsibility.

From the thirteenth century onwards the hospital had begun to come increasingly under secular jurisdiction. As cities in Europe prospered, and the bourgeoisie grew wealthy and powerful, municipal authorities tended to take over or to supplement the activities of the Church. In part this was politically motivated, a desire of the civil authorities to be independent of clerical domination or to render the ecclesiastical power subordinate to themselves. This does not mean that the clergy were eliminated. Monks and nuns continued to provide nursing care as they had done before. Administratively, the municipal authorities were responsible for the hospital facilities, but the Church might participate in some way.

Secondly, hospitals and related establishments were considered increasingly inadequate to deal with situations in which problems of health and welfare were considered from a new viewpoint. From the medieval standpoint the poor, the sick and the infirm might almost be considered necessary for the salvation of the donor of charity. They did the almsgiver a service. Such an attitude, however, accepted the beggar as a necessary part of society and tended to encourage begging. Small consideration was given to bettering the condition of the poor and the infirm. During the late Middle Ages, and especially following the Reformation, the whole approach to this problem changed.

Though the causes of poverty changed but little from the thirteenth to the sixteenth century, economic and social circumstances altered their significance and intensified their impact. As a result the condition of the poor, which was bad in the earlier period, had become worse by the early sixteenth century. Increased unemployment, higher prices, enclosures of peasant lands and related factors brought into being the problems of unemployment, vagrancy, and beggary which confronted governments from the fourteenth to the eighteenth centuries. Vagrancy appeared in the Netherlands and Germany even earlier than in England and France and then assumed increasingly large dimensions in all countries. In their endeavours to eke out a livelihood many vagrants pretended to be crippled or diseased so as to be able to beg with impunity and to obtain admission to a hospital. Some were professional beggars, frequently organized in gangs, such as those that frequented the Cours des miracles in Paris. There is little doubt that the large number of poor and sick wanderers overtaxed the facilities available in various communities. Furthermore, whether or not these vagrants were sick, there was a great deal of economic and social distress by the sixteenth century, and the problem was what to do about it. As Simon Fish put the case in 1529 in his famous Supplicacyon for the Beggars: "But whate remedy to releve us your poor sike lame and sore bedemen? To make many hospitals for the relief of the poore people? Nay truely; The moo the worse, for ever the fatte of the hole foundacion hangeth on the prestes berdes." Fish also proposed a solution— that the clergy be expropriated and the hospitals and related facilities taken in hand by the king.

In fact, this was the course followed, a course influenced essentially by the Reformation, mercantilist thought, and the rise of absolute monarchy. While the intervention of the civil authorities in matters of welfare and health before the sixteenth century has been noted, the notion that poor relief including medical care was a community, not a Church, responsibility was definitely established during the Reformation period. Those who wished to bring some order into the area of welfare and health, whether Vives in Bruges or Zwingli in Zürich, were guided by the same principles and oriented to the same goals: elimination of beggary, organization of effective agencies of public assistance, and unification of all facilities and resources (hospitals, domiciliary relief, and the like) in the hands of local or national authorities. With variations, the process and its consequences can be seen in England and on the continent.

This desire to bring some kind of order into the field of assistance went hand in hand with an equally great enthusiasm for the repression of idleness. Condemnation of idleness was, of course, not new; indolence and lassitude had been condemned in ancient and medieval thought. The main difference was that the concerns of the seventeenth century were chiefly political and economic, rather than moral. Most seventeenth-century thinkers accepted the idea that governments should use their power to compel all persons capable of engaging in production to do some work. As a result of this view, the economic literature of this period, in England and on the continent, teems with proposals for dealing with idleness. In general, the proposed remedies fall into two groups: the repression of idleness by corrective or punitive legislation, and the creation of institutions which would provide work for the poor and punishment for those who refused to work. From this viewpoint, charity in the medieval sense was to be discouraged, for it led to idleness and beggary. On the other hand, the idle poor, properly employed, would help to make the nation rich and strong. . . . .

To deal with the problems of the poor, the dependent, and the vagrant, a policy of internment and indoor relief was generally adopted, and institutions developed to put it into practice. Thus there were workhouses and houses of correction in England, Zuchthäuser in Germany, and hôpitaux généraux in France. Many of these institutions were not new creations; they evolved out of preexisting facilities and in response to problems that occurred at various times. However, it was in the later seventeenth century and in the eighteenth century that they achieved their fullest development.

The course of events in France is illuminating in this respect. From the sixteenth century on, royal action to deal with welfare and health problems occurred along two lines, one concerned with finances, the other with administrative discipline and efficiency. A series of reform regulations from 1544 on turned over the administration of each hospital to a commission composed of merchants, burghers, and artisans who had to give an annual accounting to the local representatives of the king. In addition to endowments and other sources of income, the king authorized or imposed a communal tax. The first of these measures was issued by Henri II in 1551. More-over, to insure financial stability, institutions were merged or were put under a general administrative board. As early as the reign of Henri IV plans had been made to establish such institutions for the relief of the poor and needy, but little was achieved. Finally, in 1656 a royal decree was issued founding the *Hôpital Général* of Paris. (It had been preceded by the welfare bureau of Lyon and its affiliated hospital, which dated from 1613–1614.) The pur-poses of the institution were threefold. In part they were economic: to in-crease manufactures, provide productive work for the able-bodied, and to end unemployment; in part, social: to punish wilful idleness, restore public order, and rid Paris of beggars; and in part, religious and moral: to relieve the needy, the ill and suffering, to deal with immorality and antisocial behaviour, and to provide Christian instruction.

The creation of such institutions was not limited to Paris. It was a solu-tion to the problem of poor relief which was tried all through France. Indeed, developments at Paris had been anticipated in the provinces. The *Hôpital Général* at Toulouse dated from 1647, that at Béziers from 1654, and that at Caen from 1655. Most of the provincial general hospitals were established under royal authorization. At Le Mans in 1658 all the hospitals, hostels, and *maisons-Dieu* were united into a general hospital by royal letters patent. This trend was carried further by Colbert, and slowly but steadily general hospitals came into existence throughout France.

The very nature of the functions which these institutions were intended to perform required some kind of involvement with health problems. Though the *Hôtel-Dieu* was supposed to take care of the sick, the *Hôpital Général* took care of old people, people with venereal diseases, epileptics, and the mentally ill. Thus, in the course of time the general hospital combined the characteristics of a penal institution, an asylum, a workshop, and a hospital.

An important purpose was to deal with immorality and antisocial be-haviour. All individuals who were defined as asocial or socially deviant were segregated by internment. This procedure is analogous to the manner in which the leper was treated in the medieval period. By separating such in-dividuals from society, by exiling them to the *Hôpital Général*, they were consigned to a social and psychological situation of which the dominant character is alienation. A separate socio-psychological lifespace was created for those who removed themselves from or transgressed the moral order con-sidered appropriate to their social position, occupation, or family relationship. Thus, on 20 April 1690 regulations were instituted, providing

> that children of artisans and other poor inhabitants of Paris up to the age of twenty-five, who used their parents badly, or who refused to work through laziness, or, in the case of girls who were debauched or in evident danger of

being debauched, should be shut up, the boys in the Bicêtre, the girls in the Salpêtrière. This action was to be taken on the complaint of the parents, or, if these were dead, of near relatives, or the parish priest. The wayward children were to be kept as long as the directors deemed wise and were to be released only on a written order signed by four directors.

At the same time arrangements were made to incarcerate prostitutes and women who ran bawdy houses; they were to be kept in a special section of the Salpêtrière.

The consequence of this policy was described by Tenon in his account of the Salpêtrière in 1788.

> The Salpêtrière [he wrote] is the largest hospital in Paris and possibly in Europe: this hospital is both a house for women and a prison. It receives pregnant women and girls, wet nurses and their nurselings; male children from the age of seven or eight months to four and five years of age; young girls of all ages; aged married men and women; raving lunatics, imbeciles, epileptics, paralytics, blind persons, cripples, people suffering from ringworm, incurables of all sorts, children afflicted with scrofula, and so on and so forth.
>
> At the centre of this hospital is a house of detention for women, comprising four different prisons; *le commun*, for the most dissolute girls; *la correction*, for those who are not considered hopelessly depraved; *la prison*, reserved for persons held by order of the king; and *la grande force*, for women branded by order of the courts.

In short, what had happened by the later seventeenth century was not only or simply an evolution of institutions; it was more than that. It was a change in the social perception of irrationality and madness based on criteria derived from a new view of human nature. Today, the idea of a personal self appears as an indispensable assumption of existence. Actually, like other views of human nature, it is in large measure a cultural idea, a fact within history, the product of a given era. At any given period certain criteria are employed to establish normal human nature, as well as any deviation from it.

For the seventeenth and eighteenth centuries, the touchstone was reason and its right use. Reason provided the norm; any divergence from the norm was irrational. Pascal said that he could conceive of a man without hands, feet, or head, but he added, "I cannot conceive of a man without thought; that would be a stone or a brute." Moreover, from the context in which this statement is made, it is clear that Pascal has rational thought in mind. Montaigne had still been able to accept and to discuss reason and unreason as related, interwoven facets of human behaviour. By the fourth decade of the seventeenth century, however, a sharp line of separation was being drawn between reason and unreason. Descartes, for example, recognized that reason and irrationality are encountered together, that dreams and errors of various kinds are associated with madness, but he decided to rely upon reason and to avoid the irrational. Thus, unreason and madness were exiled in thought on the basis of a conscious decision.

From this viewpoint, irrationality took on a new aspect; it could be regarded as a matter of choice, as a matter of volition. Unreason, and with it insanity, were related primarily to the quality of volition and not to the integrity of the rational mind. Endowed with reason, man was expected to behave rationally, that is, according to accepted social standards. Rational choice was his to make by virtue of his nature. Eccentric or irrational behaviour, actions which diverged from accepted norms, were considered as rooted in error or as derangements of the will and therefore subject to correction.

The World We Have Lost

PETER LASLETT

The following passages seek to define the essential characteristics of preindustrial society, which the author regards as sharply differentiated from its modern counterpart. We see a carefully controlled social environment, dominated by small units of organization in which affectionate ties prevail. The family is obviously crucial, and although the author notes the tensions that family life can create, he is preoccupied with the family's success as an emotional as well as economic unit. The essence of modernization, correspondingly, is a change in the family, and presumably a weakening of ties. Factories have replaced families as units of production. The author does not spell out the relationship, if any, between the rise of factories and changes in family structure, but he has no doubt about the outcome.

This is an intelligently nostalgic picture. The author admits the importance of material limitations, even outright misery, and acknowledges such vital aspects of preindustrial life as high mortality rates. But in terms of human relationships it is clear that the author thinks the modern world has lost a great deal. The picture of preindustrial life he paints is one of stability and close personal ties. There can be little doubt, if this picture is accurate, that most people suffered profound disruption as they entered modern society—or rather, as they were forced into it, for there is no clear motive in this preindustrial society to spontaneously seek change. Note also that the author judges preindustrial society to be rather homogeneous in its basic values. Important class differences existed, but they did not interfere with a common devotion to religion and a patriarchal family structure.

Laslett's views regarding the quality of preindustrial life and the causes and impact of change should be compared with those of Marc Bloch. Laslett is writing about a later period than Bloch. England was in many ways undergoing more rapid changes than France, in terms of the rise of market agriculture and the disruption of established religious and political patterns. Laslett himself, elsewhere in his study, points to substantial mobility in rural society. Yet he insists on the integrity and adequacy of traditional values.

In the year 1619 the bakers of London applied to the authorities for an increase in the price of bread. They sent in support of their claim a complete description of a bakery and an account of its weekly costs. There were thirteen or fourteen people in such an establishment: the baker and his wife, four paid employees who were called journeymen, two apprentices, two maidservants and the three or four children of the master baker himself. Six pounds ten shillings a week was reckoned to be the outgoings of this establishment of which only eleven shillings and eightpence went for wages: half a crown a week for each of the journeymen and tenpence for each of the maids. Far and away the greatest cost was for food: two pounds nine shillings out of the six pounds ten shillings, at five shillings a head for the baker and his wife, four shillings a head for their helpers and two shillings for their children. It cost much more in food to keep a journeyman than it cost in money; four times as much to keep a maid. Clothing was charged up too, not only for the man, wife and children, but for the apprentices as well. Even school fees were claimed as a justifiable charge on the price of bread for sale, and it cost sixpence a week for the teaching and clothing of a baker's child.

A London bakery was undoubtedly what we should call a commercial or even an industrial undertaking, turning out loaves by the thousand. Yet the business was carried on in the house of the baker himself. There was probably a *shop* as part of the house, *shop* as in *workshop* and not as meaning a retail establishment. Loaves were not ordinarily sold over the counter: they had to be carried to the open-air market and displayed on stalls. There was a garner behind the house, for which the baker paid two shillings a week in rent, and where he kept his wheat, his *sea-coal* for the fire and his store of salt. The house itself was one of those high, half-timbered overhanging structures on the narrow London street which we always think of when we remember the scene in which Shakespeare, Pepys or even Christopher Wren lived. Most of it was taken up with the living-quarters of the dozen people who worked there.

It is obvious that all these people ate in the house since the cost of their food helped to determine the production cost of the bread. Except for the journeymen they were all obliged to sleep in the house at night and live together as a family.

The only word used at that time to describe such a group of people was "family." The man at the head of the group, the entrepreneur, the employer, or the manager, was then known as the master or head of the family. He was father to some of its members and in place of father to the rest. There was no sharp distinction between his domestic and his economic functions. His wife was both his partner and his subordinate, a partner because she ran the family, took charge of the food and managed the women-servants, a subordinate because she was woman and wife, mother and in place of mother to the rest.

The paid servants of both sexes had their specified and familiar position in the family, as much part of it as the children but not quite in the same position. At that time the family was not one society only but three societies fused together: the society of man and wife, of parents and children and of master and servant. But when they were young, and servants were, for the most part, young, unmarried people, they were very close to children in their status and their function. Here is the agreement made between the parents of a boy about to become an apprentice and his future master. The boy covenants to dwell as an apprentice with his master for seven years, to keep his secrets and to obey his commandments.

> Taverns and alehouses he shall not haunt, dice, cards or any other unlawful games he shall not use, fornication with any woman he shall not commit, matrimony with any woman he shall not contract. He shall not absent himself by night or by day without his master's leave but be a true and faithful servant.

On his side, the master undertakes to teach his apprentice his "art, science or occupation with moderate correction."

> Finding and allowing unto his said servant meat, drink, apparel, washing, lodging and all other things during the said term of seven years, and to give unto his said apprentice at the end of the said term double apparel, to wit, one suit for holydays and one suit for worken days.

Apprentices, therefore, were workers who were also children, extra sons or extra daughters (for girls could be apprenticed too), clothed and educated as well as fed, obliged to obedience and forbidden to marry, unpaid and absolutely dependent until the age of twenty-one. If apprentices were workers in the position of sons and daughters, the sons and daughters of the house were workers too. John Locke laid it down in 1697 that the children of the poor must work for some part of the day when they reached the age of three. The sons and daughters of a London baker were not free to go to school for many years of their young lives, or even to play as they wished when they came back home. Soon they would find themselves doing what they could in *bolting*, that is sieving flour, or in helping the maidservant with her panniers of loaves on the way to the market stall, or in playing their small parts in preparing the never-ending succession of meals for the whole household.

We may see at once, therefore, that the world we have lost, as I have chosen to call it, was no paradise or golden age of equality, tolerance or loving kindness. It is so important that I should not be misunderstood on this point that I will say at once that the coming of industry cannot be shown to have brought economic oppression and exploitation along with it. It was there already. The patriarchal arrangements which we have begun to explore were not new in the England of Shakespeare and Elizabeth. They were as old as the Greeks, as old as European history, and not confined to Europe. And it may well be that they abused and enslaved people quite as remorselessly as the economic arrangements which had replaced them in the England of Blake and Victoria. When people could expect to live for only thirty years in all, how must a man have felt when he realized that so much of his adult life, perhaps all, must go in working for his keep and very little more in someone else's family?

But people do not recognize facts of this sort, and no one is content to expect to live as long as the majority in fact will live. Every servant in the old social world was probably quite confident that he or she would some day get married and be at the head of a new family, keeping others in subordination. If it is legitimate to use the words exploitation and oppression in thinking of the economic arrangements of the pre-industrial world, there were nevertheless differences in the manner of oppressing and exploiting. The ancient order of society was felt to be eternal and unchangeable by those who supported, enjoyed and endured it. There was no expectation of reform. How could there be when economic organization was domestic organization, and relationships were rigidly regulated by the social system, by the content of Christianity itself?

Here is a vivid contrast with social expectation in Victorian England, or in industrial countries everywhere today. Every relationship in our world which can be seen to affect our economic life is open to change, is expected indeed to change of itself, or if it does not, to be changed, made better, by an omnicompetent authority. This makes for a less stable social world, though it is only one of the features of our society which impels us all in that direction. All industrial societies, we may suppose, are far less stable than their predecessors. They lack the extraordinarily cohesive influence which familial relationships carry with them, that power of reconciling the frustrated and the discontented by emotional means. Social revolution, meaning an irreversible changing of the pattern of social relationships, never happened in traditional, patriarchal, pre-industrial human society. It was almost impossible to contemplate.

Almost, but not quite. Sir Thomas More, in the reign of Henry VIII, could follow Plato in imagining a life without privacy and money, even if he stopped short of imagining a life where children would not know their parents and where promiscuity could be a political institution. Sir William Petty, 150 years later, one of the very first of the political sociologists, could speculate about polygamy; and the England of the Tudors and the Stuarts already knew of social structures and sexual arrangements, existing in the newly discovered world, which were alarmingly different from their own. But it must have been an impossible effort of the imagination to suppose that they were anything like as satisfactory.

It will be noticed that the roles we have allotted to all the members of the capacious family of the master-baker of London in the year 1619 are, emotionally, all highly symbolic and highly satisfactory. We may feel that in a whole society organized like this, in spite of all the subordination, the exploitation and the obliteration of those who were young, or feminine, or in service, everyone belonged in a group, a family group. Everyone had his circle of affection: every relationship could be seen as a love-relationship.

Not so with us. Who could love the name of a limited company or of a government department as an apprentice could love his superbly satisfactory father-figure master, even if he were a bully and a beater, a usurer and a hypocrite? But if a family is a circle of affection, it can also be the scene of hatred. The worst tyrants among human beings, the murderers and the villains, are jealous husbands and resentful wives, possessive parents and deprived children. In the traditional, patriarchal society of Europe, where practically everyone lived out his whole life within the family, often within one family only, tension like this must have been incessant and unrelieved, incapable of release except in crisis. Men, women and children have to be very close together for a very long time to generate the emotional power which can give rise to a tragedy of Sophocles, or Shakespeare, or Racine. Conflict in such a society was between individual people, on the personal scale. Except when the Christians fought with the infidels, or Protestants fought with Catholics, clashes between masses of persons did not often arise. There could never be a situation such as that which makes our own time, as some men say, the scene of perpetual revolution.

All this is true to history only if the little knot of people making bread in Stuart London was indeed the typical social unit of the old world in its size, composition and scale. There are reasons why a baker's household might have been a little out of the ordinary, for baking was a highly traditional occupation in a society increasingly subject to economic change. We shall see, in due course, that a family of thirteen people, which was also a unit of production of thirteen, less the children quite incapable of work, was quite large for English society at that time. Only the families of the really important, the nobility and the gentry, the aldermen and the successful merchants, were ordinarily as large as this. In fact, we can take the bakery to represent the upper limit in size and scale of the group in which ordinary people lived and worked. Among the great mass of society which cultivated the land, and which will be the major preoccupation of this essay, the family group was smaller than a London craftsman's entourage. . . .

. . . One reason for feeling puzzled by our own industrial society is that the historian has never set out to tell us what society was like before industry came and seems to assume that everyone knows.

We shall have much more to say about the movement of servants from farmhouse to farmhouse in the old world, and shall return to the problem of understanding ourselves in time, in contrast with our ancestors. Let us emphasize again the scale of life in the working family of the London baker. Few persons in the old world ever found themselves in groups larger than family groups, and there were few families of more than a dozen members. The largest household so far known to us, apart from the royal court and the establishments of the nobility, lay and spiritual, is that of Sir Richard Newdigate, Baronet, in his house of Arbury within his parish of Chilvers Coton in Warwickshire, in the year 1684. There were thirty-seven people in Sir Richard's family: himself; Lady Mary Newdigate his wife; seven daughters, all under the age of sixteen; and twenty-eight servants, seventeen men and boys and eleven women and girls. This was still a family, not an institution, a staff, an office or a firm.

Everything physical was on the human scale, for the commercial worker in London, and the miner who lived and toiled in Newdigate's village of Chilvers Coton. No object in England was larger than London Bridge or St. Paul's Cathedral, no structure in the Western World to stand comparison with the Colosseum in Rome. Everything temporal was tied to the human life-span too. The death of the master baker, head of the family, ordinarily meant the end of the bakery. Of course there might be a son to succeed, but the master's surviving children would be young if he himself had lived only as long as most men. Or an apprentice might fulfil the final function of apprenticehood, substitute sonship, that is to say, and marry his master's daughter, or even his widow. Surprisingly often, the widow, if she could, would herself carry on the trade. . . .

We may pause here to point out that our argument is not complete. There was an organization in the social structure of Europe before the coming of industry which enormously exceeded the family in size and endurance. This was the Christian Church. It is true to say that the ordinary person, especially the female, never went to a gathering larger than could assemble in an ordinary house except when going to church. When we look at the aristocracy and the church from the point of view of the scale of life and the impermanence of all man-made institutions, we can see that their functions were such as make very little sense in an industrial society like our own. Complicated arrangements then existed, and still exist in England now, which were intended to make it easier for the noble family to give the impression that it had indeed always persisted. Such, for example, were those intricate rules of succession which permitted a cousin, however distant, to succeed to the title and to the headship, provided only he was in the male line. Such was the final remedy in the power of the Crown, the fountain of honour, to declare that an anomalous succession should take place. Nobility was for ever.

But the symbolic provision of permanence is only the beginning of the social functions of the church. At a time when the ability to read with understanding and to write much more than a personal letter was confined for the most part to the ruling minority, in a society which was otherwise oral in its communications, the preaching parson was the great link between the illiterate mass and the political, technical and educated world. Sitting in the 10,000 parish churches of England every Sunday morning, in groups of 20, 50, 100 or 200, the illiterate mass of the people were not only taking part in the single group activity which they ordinarily shared with others outside their own families. They were informing themselves in the only way open to them of what went on in England, Europe, and the world as a whole. The priesthood was indispensable to the religious activity of the old world, at a time when religion was still of primary interest and importance. But the priesthood was also indispensable because of its functions in social communication. . . .

Not only did the scale of their work and the size of the group which was engaged make them exceptional, the constitution of the group did too. In the baking household we have chosen as our standard, sex and age were mingled together. Fortunate children might go out to school, but adults did not usually go out to work. There was nothing to correspond to the thousands of young men on the assembly line, the hundreds of young women in the offices, the lonely lives of housekeeping wives which we now know only too well. We shall see that those who survived to old age in the much less favourable conditions for survival which then were prevalent, were surprisingly often left to live and die alone, in their tiny cottages or sometimes in the almshouses which were being built so widely in the England of the Tudors and the Stuarts. Poor-law establishments, parochial in purpose and in size, had begun their melancholy chapter in the history of the English people. But institutional life was otherwise almost unknown. There were no hotels, hostels, or blocks of flats for single persons, very few hospitals and none of the kind we are familiar with, almost no young men and women living on their own. The family group where so great a majority lived was what we should undoubtedly call a "balanced" and "healthy" group.

When we turn from the hand-made city of London to the hand-moulded immensity of rural England, we may carry the same sentimental prejudice along with us. To every farm there was a family, which spread itself over its portion of the village lands as the family of the master-craftsman filled out his manufactory. When a holding was small, and most were small as are the tiny holdings of European peasants today, a man tilled it with the help of his wife and his children. No single man, we must remember, would usually take charge of the land, any more than a single man would often be found at the head of a workshop in the city. The master of a family was expected to be a householder, whether he was a butcher, a baker, a candlestick maker or simply a husbandman, which was the universal name for one whose skill was in working the land. Marriage we must insist, and it is one of the rules which gave its character to the society of our ancestors, was the entry to full membership, in the enfolding countryside, as well as in the scattered urban centres.

But there was a difference in scale and organization of work on the land and in the town. The necessities of rural life did require recurrent groupings of households for common economic purposes, occasionally something like a crowd of men, women and children working together for days on end. Where the ground was still being tilled as open fields, and each household had a number of strips scattered all over the whole open area and not a compact collection of enclosures, ploughing was co-operative, as were many other operations, above all harvesting, and this continued even after enclosure. We do not yet know how important this element of enforced common activity was in the life of the English rural community on the eve of industrialization, or how much difference enclosure made in this respect. But whatever the situation was, the economic transformation of the eighteenth and nineteenth centuries destroyed communality altogether in English rural life. The group of men from several farmsteads working the heavy plough in springtime, the bevy of harvesters from every house in the village wading into the high standing grass to begin the cutting of the hay, had no successors in large-scale economic activity. For the arrangement of these groups was entirely different in principle from the arrangement of a factory, or a firm, or even of a collective farm.

Both before and after enclosure, some peasants did well: their crops were heavier and they had more land to till. To provide the extra labour needed then, the farming householder, like the successful craftsman, would extend his working family by taking on young men and women as servants to live with him and work the fields. This he would have to do, even if the land which he was farming was not his own but rented from the great family in the manor house. Sometimes, we have found, he would prefer to send out his own children as servants and bring in other children and young men to do the work. This is one of the few glimpses we can get into the quality of the emotional life of the family at this time, for it shows that parents may have been unwilling to submit children of their own to the discipline of work at home. It meant, too, that servants were not simply the perquisites of wealth and position. A quarter, or a third, of all the families in the country contained servants in Stuart times, and this meant that very humble people had them as well as the titled and the wealthy. Most of the servants, moreover, male or female, in the great house and in the small, were engaged in working the land.

The boys and the men would do the ploughing, hedging, carting and the heavy, skilled work of the harvest. The women and the girls would keep the house, prepare the meals, make the butter and the cheese, the bread and the beer, and would also look after the cattle and take the fruit to market. At harvest-time, from June to October, every hand was occupied and every back was bent. These were the decisive months for the whole population in our damp northern climate, with its one harvest in a season and reliance on one or two standard crops. So critical was the winning of the grain for bread that the first rule of gentility (a gentleman never worked with his hands for his living) might be abrogated. . . .

The factory won its victory by outproducing the working family, taking away the market for the products of hand-labour and cutting prices to the point where the craftsman had either to starve or take a job under factory discipline himself. It was no sudden, complete and final triumph, for the seamstresses were working in the garrets right up to the twentieth century, and the horrors of sweated labour which so alarmed our grandfathers took place amongst the out-workers, not on the factory floor. It was not a transformation which affected only commerce, industry and the towns, for the hand-work of the cottages disappeared entirely, till, by the year 1920, rural England was an agrarian remnant, an almost lifeless shell. The process was not English alone, at any point in its development, and its effects on the Continent of Europe were in some ways more obviously devastating than ever they were amongst our people. But ours was the society which first ventured into the industrial era, and English men and women were the first who had to try to find a home for themselves in a world where family and household seemed to have no place.

But Marx and the historians who have followed him were surely wrong to call this process by the simple name of the triumph of capitalism, the rise and victory of the bourgeoisie. The presence of capital, we have seen, was the very circumstance which made it possible in earlier times for the working family to preserve its independence both on the land and in the cities, linking together the scattered households of the workers in such a way that no one had to make the daily double journey from home to workshop, from suburb to office and factory. Capitalism, however defined, did not begin at the time when the working household was endangered by the beginnings of the factory system, and economic inequality was not the product of the social transformation which so quickly followed after. Though the enormous, insolent wealth of the new commercial and industrial fortunes emphasized the iniquity of the division between rich and poor, it is doubtful whether Victorian England was any worse in this respect than the England of the Tudors and the Stuarts. It was not the fact of capitalism alone, not simply the concentration of the means of production in the hands of the few and the reduction of the rest to a position of dependence, which opened wide the social gulf, though the writers of the eighteenth and nineteenth centuries give us ample evidence that this was observed and was resented—by the dispossessed peasantry in England especially. More important, it is suggested, far more likely a source for the feeling that there is a world which once we all possessed, a world now passed away, is the fact of the transformation of the family life of everyone which industrialism brought with it.

In the vague and difficult verbiage of our own generation, we can say that the removal of the economic functions from the patriarchal family at the point of industrialization created a mass society. It turned the people who worked into a mass of undifferentiated equals, working in a factory or scattered between the factories and mines, bereft forever of the feeling that work, a family affair, carried with it. The Marxist historical sociology presents this as the growth of class consciousness amongst the proletariat, and this is an important historical truth. But because it belongs with the large-scale class model for all social change it can also be misleading, as we shall hope to show. Moreover it has tended to divert attention from the structural function of the family in the preindustrial world, and made impossible up till now a proper, informed contrast between our world and the lost world we have to analyse. . . .

European society is of the patriarchal type, and with some variations, of which the feudal went the furthest, it remained patriarchal in its institutions right up to the coming of the factories, the offices and the rest. European patriarchalism, we may notice, was of a rather surprising kind, for it was marked by the independence of the nuclear family, man, wife and children, not by the extended family of relatives living together in a group of several generations under the same patriarchal head. Yet society was patriarchal, nevertheless, right up to the time of industrial transformation: it can now no longer be said to be patriarchal at all, except vestigially and in its emotional predisposition. The time has now come to divide our European past in a simpler way with industrialization as the point of critical change.

The word alienation is part of the cant of the mid-twentieth century and it began as an attempt to describe the separation of the worker from his world of work. We need not accept all that this expression has come to convey in order to recognize that it does point to something vital to us all in relation to our past. Time was when the whole of life went forward in the family, in a circle of loved, familiar faces, known and fondled objects, all to human size. That time has gone for ever. It makes us very different from our ancestors.

. . . In every one of the village communities too, the families of craftsmen, labourers and paupers tended to be smaller than the families of yeomen, and those of the gentry to be largest. The traffic in children from the humbler to the more successful families shows up in the relative numbers in the various groups. Poverty, in our day, or, at least, in the very recent past, was associated with large numbers of children, but . . . in the seventeenth century exactly the reverse was true. The richer you were, the more children you had in your household. In [the village of Goodnestone] in 1676, the gentry with children had an average of 3.5 in their families, the yeomen 2.9, the tradesmen 2.3, the labourers 2.1 and the paupers 1.8.

These figures from Goodnestone are too good to be true and it is common enough to find humble families with many children at home, too many for the meagre resources of the wage-earner and a promise of destitution for his widow if he should die too soon. Nevertheless, the association of few children with modest position and resources is almost as marked a feature of social structure in the traditional world as the association of smaller families generally with the poor. It was not simply a matter of the poor offering up their children to the rich as servants; they probably also had fewer children born to them, and of those which were born, fewer survived. It is likely that works on the expectation of life and size of the biological family will confirm what early impressions seem to show, which is that poor men and their wives could not expect to live together long enough to have as many offspring as the rich. This loss of potential labour-power was a matter of consequence, for it always must be remembered that the actual work on most of the plots of land was done by the working family, the man, his wife and children.

At harvest-time, of course, there was a difference: the individual farming family could no longer cope with the work. From the making of the hay in June until the winning of the corn and pease in late September, every able-bodied person in the village community was at work on everyone's land. How much co-operation there was is difficult to say, but when the crisis of the agricultural year came round, right up to the time of mechanized farming, the village acted as a community. When all was in, there was harvest home.

> It is usual, in most places, after they get all the pease pulled or the last grain down, to invite all the workfolks and their wives (that helped them that harvest) to supper, and then they have puddings, bacon, or boiled beef, flesh or apple pies, and then cream brought in platters, and every one a spoon; then after all they have hot cakes and ale; for they bake cakes and send for ale against that time: some will cut their cake and put it into the cream, and this feast is called cream-pot, or cream-kit; for on the morning that they get all done the workfolks will ask their dames if they have good store of cream and say they must have the cream-kit anon.

This was the Yorkshire custom in the 1640's when it was necessary, at harvest-time, to go even beyond the carpenters, the wheelwrights and the millers, in order to bring in the sheaves off the fields. The richer men had to make a home in the barns during harvest for folk, pastoral in their ways, who came down from the wild moorland. Migration of labour at harvest was common enough in the eighteenth century, but eating and drinking together was a universal characteristic of rural life at all times. Whatever the churchwardens or the overseers of the poor did, when the church-bell was rung in celebration, or the churchyard mowed, there was an entry in the ill-written accounts for ale drunk on the occasion. . . . The meticulous, unpopular Rector of Clayworth in the last quarter of the seventeenth century, entertained the *husbandry* of the two settlements in his parish separately to dinner every year.

When the curate of Goodnestone returned the names of all his parishioners in April, 1676, "according to their families, according to their quality and according to their religion," he did as he was bid and told his lordship, the bishop, how many of them had been to holy communion that Eastertide. Apart from sixteen exceptions every person in the community known by their priest to be qualified for the sacrament had actually taken it at some time during the festival, which fell in that year between March 19th and 26th: 128 people communicated that is to say, out of a population of 281. Even the defaulters had promised to make amends at Whitsuntide, all but the one family in the village which was nonconformist. But William Wanstall, senior, one of the absentees, was given no such grace; he had been "excluded the Holy Sacrament for his notorious drunkenness, but since hath promised reformation." Francis Nicholson, the priest-in-charge, was evidently a devoted pastor, for he could give an account of every one of the absentees. Mrs. Elizabeth Richards, the widowed head of one of the households of gentry, was excused as "melancholy," and Barbara Pain since she was "under a dismal calamity, the unnatural death of her husband," who had left her at the head of a yeoman family, three children and two servants.

This . . . draws attention to a feature of the village community and of the whole of the world we have now half-forgotten which has scarcely been mentioned so far. All our ancestors were literal Christian believers, all of the time. Not only zealous priests, such as Francis Nicholson, not only serious-minded laymen, but also the intellectuals and the publicly responsible looked on the Christian religion as the explanation of life, and on religious service as its proper end. Not everyone was equally devout, of course, and it would be simple-minded to suppose that none of these villagers ever had their doubts. Much of their devotion must have been formal, and some of it mere conformity. But their world was a Christian world and their religious activity was spontaneous, not forced on them from above. When Francis Nicholson refused the cup to William Wanstall, in March, 1676, the scores of other people in the church that morning no doubt approved of what he did, as no doubt Wanstall deserved this very public rebuke. When William Sampson, the formidable Rector of Clayworth, did exactly the same thing in April, 1679, to Ralph Meers and Anne Fenton "upon a common fame that they lived and lodged together, not being married," he also had the community behind him. He knew what he was doing too, for Anne Fenton's first baby was christened two months later, only a week or two, presumably, after she had married Ralph Meers.

It has been shown only very recently how it came about that the mass of the English people lost their Christian belief, and how religion came to be a middle-class matter. When the arrival of industry created huge societies of persons in the towns with an entirely different outlook from these Stuart villagers, practically no one went to church, not if he was working class and was left untouched by religious emotion. Christianity was no longer in the social air which everyone breathed together, rich and poor, gentleman, husbandman, artificer, labourer and pauper. So much has been written about the abuses of the clergy in earlier times, so much about the controversies and doubts, about the revivals, especially the Wesleyan revival, that the religious attitude of common folk has been lost sight of. Perhaps the twelve labourers who lived at Goodnestone in 1676 did not know very clearly what Our Lord's Supper meant, and perhaps they felt that it would displease Squire Hales if they stayed away, but every single one of them took communion. Their descendants in the slums of London in the 1830's, '40's and '50's did not do so: they already looked on Christianity as belonging to the rural world which they had lost. It was something for their employers, something for the respectable, which, perhaps, they might go in for if ever they attained respectability and comfort. This was not true of the hard-working, needy, half-starved labourers of pre-industrial times.

Louis XIV
and Twenty Million Frenchmen

PIERRE GOUBERT

Here is a different approach to rural and preindustrial society from that taken by Bloch and Laslett. Goubert might argue with Laslett about the social structure of preindustrial society, for he sees clearer class distinctions than Laslett does, but the basic difference between the two is not primarily a question of fact: the main issue is one of emphasis. No one denies that preindustrial society was poor or that it fostered great inequality. Goubert, however, finds in these characteristics the essence of preindustrial life. Is he applying inappropriate standards, drawn perhaps from a modern concern for material well-being? Or does he genuinely capture the mood of premodern people themselves, a mood that not infrequently caused riots and unrest? Goubert's interpretation certainly complicates any nostalgic judgment of rural life. It might also suggest reasons for some rural people to welcome the new society that industrialization was to create a century later. Possibly industrial life, although unpleasant, was less unpleasant than preindustrial life for the common people. Again, much depends on how we evaluate perindustrial society itself.

There was in the kingdom of France a traditional distinction between those who prayed, those who fought and those who toiled. The last of these were useful and consequently base. For a long time, at least since Loyseau, the Third Estate had been held to comprise officials, tradesmen and bourgeois, while right at the bottom were the most contemptible of all, the "rude mechanicals" who worked with their hands: artisans, some tens of thousands of urban workers and the vast mass of the peasantry.

Society, like the State and the economy, rested on the most numerous, dependent and eminently productive section of the community: the peasantry. The peasants were less a social class than a complex group. What they had in common was their habitat, their occupations, the framework of dependency within which they were held and the fact of enabling the three real estates of the realm to live and prosper.

The working of the land was wholly in the hands of the peasantry which—allowing for a good deal of regional variation—owned less than half of it. Except for the very few remaining freeholds, peasant property was not of the "Roman" type but manorial, that is to say that it was never independent. It is fashionable among royalist historians to assert the peasant's right to sell, lease, exchange, give or bequeath his land and this was true up to a point, but only with the consent of his overlord and after payment of what were frequently crippling dues and bearing in mind the fact that the *seigneur* always could, and often did, withdraw his consent. (It was quite within his rights to substitute himself as purchaser and at the same price.) It is further maintained nowadays that the peasants' feudal dues, which had been fixed for a long time, had dwindled into insignificance with the decline in the value of money. This is true of the old financial payments made in direct rents but false as regards all other dues which were often levied in kind and in particular of *rentes* and *champarts*; the last alone currently amounted to a tenth and sometimes a third of the crop. The feudal nature of his holding was to the peasant at the same time an annoyance and a burden, aggravated by the amazing variation in local conditions.

It seems probable that the small part of French territory which did belong to four-fifths of its inhabitants was divided extremely unfairly. The few serious studies which have been made of some provinces lead to the following conclusions. Not many peasants were altogether landless. About a tenth possessed the few hectares (varying from one region to the next) which meant economic security for their families. The vast majority had only a few scattered plots, often the poorest land in the district, and were compelled to find other means of livelihood. The peasants who were really rich and powerful were those who farmed great estates and manors who were to some extent the overseers and agents of the great landowners. These conclusions are valid at least for the Ile-de-France and Picardy, though they have still to be confirmed elsewhere. A village of a hundred families would include one or two big farmers whose ploughs, teams, holdings and credit made them powerful men in the locality, a dozen or so more or less independent labouring men and the same number of poor souls whose only possessions were their hovel, their patch of ground or their ewe or who were frankly beggars. The remainder, farm hands, casual labourers, vineyard workers, woodmen and weavers were all humble folk scraping a meagre living from tiny holdings and turning their hands to any trade that came their way. The tools, livestock and employment on which the entire village depended for a livelihood, at least in good years, were in the hands of the dozen or so "big men" and even, in some cases, of a single "cock" of the village. Nothing could have been less egalitarian than a French village community. "Jacques Bonhomme" never existed except in the minds of novelists and pamphleteers. Village administration, which was more energetic and effective than that of our modern councils, was naturally in the hands of the farmers and labouring men who formed the "better part" of the local assemblies. The village community levied taxes from all its members towards the upkeep of the church, priest's house, grave-yard, schoolhouse and teacher, and for the communal shepherd, or shepherds, and wardens and keepers to watch over the crops or vineyards. In many cases the local village community was combined with the religious one of the parish to form a basic administrative unit of the kingdom in matters concerning *bailliages*, elections, salt stores and control of woods and forests and so forth. More rarely it was identified with the *seigneurie*.

This, with the village and the parish, constituted the third social group to which the peasant belonged. As we know, the *seigneur*, whether individual or collective, nobleman or *roturier*, clergy or layman, enjoyed a great many rights, honorary or otherwise, which varied endlessly from place to place and were persistently confused with the privileges of nobility. (A fact extremely convenient for the *faux nobles*, *seigneurs* of long standing who probably formed the bulk of the French nobility.) These seigneurial dues might be slight or they might be ruinous and were generally substantial but they were invariably a burden, the extent of which varied according to the region, the *seigneur* and his collector. In the long sequence of peasant revolts which go to make up the history of rural France in the seventeenth century it is as common to find the peasants allied with the *seigneur* against the king—as, for instance, in Auvergne—as it is the opposite—notably in Brittany and Picardy. Even an absentee *seigneur* often made his authority felt through the severity and unlimited powers of his collectors, intendants, judges, bailiffs, seneschals, clerks and fiscal attorneys, who were not always remarkable for their honesty. Insufficient study has been devoted to the seigneurial courts which were numerous, busy and basic to an understanding of rural life. They clearly served a useful purpose to their clients but sometimes at the cost of substantial fees and the imposition of large fines for trivial offences.

The parish priest was an inseparable part of rural life in 1661. He played an important, although variable role and he, too, took his share of the country's resources, for his own support and for the maintenance of church buildings and furniture. This was rarely in the form of major tithes (on corn etc.) which went to more powerful men than himself, but for the most part in small levies which were not easy to collect and in casual sums for the various offices of his calling.

This meant that there were four interested parties preying on the labour and income of the peasants: the local community, the Church, the *seigneur* and the king. The last of these was the most diverse and also the most oppressive, varying from simple, direct methods such as the *taille*, the *gabelle* and a number of additional taxes, to the more complex and equally burdensome host of indirect levies, the most loathed of which were the *aides* on liquor. In theory these were an extraordinary and purely temporary measure, as were the dues paid for the food and lodging of military personnel, although even these were not so harsh as the actual billeting of a swaggering, thieving soldiery which was dreaded almost as much as the plague and had turned up all too often in the past twenty-five years.

The levies raised in kind, whether they were collected or required to be delivered, difficult as they were, were the easiest to manage. For the rest, money had to be found somehow by dint of piece work, day labouring and the marketing of small items such as a calf, a few fleeces, some lambs or a clutch of eggs or chickens if these could be raised. The poorer peasants borrowed to raise the money, always from the same people: the better-off labourer, the tax collector or any scrivener, court official or tradesman prepared to advance the price of a piece of cloth or a few dozen nails. The debt remained to be paid, entered on a scrap of paper, with interest added in advance, and registered officially in the presence of a notary or before a court of law. The debtor did his best to pay it back in kind and the partial or complete repayment of these small IOUs was often his chief reward. One bad harvest, a visitation by the soldiers, an epidemic or the death of a cow or a few sheep could mean a swift rise in the amount of the debt and eventual foreclosure. Anyone who has gone through the inventories compiled after the deaths of labourers of the time finds the monotonous repetition of the same lists of liabilities, cutting into or even wiping out the assets, becoming an obsession. In order to satisfy the collectors of rents and taxes, the peasants fell victim to a host of creditors, some local but more often townsmen, a few in the church but the majority belonging to the *bourgeoisie*. When times were particularly hard, as they were during the Frondes, this system resulted in the wholesale dispossession of country folk by their creditors and in the passage of numerous smallholdings into wealthy hands to form the basis of large estates, especially in the vicinity of prosperous towns and abbeys. In this way a considerable portion of the income earned by the peasants of the kingdom was swallowed up simply in paying back loans. A number of attempts have been made to calculate exactly how large this portion was, but the results vary according to place, the attitudes of those engaged in the calculation and, above all, the year. Setting aside the possibility of vast discrepancies in time and place, it may be put forward as a general rule that the poorer French peasants hardly ever kept more than half the gross product of their labours for themselves. This was not in fact so very little if we think for a moment of the Spanish peasants, of the serfs of Prussia or Muscovy, of the incredible toll of four fifths of the total produce customarily exacted from tenant farmers in Muslim lands, of the appalling conditions of Chinese and Japanese peasants as revealed in recent studies, or of the North American Indians, driven from their own lands at gunpoint by their god-fearing conquerors.

The life of the small minority of urban workers, whom the peasants outnumbered by twenty to one, seems to have been much closer to the social conditions with which we are familiar. These were typical of the traditional type of the proletariat, owning neither land nor houses, living in rented accommodation and with practically no furniture or linen to their names. They lived entirely on their earnings, paid on a piece work rate, though sometimes by the day and occasionally including some food. The money, like the job itself, was always uncertain. In practice, a system of advances on the part of the employers turned these workers of the Grand Siècle into a class—for that is what they were—of permanent debtors, entirely at the mercy of their masters. They might or might not belong to the so-called corporative institutions (the word corporation is an English one and a good deal later than Louis XIV), but these were more like religious brotherhoods in appearance, or occasionally a means of self-protection: in general they were dominated by the employers and without any real influence. There are known to have been none in rural areas and we must therefore disabuse ourselves of the twentieth-century idea that society in the seventeenth century was made up of corporations. This urban proletariat suffered from a very real degree of exploitation which often took the form of a subtle cheating in the matter of goods, hours of work or the nature of remuneration—workers were paid with lengths of unsaleable cloth, in bad coin which was not easy to get rid of, in false measures of flour and so forth. More often than not they worked from home or were employed by the day. Workshops employing labour on a large scale were the exception and there is little reliable evidence of the so-called patriarchal care of a "good master." The profits earned by these methods did not often go to those who supervised the work, who were themselves simply links in the chain of an industrial hierarchy at the top of which were usually the powerful merchants who were the chief beneficiaries of the system.

In practice, although the poverty of the urban working class was frequently striking and better known than the sufferings of the peasants, it may well have been less dire. On the one hand, the workers in the cities had the advantage of organized charities of long standing which had been substantially improved by the recent expansion of the hospitals (first in Lyons, then in Beauvais, in 1653 and Paris in 1655) while on the other, the workers themselves possessed some means of putting pressure on their employers through the spontaneous formation of their own secret societies, many of which were very powerful. This was especially true in times when there was a heavy demand coupled with a shortage of skilled labour, such as occurred as a sequel to various demographic and economic crises. Finally, at this period townsmen were privileged in paying substantially fewer taxes than the peasants. Naturally they were not liable to tithes and generally got off more lightly in the matter of seigneurial dues. The worst troubles of the urban poor, shortages and unemployment, generally came together. In spite of some valiant efforts, private and public charity was unable to cope with really desperate crises in employment and rising prices and the workers, huddled in their wretched dwellings, eating what scraps they could and abandoned by all save a handful of doctors and priests, died like flies. This in itself, however, helped to solve the problems of shortage of food and work. The survivors could look forward to a few easy years before the next crisis occurred. And so, in 1661, the poor people of the towns were beginning to forget the recent troubles of the Frondes and were once more able to make an honest living while they waited for what new disaster should lie in wait for them.

Fifteen million peasants, therefore, together with a tenth or a twentieth of that number of workers (the title of journeyman had fallen into disuse) made up the productive force of the realm and made some kind of a living, mostly rather poor but occasionally quite good, punctuated every now and then by appalling periods of crisis. Taking into account time, place and attitude of mind, they should probably be regarded as among the more fortunate of the world's populations. If they did sometimes complain or resort here and there to active rebellion triggered off by a new tax, an unexpected shortage, a false rumour or some more or less well-founded apprehension, these revolts were never more than local or regional affairs, with little or no organization, and only became at all serious when some other sector of society —usually the nobility—began to take a positive interest.

These popular risings, the existence, duration and gravity of which is no longer in dispute, were regularly concluded by the triumph of order as symbolized by the king's army. They had no serious effect on the comparatively simple basis of society.

If, for the sake of brevity, we discount the middle class which was still very small although showing signs of development among the small shopkeepers, craftsmen and minor tradespeople, it would be fair to say that, as a general rule, nine out of ten of King Louis' subjects worked hard and thanklessly with their hands in order to permit the tenth to devote himself comfortably to the life of bourgeois, nobleman or mere idler. Directly or indirectly, this tenth of the population lived to a greater or lesser extent on the vast revenues of the land, scraped from the soil of the kingdom by the inhabitants of the countryside and swelled and transformed by their labour and those of the workers in the towns. To one of these numerous classes of *rentier* belonged nearly all the nobility, most of the clergy and the whole of the bourgeoisie, all those privileged persons in fact who also enjoyed the benefits of their own special legal system, the *leges privatae*.

Premodern Families

DAVID HUNT

Much of our image of premodern society depends on an evaluation of the family. A sense that family life is decaying goes back to the beginning of industrialization and continues to the present day, making it sometimes difficult to understand how anything remains to deteriorate further. The family as an economic unit has undoubtedly declined. The question is, what has happened to it as a unit of affection?

Peter Laslett stressed the bonds of love that united the family. More recent work, however, emphasizes the tensions that existed within the family. There is evidence of serious discord between young adults and their parents, as the young people generally could not marry or even enjoy adult status until their parents died or retired, leaving them with the land. Laslett himself suggests one possible result of this friction: the practice of putting children into the service of other families.

There is also serious question about the attitudes toward and the treatment of young children in the early modern family. The following selection relies for its evidence primarily on documents from the upper classes, particularly the account of the upbringing of Louis XIII when he was dauphin. But the author generalizes about French society as a whole, a dangerous practice but perhaps necessary in this murky area. He also applies some of the theories of modern psychology to a decidedly unmodern family structure. This approach, too, can be criticized; it might be argued that premodern families produced a different set of psychological problems. (Hunt clearly suggests they produced a different personality, but he bases his views on modern notions of personality.) If we cannot apply psychological theories to the past, though, we clearly restrict our claims to a full knowledge of history.

Hunt's picture, if correct, has a number of implications for the history of modernization. In contrast to Laslett's view, it suggests that in the seventeenth century the family as an affectionate unit was barely developed. In other words, the picture of preindustrial life as emotionally and psychologically satisfying must be seriously qualified—there may not have been as much for industrialization to disrupt as some authorities claim. And as a more affectionate family did develop, it may well have added important new dimensions to human experience, thus serving as some compensation for whatever new stresses modernization did produce.

At the same time, certain aspects of family life had to change before modernization was possible. In particular, there is evidence that the extremely authoritarian treatment of children, designed to break their will and to retard individual initiative and innovation, did begin to change in the eighteenth century. Swaddling (tightly wrapping an infant in strips of cloth), for example, was abandoned in France. It is also possible that the affection for young children increased.

Only the outlines of these changes have as yet been established, but they have important implications. Why did they occur? Some historians have argued that in the late seventeenth century the upper classes began to develop new emotions about young children and that these new attitudes filtered down to the lower classes. David Hunt mentions that the thinkers of the Enlightenment urged greater affection and specifically criticized practices such as swaddling. Declining child mortality rates in the eighteenth century may have encouraged parents to make a greater emotional investment in their children. The reasons are not fully clear, and we cannot at this point be sure that the lower-class outlook toward children did actually change significantly during the eighteenth century. Again the question is whether the common people began to revise their own attitudes before they were caught up in externally imposed change. In any event, the long-term changes in behavior toward children suggest the need to reinterpret the role of the family in modernization.

For every new-born infant, whether he was from a rich family or a poor one, whether he was raised by a nurse, a governess, or by his parents, the major difficulty in the first months of life was getting enough to eat. Without bottles or good baby foods, adults were very hard pressed to nourish children fully and safely. Our effort to understand childhood in the seventeenth century ought to begin with a discussion of this fundamental issue.

The experience of Louis XIII, as recorded by Héroard, provides a good starting point. From the beginning, the dauphin had feeding problems. The difficulty was first attributed to the "fiber" (*filet*) under the infant's tongue. His surgeon, Jacques Guillemeau, cut this fiber in the hope of making it easier for the young prince to suck properly. In the days that followed, attention shifted to the nurse. She did not seem to have enough milk to satisfy the baby, who sucked in "such great gulps . . . that he drew more in on one try than others did in three." The woman attempted to correct this deficiency by eating more than usual, a tactic which succeeded only in giving her an upset stomach. A supplementary nurse was brought in and then almost immediately dismissed because enemies at court managed to discredit her with the queen. When Louis was eleven weeks old, and obviously undernourished, a medical conference was summoned to consider further remedies. This situation gives occasion for some sober thought. With unlimited resources at their disposal, and with the child enjoying the best possible living conditions available at that time, the doctors nonetheless found themselves confronted with a case of virtual starvation: the muscles of the dauphin's chest were "completely wasted away," and his neck was so thin that the folds in the skin had disappeared. A third nurse arrived, but she lasted only a short time; people

Excerpts from Chapter Six of *Parents and Children in History: The Psychology of Family Life in Early Modern France* by David Hunt, © 1970 by Basic Books, Inc., Publishers, New York.

thought she was not "clean." The fourth and permanent nurse was not in place until the baby was sixteen weeks old.

This account is in no way extraordinary. For example, the operation on the dauphin's tongue was routinely performed. Almost all the medical authorities mentioned it, with Guillemeau giving the fullest explanation:

> In children that are newly borne there are commonly found two strings: the one comes from the bottome of the tongue, and reacheth to the very tip and end thereof. This string is very slender and soft and it hindreth the child from taking the nipple . . . so that he cannot sucke well. This string must be cut with a sizzer within a few daies after he is borne.

Paré agreed with this advice, adding that, if not cut, the "string" would later cause the child to stutter. These comments were not dictated by the surgeon's desire for an extra commission; Vallambert's remark that the cutting was well performed with one's thumbnail indicates that the doctors thought anyone could do the job. One folklorist has maintained that the custom of cutting the infant's *filet* persisted into the twentieth century in rural France.

The trouble with the nurses was also common, and in fact Louis' appetites were rather modest when compared to those of other children in the royal line. Michelet claimed that as an infant Henri IV went through eight nurses; Louis XIV may have had as many as nine. In the *livres de raison*, several families hired and discarded one nurse after another because no one among them was able to satisfy the demands of the infant she had been contracted to feed. These accounts give us another perspective on the use of the nurse. In a situation where breastfeeding was clearly the best and the safest way to nourish children, the financial ability to employ a nurse, or better yet a whole string of them, was a major advantage for a family anxious about the welfare of its offspring. If something happened to the mother nursing her own children, if she became ill or if another pregnancy interrupted the regime of breastfeeding (it was felt that carrying a child and feeding one at the same time was too taxing an undertaking for a woman to attempt), she could fall back on her family's economic reserves and bring in a nurse to help out. In a number of cases, the mother shared from the moment of birth feeding chores with a nurse, so that there were always two women available to her infant.

Since their families could not afford nurses, most children must have been forced to work even harder than the dauphin to get enough to eat. Mothers seem to have felt that, because of their many other duties, they were not in a position to devote a great deal of time even to very young children. The medical literature was almost unanimously in favor of feeding children on demand, but of all the pieces of advice offered by the experts this suggestion was among the most academic. The doctors indicate that the common practice was to limit feeding to particular times and places determined by the women rather than by their offspring. Even if the poor mother managed to stay with her child at all times, it was thought that she still would not have enough milk to satisfy him. As Vallambert observed: "Because of their continual labor and poor life, [these mothers] do not have a lot of milk, so that they would not be capable of feeding the child if he did not take other nourishment in addition to the milk from the breast."

This "other nourishment" was "gruel" (*bouillie*), a combination of cow's or goat's milk with wheat flour or the crumbs of white bread soaked in water. The mixture was to be baked until it thickened, then served to the infant on his mother's or nurse's finger. This staple appears to have been very widely used. Dionis commented: "There are no women who do not know how to make *bouillie*." Yet the doctors were very suspicious of it. *Bouillie* was too "viscous and thick," causing "indigestion and constipation." Women made the mixture carelessly, not sifting the flour or neglecting the baking stage.

However, in a characteristic way, these experts would break their discussion in two parts. Recognizing the strength of the custom, and apparently deciding to make the best of a bad situation, they would add all sorts of recommendations on the use of *bouillie*, for example, that egg yolk or honey added to the mixture would serve as a purgative, counteracting the "obstruction" normally caused by the food. Several of them were content with very modest prohibitions against its use, forbidding *bouillie* in the first two weeks of a child's life. Mauriceau's belief that it should not be added to the infant's diet until the second or third month seems utopian by comparison.

Badly prepared *bouillie*, fed to the infant on the end of his mother's finger, must have created serious problems for untested digestive systems. However, the use of this staple was unavoidable:

> Long before the first teeth appear, even before the age of three months, . . . the women of the countryside, and the other poor women of the towns [give *bouillie* to their children] because if the latter took no other nourishment besides milk, they would not be able to go so long without sucking as they do, during the time when mothers are absent and held down by their work.

Even the dauphin was given *bouillie* only eighteen days after birth. Here, as elsewhere, the experience of the most precious child in the kingdom enables us to imagine the even more somber circumstances of his less fortunate peers. A squad of nurses barely managed to feed the dauphin, and his diet had to be filled out with *bouillie* before he was three weeks old. In spite of all the efforts of the household, Louis almost succumbed. We might well wonder how other children survived the precarious first months of life.

In fact, when the infant did not get enough milk at the breast and was unable to digest the *bouillie*, he starved. The willingness to have children suckled by farm animals (a practice condoned in the medical literature) indicates the gravity of the food problem. In this respect, the story of the feeding of children represents very well the insecurity of their situation as a whole. For whatever reason, a shocking number of children died. This mortality rate has been fairly conclusively documented. In one rural area during the seventeenth century, more than one-quarter of the children born at a given time did not reach the age of one, and almost a half died before the age of four. There are no equally reliable statistics for urban areas within France during this period, but from what we know of European cities in general, it seems safe to conclude that rates there would have been at least as high. The fact that infants were so vulnerable, that it was tremendously difficult to feed them properly and to protect them from disease and death, is the fundamental precondition which we of a more comfortable milieu must grasp if we are to understand what childhood was like in the seventeenth century. . . .

With these thoughts in mind, it is interesting to turn to actual descriptions of very small children in the seventeenth century. In fact, grownups had a highly developed awareness of the infant's tireless capacity for appropriation, of his tenacious parasitism. The picture Héroard sketched of a greedy Louis gulping in huge swallows of milk is not without a tinge of the sinister. It was commonly believed that birth was prompted by the hunger of the infant who, because he could no longer satisfy himself in the womb, tried "with great impetuousness to get out." Avarice was the child's principal trait: "All children are naturally very greedy and gluttonous." At the same time that they called for feeding on demand, the doctors cautioned mothers against overfeeding. While being indulgent, they could not let the unquenchable appetite of the infant hold full sway.

These opinions take on their full significance when we note that the experts thought the mother's milk was actually whitened blood. They do not seem to have understood the fact that secretion of milk in the mother's body is a self-sustaining process designed specifically to meet the special demands of the new-born infant. The nursing situation was not seen as a cooperative effort, but as a struggle in which the interests of the two parties were at least to some extent at odds. In fact, the infant prospered at the expense of his mother, from whose body he sucked the precious substance he needed for his own survival. These views explain why breastfeeding was seen as a debilitating experience for a woman, why she was counseled to hire a nurse after a difficult delivery, or if she again became pregnant. Only the healthy mother could afford to sacrifice a part of herself for the welfare of her children.

In a world where people believed that resources of all kinds were fixed and in short supply, the prosperity of one person or group was always linked to the bad luck of others. From this perspective, adults were naturally disturbed by the incessant demands of small children. For example, I think that such sentiments underlie the story recorded by Louise Bourgeois about a Strasburg mother who fell asleep while nursing her child. A snake with poisonous fangs attached itself to her breast and began to suck. The woman and her husband could not remove the animal for fear that it would bite, and for ten months it continued to suck, growing to monstrous proportions on the strength of this nourishment. Bourgeois thought the incident showed "how much substance there is in woman's milk." The mother was forced to put her child out to nurse and to go everywhere with the unwelcome guest, carrying it in a basket. The child at the breast had been transformed into a serpent, symbol of evil. At the end of the story, only the magic charms of a sorceress succeeded in tempting away this covetous intruder.

The fear of being bitten expressed in the story was manifested more generally by adults in a great deal of anxiety about teething. Parents reacted very specifically to this step in infantile development and regarded teething as a serious disease which might lead to all sorts of complications: diarrhea, fevers, epilepsy, spasms, and even death. Paré wrote:

> Monseigneur de Nemours sent to fetch me to anatomize his dead son, aged eight months or thereabouts, whose teeth had not erupted. Having diligently searched for the cause of his death, I could not find any, if not that his gums were very hard, thick and swollen; having cut through them, I found all his teeth ready to come out, if only someone had cut his gums. So it was decided by the doctors present and by me that the sole cause of his death was that nature had not been strong enough to pierce the gums and push the teeth out.

Remedies abounded for this "disease," and parents were advised to rub the sore gums with all sorts of magical panaceas. If this did not help, Guillemeau suggested: "Rub the legs, thighs, shoulders, backe and nape of the child's necke, drawing still downwards, thereby to alter and turne the course of humours which fall downe upon the gummes and passages of the throat." As a last resort, the surgeon was supposed to cut the gums so that the teeth might more easily emerge.

In these comments, doctors stress the fact that teeth are the infant's first aggressive tools, although they limit themselves to discussing the ways in which children themselves can be harmed by such sharp instruments. However, I think that the tone of the discussion, the awe with which doctors analyze the eruption of teeth, indicate an underlying fear of the child's biting impulses, the potentially dangerous use he can make of his mouth. In this respect, the interpretation of teething is consistent with the tendency to see children as gluttonous little animals and with the belief that they were sucking away the mother's blood. Collecting together these images, we have a picture of the small child as a predatory and frightening creature capable of harming the woman whose duty it was to care for him. Returning to Erikson's hypothesis, we can say that in the eyes of his elders the seventeenth-century infant was an "oral sadist."

I have no doubt that similar themes appear in the childrearing literature of all cultures. In fact, they are built into the breastfeeding relationship: the infant does suck with striking intensity, because his life depends on it; women are to some extent tied down by the demands of their very small offspring; and breastfeeding is always complicated by the child's teething. At the same time, I believe that images of the child as a greedy little animal had a special power in the seventeenth century and that they exerted a relatively pronounced negative influence on efforts to feed the very young.

I picture a mother, who herself probably did not get enough to eat, and who was forced to work long and difficult hours, turning to the task of breastfeeding with mixed feelings. The child was a parasite; he did nothing and yet his appetites seemed to be endless. He was sucking a vital fluid out of her already depleted body. This situation must have been tremendously difficult for mothers to tolerate. In turn, children sensed the anxiety of their providers, perhaps in the tense way they were held, in the tentativeness of the breast being offered to them. Aware of the unreliability of this source of life, they redoubled their efforts to "get" as much as possible. These efforts impressed mothers as especially gluttonous and devouring, and in reaction they developed an image of children as greedy little animals, who were harmful to their guardians. These fantasies worked to undermine the resolution of mothers, whose gathering ambivalence would be communicated to children, who in turn would become all the more peremptory in their demands for more milk.

Some hypothesis along these lines is necessary to account for the frequent breakdown in efforts to feed little children. The poverty of the society, while it provided the necessary, and very powerful, initial impetus for the process by which mother and child became wary of each other, is not in itself a sufficient explanation for the problem. Mothers in equally poor societies manage to keep their children close by and to feed them on demand. Medically speaking, there is no reason why a woman, even if she is relatively undernourished, cannot adequately breastfeed a child. Further, we know that lactation does not weaken mothers who undertake it. This analyis is not intended as a critique of seventeenth-century mothers. Given their situation, it is entirely natural that they should have been ambivalent about children. My point is that economic or physiological arguments do not in themselves explain the great difficulty experienced in getting enough food into the child's belly. These difficulties make sense only if we picture the specifically economic factors overlaid with a set of disturbing fantasies about children at the breast. The problem was first of all in the seventeenth-century economy, but at the same time it was also in the minds and the deportment of parents.

This point is clearly illustrated in the royal court, and in the houses of the rich, where nurses, who almost certainly got enough to eat, were often unable to produce enough milk for the children they were supposed to breastfeed. Poor living conditions cannot explain these failures which the literature documents with such regularity and which adults of the time seem to have accepted as a matter of course. The situation of the nurse must have created conflicts of its own. Given their low status, and the constant critical scrutiny of people like Héroard, who were alert to any sign of their inadequacy as providers, these women may well have had trouble relaxing and devoting themselves wholeheartedly to the task of feeding the children of their superiors. On the other hand, I suspect that some part of the problem was independent of the woman's identity as a nurse, but instead grew out of her image of children, her sense of them as demanding and dangerous little animals, a sense she shared with all other mothers, of the time. . . . In his analysis of the first phase of childhood growth, Erik Erikson maintains that the incorporative mode of behavior is expressed most obviously through the mouth, but that it is also manifested in the activity of the infantile organism as a whole. The child must be seen as a personality, facing a total existential situation, and not simply as an oral creature who must be fed. By contrast, in the seventeenth century infantile experience was grasped by adults primarily in terms of feeding. The discussion of the doctors concentrated heavily on the problem of how best to nourish the child. In the same spirit, parents contracted with nurses to serve simply as suppliers of milk, rather than as maternal figures in a broader sense, because they believed that the infant's alimentary needs were the only ones worthy of serious attention. The fact that small children needed conversation, companionship, and play, as well as nourishment of a more tangible sort, was not well understood by adults of the period.

Of course parents were amused and diverted by infants and did take notice of them in situations other than those connected with feeding. On the other hand, I think it is significant that in the seventeenth century the notion of "playing" with children had an ambiguous ring. Some critics thought that in this play adults betrayed a careless, self-indulgent attitude. In casting about for the words to describe their impressions, these observers hit upon a comparison which we have already encountered in the discussion of feeding: parents treated children like pets, or little animals. Montaigne argued: "We have loved [infants] for our own amusement, like monkeys, not like human beings." And Fleury commented: "It is as if the poor children had been made only to amuse the adults, like little dogs or little monkeys."

This comparison of the child to an animal is something more than a useful device, a way of characterizing the infant at the breast. The image appears throughout seventeenth-century literature on children. In a total sense, the small child was an intermediate being, not really an animal (although he might often be compared to one), but on the other hand not really human either. This quasi-evolutionary model of the ages of life was so ingrained that adults often hardly noticed its presence in their own speech. Thus in describing the battle of Paris, Jean Burel wrote that the Parisians "were besieged by the King of Navarre so closely that they were forced to eat animals: dogs, horses, everything right up to, and almost including, little children." In the chain of being, a separate link—infancy—connected the animal and the human worlds without belonging completely to either one.

I have already argued that, with respect to the specifically oral forms of this image of the child as little animal, in an area where infant survival was very much at stake, parents struggled with their negative feelings and managed to stay in touch with their offspring. Once the child had been safely fed, however, it is possible that adults gave vent to their aversion and disgust and treated the infant with the callousness which his subhuman station deserved. We must try to ascertain whether the feeding of infants was somehow special, or if, on the other hand, parental attitudes in that area carried over into the whole of relations with the child during the first year of life.

I think the best way to approach this problem is through an examination of the practice of swaddling. The eighteenth-century philosophes have already experimented with a similar tactic. In turning their attention to child-rearing, they found evidence of negligence on every side, but nowhere more obnoxiously manifested than in the practice of swaddling. In detailing the evils of the custom, these critics conjured up a whole gallery of cruel images: the infant was wrapped up tight and tossed "in a corner"; or the nurse hung a crying baby in swaddling clothes from a nail on the wall, so that the bands tightened, suffocating the child and choking off his cries; or the nurse placed the swaddled baby in his cradle and rocked him until he fell into a groggy sleep. In all these instances, swaddling represented a general point of view toward children, a deficiency in that sympathy or generosity which the philosophes thought a child had a right to expect from his elders. While reserving judgment on the exact meaning of the practice, I follow the eighteenth-century critics by discussing swaddling in this symbolic sense, as a key to understanding what adults thought of the first stage of life.

The swaddling of infants, which to us is one of the most exotic features of childrearing in the seventeenth century, was utterly taken for granted by the adults of that period. Doctors, who showed such a lively interest in the various controversial issues of childrearing, barely took notice of swaddling and offered only a few scraps of advice on the subject; as Mauriceau put it, "There are no women who do not know all about something which is so common." In describing Louis' birth, Héroard mentions that the infant was swaddled soon after being washed and fed, but he never refers to the clothes again. In an account otherwise rich in detail, there is nothing on the regime of swaddling: how the wrapping was done, when during the day the clothes were removed, not even a hint as to when in the life of the dauphin the practice was terminated. Although swaddling has almost completely disappeared in modern France, the custom was once so deeply rooted in everyday life that it was put into practice almost automatically. This combination of factors makes it a particularly useful, as well as difficult, subject for the historian interested in the distinctive qualities of childrearing in the old regime.

The swaddling band (called the *maillot*) was a roll of cloth about two inches across. The infant was wrapped up with this length of cloth, arms straight at his sides and legs extended, with a few extra turns around the head to hold it steady, so that only a small circle of his face would be left exposed. Doctors advised that the pressure of the band should be equal on all parts of the body, to avoid crippling the infant, and that especial care should be taken in wrapping the chest and stomach so that breathing would not be impeded. The swaddling was left in place at all times during the first weeks of an infant's life except when it was necessary to clean and change him. Vallambert suggested that if an infant cried excessively, one could "unswaddle him, and massage and move his limbs, for that often causes the crying and the screaming to stop." At some time early in his life (according to doctors, between the first and fourth month), the infant's arms would be freed and the wrappings applied only to his legs and torso. Finally, when he was eight or nine months old, or at the latest around his first birthday, the infant would be left unswaddled for good.

Intuitively—and wrongly—we imagine that such a regime would leave infants deformed or retarded. Actual details on the physical development of babies in the seventeenth century are very scarce, but Héroard's *Journal* does suggest something of the dauphin's progress in this respect and helps to show that swaddling did not stunt the growth of children. At first, the doctor describes Louis performing acts compatible with a regime of swaddling: listening, staring, speaking, laughing. At four months, Louis was "playing" with the king and queen, and in one session Henri studied the feet of his son, which, he had been told, resembled his own. At five and a half months, "he dances gaily to the sound of a violin." Obviously this was not real dancing, but perhaps some rhythmic movement of the arms. A week later, he stretched out his hand for an object (a book) for the first time. Louis was throwing things at the age of six months and was also being put to bed with his arms free (it will be remembered that while he was teething Héroard sat up holding his hand). At eight months, the dauphin was fitted for his first pair of shoes, and six weeks later the "leading strings" (*lisières*), which would be used by adults to help him learn to walk, were attached to his clothes.

This circumstantial evidence seems to fit well enough the schedule suggested by the doctors. No later than five and a half months after his birth, Louis' arms were left unswaddled so that he was free to "dance," to grasp a book, to be held by the hand. In fact, he may have been completely unswaddled by this time since Henri IV was able to study his feet; but it is also possible that the dauphin was specially unwrapped for his parents' visit. In any case, the *maillot* was definitively discarded by eight or nine months when Louis was fitted for shoes and *lisières*.

Swaddling had little effect on subsequent motor development. Apparently children did not spend much time crawling. There are almost no pictorial representations of a stage between swaddling and walking, and, on the other hand, every effort seems to have been made to help children learn how to walk. Around his first birthday, the dauphin was indeed walking with "firmness, held under the arms." When Louis was nineteen months old, Héroard describes him running, and in going from place to place he was now led (*mené*) as often as carried (*porté*). The descriptions offered of his play corroborate the impression of the dauphin's rapidly growing dexterity, "fencing" with Héroard (ten months), playing the violin and the drum (about a year and a half), and striking a blow of fifty-five paces with his "bat" (*palemail*) when he was just over two.

Swaddling obviously did not cripple children. In fact the practice performed a number of positive functions. From the recent literature on the subject, we know that (like a high-walled cradle or a play-pen) swaddling limits potentially dangerous motor activity; that (like a carriage) it makes children easier to carry; and that it provides a measure of security and reassurance by relieving the infant of responsibility for the control of his limbs in a period when he does not yet have sufficient physical mastery to handle the job completely on his own.

All of these reasons may have been considered in the seventeenth century, but they were not mentioned by experts in their terse discussions of the practice. Among the reasons which were given for swaddling, the first and most important seems to have been that it kept the baby warm:

> Nor then forget that wrappers be at hand,
> Soft flannels, linen, and the swaddling band,
> T'enwrap the babe, by many a circling fold,
> In equal lines, and thus defend from cold.

This function was very important; we are dealing with a world in which even the royal palaces were so poorly insulated that children had to be admonished to stay close to the fireplace on the coldest days. One doctor cautioned against freeing the child's arms during the winter. Even if he was past the age of three or four months, the baby was to remain fully swaddled "until he is older and it is not so cold."

Doctors also argued that swaddling was necessary to help the infant's limbs grow straight. Apparently this belief in the effectiveness of the wrapping is not unfounded, especially when one considers the prevalence of rickets among young children at that time. There was also some notion that swaddling prevented the child from hurting himself by striking a hard object or by falling. More generally, swaddling immobilized the child under reasonably beneficial circumstances and thus served as a substitute for the constant attention which the unhindered baby would have required from its elders. This substitution may often have been dictated by a lack of interest in children and could therefore be interpreted (in the tradition of the philosophes) as a sign of parental neglect. However, in this respect as in others, we must be careful to distinguish matters of choice from those of necessity. For many poor women, the *maillot*, no less than *bouillie*, was an essential device which enabled them to spend long periods of time at work and away from their infants. For any society which could not afford to be too child-centered, swaddling, or some other practice which relieved adults of the need for constant supervision of children, was inevitable and can hardly be construed as a sign of some special parental malice and neglect.

In fact, swaddling can be interpreted as an antidote to the more extreme forms of parental ambivalence. We have seen how much contempt adults were likely to feel for children and how they seemed to regard their offspring as little animals. Swaddling allowed parents to defend against the consequences of their own distaste. This distinctive custom helped to place infants. It defined with a more reassuring precision the limbo of childhood, leaving it distinct from the sphere of adult life, but also firmly marking it off from the animal kingdom. As Mauriceau observed, children were swaddled for fear they would otherwise never learn to stand erect, but would always crawl on all fours like little animals. Swaddling embodied the promise of a future humanity and saved infants from a descent to that animal world into which their own strangeness and frailty threatened to propel them.

In the same spirit, adults wanted children either in swaddling clothes or walking on two feet. Crawling was discouraged precisely because it made more ambiguous that distinction between infants and animals which adults knew in their hearts they had to maintain. We have already seen how a kind of collective repression protected parents from their fear of the predatory appetites of growing infants. With its numerous benefits, and as a means of defining the first stage of life, swaddling operated on an even more general plane as a way of caring for infants and at the same time of binding up the anxiety which adults experienced in dealing with the animality of small children. . . .

I would maintain that in the seventeenth century people felt strongly the contrast between the loyalties and duties incumbent upon them as a consequence of their station in society on the one hand, and their natural inclinations on the other. Institutional arrangements always implied a gradation of rank and were thus held to be incompatible with friendship, in which equality between the partners was so important. Far from accepting the fact that personal relations were almost always arranged according to hierarchical principles, individuals were made acutely uncomfortable by this situation. In personal letters, writers often distinguished sincere and spontaneous affection from the more perfunctory good will which went with the formal relationship to their correspondent. Thus Madame de Sévigné, in sending good wishes to her daughter, stipulated that, "In this case, maternal love plays less of a part than inclination."

As the quote indicates, the family was caught up in this system. To be a brother, son, or wife was a status, with its special obligations, its place in a grid of rule and submission. Members of the family were supposed to love one another; paternal, maternal, fraternal love were all often cited as models of human fellow feeling. At the same time, even within the family, it was terribly hard to imagine a relationship of mutual affection which was not simultaneously one of ruler and ruled. Like the bond between master and servant, between seigneur and peasant, between king and subject, family ties, while steeped in a folklore of pious harmony, implied as well the power to dominate others, to claim rewards, or, on the contrary, the awareness of a helpless dependence.

This line of argument will help to explain further the distinction which, as we have seen, observers made with such clarity between marriages of love and those of interest. Marriages of love implied spontaneous affection between the two lovers, who were concerned primarily with their own happiness. Marriage of interest involved social and financial considerations to be arranged for the benefit of families. These observers understood very well that in a social system which attempted to subordinate the wishes of marriageable children to the ambitions of their parents, and in which the wife was regarded simply as the means of cementing alliances between families, marriage could not at the same time be expected to provide for the happiness and the emotional satisfaction of the partners.

Fraternal relations were compromised by similar pressures. As the dauphin was being forced to acknowledge himself as his father's valet, it was also being pointed out to him that his brothers, who were younger and hence subordinate, would serve him just as he served the king. Books of etiquette often struggled with the problem of fraternal affection and the rights of primogeniture. How do you reconcile "natural" ties with the principle which arranges brothers one above the other in a hierarchy of prerogatives? Corneille built the play *Rodogune* around this dilemma. The twins Seleucus and Antiochus are the model of fraternity. Since they do not know who is older (the oddity of the situation demonstrates how hard it was in the seventeenth century to conceive of real equality), they can be familiar and trusting in relations with one another. Their mother, however, decides to disclose the order of birth, and the two brothers are thrown into a panic. They know that if this information is revealed, one will become the arrogant master, the other, his resentful servant (full of "shame and envy"), and their accord will be ruined.

We can see that gradations of rank within the household were interpreted simply as a matter of power and of usage, and that people believed this situation discouraged close and mutually satisfying relationships among family members. Ideally, those of lower rank should have accepted the eminence of their superiors and been warmed by the benefits they received from an admittedly unequal partnership. In fact, inequality within the domestic unit filled people not with love and warmth, but with resentment and a feeling of "shame and envy."

Among the members of the family, the infant is the most prone to these feelings. His physical and intellectual inferiority is a basic fact of nature as is his subjection to the will of older, stronger adults. Precisely because it is so completely unearned by any merit, but instead is derived from an amoral biological fact, parental authority might legitimately be expected to embody whatever sense of justice adults profess to respect. The child has to obey; in what ways do grownups persuade him that he ought to obey?

It seems to me that no one could deny the paramount importance of force and intimidation in the upbringing of the dauphin. The beating Louis received at the hands of his father demonstrated the lengths to which adults were willing to carry the matter: an obstinate child was in physical danger. Grownups relied heavily on their ability to frighten the young prince. They rightly assumed that he remembered what had happened the last time he had been too defiant. Childish fears were exploited in a variety of petty ways. For example, when it was discovered that Louis was afraid of someone (a hunchbacked member of the guard, or a mason in the king's service), that person would be summoned whenever it was necessary to make Louis toe the line.

The whippings continued, gradually settling into a fixed ritual. Louis was beaten first thing in the morning the day after his infractions: "Scarcely were his eyes open when he was whipped." Often he would get up early and hide or block the door in order to avoid these sessions. When it became impossible for Madame de Montglat to handle the dauphin, his father instructed soldiers of the guard to hold him while the whippings were administered. Louis was beaten even after becoming king of France, and at the age of ten, he still had nightmares about being whipped. As late as January, 1614, adults continued to threaten Louis with the switch, but by this time his physical development was at last putting a stop to such means of punishment.

As I suggested earlier, formalized coercion was probably better for the infant than the erratic and unrestrained cruelty which no doubt characterized discipline in families where parents had to deal directly with their offspring. But even in the royal household, it is obvious that fear was one of the principal forces steering the child into that social role which adults required him to assume. Such fear was not incompatible with love. Louis always demonstrated an intense feeling for his father, and it would be foolish to pretend that their relationship was entirely negative. Yet this love (corresponding to the sentiment which many historians have thought tied together master and servant in the old regime) does not change the fact that terrorizing children was inhumane and wrong. At the core of its domestic life, I think we find a telling indictment of the old regime.

We now have a better idea of how life cycles "interlocked" in the seventeenth century. It is no accident that fathers whipped their sons for their own good, because they themselves were whipped as children. These fathers had been thwarted in their own infantile efforts to be autonomous. Punished for attempting to establish selfhood, and deprived of control over their bodies, they were left with a pervasive sense of shame and doubt. Such sentiments fit the adult life they could lead in a hierarchical society indifferent to the dignity of the individual and held together principally by coercive means. In turn, people formed along these lines were necessarily going to respond to their children's search for independence with rigid counterassertions and panicky violence. The inability of the king himself, the only man in the society who was without a master, to break out of this vicious circle attests to the power of the cycle of unfreedom.

The Spread of Urban Values

E. A. WRIGLEY

The following essay deals with one of the central changes in popular mentality brought about by modernization, the diffusion of an urban outlook and an urban economic network. Here again the beginnings of change antedated some of the more obvious phenomena of modernization, such as the industrial revolution. In England, at least, where the industrial revolution began, the popular mentality had to be altered before industrialization was possible. But the spread of urban influence raised a host of difficult problems. London became the center of an increasingly compelling economic nexus, which could draw people into commercial operations against their will. Or, more subtly, decisions could be made to participate in a limited fashion in the urban economy with no intention of yielding to the broader urban pressures which inevitably changed fundamental values and behavior patterns. The common people are not presented as passive subjects in this article, but they are seen undergoing profound changes. Perhaps the basic question is, what caused the changes in the first place? Were immigrants attracted or forced into the orbit of London? Were they escaping hardship or lured into disruption, or perhaps both? And we must remember that these changes, whatever their meaning, occurred before the mid-eighteenth century. The further question is, what kind of a population did the changes prepare for the advent of outright industrialization? The industrial revolution may have flowed from previous alterations in outlook, or it may have jolted a dynamic but still basically traditional society.

Towards the end of the seventeenth century London became the largest city in Europe. The population of Paris had reached about 400,000 by the beginning of the seventeenth century and was nearing 500,000 towards its end, but thereafter grew very little for a further century. At the time of the 1801 census its population was still just less than 550,000. London, on the other hand, grew rapidly throughout the seventeenth and eighteenth centuries. Its exact population at any time before the first census is a matter for argument but in round figures it appears to have grown from about 200,000 in 1600 to perhaps 400,000 in 1650, 575,000 by the end of the century,

From E. A. Wrigley, "A Simple Model of London's Importance in Changing English Society and Economy 1650–1750" in *Past and Present*, no. 37, July 1967, pp. 44–67. World Copyright: The Past and Present Society, Corpus Christi College Oxford. This article is reprinted with the permission of the Society and the author from *Past and Present*, a journal of historical studies, no. 37.

675,000 in 1750 and 900,000 in 1800. London and Paris were much larger than other cities in Europe during these two centuries and each was very much larger than any rival in the same country. The contrast between the size and rates of growth of the two cities is particularly striking when it is borne in mind that until the last half of the eighteenth century, when the rate of growth of population in England increased sharply, the total population of France was about four times as large as that of England. In 1650 about 2½ per cent of the population of France lived in Paris; in 1750 the figure was little changed. London, on the other hand, housed about 7 per cent of England's total population in 1650 and about 11 per cent in 1750. Only in Holland does any one city appear to have contained such a high percentage of the total national population. Amsterdam in 1650 was already a city of about 150,000 people and contained 8 per cent of the Dutch total. But Amsterdam by this time had ceased to grow quickly and a century later had increased only to about 200,000, or 9 per cent of the total.

These rough facts suggest immediately that it may be valuable to look more closely at the rapid growth of London between 1650 and 1750. Anything which distinguished England from other parts of Europe during the century preceding the industrial revolution is necessarily a subject of particular interest since it may help to throw light on the origins of that extraordinary and momentous period of rapid change which has transformed country after country across the face of the globe.

It is convenient to begin by examining first some demographic aspects of the rapid growth of population which took place in London. . . .

In any population it is normally the young and single who migrate most readily. There is a growing volume of evidence that in England in the seventeenth and eighteenth centuries mobility before marriage was very high but was reduced once marriage had taken place. In view of this, let us assume, as a part of the demographic model of London's growth, that the mean age of those migrating into London was twenty years. Given the mortality conditions of the day any large group of twenty-year-olds coming into London would represent the survivors of a birth population at least half as large again. Some 12,000 births, therefore, in the rest of England and elsewhere were earmarked, as it were, each year to make it possible for London's population to grow as it did during this period. Once again this is a very rough figure, too high for a part of the century, too low for the later decades, but useful as a means of illustrating the nature of the general demographic relationship between London and the rest of the country. . . .

On the other hand, all the calculations made above are based on figures of *net* immigration into London. The gross figures must certainly have been considerably higher since there was at all times a flow of migrants out of London as well as a heavier flow inward. If therefore one were attempting to estimate the proportion of the total adult population of England who had at some stage in their lives had direct experience of life in the great city, a sixth or an even higher fraction is as plausible a guess as any other.

   If it is fair to assume that one adult in six in England in this period had had direct experience of London life, it is probably also fair to assume that this must have acted as a powerful solvent of the customs, prejudices and modes of action of traditional, rural England. The leaven of change would have a much better chance of transforming the lump than in, say, France even if living in Paris produced the same change of attitude and action as living in London since there were proportionately four or five times fewer Frenchmen caught up in Parisian life than Englishmen in London life. Possibly there is a threshold level in a situation of this type, beneath which the values and attitudes of a traditional, rural society are very little affected by the existence of a large city, but above which a sufficiently large proportion of the population is exposed to a different way of life to effect a slow transformation in rural society. Too little is known of the sociological differences between life in London and life in provincial England to afford a clear perception of the impact of London's growth upon the country as a whole. Some things, however, are already known, and other points can be adumbrated in the hope that more research will resolve present uncertainties.

   London was so very much bigger than any other town in the country that the lives of the inhabitants of London were inevitably very different from the lives of men living in the middle rank of towns, such as Leicester or Derby, where local landed society could continue to dominate many aspects of town life and the ties with the surrounding countryside were ancient and intimate. Family life in London, at least for the very large number who had come to London from elsewhere, was necessarily different from the family life of those who lived within five or ten miles of their birthplace all their lives. Near relatives were less likely to live close at hand. Households in the central parts of London were larger on average than those in provincial England. And this was not because the conjugal families contained more children but because other members of the households were more numerous. There were many more lodgers than in the countryside, as well as servants, apprentices and other kin in varying proportions according to the social type of the parish.

   Outside the household, moreover, a far higher proportion of day-to-day contacts was inevitably casual. Urban sociologists describe the characteristic tendency of modern city life to cause individuals in these circumstances to be treated not as occupying an invariable status position in the community, but in terms of the rôle associated with the particular transaction which gave rise to the fleeting contact. They stress the encouragement which city life gives to what Weber called "rational" as opposed to "traditional" patterns of action and the tendency for contract to replace custom. The " 'aping' of one's betters" which often attracted unfavourable comment at the time, and which has sometimes been seen as a powerful influence in establishing new patterns of consumption, is a common product of social situations like that in which the inhabitants of London found themselves at this period. Coleman has recently suggested that in the seventeenth century there was probably a backward-sloping supply curve for labour. It would be fascinating to know how far the new patterns of consumption behaviour established in London may have helped to reduce any preference for leisure rather than high earnings. There is much literary evidence of the shiftless and disorderly behaviour of many members of London's population at this time, but there were important countervailing influences at work upon the bulk of the population. The shop, a most important, new influence upon consumer behaviour, was a normal feature of the London scene by the latter half of the seventeenth century. Sugar, tea and tobacco had become articles of mass consumption by the early eighteenth century. Life in London probably encouraged a certain educational achievement in a wider spectrum of the population than might be expected. In 1838–9 fewer men and women were unable to sign their names on marriage than anywhere else in the country (marks were made as a substitute for signatures by only 12 per cent of grooms and 24 per cent of brides, whereas the national averages were 33 per cent and 49 per cent respectively). How long this differential had existed is not yet known but if it proves to have been true of earlier periods in London's history also, it suggests that the London environment put a high premium on at least a minimum degree of literacy.

There were many ways in which seventeenth-century London differed from a modern city. Glass, for example, notes that in 1695 the proportion of wealthy and substantial households was highest near the centre of London and tended to fall with distance from the centre, being very low outside the city walls (apart from St. Dunstan in the West). "This kind of gradient is in contrast to that found in the modern city, in which the centrifugal movement of population has occurred particularly among the middle classes." In this respect London was still in 1695 a pre-industrial city, but in general London was far removed from the classical type of pre-industrial city. Sjoberg's account of the typical pre-industrial city may serve as a means of underlining the "modernity" of London at this period. He draws illustrative material not only from the cities of Asia today, from ancient Mesopotamia and the Near East, and from the classical cultures of the Mediterranean, but also from medieval Europe.

Sjoberg's pre-industrial city is fed because the city houses the ruling élite. The élite "induces the peasantry to increase its production and relinquish some of its harvest to the urban community." It "must persuade many persons subsisting, relative to industrial standards, on the very margins of existence, under conditions of near starvation or malnutrition, to surrender food and other items that they themselves could readily use." The farmer "brings his produce to the urban centers at irregular intervals and in varying amounts."

Within the city the merchants, those responsible for the organization of much of its economic life, are "ideally excluded from membership of the elite." A few manage to achieve high status under sufferance, but "most are unequivocally in the lower class or outcaste groups." The chief reason for excluding merchants is that they necessarily meet all types of people, making casual contacts with men in all positions, and are therefore a menace to the stability of the existing societal arrangements. Men are largely indifferent to the discipline of the clock and only half attentive to the passage of time. Almost all transactions, however trivial, are concluded only after long haggling. There is little specialization of function in craft industrial production, though a good deal of product specialization.

In the pre-industrial city the dominant type of family is the extended family, though necessity may prevent it developing so fully in the lower classes as in the élite. Marriage takes place early, and before marriage a man does not reach full adult status. On marriage the bride normally expects to move into the household of her husband's family. "However, as industrial-urbanization becomes firmly entrenched, the large extended household is no longer the ideal toward which people strive. The conjugal family system now becomes the accepted, and often the preferred norm." This occurs because "a fluid, flexible, small family unit is necessarily the dominant form in a social order characterized by extensive social and spatial mobility."

In his anxiety to correct the naive assumptions of some sociologists about cities in the past and in the developing world today, Sjoberg may well have been tempted to straitjacket his material at times in a way which does violence to history. At all events not only London but all England had moved far from his archetypal pre-industrial society by the seventeenth century. The conjugal family system was firmly established in England at that time. On marriage a man and his wife set up a new household. And both sexes married late, later than in England today, and far later than in extra-European societies in which marriage, for women at least, almost invariably occurred at or even before puberty. Where three generations did live together in the same household this was not usually because a son on marriage brought his wife to his parents' home, but because a grandparent came to live in the household of a married son or daughter when no longer able to look after himself or herself, for example on the death of a spouse.

London shared these sociological and demographic characteristics with the rest of the country. Three-generational households were possibly rather commoner in the wealthier parts of London than was usual elsewhere but everywhere the conjugal family appears to have been the dominant form. The status of merchants in London varied with their wealth but it would be difficult to argue that they were largely excluded from the ruling élite. The provisioning of London was secured by an elaborate and sophisticated set of economic institutions and activities and many of the farmers who sent their produce to the London market geared their land to commodity production in a thoroughly "modern" fashion. In short, whereas pre-industrial cities might grow large and powerful without in any way undermining the structure of traditional society, a city like London in the later seventeenth century was so constituted sociologically, demographically and economically that it could well reinforce and accelerate incipient change.

What might be called the demonstration effect of London's wealth and growth, for instance, played an important part in engendering changes elsewhere. London contained many men of great wealth and power whose sources of wealth did not lie in the land and who found it possible to maintain power and status without acquiring large landed estates. Indeed in as much as it was the backing of London which assured the Parliamentary armies of success in their struggle with the king, London could be said at the beginning of the century 1650–1750 to have shown that it possessed the power necessary to sway the rest of the country to its will. In the provinces in the later seventeenth and early eighteenth centuries there were increasingly large numbers of men of wealth and position who stood outside the traditional landed system. These were the group whom Everitt has recently termed the "pseudo-gentry." They formed "that class of leisured and predominantly urban families who, by their manner of life, were commonly regarded as gentry, though they were not supported by a landed estate." Their links with London were close and their journeys thither frequent. They were urban in their habit of life but would have been powerless to protect their position in society if London had not existed. London both provided them with a pattern of behaviour, and, because of its immense economic strength and prestige, protected them from any hostility on the part of the traditional elements in society. London was, as it were, both their normative reference group and their guarantee against the withdrawal of status respect.

The social and economic changes of the seventeenth and eighteenth centuries reached their culmination in the industrial revolution. Although this was far more than simply an economic phenomenon, economic change was what defined it. It is natural, therefore, to consider the strictly economic effects of London's rapid growth as well as the demographic and sociological changes which accompanied it.

The importance of the London food market in promoting change in the agriculture of Kent and East Anglia from an early date has long been recognized. Fisher showed how even during the century before 1650 London was large enough to exercise a great influence upon the agriculture of the surrounding counties, causing a rapid spread of market gardening, increasing local specialization, and encouraging the wholesalers to move back up the chain of production and exchange to engage directly in the production of food, or to sink capital in the improvement of productive facilities. The influence of the London food market was "not merely in the direction of increased production but also in that of specialization, and in that direction lay agricultural progress"—"Poulterers made loans to warreners and themselves bred poultry. Fruiterers helped to establish orchards and leased them when established. Butchers themselves became graziers." Between 1650 and 1750 it is reasonable to suppose that the demand for food in the London market must have increased by about three-quarters since population increased roughly in that proportion. The increased demand was met from home sources rather than by import, and it follows that all those changes which Fisher observed in the preceding century were spread over a larger area and intensified.

Once more it is interesting to work initially in terms of a very crude model and review its implications, though in this case the orders of magnitude assumed are even more open to question than those embodied in the demographic model used earlier. Suppose, firstly, that in 1650 the population of London was 400,000 and the population of the rest of the country 5,100,000 and that in the country outside the metropolis the proportion of the male labour force engaged in agriculture was 60 per cent. This would imply that 3,060,000 were dependent on agriculture (those directly employed plus their families), and that every 100 farming families supported a total of 80 families who earned their living in other ways. If in the next century the population of London rose to 675,000 and that of the whole country to 6,140,000 but the proportion engaged in agriculture outside the capital remained the same, then the agricultural population in 1750 would have numbered 3,279,000 and every 100 farming families would have supported 87 other families. This in turn would imply a rise in agricultural productivity per head of about four per cent. This figure is certainly too low, however, since this was a century of rising exports of grain, especially after 1700. By 1750 exports formed about six per cent of total grain production; at the beginning of the century they were only a little over one per cent. Grain was not, of course, the only product of agriculture, but there were parallel movements in some other agricultural products. Imports of wool, for example, fell markedly in the early eighteenth century, while domestic production rose. There was a sharp rise in the production of mutton, though not of beef, and some minor agricultural products, notably hops, were grown in greater quantities. All in all it is reasonable to suppose that these changes represent a rise of not less than five per cent in agricultural productivity per head. This, in combination with the rise which must have occurred in meeting London's demands, suggests a rise of about ten per cent in agricultural productivity per head.

A rise of ten per cent in productivity is far from trivial. It could have released a substantial amount of purchasing power into other channels as the price of foodstuffs fell and at the same time have made it possible for a substantially higher proportion of the population to be drawn into secondary and tertiary employment. The rise, however, is almost certainly understated at ten per cent, since the percentage of the total labour force outside the capital engaged in agriculture probably fell somewhat, implying a still steeper rise in agricultural productivity per head. . . . Deane and Cole suggest that the rise may have been as high as twenty-five per cent in the first half of the eighteenth century alone. But a rise in agricultural productivity even of this magnitude is a formidable achievement and goes far to suggesting how a pre-industrial economy can slowly lever itself up by its own bootstraps to the point where a rapid growth of secondary industry can occur. The fact that income elasticity of demand for food is substantially less than unity makes it easy to understand how grain prices might sag in these circumstances and how considerable the diversion of purchasing power into the products of secondary industry may have been.

It does not follow from the above, of course, that the considerable rise in agricultural productivity per head which appears to have taken place was due to London's growth in its entirety. What can be said is that the steady growth in demand for food in London as population there increased, necessarily caused great changes in the methods used on farms over a wider and wider area, in the commercial organization of the food market, and in the transport of food. It must also have tended to increase the proportion of people living outside London who were not engaged directly in agriculture since tertiary employment was sure to increase in these circumstances. Drovers, carters, badgers, brokers, cattle dealers, corn chandlers, hostlers, inn-keepers and the like grew more and more numerous as larger and larger fractions of the year's flocks and crops were consumed at a distance from the areas in which they were produced. As yet it is difficult to quantify the changes in employment structure satisfactorily, but many parish registers began regularly to record occupations from the later seventeenth or early eighteenth centuries onwards, and it is therefore a fairly straightforward matter to produce a picture of changing employment structure for this period for many parts of the country, given sufficient time and effort. Such an exercise may well reveal not only a slow fall in the proportion of men directly employed on the land, but also differences in the timing and speed of change related to the accessibility of the market.

There were other ways in which the immense demands of the London market helped to promote economic and technological changes in the structure of English production during this period. The inhabitants of London needed fuel as well as food, and before the end of the sixteenth century they were beginning to abandon wood for coal as the chief source of domestic fuel. The annual shipment of coal south along the coast from Tyneside and Wearside had reached about 650,000 tons by 1750, having doubled in the preceding hundred years. This represented a very substantial fraction of the total production of coal in the north-east, and perhaps as much as a sixth of the total national production. Coal production in England was on a much larger scale during these years than in any other country in Europe, and the coal industry was the forcing house for many of the technical improvements which were to come to a fuller fruition during the classical years of the industrial revolution. Newcomen's engine was developed largely to meet the drainage problem in coal mines and found its largest sale among mine owners. And it was in the Newcastle area that the first railways were constructed to enable horses to pull much heavier loads from the pitheads to the coal staithes. The first beginnings of the new technology of the steam engine and the railway lay in the eighteenth-century coal mining industry, and one of its chief supports in turn was the large and steadily growing demand for coal afforded by the London coal market. . . .

London's importance as a centre of consumption, which prompted Defoe in 1724 to write of the "general dependence of the whole country upon the city of London . . . for the consumption of its produce" sprang not only from its size but also from the relatively high level of wages prevailing there. Gilboy's work on eighteenth-century wage rates provides evidence of this. "The London laborer had the highest wages of any group we have examined. In the first part of the century, at least, he had surplus income to spend and there is every indication that real wages improved as the century progressed." When George remarked that "as early as 1751 it was said that the shoes sold in London were chiefly made in the country where labour was cheaper," she was touching upon a general phenomenon. Men and women were put in work over much of the home counties and Midlands because their labour was much cheaper than the labour of London artisans and journeymen. The existence of a mass of relatively well paid labour in London played a major part in creating new levels of real wages and new standards of consumption in the century after the Restoration, when "there was a rise in internal demand which permanently affected the level of expectation of most classes in English society."

Access to the London market was the making of many a manufacturer and a forcing house of change in methods of manufacture, in marketing techniques and in systems of distribution. Josiah Wedgwood was drawn thither.

> [He] was quick to realize the value of a warehouse in London. For high quality goods he needed a market accustomed to "fine prices." He was not likely to find it in the annual market fairs of Staffordshire—the time-honoured *entrepôt* of their county's pots—nor among the country folk who haggled over their wares straight from the crateman's back or the hawker's basket, and to whom expense was the controlling factor in deciding their custom.

But this did not isolate him from mass markets. Once having secured the custom of the London élite he was able also to sell his less expensive lines to the middle and lower classes. He studied closely the idiosyncrasies of each group at home and abroad and produced goods designed to appeal peculiarly to each of them.

> By these means Wedgwood had created an enormous demand for his ware both ornamental and useful. The upper classes bought both, but mainly the expensive ornamental wares, and in imitation of their social superiors the lower classes bought the useful.

Moreover, his efforts to command a countrywide market drew him into canal construction and the promotion of turnpike trusts.

Wedgwood was one of the most original and successful entrepreneurs of his age. The actions of his fellows seldom show the same appreciation of the opportunities for new methods. And his product may have lent itself more than most to illustrating the sense in which a triumph in London opened up the markets of the whole country. Yet it is reasonable to quote his example, for his success hinged upon an economic and social fact of importance before Wedgwood's time—through the London market the whole country might be won.

> For a fashionable appeal in London had a vital influence even in the depths of the provinces. The woman in Newcastle upon Tyne who insisted on a dinner service of "Arabesque Border" before her local shopkeeper had even heard of it, wanted it because it was "much used in London at present," and she steadfastly "declin'd taking any till she had seen that pattern."

The London market, of course, supported many industries within the city itself. Silk weaving at Spitalfields, brewing, gin manufacture, watch and clock making, cabinet making, the manufacture of soap, glass and furniture, and a wide range of luxury industries have all received notice. They all added to the economic weight of London, and furthered its growth, though few of them produced striking technological advances or were transformed into path-breaking industries during the industrial revolution. They were impressive in their range but were not for the most part greatly different in kind from the industries to be found in large cities elsewhere in Europe.

London's prime economic foundation, however, had long been her trade rather than her industry. English trade expanded greatly during the century and London enjoyed the lion's share of it. It has been estimated that a quarter of the population depended directly on employment in port trades in 1700 and, allowing for the multiplier effect of this employment, "it is clear that the greatness of London depended, before everything else, on the activity in the port of London." London's merchants, not her manufacturers, dominated her activities economically and politically, and it has long been a momentous question how best to conceive the mechanism by which the large fortunes made in London from commerce helped to transform the national economy.

Many London merchants bought land in the country. Some in doing so hastened agricultural change. The banking and general commercial facilities of London were available to men throughout England and played some part in financing the agricultural and industrial changes which occurred in many parts of the country. The success of the London merchants fostered a change of attitude towards trade. It helped to fulfil one of the necessary conditions of rapid economic growth in Leibenstein's analysis—that "the rate of growth of the new entrepreneurial class must be sufficiently rapid and its success, power and importance sufficiently evident so that entrepreneurship, in some form or other, becomes an 'honorific' mode of life in men's minds." But it is doubtful whether the prime connection between the growth of London and the great changes going forward outside London is to be sought in points of this type. London's trading pre-eminence is perhaps better conceived as acting more powerfully at one remove. It was the fact that the growth of her trading wealth enabled London herself to grow, to develop as a centre of consumption, and to dominate English society, which formed her greatest contribution to the total process of change in the country as a whole. The relationship between rising trading wealth and economic and social change outside London was primarily, as it were, indirect, springing from the changes which the steady growth of London provoked elsewhere in ways already discussed. While other big European cities during this century could do little more than maintain their population size, London almost doubled her population. Already as large as any other European city in 1650, it was much larger than any rival a century later. In order to meet the food and fuel requirements of a city of this size old methods in many cases were simply inadequate. And the new methods developed often produced those substantial increases in productivity per head which form the most promising base for a continuing beneficent spiral of economic activity.

It is always well to be chary of accepting explanations which explain too much. The industrial revolution in England was a vastly complex congerie of changes so diverse that it would be absurd to suppose that any one development of earlier times can serve to explain more than a part of it. It will not do to pyramid everything upon changes in the supply of capital, or the burgeoning of Nonconformist entrepreneurship, or an increase in upward social mobility. Complicated results had, in this case at least, complicated origins. It is therefore no part of this argument that the growth of London in the century before 1750 was the sole engine of change in the country, to which all the chief preconditions of the industrial revolution can be traced. But London's growth is a fine vantage point from which to review much that was happening. The period between the rapid rise in population and economic activity which ended early in the seventeenth century and the onset of renewed rapid growth of population and production in the last third of the eighteenth century has remained something of an enigma in economic history. It was a period in which population grew little if at all over the country as a whole. In some areas for long periods it was probably falling. Many of the chief indices of production, when estimates of them are possible, show comparatively little change and certainly grew much less spectacularly than either before or after. There was a slow, if cumulatively important, improvement in agricultural productivity because of the introduction of new crops like roots and clover, and because there was both a slow drift of land into enclosure and increasing flexibility of land use in the champion areas. Trade and industry expanded but in general at a modest rate.

How then should this period be understood? It was immediately followed by a period which saw the birth of a radically new economic system, the transition from the pre-industrial to the industrial world. Was England in 1750 greatly improved when compared with the England of the Commonwealth as a springboard for rapid economic and social change? Was the triggering off of the period of rapid growth connected, as it were, in great depth with the preceding period, or could it have occurred almost equally readily at a considerably earlier period? It is against a background of questions of this type that the growth of London appears so strategically important.

There were a number of developments tending to promote economic change and growth in the hundred years 1650–1750. Apart from the growth of London, for example, there were the agricultural advances which improved animal husbandry and lay behind the secular tendency of grain prices to fall (thus helping real wages to rise where money wages were unchanged or improved). Or again there is the probability that because of stable numbers and a modest increase in production the national product/population ratio rose significantly. The idea of critical mass has been invoked recently as a concept of value in conveying the nature of the importance of cumulative slow change in the period immediately preceding rapid industrialization. It could be used appropriately of any of these progressive changes, but is particularly telling when related to London's growth. It is not so much that London's growth was independently more important than the other major changes which modified English economy and society during the century, as that it is a most convenient point of entry into the study of the whole range of changes which took place, especially since some aspects of London's growth can be quantified fairly satisfactorily. Both the changes in agriculture which took place and the failure of national population to increase are closely intertwined with the growth of London, but not with each other. Demographically the existence of London counterbalanced any "natural" growth of population in much of the rest of the country, and the necessity of feeding London created market conditions over great tracts of England which fostered agricultural improvement and reduced economic regionalism. The absence or slightness of population growth overall, had it not been for London's expansion, might well have inhibited agricultural change.

It is possible to write out a check-list of changes which by their occurrence in a traditional and predominantly agricultural society tend to promote social and economic change and may succeed in engendering the magic "takeoff." On any such list the following items are likely to appear (the list is far from being exhaustive).

A. *Economic Changes*

1. The creation of a single national market (or at least very much larger regional markets) for a wide range of goods and services, so that specialization of function may be developed and economies of scale exploited.

2. The fostering of changes in agricultural methods which increase the productivity of those engaged in agriculture so that the cost of foodstuffs will fall and real wages rise; so that a rising proportion of the workforce can find employment in secondary and tertiary activities without prejudicing the supply of food or raising its price inordinately; and possibly so that a larger export income can be derived from the sale of surplus food supplies abroad.

3. The development of new sources of raw material supply which are not subject to the problem of rising marginal costs of production in the manner characteristic of raw materials in pre-industrial economies. This occurs when mineral raw materials are substituted for animal or vegetable products (for example, coal for wood) and may well be accompanied by important technological changes contrived to overcome novel production problems (for example, the Newcomen engine or the coke-fired blast furnace).

4. The provision of a wider range of commercial and credit facilities so that the latent strengths of the economy can be more expertly, quickly and cheaply mobilized. Under this head might fall, for example, the cluster of changes accompanying and reflected in the establishment and development of the Bank of England.

5. The creation of a better transport network to reduce the cost of moving goods from place to place; to make it possible for goods to move freely at all seasons of the year in spite of inclement weather; to shorten the time involved and so to economize in the capital locked up in goods in transit; and more generally to foster all the changes of the type mentioned in (1) above.

6. The securing of a steady rise in real incomes so that the volume of effective demand rises *in toto* and its composition changes with the diversion of an increased fraction of the total purchasing power into the market for the products of industry. This is closely connected with (2) above.

B. *Demographic changes*

7. The interplay between fertility, mortality and nuptiality must be such that population does not expand too rapidly and this must hold true for some time after real incomes per head have begun to trend upwards. If this is not so, the cycle of events which is often termed Malthusian can hardly be avoided—there is a great danger that real incomes will be depressed and economic growth will peter out. This happened often enough before the industrial revolution. . . . Too rapid population growth can, of course, be

avoided by the existence of areas of surplus mortality which counterbalance those of surplus fertility as well as by the existence of a rough balance of births and deaths in each area throughout the country.

C. Sociological changes

8. The steady spread of environments in which the socialization process produces individuals "rationally" rather than "traditionally" oriented in their values and patterns of action.

9. The establishment of conditions in which upward social mobility need not necessarily lead to what might be called the recirculation of ability within traditional society but can also produce a steady strengthening of new groups who do not subscribe to the same priorities or use their wealth and status in the same ways as the upper levels of traditional society.

10. The spread of the practice of aping one's betters. When consumption habits become more fluid and the new styles and wants of the upper ranks are rapidly suffused throughout the lower ranks of society, men experience a stronger spur to improve their incomes, and the first steps are taken towards the era of uniform, mass consumption. To be aware that a change in one's pattern of life is possible and to consider it desirable is a vital first step to the securing of the change itself. No doubt this awareness is never wholly absent, but it may be present in widely varying intensities and its increase is an important stimulant to economic change.

This check-list is, of course, also a catalogue of the ways in which the growth of London may have promoted social and economic change in England in the period between the dying away of the economic upthrust of Elizabethan and early Stuart times and the sharp acceleration at the end of the eighteenth century. . . .*

---

*[In the final four pages Dr. Wrigley represents the check-list diagrammatically and discusses interconnections between various items on the list.]

P A R T 2

Early Industrialization,
1750-1850

The rate of change in western Europe greatly increased after 1750. The industrial revolution began in England in the later eighteenth century and spread to France and other nearby countries after 1820. Its central feature was the application of power machinery to manufacturing, but it involved much more than this. The introduction of machines and factories necessarily imposed new systems of work. Rapidly rising production required new forms of consumption. Industrialization led to urbanization; many cities grew phenomenally. People were on the move. In the cities they found themselves surrounded by strangers, other new arrivals, and an unfamiliar new environment. Urban life had always been different from rural. Now more people than ever before would experience these differences, ranging from greater sexual activity to greater literacy.

The industrial revolution was in part the product of other developments affecting the common people. Most important, the population began to increase rapidly in the eighteenth century. This forced people to seek new ways of making a living. Parents at all levels of society had to figure out what to do with and for children who in the past would not have survived. These same children, as they reached adulthood, often had to seek new livelihoods, for there were not enough traditional jobs to go around. Here was a powerful disruptive force, challenging every social group and institution.

Partly because of population pressure, many economic activities became increasingly commercialized. Domestic manufacturing spread—here was one means of supporting excess rural labor. More and more peasants became involved with production for the market. By specializing in cash crops, they could hope to support growing families. In the cities, many artisan masters altered their business methods, treating their journeymen as paid employees rather than as fellow craftsmen. Journeymen found it harder to become masters, because established masters reserved their places for their own children. This general commercialization of the economy affected far more people than did the early stages of the industrial revolution itself and very likely was profoundly disturbing to people accustomed to traditional economic relationships. Even the necessity of dealing with strangers, which commercialization required of peasants engaged in market agriculture or domestic manufacturing, may have been upsetting.

Obviously, then, the leading question for this period of European history concerns the impact of change. Was change simply imposed on the common people? Many peasants entered cities and factories only with the greatest reluctance, because population pressure and other economic factors left them no other means of earning a living. Many of these people endured a massive deterioration in their conditions before making a move. But other peasants may have been more eager for a change. Tensions with their parents (most migrants to the city were in their late teens or early twenties, an age at which disputes in a peasant household were particularly likely) or an active desire for a better life may have drawn them away from the countryside. Without question, some of the forces of change were beyond the control of the common people, but there may have been positive attractions as well. There are signs, too, that rural values themselves were changing, leaving some people better able to cope with a new life style.

Furthermore, although the industrial revolution brought about a huge and rapid transformation, it did not occur overnight. We must not imagine there were modern factory conditions during this period. Early factories were small and sometimes rather informal. Many factories had no more than twenty workers and therefore were not necessarily impersonal or rigidly organized. Actually, most people were not working in factories at all, but rather in agriculture or in the crafts. Life for peasants and artisans was changing, but traditions yielded slowly. The common people themselves found ways to modify the shock of new conditions. Most people who moved to cities in this early period did so gradually: one generation moved to a village closer to a big city, the next to the city outskirts, and so on. Factory workers found ways to take time off so that they would not have to surrender their own notions of work and leisure completely.

So along with the shock and disturbance of change, we must consider successful resistance and positive adaptation. Which reaction predominated depended on the particular circumstances—specific economic conditions, for example—and personality types. Few people could adapt to the new life without regret; but probably most people were not completely confused by it either. Even in their outright protests the common people began to show signs of accepting the industrial system, for protest gradually moved away from traditional goals toward demands for greater rewards within the new social order.

Bibliography

On population growth, E. A. Wrigley, *Population and History* (New York, 1969), is an excellent general introduction. Several explanations of population growth that differ from that of William Langer are presented in Michael Drake, ed., *Population in Industrialization* (New York, 1969). Another convenient survey is Carlo Cipolla, *Economic History of World Population* (Baltimore, 1962). These demographic studies, in discussing rising fertility rates in the eighteenth century, bear some relation also to the history of sex, which unfortunately lacks much bibliography of its own.

Despite the currency of generalizations about the middle class, there have been surprisingly few general studies. Charles Morazé, *The Triumph of the Middle Classes* (New York, 1968), interprets modern history in the light of middle-class ascendancy. Reinhard Bendix, *Work and Authority in Industry: Ideologies of Management in the Course of Industrial Labor* (New York, 1956), studies a variety of approaches developed by employers to deal with industrial workers. The question of what the middle class was, and therefore how unified its approach to the working class was, needs further exploration; outlines of the debate can be followed in Lenore O'Boyle, "The Middle Class in Western Europe," *Americal Historical Review* (1966), pp. 826–45, and Alfred Cobban, "The 'Middle Class' in France, 1816–1848," *French Historical Studies* (1967), pp. 42–51.

Very little work is yet available on the history of crime. Louis Chevalier, *Dangerous Classes and Laboring Classes* (New York, 1972), deals, like Tobias, with qualitative evidence rather than firm statistics. He believes that crime rose in Paris before 1850 and that middle-class fear of crime increased even more. Two novels convey the flavor of traditional big-city crime: Victor Hugo, *Notre Dame de Paris*, and Charles Dickens, *Oliver Twist*. On both protest and crime, the essays in Hugh D. Graham and Ted R. Gurr, eds., *Violence in America* (New York, 1970), are suggestive; some deal with Europe directly. For some changes in criminal patterns in the twentieth century see F. H. McClintock and N. Howard Avison, *Crime in England and Wales* (New York, 1969).

A rich literature is developing on pre- and early industrial protest. A good general statement is George F. Rudé, *The Crowd in History, 1730–1848* (New York, 1964). See also Eric J. Hobsbawm, *Primitive Rebels* (New York, 1965). Specific studies are Malcolm I. Thomis, *The Luddites: Machine-Breaking in Regency England* (Hamden, Conn., 1971), and Eric J. Hobsbawm and George Rudé, *Captain Swing* (New York, 1968). Peter N. Stearns, *Revolutionary Syndicalism and French Labor* (New Brunswick, N.J., 1971), dealing with a later period, questions the suddenness of the transition to modern protest. Priscilla Robertson, *Revolutions of 1848: A Social Study* (Princeton, N.J., 1952), is a standard survey of the period covered in Tilly's essay. See also Georges Duveau, *1848: The Making of a Revolution* (New York, 1966).

The Population Revolution

WILLIAM LANGER

The massive increase in population that began in western and central Europe around the middle of the eighteenth century was the most obvious stimulus for change in other aspects of life. It provided new markets and an expanded labor force and caused growing competition for the number of "places" society had to offer. Prestigious government positions did not increase as rapidly as did the population that might aspire to them. The same was true, at a lower social level, of secure artisan jobs. The population surge was profoundly unsettling. By increasing competition for jobs and land, it caused great grievance and was one of the major factors leading to the wave of revolutions that swept Europe at the end of the eighteenth century—revolutions that in turn furthered political modernization. Population increase seems the best single explanation for the various innovations that more directly launched the modernization process in Europe by prompting at least a significant minority of people to think in new ways and aspire to new goals.

What caused this population rise? A variety of factors, surely. But were these factors largely independent of human choice, or were prior changes in values responsible?

One line of argument stresses that a new, perhaps more affectionate attitude toward the family, leading people to marry early and have more babies, was the most important cause of the population revolution. It has also been argued that economic changes and dislocations—the enclosure movement, the spread of new industry—broke down traditional barriers to large families.

William Langer takes a different view, although he acknowledges that the change in family patterns had a limited role to play. Langer paints a bleak picture of the common people in the later eighteenth century: trapped in growing misery, which the new food crops, particularly the potato, ironically allowed them to survive, the lower classes responded by increasing their traditional use of infanticide and abandonment—yet the population kept growing. Europeans were caught in a dilemma they could not understand. To be sure they had made a decision, encouraged in some cases by their governments, to plant new crops, but having done this they lost control of their lot as an unprecedented percentage of children survived into adulthood. Population increase was virtually a worldwide phenomenon in the eighteenth century, although Europe's rate was higher than that in most other places. In this sense, even Langer's generalization may be judged inadequate, for the potato did not spread so widely (though some other new world crops did). More important, population increase outside Europe and North America did not stimulate modernization. Only in Europe did industrialization and new political forms directly follow.

This means that some aspects of European culture—either traditional culture or more recent developments—were distinctively appropriate for modernization, when triggered by the demographic revolution.

The use of the dramatic term "explosion" in discussions of the present-day population problem may serve to attract attention and underline the gravity of the situation, but it is obviously a misnomer. The growth of population is never actually explosive, and as for the current spectacular increase, it is really only the latest phase of a development that goes back to the mid-eighteenth century.

Prior to that time the history of European population had been one of slow and fitful growth. It now took a sudden spurt and thenceforth continued to increase at a high rate. From an estimated 140,000,000 in 1750 it rose to 188,000,000 in 1800, to 266,000,000 in 1850, and eventually to 400,000,000 in 1900. The rate of increase was not uniform for all parts of the Continent, but it was everywhere strikingly high. Even in Spain, where there had been a remarkable loss of population in the seventeenth century, the population grew from 6,100,000 in 1725 to 10,400,000 in 1787 and 12,300,000 in 1833.

This tremendous change in terms of European society has received far less attention from historians than it deserves. In the early nineteenth century it troubled the Reverend Thomas Malthus and precipitated a formidable controversy over the problem of overpopulation and the possible remedies therefor. But the discussion remained inconclusive until reopened in more recent times by British scholars, making use of the rather voluminous English records and directing their attention almost exclusively to their own national history. It is not unlikely that this focusing on the British scene has had the effect of distorting the issue, which after all was a general European one.

The point of departure for recent attacks on the problem was the publication, in the same year, of two closely related books: G. T. Griffith's *Population Problems in the Age of Malthus* (Cambridge, Eng., 1926) and M. C. Buer's *Health, Wealth and Population in the Early Days of the Industrial Revolution* (London, 1926). To these should be added the keen corrective criticism of T. H. Marshall's essay, "The Population Problem during the Industrial Revolution."

Taken together, these writings provided a coherent, comprehensive analysis. Based on the proposition that the unusual increase of the population in the late eighteenth century was due primarily to a marked decline in the death rate, they attempted to show that this decline must, in turn, have been

From William Langer, "Europe's Initial Population Explosion," *American Historical Review*, Vol. 69, No. 1 (October 1963), pp. 1–5, 6, 7–9, 9–10, 11–12, 13–14, 16. Reprinted by permission of William Langer.

due to an alleviation of the horrors of war, to a reduction in the number and severity of famines, to an improvement in the food supply, and finally to a falling off of disease as a result of advancing medical knowledge and better sanitation.

These conclusions were not seriously challenged until after the Second World War, when a number of demographic and sociological analyses by British and American scholars called various items of the accepted theory seriously into question. Because of the inadequacy of the statistical data some aspects of the problem can probably never be disposed of definitively. However, the very foundation of the Griffith thesis has now been badly sapped. A number of specialists have come to the conclusion that the spectacular rise in the European population may have been due not so much to a reduction in the death rate as to a significant rise in the birth rate which, according to Griffith, did not vary greatly throughout the period.

From these excellent studies of fertility and mortality there has not, however, emerged any satisfactory explanation to replace the argumentation of Griffith and Buer about underlying causes. It may not be amiss, then, for a historian to join the debate, even though he must disclaim at the outset any professional competence in demography or statistics.

From the strictly historical standpoint none of the previous interpretations of the initial spurt of the European population has been satisfactory. At the time it was commonly thought that the so-called "Industrial Revolution," with its high requirement for child labor, may have induced larger families. This explication could at best apply primarily to Britain, where the demographic revolution was roughly contemporaneous with industrialization. Since the rate of population increase was just as striking in completely unindustrialized countries like Russia, a less parochial explanation was clearly required. At the present time it seems more likely that industrialization saved Europe from some of the more alarming consequences of overpopulation.

Griffith's theses, inspired by Malthusian doctrine, are unacceptable, for the historical evidence provides little support for the notion of a marked decline in the death rate. Take, for instance, the mortality occasioned by war. Granted that no conflict of the eighteenth or early nineteenth centuries was as deadly as the Thirty Years' War is reputed to have been, there is yet no evidence of a difference so marked as to have made a profound change in the pattern of population. It is well known that nations usually recover quickly from the manpower losses of war. If it were not so, the bloody conflicts of the French revolutionary and Napoleonic periods should have had a distinctly retarding effect on the growth of the European population.

Not much more can be said of the argument on food supply. What reason is there to suppose that Europe suffered less from famine? We know that there were severe famines in the first half of the eighteenth century and that the years 1769–1774 were positively calamitous in terms of crop failures. The early 1790's and the years immediately following the peace in 1815 were almost as bad, while at much later periods (1837–1839, 1846–1849) all Europe suffered from acute food shortages. Even in Western and Central Europe famine was a constant threat until the railroads provided rapid, large-scale transportation.

Griffith was convinced that the important advances in agronomy (rotation of crops, winter feeding of cattle, systematic manuring, improved breeding of livestock, and so forth) as well as the practice of enclosure all made for more productive farming and greatly enhanced the food supply. But even in Britain, where agriculture was more advanced than elsewhere, these improvements did not make themselves generally felt until the mid-nineteenth century. There were many progressive landlords, on the Continent as in Britain, and no doubt there was improvement in grain production, but it was too slow, and grain imports were too slight to have had a decisive bearing on the rate of population growth. Even in mid-nineteenth-century Britain the three-field system was still prevalent, ploughs and other implements were old-fashioned and inefficient, grain was still cut by sickle or scythe and threshed with the flail, and ground drainage was primitive. Of course, more land had been brought under cultivation, but the available data reflect only a modest increase in the yield of grain per acre in this period.

Crucial to the argumentation of Griffith and Buer was the proposition that improved health entailed a significant reduction in the death rate. The disappearance of bubonic plague, the falling off of other diseases, the advances in medical knowledge and practice (especially in midwifery), and progress in sanitation were in turn alleged to have produced the greater health of the people.

No one would deny that the disappearance of plague in the late seventeenth and early eighteenth centuries rid the Europeans of their most mortal enemy, and so reacted favorably on the development of the population. For the repeated plague epidemics had been fearfully destructive of life, especially in the towns. In the Black Death of 1348–1349 fully a quarter of the population had been carried away, while even as late as the epidemic of 1709–1710 from one-third to one-half of the inhabitants of cities such as Copenhagen and Danzig fell victims. In Marseilles in 1720 there were 40,000 dead in a total population of 90,000. In Messina in 1743 over 60 per cent of the population was carried off.

But whatever may have been the gains from the disappearance of plague they were largely wiped out by the high mortality of other diseases, notably smallpox, typhus, cholera, measles, scarlet fever, influenza, and tuberculosis. Of these great killers smallpox flourished particularly in the eighteenth century and tuberculosis in the eighteenth and nineteenth, while the deadly Asiatic cholera was a newcomer in 1830–1832.

Smallpox, though it reached up on occasions to strike adults, even of high estate, was primarily a disease of infancy and early childhood, responsible for one-third to one-half of all deaths of children under five. In 1721 the practice of inoculating children with the disease, in order to produce a mild case and create immunity, was introduced into England. It was rather widely used by the upper classes, but quite obviously had little effect on the epidemiology of the disease. There appears to have been a gradual falling off of the disease after 1780, but even the introduction of vaccination by Edward Jenner in 1798 did not entirely exorcise the smallpox threat, though vaccination was offered gratuitously to thousands of children and was made compulsory in England in 1853. Mortality remained high, especially in the epidemics of 1817–1819, 1825–1827, 1837–1840, and 1847–1849. In the last great epidemic (1871–1872), when most people had already been vaccinated, the toll was exceedingly heavy: 23,062 deaths in England and Wales, 56,826 in Prussia in 1871 and 61,109 in 1872. Small wonder that opponents of vaccination stamped it a dangerous and futile procedure. . . .

Considering the terrible and continuing ravages of disease in the days before the fundamental discoveries of Louis Pasteur and Robert Koch, it is hard to see how anyone could suppose that there was an amelioration of health conditions in the eighteenth century sufficient to account for a marked decline in the death rate.

Recent studies have pretty well disposed also of the favorite Griffith-Buer theme, that advances in medical knowledge and practice served to reduce mortality, especially among young children. Doctors and hospitals were quite incompetent to deal with infectious disease. The supposed reduction in child mortality was certainly not reflected in the fact that as late as 1840 half or almost half of the children born in cities like Manchester or even Paris were still dying under the age of five. . . .

In this context it may be said that in Europe conditions of life among both the rural and urban lower classes—that is, of the vast majority of the population—can rarely have been as bad as they were in the early nineteenth century. Overworked, atrociously housed, undernourished, disease-ridden, the masses lived in a misery that defies the modern imagination. This situation in itself should have drastically influenced the population pattern, but two items in particular must have had a really significant bearing. First, drunkenness: this period must surely have been the golden age of inebriation, especially in the northern countries. The per capita consumption of spirits, on the increase since the sixteenth century, reached unprecedented figures. In Sweden, perhaps the worst-afflicted country, it was estimated at ten gallons of *branvin* and *akvavit* per annum. Everywhere ginshops abounded. London alone counted 447 taverns and 8,659 ginshops in 1836, some of which at least were visited by as many as 5,000–6,000 men, women, and children in a single day.

So grave was the problem of intemperance in 1830 that European rulers welcomed emissaries of the American temperance movement and gave full support to their efforts to organize the fight against the liquor menace. To what extent drunkenness may have affected the life expectancy of its addicts, we can only conjecture. At the very least the excessive use of strong liquor is known to enhance susceptibility to respiratory infections and is often the determining factor in cirrhosis of the liver.

Of even greater and more obvious bearing was what Malthus euphemistically called "bad nursing of children" and what in honesty must be termed disguised infanticide. It was certainly prevalent in the late eighteenth and nineteenth centuries and seems to have been constantly on the increase.

In the cities it was common practice to confide babies to old women nurses or caretakers. The least offense of these "Angelmakers," as they were called in Berlin, was to give the children gin to keep them quiet. For the rest we have the following testimony from Benjamin Disraeli's novel *Sybil* (1845), for which he drew on a large fund of sociological data: "Laudanum and treacle, administered in the shape of some popular elixir, affords these innocents a brief taste of the sweets of existence and, keeping them quiet, prepares them for the silence of their impending grave." "Infanticide," he adds, "is practised as extensively and as legally in England as it is on the banks of the Ganges; a circumstance which apparently has not yet engaged the attention of the Society for the Propagation of the Gospel in Foreign Parts."

It was also customary in these years to send babies into the country to be nursed by peasant women. The well-to-do made their own arrangements, while the lower classes turned their offspring over to charitable nursing bureaus or left them at the foundling hospitals or orphanages that existed in all large cities. Of the operation of these foundling hospitals a good deal is known, and from this knowledge it is possible to infer the fate of thousands of babies that were sent to the provinces for care.

The middle and late eighteenth century was marked by a startling rise in the rate of illegitimacy, the reasons for which have little bearing on the present argument. But so many of the unwanted babies were being abandoned, smothered, or otherwise disposed of that Napoleon in 1811 decreed that the foundling hospitals should be provided with a turntable device, so that babies could be left at these institutions without the parent being recognized or subjected to embarrassing questions. This convenient arrangement was imitated in many countries and was taken full advantage of by the mothers in question. In many cities the authorities complained that unmarried mothers from far and wide were coming to town to deposit their unwanted babies in the accommodating foundling hospitals. The statistics show that of the thousands of children thus abandoned, more than half were the offspring of married couples.

There is good reason to suppose that those in charge of these institutions did the best they could with what soon became an unmanageable problem. Very few of the children could be cared for in the hospitals themselves. The great majority was sent to peasant nurses in the provinces. In any case, most of these children died within a short time, either of malnutrition or neglect or from the long, rough journey to the country.

The figures for this traffic, available for many cities, are truly shocking. In all of France fully 127,507 children were abandoned in the year 1833. Anywhere from 20 to 30 per cent of all children born were left to their fate. The figures for Paris suggest that in the years 1817–1820 the "foundlings" comprised fully 36 per cent of all births. In some of the Italian hospitals the mortality (under one year of age) ran to 80 or 90 per cent. In Paris the *Maison de la Couche* reported that of 4,779 babies admitted in 1818, 2,370 died in the first three months and another 956 within the first year. . . .

. . . In the light of the available data one is almost forced to admit that the proposal, seriously advanced at the time, that unwanted babies be painlessly asphyxiated in small gas chambers, was definitely humanitarian. Certainly the entire problem of infanticide in the days before widespread practice of contraception deserves further attention and study. It was undoubtedly a major factor in holding down the population, strangely enough in the very period when the tide of population was so rapidly rising.

Summing up, it would seem that in the days of the initial population explosion one can discern many forces working against a major increase and few if any operating in the opposite direction. It is obviously necessary, then, to discover one or more further factors to which a major influence can fairly be attributed.

If indeed the birth rate was rising, this was presumably due primarily to earlier marriage and to marriage on the part of a growing proportion of the adult population. Even slight variations would, in these matters, entail significant changes in the birth rate.

Unfortunately the marriage practices of this period have not been much investigated. Under the feudal system the seigneur frequently withheld his consent to the marriage of able-bodied and intelligent young people whom he had selected for domestic service in the manor house. Likewise under the guild system the master had authority to prevent or defer the marriage of apprentices and artisans. Whether for these reasons or for others of which we have no knowledge, there appears to have been a distinct decline in the number of marriages and a rise in the age of marriage in the late seventeenth and early eighteenth centuries. Some writers have even spoken of a "crise de nuptialité" in this period. But by the mid-eighteenth century the old regime was breaking down, soon to be given the *coup de grâce* by the French Revolution. With the personal emancipation of the peasantry and the liquidation of the guild system, the common people were freer to marry, and evidently did so at an early age. There is, in fact, some indication that the duration of marriages was extended by as much as three years, at least in some localities. . . .

Marriage practices, though obviously important, seem hardly to provide a complete explanation of the population growth. To discover a further, possibly decisive factor, it is necessary to return to consideration of the food supply, recalling the proposition advanced by the physiocrats and heavily underlined by Malthus, that the number of inhabitants depends on the means of subsistence—more food brings more mouths. That population tends to rise and absorb any new increment of the food supply is familiar to us from the history of underdeveloped societies. Historically it has been demonstrated by studies of the relationship between harvest conditions on the one hand and marriage and birth rates on the other. In Sweden, for example, where careful statistics were kept as long ago as the seventeenth century, the annual excess of births over deaths in the eighteenth century was only 2 per thousand after a poor crop, but 6.5 after an average harvest, and 8.4 after a bumper crop. Invariably, and as late as the mid-nineteenth century, high wheat prices have been reflected in a low marriage and to some extent in a low birth rate.

The addition of an important new item to the existing crops would necessarily have the same effect as a bumper crop. Such a new item—one of the greatest importance—was the common potato, a vegetable of exceptionally high food value, providing a palatable and satisfying, albeit a monotonous diet. Ten pounds of potatoes a day would give a man 3,400 calories—more than modern nutritionists consider necessary—plus a substantial amount of nonanimal protein and an abundant supply of vitamins. Furthermore, the potato could be grown on even minute patches of poor or marginal land, with the most primitive implements and with a minimum of effort. Its yield was usually abundant. The produce of a single acre (the equivalent in food value of two to four acres sown to grain) would support a family of six or even eight, as well as the traditional cow or pig, for a full year. The yield in terms of nutriment exceeded that of any other plant of the Temperate Zone.

The qualities of the potato were such as to arouse enthusiastic admiration among agronomists and government officials. It was spoken of as "the greatest blessing that the soil produces," "the miracle of agriculture," and "the greatest gift of the New World to the Old." The eminent Polish poet, Adam Mickiewicz, writing as a young man in the hard and hungry years following the Napoleonic Wars, composed a poem entitled *Kartofla*, celebrating this humble vegetable which, while other plants died in drought and frost, lay hidden in the ground and eventually saved mankind from starvation.

The history of the potato in Europe is most fully known as it touches Ireland, where in fact it became crucial in the diet of the people. It was introduced there about the year 1600 and before the end of the seventeenth century had been generally adopted by the peasantry. By the end of the eighteenth century the common man was eating little else:

> Day after day, three times a day, people ate salted, boiled potatoes, probably washing them down with milk, flavouring them, if they were fortunate, with an onion or a bit of lard, with boiled seaweed or a scrap of salted fish.

Because this was so, Ireland provides a simple, laboratory case. There were in Ireland no industrial revolution and no war, but also no fundamental change in the pattern of famine or disease. The unspeakable poverty of the country should, it would seem, have militated against any considerable population increase. Yet the population did increase from 3,200,000 in 1754 to 8,175,000 in 1846, not counting some 1,750,000 who emigrated before the great potato famine in 1845–1847.

It was perfectly obvious to contemporaries, as it is to modern scholars, that this Irish population could exist only because of the potato. Poverty-stricken though it might be, the Irish peasantry was noteworthy for its fine physique. Clearly people were doing very well physiologically on their potato fare. Young people rented an acre or less for a potato patch. On the strength of this they married young and had large families. . . .

Why should not the impact of the potato have been much the same in Britain and on the Continent as in Ireland? If it made possible the support of a family on a small parcel of indifferent soil, frequently on that part of the land that lay fallow, and thereby encouraged early marriage, why should it not in large part explain the unusual rise in the population anywhere?

A definitive answer is impossible partly because the history of potato culture has not been intensively studied, and partly because the situation in other countries was rarely if ever as simple or as parlous as that of Ireland. The most nearly comparable situation was that obtaining in the Scottish Highlands and the Hebrides, where the potato proved to be "the most beneficial and the most popular innovation in Scottish agriculture of the eighteenth century." By 1740 the potato had become a field crop in some sections, grown in poor soil and sand drift and soon becoming the principal food of the population, much as in Ireland. In these areas also the spread of potato culture ran parallel to a marked expansion of the population.

In the Scottish Lowlands, as in England, the potato met with greater resistance. Scottish peasants hesitated to make use of a plant not mentioned in the Bible, and it was feared in many places that the potato might bring on leprosy. In southern England in particular, the peasants suspected that the potato would tend to depress the standard of living to the level of that of the Irish. Nonetheless the potato, having in the early seventeenth century been a delicacy grown in the gardens of the rich, was strongly urged in the 1670's as a food for the poor. In Lancashire it was grown as a field crop before 1700. During the ensuing century it established itself, even in the south, as an important item in the peasant's and worker's diet. The lower classes continued to prefer wheat bread, but growing distress forced the acceptance of the potato which was, in fact, the only important addition to the common man's limited diet in the course of centuries. Long before the end of the eighteenth century large quantities of potatoes were being grown around London and other large cities. By and large the spread of the potato culture everywhere corresponded with the rapid increase of the population.

Much less is known of the potato's history on the Continent. It was introduced in Spain from South America in the late sixteenth century and quickly taken to Italy, Germany, and the Low Countries. As in England, it was cultivated by the rich in the seventeenth century and gradually adopted by the common people in the eighteenth. It appears to have been grown quite commonly in some sections of Saxony even before the eighteenth century, while in some parts of southern Germany it became common in the period after the War of the Spanish Succession. In several instances soldiers campaigning in foreign lands came to know and appreciate its qualities.

One of the greatest champions of the potato was Frederick the Great, who throughout his reign kept urging its value as food for the poor, prodding his officials to see that it was planted by the peasants, and providing excellent instructions as to its culture and preparation. He met at first with much resistance, but after the crop failures of 1770 and 1772 even the most hidebound peasantry came to accept it. They were impressed by the fact that the potato thrived in wet seasons, when the wheat crop suffered, and that the potato did well in sandy soil. They also realized that it would make an excellent salad and that it went exceptionally well with herring. . . . Any conclusion to be drawn from these data must be tentative. The great upswing in the European population beginning around the middle of the eighteenth century can never be explained with any high degree of assurance or finality. It is extremely difficult to demonstrate whether it was due primarily to a decline in the death rate or to a rise in the birth rate. And beyond any such demonstration would lie the further question of the forces making for such demographic change. It is most unlikely that any single factor would account for it. Thus far the many explanations that have been advanced seem woefully inadequate. It seems altogether probable, therefore, that the introduction and general adoption of the potato played a major role.

A Sexual Revolution?

EDWARD SHORTER

One of the first decisive changes in the traditional outlook of the common man in Europe and North America may have concerned sex. A number of historians are now claiming that peasant society, at least in northern and western Europe, was quite prudish. Marriage occurred rather late, and premarital sex was frowned upon. (Here is another aspect of preindustrial family life that might raise important questions about the satisfactions it provided.) During the eighteenth century, however, a number of changes began to occur. The age at which puberty was attained gradually lowered. Choirboys, for example, found their voices changing at around the age of fifteen instead of the traditional eighteen—to the detriment of sacred music. Undoubtedly, improved food supplies were largely responsible for this change, but new sexual expectations may have played a role as well, for scientists have discovered that psychological factors as well as a better diet are involved in bringing about an earlier onset of puberty. Earlier marriages became more common. In addition, the conception cycle changed. Instead of bunching the conception of children at a few peak periods during the year, particularly during the late spring, as was traditional in rural society, villagers began to space them out more regularly through the year, which at least implies more regular sexual intercourse. And, as the following section outlines, there were other important changes in sexual behavior that began in the eighteenth century and continued as the modernization process advanced.

Obviously, any judgments about sexual change must be in large part speculative. We know with a fair degree of certainty that the rate of illegitimate births increased; we can only surmise the extent to which this represented a change in values, a new sense of the individual ego.

Edward Shorter confirms the impression that a basic revision of outlook was at least beginning among the common people in the eighteenth century, before the full onslaught of industrialization and urbanization occurred. In seeking the causes of this revision, Shorter looks primarily to prior economic changes and the related extension of urban influences. These in turn altered family relationships by loosening traditional parental control and, perhaps, increasing the importance of sexual compatibility between man and wife (it must be remembered that the marriage age was dropping even as illegitimacy was on the rise). This is a plausible explanation, but it leaves open the question of what caused the economic changes.

Even so, the recognition that lower-class attitudes began to "modernize" this early helps us approach the next question, the impact of the industrial revolution. For here the central issue is whether the lower classes could adapt positively, or whether they were completely confused and alienated for a long time. The fact that some adaptation had already begun in response to more limited changes may help us to answer the question. If the common people were becoming more individualistic, if indeed they found greater pleasure in sex, perhaps they were at least partially prepared to face still greater changes.

. . . Sexuality in traditional society may be thought of as a great iceberg, frozen by the command of custom, by the need of the surrounding community for stability at the cost of individuality, and by the dismal grind of daily life. Its thawing in England and Western Europe occurred roughly between the middle of the eighteenth and the end of the nineteenth centuries, when a revolution in eroticism took place, specifically among the lower classes, in the direction of libertine sexual behavior. One by one, great chunks—such as premarital sexuality, extra- and intra-marital sexual styles, and the realm of the choice of partners—began falling away from the mass and melting into the swift streams of modern sexuality.

This article considers the crumbling of only a small chunk of the ice: premarital sexuality among young people, studied from the evidence of illegitimacy. However, in other realms of sexuality, a liberalization was simultaneously in progress. There is evidence that masturbation was increasing in those years. The first transvestite appears in Berlin police blotters in 1823. Prostitution in Paris tripled in the first half of the nineteenth century. And, between 1830 and 1855, reported rapes in France and England climbed by over 50 per cent. It is not the concern of this paper, however, to pin down qualitatively these other developments. This is a task reserved for future research based upon a content analysis of pornographic literature and a statistical study of the dossiers of sexual offenders in France and Germany.

What is meant by "liberalization" or "sexual revolution"? With these terms I wish to indicate a change in either, or both, the quantity and quality of sexual activity. Quantity refers to how often people have intercourse and with whom—premarital, extramarital, and marital. By quality I mean to locate the style of activity upon a spectrum running from genital to "polymorphous" sexuality: A genital orientation is the concentration of libidinal gratifications in the genitals alone; polymorphous is the discovery of other areas of the body to be erogenous zones. Liberalization will thus be understood as an increase in the quantity of sexual activity or a shift on the quality spectrum from genital to polymorphous gratification.

Premarital adolescent sexuality, basically a "quantitative" subject, is the easiest portion of the sexual revolution to deal with because reliable statistics pertaining to the behavior of common people may be found and correlated with other indicators of social and economic transformation. Before

From Edward Shorter, "Illegitimacy, Sexual Revolution, and Social Change in Modern Europe." Reprinted from *The Journal of Interdisciplinary History*, II (Autumn, 1971), 237–238; 240–253, by permission of *The Journal of Interdisciplinary History* and The M.I.T. Press, Cambridge, Massachusetts. Copyright © 1971 by the Massachusetts Institute of Technology and the editors of *The Journal of Interdisciplinary History*.

1825 data on illegitimacy were accurately preserved in parish registers through-out Europe. And nineteenth-century government statisticians meticulously noted in their annual reports not only the movement of the population, but also the number of illegitimate children born in the various districts of their lands. New insights into the intimate realms of popular life may be gained from these statistics.

Starting around the mid-eighteenth century a dramatic increase in the percentage of illegitimate births commenced all over Europe; illegitimacy further accelerated around the time of the French Revolution, and continued to increase until approximately the mid-nineteenth century. This illegitimacy explosion clearly indicates that a greater number of young people—adults in their early twenties, to go by the statistics on the age of women at the birth of their first illegitimate child—were engaging in premarital sex more often than before. There were slip-ups, and the birth of illegitimate children re-sulted. . . .

[Of equal interest as an index of social activity is] the number of children born within eight months of their parents' marriage. In virtually every com-munity we know about, prenuptial conceptions rose along with illegitimate births. . . . The simultaneous upward march of illegitimacy and prenuptial pregnancy means that the rise in illegitimacy itself was *not* merely the result of increasing delay in marriage, with the level of intercourse remaining stable. Rather, if both bastardy and prebridal pregnancy rose, there is an almost complete certainty that the total volume of premarital intercourse was rising. This demonstrates that engaged couples were copulating before marriage more often than before, and that many more casual sexual alliances were being constituted than in the past.

Finally, we should inspect the rough outlines of traditional sexuality. By "traditional" I refer to European rural and small-town society between 1500 and 1700. It was a period of cultural homogeneity in which all popular strata behaved more or less the same, having similar social and sexual values, the same concepts of authority and hierarchy, and an identical appreciation of custom and tradition in their primary social goal, the maintenance of static community life. We have numerous testimonies to the quality of peasant and burgher sex life, but almost none to that of the lower classes (domestic ser-vants, laborers, journeymen, and the industrious poor). But I think it is safe to assume that the comportment of the two strata was similar. Möller has portrayed sex life among the *Klienbürgertum* in the 1700s: man on top, no foreplay, quick ejaculation, and indifference to partner's orgasm. The gamut seems paper-thin, and the more exotic perversities which delighted the upper classes were doubtless unheard of and unimagined in provincial backwaters. More importantly, people were either chaste before marriage, or began sleep-ing together only after the engagement was sealed. This is the situation from which the great liberalization emerged.

A Typology of Illegitimacy

In order to understand why an increasing number of illegitimate children were born, two questions must be asked: (1) Why did the level of intercourse outside of marriage rise, thereby increasing the incidence of premarital conceptions? (2) Why did a greater percentage of conceptions fail to lead to marriage—why did more of this increased sexual activity result specifically in illegitimacy? To answer the first question one must distinguish, in a general way, among the reasons for having sex; to answer the second requires an understanding of the social situation in which a couple found themselves —for the stability and durability of their own relationship, and the firmness of their integration into the social order about them, would determine whether they would marry before the child was born.

The reader must be warned of the speculative character of my answers to these two questions. The explanations of shifts in sexual mentalities and the typologies of interpersonal relationships from one period to the next are preliminary efforts to make sense of badly fragmented and scattered information on intimate life. The arguments that follow thus are not to be understood as hard statements of fact, but rather as informed guesses about the likely course of events. Only the hope of spurring further research justifies this kind of speculative enterprise, for we are unable to determine what kinds of evidence to seek out until we have arguments that specify exactly what is to be sought.

As a first imprudent step, let us assume that people have intercourse for one of two reasons. They may wish to use their sexuality as a tool for achieving some ulterior external objective, such as obtaining a suitable marriage partner and setting up a home, or avoiding trouble with a superior. If they have such motives in mind as they climb into bed, they are using sex in a *manipulative* fashion. Alternatively, they may be intent upon developing their personalities as fully as possible, upon acquiring self-insight and self-awareness, and, accordingly, think of sex as an integral component of their humanity. For such people, sex is a way of expressing the wish to be free, for the egoism of unconstrained sexuality is a direct assault upon the inhibiting community authority structures about them. I call this *expressive* sexuality. This level of intercourse is higher than that for the manipulative variety because self-expression is an ongoing objective, whereas once the object is attained to which manipulative sexuality was employed, the person may lapse into the unerotic torpor society has ordained as proper. Expressiveness means a lot of sex; manipulativeness means little.

But what about the sex drive? It is always with us, a dark motor of human biology moving men and women to intercourse in all times and all places. Yet its position in the hierarchy of *conscious* needs and impulses is by no means constant, but is rather a function of social and cultural variables which change from one time and place to another. Gagnon and Simon have shown for twentieth-century America that social structure and cultural stances interpose themselves between the steady thrust of the libido and the act of intercourse. My point is that such factors constituted "reasons for intercourse" in nineteenth-century Europe as well. Specifically, there are two: the conscious wish to use sex as a means of manipulating other people to perform non-sexual acts, and the conscious wish to use sex as a spotlight in the introspective search for identity. Changes in these reasons for intercourse suggest that the history of the sexual revolution in Europe may be written as the transformation of lower-class eroticism from manipulation to expression.

But if the social order about the expressive couple remains the same, they will doubtless get married and appear in the records of the statisticians only as contributors to the legitimate birth rate. In order to see why the child whom they conceive is born a bastard, we must look at the stability of their relationship. Instability may result when one of the partners in a relationship (normally the male) is using his social or economic authority to exploit the other sexually (usually the female). In such a case, marriage is unlikely to follow pregnancy. The likelihood of a subsequent marriage is also reduced when the partners are caught up in a society undergoing rapid flux, so that either the establishment of a family household is impossible, or the male can easily escape the consequences of impregnation by fleeing. The notion of stability in the social situation of the couple therefore incorporates several possibilities.

These two variables—the nature of sexuality (expressive vs. manipulative) and the nature of the couple's social situation (stable vs. unstable)—are strategic in accounting for the illegitimacy explosion in Europe. Because each has its own history (although both must be considered together) we may construct a table which cross-classifies and derives four different situations resulting in the birth of an illegitimate child:

Table 1
The Types of Illegitimacy

	Expressive sexuality	*Manipulative sexuality*
Stable social situation	True love	Peasant-bundling
Unstable social situation	Hit-and-run	Master–servant exploitation

"Peasant-bundling" illegitimacy lies at the intersection of instrumental sexuality and a stable social situation: persons with things on their mind other than sex whose cohabitation is sanctioned by custom. "Master–servant exploitation" denotes the coercion of women into bed by men who use their power as employers or social superiors to wrest sexual favors from them. Less than rape, the woman consents to being exploited in order to exist in peace with her superiors. There is little question of marriage when pregnancy ensues, a sign of the instability inherent both in the relationship and in the society which permits this kind of illicit exercise of authority. "Hit-and-run" illegitimacy identifies temporary liaisons where the partners articulate romantic sentiments and substantial ego awareness, and thereby are sexually expressive, yet are not inclined to remain together after a conception has taken place, or are prohibited by the force of events from doing so. Finally, in "true love" illegitimacy the psychological orientation of the partners is roughly the same as with the hit-and-run situation (although the couple may come more quickly to think of itself as a domestic unit), yet both their intent and their social environment conspire to permit a swift subsequent wedding and the establishment of a household. The child is technically illegitimate, but, like the offspring of peasant bundlers, is soon enmeshed in orderly family life. Children born of master–servant and of hit-and-run unions are more enduringly illegitimate.

All four types of illegitimacy were present in European society at all stages of historical development, but, in some epochs, some types were more prevalent than others. The explosion of bastardy may be written as the supplanting of peasant-bundling and master–servant exploitation by hit-and-run and true-love illegitimacy as the predominant types. This transition came about because popular premarital sexuality shifted from manipulative to expressive, thus elevating the number of conceptions, and because inconstancy crept into the couples' intentions toward each other, and instability into the structure of the social order in which they found themselves. The result was to make more premarital conceptions into illegitimate births.

These four types represent, in fact, four distinct historical stages in the unfolding of illegitimacy, one giving way to the next in a neat chronological progression.

Stage I. Peasant-bundling was the paramount form of illegitimacy in Europe before the eighteenth century. England and Europe had always known some bastardy, on the order of 1 or 2 per cent of all births, and most parish registers turned up an isolated illegitimate child or two in the course of a decade. But these children, when not the offspring of the poor servant girl raped by the village half-wit, stemmed normally from engaged peasant couples who commenced sleeping together before marriage, as was customary, yet delayed the marriage too long. Social authorities in these village and small-town communities put enormous pressure upon hesitant males to wed their swollen fiancées, being persuasive only because the seducer had been, and would continue to be, resident locally and dependent upon the good will of his social betters.

I have not seen data on the legitimation of illegitimate children before 1800, so the characterization cannot be made exactly. Yet excellent information on prenuptial conception and illegitimacy convince me that this portrait must be essentially accurate.

Stage II.   Master–servant exploitation became an even brighter thread in illegitimacy as the seventeenth century gave way to the eighteenth. Manipulativeness continued paramount in lower-class eroticism; the change seems to have been that people in positions of influence and authority were able, as they had not been before, to take advantage of their exalted stations. We must keep in mind that these little dramas of exploitation happened mostly within the context of lower-class life. At that humble level, the authority of the oldest journeyman of the master tanner, for example, may have been minimal in absolute terms, yet to the girl who swept out the shop it must have appeared commanding. The abuse of social and economic power to sexual ends doubtless was more difficult in the good old days, with the rest of the community watching vigilantly for disfunctions in the smooth mechanisms of prerogatives and obligations, but the stirrings of social change weakened traditional control over such goings on.

Among the evidence for this characterization is Solé's work on the city of Grenoble in the late seventeenth century. He noted that around half of the illegitimate births (illegitimacy was around 3 per cent of all births) were the work of men who held the mothers of the bastards in some kind of thralldom, as masters of domestic servants or employers of female wage labor. And many of the cases of "rapt" coming before the judiciary of Angoulême in 1643–44 involved the master's sexual violation of the servant. "The most common case is that of the farmers (*laboureurs à bœufs*) or village officials who, upon becoming widowers, take as servants a young girl from the parish. They speak to her vaguely of marriage, then when a birth approaches chase her from the house. . . ." In the early 1700s, the illegitimacy ratio in numerous urban communities had just begun to rise, whereas that in small rural communities continued at an infinitesimal level, a statistical demonstration of a rise in Stage II illegitimacy. But a detailed study of fathership in parish register data is needed to confirm our picture of master–servant exploitation.

A number of large-scale social changes intervened between Stages II and III, running roughly from 1750, which had the end effect of giving lower-class people a new conception of self and thus an expressive notion of sexuality. The fabric of lower-class life was thus shaken in a way that substantially decreased a pregnant girl's chances of getting married.

Stage III.   Hit-and-run illegitimacy typified a period when young people swooned romantically through a social landscape of disorder and flux. There was much intercourse, but people were stepping out of their old places en route to new ones, and temporary cohabitations often failed to turn into permanent concubinages. This combination of circumstances raised illegitimacy to historic heights, for the years 1790–1860 were, in virtually every society or community we know about, the peak period of illegitimacy. . . .

Time-series data on legitimation demonstrate that only a quarter to a third of all illegitimate children were subsequently legitimated by the *inter*-marriage of their parents. The other two-thirds either died, typically a consequence of indifferent care and the lack of a secure home, or remained un-legitimated—by definition outside of a glowing familial hearth. Some mothers eventually found husbands other than the fathers of their children; their bastards would then be raised in a domestic atmosphere, but rarely would their new stepfathers adopt them. Legitimation statistics point to an unsettledness in the sexual relations between men and women, hence the sobriquet "hit-and-run."

Stage IV.   From about 1875, the reintegration of the lower classes into the structure of civil society appears to have removed the transient quality from romantic relationships, leaving their expressive nature unimpaired. Stable communities developed in the sprawling worker quarters of industrial cities; a cohesive lower-class subculture with distinctive values and symbols became elaborated in distinction to the bourgeois society. Outside society accepted placidly the idea of early worker marriage, and, within premarital liaisons themselves, thoughts of subsequent marriage were present at the beginning.

During this stage illegitimacy ratios declined somewhat from their Stage III heights, although they did not return to the low levels of traditional society. And legitimation rates rose steadily during the last third of the century, a sign that couples who coalesced briefly for intercourse were staying together with connubial intent. The modern pattern of cohabitation is between social and economic equals, not between unequals, as in Stage II. The only survey I have been able to find of illegitimate fatherhood late in the century demonstrates that the seducers came from similar social stations as the seduced, which implies a growth of romantic, expressive sexuality in place of the manipulative, instrumental sort.

These portraits of the four stages are meant as ideal types suggesting the sequence of events most places would experience. I do not intend to argue that the infinitely disparate cities and regions of Western Europe marched in lockstep, for the timing of each of these stages would vary from one place to another, depending on events. But the illegitimacy explosion sooner or later came to Breslau and Liverpool, to the Scottish lowlands and the Zurich highlands. Exactly when depended upon the pace of modernization.

Social Change and the Wish To Be Free

What touched off the wish to be free—the great drift toward individual innovation and autonomy at the cost of community custom and hierarchy— is one of the most vexing problems of modern scholarship, and a solution to it does not lie within the scope of this paper. Weinstein and Platt state that at the psychoanalytic level, the separation of home and workplace was responsible, for as the father exchanged his continuing presence within the family circle for workaday employment outside, certain emotional connections caused sons to rebel against their fathers' authority. With fathers no longer emotionally nurturant, male children no longer had to obey them. Classical sociology provides other answers: Marx with his insistence upon the capitalist economy as the generator of proletarian rebellion, de Tocqueville with his assertion that equality had proven too much of a good thing. The matter is still unclarified, and my puzzlement is as great as anyone's. But the pattern of takeoff in illegitimacy ratios, and the correlates of illegitimacy with other socioeconomic variables, suggest a partial answer to the question.

It is in the area of changes which enhanced the individual's sense of self and which correspondingly broke down allegiances to custom and to the community that we must seek the motor of the wish to be free. At many levels of social relations and of psychodynamics, sexual freedom threatens the maintenance of community life because of the radical privatism and "egoism" it instills in individuals. (The classic European tradition of conservatism was intensely aware of the nature of this threat, and often damned libertine sexual behavior as "Egoismus.") Following accepted practice in the study of modernization, I shall call those areas of the economy and society effecting such changes in individual mentalities the "modern" sector. A case can be made that exposure to the modern sector at least sensitizes the population to the values of individual self-development and precipitates a readiness to experiment with new life styles and personality configurations, which then leads to action, *should all other things be equal.*

Most corrosive of the traditional communitarian order was the modern marketplace economy. This insight into the individualizing impact of capitalism upon the *local* arenas is almost as old as the free marketplace itself. . . . The notion of the individual as an isolated actor in the economy hell-bent upon maximizing his own profit was the diametric opposite of concepts binding together the traditional local corporation, be it a small-town guild or open-field village. The reality, of course, was quite different from the classical *laissez-faire* model, yet it is likely that the concept was constantly in the thoughts of those involved in wage negotiations, for example, or those who offered their services in a competitive labor market. To be sure, Western Europe had known *export* capitalism, the fabrication of goods for non-local sale, since the Middle Ages, but free markets within the *local* economy date from the eighteenth century in France and England, and from the early nineteenth in Germany.

In the context of sexual history, however, a free market economy meant something a little more precise than the general exchange of goods and services regulated only by the price mechanism. In the countryside it meant agricultural capitalism and the rationalization of husbandry. The laborers and live-in hired hands who worked for improving farmers all over Europe were highly prone to illegitimacy. This is no less true of such English areas of agricultural modernization as Norfolk, Surrey, and Sussex, as it is of French departments—the Somme, the Eure, and the Pas-de-Calais—employing numerous rural wage laborers. In Germany, the great farms of Mecklenburg and Niederbayern employed workers among whom illegitimacy flourished. Parish data from the late eighteenth century are still not abundant enough to tell if the accumulation of an agricultural proletariat produced a corresponding initial increase in bastardy, but I suspect that this finding will turn up in the work that E. A. Wrigley and Louis Henry are now directing for England and France.

In towns, a free market economy meant capitalism in the form of factory industry. A distinctive feature of factory worker life in the 1800s was staggering rates of illegitimacy. In France, local studies of industrial towns have established that female factory workers were substantially over-represented among unwed mothers in proportion to the population. In Dresden and Munich, an illegitimate child often accompanied worker parents to the altar. Yet these are only examples; the systematic statistical analysis required to demonstrate such hypotheses is inordinately difficult to obtain because: (1) as noted, we simply do not know about the development of illegitimacy over time in a sufficient number of municipalities to permit us to isolate the impact of factory industrialization; and (2) what appears to be the effect of factory industry may, in fact, be the effect of residence in a city.

The fact that the single group most prone to illegitimacy was urban domestic servants gives pause to attaching too much importance to factories and to the modern economy. I have argued elsewhere that urbanity itself constitutes an important independent variable in accounting for the distribution of illegitimacy, but I was unable then, and still cannot now, fit the impact of the city into a neat theoretical structure. We can see the city accelerating illegitimacy by reducing the chances that an impregnation will eventuate in marriage. But does urban residence by itself shift lower-class mentalities from manipulativeness to expressiveness? What difference the city makes is one of the big questions in modern social science, and another unresolved puzzle in this paper.

Among the empirical evidence I can offer on this subject is that illegitimacy began to turn upward in the cities first, spreading to the villages only later. In every city in England and the continent for which data are available, the upsurge in illegitimacy commenced around 1750 or before. . . . Second, except in England cities had much higher illegitimacy ratios than surrounding rural areas. Yet such illegitimacy may have been solely due to the fact that there were more single women in the cities than in the countryside. And, because of all of these urban maidservants, seamstresses, and the like, a higher proportion of all urban births were illegitimate than in the countryside. But that does not mean that the typical urban girl would be more likely than the typical country girl to behave immorally and produce illegitimate children. Maybe no differences existed in the morality of young women in the city and the country. Further research will clarify this question.

English cities are a puzzling case apart, for their illegitimacy *ratios* were often beneath those of the surrounding countryside. In London, for example, illegitimacy in 1859 was an unbelievably low 4 per cent of all births. (In Vienna in 1864, illegitimate births exceeded the legitimate.) Either something about English cities, such as their great prostitution, made them remarkably different from their continental counterparts, or many births were not being registered as bastards (something that could easily have happened in English vital statistics registration).

The final sensitizing variable crucial in value change appears to be exposure to primary education. Formal education, if only of a rudimentary sort, is calculated precisely to give the individual a sense of self by teaching logical thought. Learning to read requires the acquisition of linear logic, which mode of thought then surely spreads to other intellectual processes and levels of perception, to say nothing of the logical capacities instilled by other kinds of formal education. Logic and rationality are just other words for ego control, the psychostructural state of mind whence expressive sexuality flows. It is surely significant that the illegitimacy explosion coincided closely in time with the spread of primary education, and in space with the diffusion of literacy among the population.

To review a provisional reconstruction of the psychodynamics of the sexual revolution: It appears that liberal sexual attitudes probably flowed from heightened ego awareness and from weakened superego controls. Traditional European society internalized anti-sexual values which commanded repression. But, when new values began to replace old ones, the superego restrictions on gratification gave way to the demands of the ego for individual self-fulfillment, and it was but a short logical step to see sexual fulfillment as integral to this larger personality objective. I do not mean that people became "sexualized" human beings; instead they became pluralized, seeing sex as an intrinsic part of their humanity. This makes the sexual revolution an integrated movement of self-awareness, not a turbulent unleashing of carnality. If my argument is correct, behind this wish to be free lay the market economy, evoking ego orientation from those caught up in it, and primary education, stressing logical thought and control of the external world.

Middle Class Outlook

CHARLES MORAZÉ

As the lower classes became involved in more commercial relationships, and particularly as large numbers came to the cities and entered factories, they came into contact with the middle-class world. The people to whom they sold their produce and from whom they bought the goods they no longer made themselves, the people who served as factory employers, were for the most part members of the middle class. Hence their attitude toward and treatment of the lower classes played an important part in shaping the new environment in which the common people lived.

The middle-class outlook resulted from a number of factors. It was strongly influenced by rationalist thought, which, as we have seen, had even earlier altered public opinion toward the insane. It was in part determined by the necessities of industrialization, for there was a need to train a reliable work force. The doctrines of liberalism best describe the middle-class view. Liberalism reflected the belief in man's rationality and individual responsibility. It could lead easily to a condemnation of the poor; but it could also lead to optimistic and very new efforts to improve the lot of the poor, especially through education. So the implications of liberalism itself are ambiguous. Furthermore, the middle class was a varied group, wedded to no single theory. It retained considerable traditionalism in its approach to the lower classes—as in a frequent insistence that "the poor will always be with us." This could excuse harsh treatment and apathy, but it could also motivate traditional charity. Many elements of this complex mixture of values have persisted into more recent times, for the middle class continues to define much of the framework in which the common people live.

The following passage outlines the middle-class outlook during the 1830s in France, when the industrial revolution was beginning to take hold. The regime newly installed after the revolution of 1830 was moderately liberal, and government ministers like Francois Guizot wrote in defense of middle-class interests and values.

The upper bourgeoisie was satisfied: "France," declared Guizot, the Minister of the Interior of the new regime, in September 1830, "wants improvement and progress, but a calm improvement, a regular progress. Content with the regime it has just won, it aspires above all to consolidate it. Let the

Translated by Peter Meyers from Charles Morazé, La France Bourgeoise (Paris: Librairie Armand Colin, 1952), pp. 86–87, 88–90. Reprinted by permission of Librairie Armand Colin.

partisans of progress, civilization and liberty be reassured: their repose will not be troubled." This was the guiding doctrine.

There is no longer any question of fraternity. The national guard replaced it with "public right" as the third word in its motto. But what of equality? Guizot did not talk of it; no one in the government talked of it. But Mrs. Guizot informs us quite clearly: "In spite of its mistakes and its moral weakness, the previous century had one new and great virtue, for it loved all men. . . ." And she spoke of this idea as holy and powerful; but the conclusion she derived is this: "Under the name of equality, the idea has been strangely interpreted, disfigured, travestied, obscured, rendered immoral and odious. . . . For it is folly always to want to act on a grand scale," the minister's wife explained, referring also to the "moral danger which is attached to unduly brilliant projects" which lead to a "disdain of smaller works which are much more certain, which indeed alone are certain." In her hands "humanity" is colored by religion and becomes "charity."

Liberty in order, progress in repose cause boredom, and the solution to boredom is charitable work. This is what the example of the Guizot family proves. An admirable example of old bourgeois virtues. The salons, the last vestiges of old regime society, gradually disappeared. . . . It is in his own home the head of the family, tired by the day's work, finds a reliable happiness. The larger world has no attraction. Diderot's bourgeois dream is realized. In what time and what place was there more happiness, wrote Elisa Guizot, than in France "where the father received more affection and tender respect, the husband more confidence, the son more gentle guidance, the whole society more care and protection. Let us thank the Lord, while showing compassion toward the poor—but a limited compassion, severly regulated by the principles of the new economists."

At last, the air was cleared, order assured, the family consolidated, so each could turn to his own affairs. Supported by Guizot, the *Journal des Débats* advocated the politics of resistance with a youthful intelligence; the regime built on wealth could count on favorable elections. Thus, all attention could focus on business. In fact, after the end of the imperial experience which was the period of past growth, it was only now that an upsurge of activity spread little by little throughout the country. Each year new stocks appeared on the quotations of the Bourse, forcing an enlargement of the building. The textile industry especially extended and transformed the workings of the exchange. The hard-working class—by this one meant the *bourgeoisie*—is well paid for its troubles and its diligence.

Nothing supposedly is gained without effort. Did those who criticized the wealthy realize that commercial success was only the just reward for hard work? At the Academy of Moral Sciences, the economist Dunoyer upbraided one critic whose sensibilities revolted at the sight of "such penury for some, such superfluous abundance for others. This surprising outburst of passion is certainly not well-informed. In truth, nothing is less astonishing or less unjust than the differences in the rewards going to the capitalist and worker. To appreciate this, one needs only consider that there is accumulated labor in the sum that the capitalist provides, as compared to the worker who contributes only his daily labor. . . ."

A few rare spirits were disturbed about the growing misery, the moral and physical consequences of the awful daily torture which the progress of industry inflicted on the poorest classes. But what was to be done? Some proposed slowing progress, halting science, discouraging new discoveries. A naive, utopian solution. Others, indeed the majority, thought that all this should be accelerated, for from the perfecting of technology the well-being of all would definitively result. As the benefits of civilization increased, they would spread to the level of the humblest people. But population might continue to increase indefinitely, and Ricardo judged that the supply of labor would always be higher than demand and would thus produce low wages and famine. The Neo-Malthusian movement thus urged limitation of birth. And everyone agreed in praising charity, carefully regulated charity that is, and in recommending savings, prudence, careful habits and celibacy to the workers, insofar as workers were capable of these virtues. But no one went on to examine the bases of the liberty in whose name property had gained its rights; no one recalled the rights of equality and fraternity, because property was according to Voltaire a natural right, recognized from China to Peru, and inequality was not less so, by an irreversible decree of providence.

It is particularly remarkable that no one even took up the problem of the legitimacy of industrial profits. Adam Smith had posed this problem, but in choosing him as their guide the economists of the liberal tradition ignored this aspect of his observations. . . . To satisfy its economic needs the ruling class set up the regime it wanted, which prepared the laws that were useful to this class. Once the regime was established, its principles took on a sacred and universal character; to sustain and defend them became moral, to attack them, immoral. The new parliamentary regime thus sanctified class interests by calling them principles. This sophism naturally was perceived by a few rare minds. The middle class did not perceive it, which allowed it to adjust without scruples to the misery of the working classes.

Thus, "whatever the condition of the worker may be, it is not up to the industrialist to improve it." Orders determine general business activity; if the price drops because of competition, it must lead to a general decline. Unequal division of the benefits? The owner offers the worker all the salary that he can, since it is more to his advantage to have his employees working, than to turn down orders. And besides, if the owner would prefer to lose business rather than provide work "no power in the world" can force him to give work to his laborers. Such were the contemplations of the minister of commerce, the count of Agoult, based on the self-evident nature of things.

In fact, the most pessimistic economists still had an optimistic view of things when they claimed that salaries were necessarily reduced to the absolute minimum. Very often they were even lower. One industrialist of Rouen swore, in 1831, that 60 out of 100 workers in a spinning mill did not attain the absolute minimum. But he claimed that the total wages paid were enough to support the whole labor force, although he noted one necessary precondition for this, no unemployment. But unemployment was a frequent occurrence. In a family where all worked, one paid the father enough to live, the wife and children only the cost of food. Every household, especially if burdened with young children, was thus condemned to the most extreme misery. It was "regulated charity" that relieved such hardship, but the employer in no way considered himself responsible for the suffering, even claiming it to be a necessity, a natural inequality which, very often, had even ceased to trouble him.

One found the same indifference toward the organization of work in the factory. There was no systematic effort to improve working conditions, no concern over the length of the working day or the availability of work (which continued to be assigned on a day to day basis), nor on questions of safer machinery or healthier air in the shops. Villermé in an inquiry recognized that such interests were considered very extraordinary in 1830. Thus progress, that famous concept which the 18th century interpreted in an abstract or general sense, was made precise, was harshly realized in the concrete notion of industrial advance. It was always unlimited and held to be a natural law. One always hoped that it would lead to material improvement for all, but one was resigned to sacrifice a large segment of the working class for it.

All the investigators, the philanthropists, who turned to these problems around 1830, agreed that the majority of employers did not conceive that they had any particular duties toward their workers, not even over questions of morality. Rare were those who, for instance, separated the men from the women in the factories, a cohabitation that was deplored by the moralists because it led to all sorts of depravities. But the inquiries also revealed that the employers were all the more harsh if their businesses were of recent origin or if they were low on the ladder to wealth.

And this suggests an evolutionary factor. As overall wealth progressed, not only was the material condition of the worker improved but also the employer felt himself morally bound by the obligations of his situation. And this progressive enrichment was accompanied by movements of social classes: individual and group advance reinforced the upper levels of the bourgeoisie while the lower levels multiplied their efforts to ascend in their turn. This was the new form of equality and the social basis of the reform movement which marked the last years of the regime. . . . But the common people, who had aided the revolution of 1830, made the revolution of 1848 and transformed this aspiration into a social revolution.

Changing Forms of Protest

CHARLES TILLY

By the end of the Middle Ages the common people of western Europe had developed a standard form of protest—they could riot against deteriorating economic conditions and against more general encroachments on their rights. With the onset of modernization many groups stepped up their rate of protest, but they did not for the most part change its nature. Protest still largely took the form of riots in the name of past rights. The protesters sought the restoration of a previous standard of living or of previous rights to the land or to guild protection. The groups that protested most frequently were not those who were most directly involved with modernization; hence artisans struck and rioted far more often than factory workers. They still had a sense of the traditional community, which is why their protest continued to appeal to past values.

The following essay discusses the transition from premodern to modern protest, which Tilly claims was quite sudden in France. The transition came about as more modernized segments of the lower classes were brought into the protest arena. This in turn led to a major change in outlook, for it linked the common people to new kinds of ideologies and political values. Protesters now talked in terms of progress and new rights.

The new kind of protest could be vigorous and bitter, but it did for the most part work within the framework of a modernizing society rather than rebel against it. Its goals—material progress, new political rights—reflected values that had already developed in the middle class. By the later nineteenth century, and certainly through the twentieth century, lower-class protest, primarily in the form of strikes and political activity, became more frequent than it had ever been before the industrial revolution. But in the advanced industrial nations, it usually fell short of outright revolution. There are many reasons for this; among them may be the fact that although the protesters had learned to ask for more within the modern scheme of values, they were no longer seeking a distinctive set of values of their own.

Around the middle of the nineteenth century the character of collective violence in France changed rapidly, thoroughly, and definitively. The forms of violence evolved before and after that turbulent moment, but never so fast. Exactly how the change to newer forms of conflict occurred varied from

Excerpted by permission of the publishers from pp. 139–40, 145–61 and 162–63 of Melvin Richter, ed. *Essays in Theory and History: An Approach to the Social Sciences*, Cambridge, Mass.: Harvard University Press, Copyright, 1970, by the President and Fellows of Harvard College.

sector to sector and region to region within French society, but it occurred almost everywhere. From a country in which local food riots, scattered machine-breaking, sporadic protests against such government measures as taxation and conscription, and mass trespassing in rural properties were the predominant varieties of collective violence, France transformed herself into a nation of organized demonstrations, bloody strikes, and sophisticated attempts at revolution. Despite the shift to apparently more formidable types of rebellion, collective violence became a less reliable means of seizing power or of changing public policy. It all happened in little more than twenty years.

Those twenty-odd years, moreover, spanned the country's first great surge of industrial expansion and urban growth. They included the knitting together of the nation by railroad and telegraph. They contained the advent of universal manhood suffrage, the emergence of political parties, and the formation of trade unions. They even saw a crucial and durable switch from high fertility toward low fertility.

In a short generation the quality of social life and the style of political life in France took on many of the features we customarily call "modern." What is more, in many parts of France the pattern of political action stamped in the mid-nineteenth century endured well into the twentieth. Writing of the momentous changes in the political life of the Alpine region from 1848 through 1851, for example, Philippe Vigier says:

> It is not just a matter of a political *prise de conscience* on the part of the rural masses (or at least a good part of them) as a result of the establishment of universal suffrage. That *prise de conscience* was accompanied by *prises de position* which have marked the population of these areas up to the present day: those four years were enough to create a republican tradition which . . . permitted the regime produced by the Revolution of September 4th to take a solid hold in the Alpine region in 1871—thus aiding powerfully in the strengthening of the Republic in the country as a whole.

It was a time of profound political transformations. The nature of collective violence changed in step with those transformations. In most of these respects the quarter century from 1845 to 1870 was more decisive than the quarter century of the great French Revolution. . . .

In France the mid-century peak of violence was actually due to the nearly simultaneous rise of two rather different kinds of collective violence: one backward-looking, local in scope, resistant to demands from the center; the other forward-looking, broad in scope, taking the existence of a central power as its premise. Tax rebellions, food riots, and machine-breaking exemplify the first type. Violent strikes and demonstrations belong to the second.

How should we label these types of protest? It obscures the point slightly to call the first "prepolitical" and the second "political." They were *both* political, in the sense that they expressed opposition to the way power was being used and were seen by those in power as challenges to the established order. Nonetheless, the second type did much more regularly flow out of the activities of durably, even formally, organized groups contending for power and did more frequently involve explicit statements of allegiance to an articulated ideology or program.

Nor will it do to distinguish simply between "industrial" and "preindustrial" disturbances. That sort of labeling not only inserts an evolutionary assumption into the basic definition, but also imputes a timeless, primitive character to the tax rebellion or the food riot.

To be sure, the earlier nineteenth century *did* see some collective violence in ancient forms—destructive panics in Poitou, brawls of rival groups in compaignons in Bordeaux, vendettas and mass banditry in Corsica, religious warfare in Albi and Nîmes. These forms of violence better deserve the term "pre-industrial." But they were rare. They were far outnumbered by the food riots, tax rebellions, machine-breaking, and rural trespassing of the time. They resembled those characteristic disturbances in being local in scope, simple in structure, and largely rural in location. They differed in having virtually no political content and only a tenuous connection with the great changes sweeping over French society.

For these reasons we would do better to distinguish three types of collective violence: "primitive," "reactionary," and "modern." In nineteenth-century France none of the three was the work of masses uprooted by industrialization, although "reactionary" food riots or tax rebellions attracted many men whose livelihood the growth of an urban, industrial, capitalist nation was destroying. None of the three was intrinsically larger or more destructive than the other, although the "modern" violent demonstration or strike occasionally mobilized masses of men inconceivable in the heyday of the informal political disturbance. Yet it is roughly accurate to think of the primitive political disturbance as a standard response to local tyrannies and communal rivalries, the reactionary political disturbance as a characteristic form of resistance to the emergence of a centralized nation-state, and the modern political disturbance as the centralized nation-state's ordinary expression.

With these distinctions in place I can state a bit more clearly the nature of the change which calls for explanation: during the nineteenth century primitive disturbances were rare and becoming rarer; there was no apparent order to their fluctuations. In terms of frequency of occurrence, reactionary disturbances were by far the predominant form of collective violence in France up to the middle of the century. They were especially common in years of revolution, even if we exclude the events directly connected with the transfer of power. They reached their nineteenth-century height in the years 1847 to 1851. After that, this whole class of collective violence virtually disappeared.

Modern disturbances had occurred before the nineteenth century. They had, indeed, played crucial parts in the Revolution and other early struggles for power. But, proportionately speaking, they were exceedingly rare until a slow growth after 1830 gave way to a great spurt with the Revolution of 1848. By the 1860's the modern forms of collective violence were overwhelmingly predominant. The questions are: Why did the transition occur? And why the mid-century peak for both the reactionary and the modern forms?

Like England in the first third of the century and Italy in the last decade of the century, the France of the nineteenth century's middle years produced an incessant stream of violent disturbances. The understandable tendency of the largest and most influential of these disturbances to monopolize historical attention makes them seem much rarer and more like drastic breaks with routine political life than they actually were. On the whole the makers of collective violence were solid little people with strong social attachments rather than unstable individuals cut loose by industrialization or urbanization; their violent protests grew out of other less dramatic forms of political activity.

In the earlier part of the century France's collective violence took five main forms, four of them frequent and widespread, the fifth rarer but acutely important. The common forms were the food riot, the attack on machines, violent resistance to government controls (especially taxation), and the devastation of fields or forest. The rarer type was the urban rebellion. The first four were "reactionary," the fifth more nearly modern.

It may be helpful to sketch one of them. Let us consider the food riot. On the surface the food riot appears to be impulsive, purely local, unpolitical, irrelevant to modernization. In fact it sums up the essential features of the reactionary political disturbance.

Men have complained about shortages and high prices of food since food has been in the market. But the distinctive pattern of behavior we know as the Western European food riot seems to have taken shape during the sixteenth and seventeenth centuries. It remained the most frequent form of collective violence in some parts of Europe at the end of the nineteenth century. More exactly, it took two shapes—one urban and one rural. In the cities, at times when the bread supply shrank and the price of bread rose, men, women, and children would gather, grumbling, outside the shops of bakers or grain merchants presumed to be profiteering or hoarding. Often they demanded food at what they considered a just price—bread at ten sous—and reviled the city officials for their inaction. Sometimes they beat up the merchant. More often they broke into the shop, seized the grain or bread, then sold it publicly at the proclaimed just price. Later (if the troops had not already intervened) they went home peacefully.

A report from Auch, in June 1832, ran as follows:

> Troubles of a distressing nature broke out last week at many fairs and markets of the department of Gers. A little riot broke out at Mauzevin

on the twenty-eighth of May; it was quickly put down by the energetic cooperation of the police and the National Guard. Last Friday, fair day at Fleurance, the evil intentions of a few people produced a sort of uprising in the course of which a number of grain merchants were manhandled. A few wagons loaded with grain were dumped and sacks of grain opened or cut. The police of Lectoure . . . being too few to subdue the agitators, it was necessary to call on the National Guard to restore order. There were four arrests at Fleurance.

Finally, the market at Auch on Saturday the second of June was troubled by insults and threats to certain grain merchants, who were weak enough to give in to that violence and turn over their grain at the price of 25 francs the hectoliter, instead of the 27 or 28 francs which was its true price. . . .

The mayor of Auch published the following proclamation Sunday morning:

Considering the report submitted to him the second of this month by the *commissaire* of police, stating that the sales of grain which took place at the market of that date were the result of the threats and violence of a public blind to its own interest; considering that such conduct cannot be tolerated by an administration which intends to be strong as it intends to be just.

Declares as follows: In no respect will the price of bread announced in the list of 26 May be changed this week, since yesterday's price list was not established by legal means.

The mayor himself concedes that the muncipality has the duty to set the price; the issue is whether it is doing its work properly and whether unenlightened people have the right to take the law into their own hands.

This predominantly urban version of the food riot sometimes occurred in the country as well, with the added fillip that the accused hoarder was then frequently a rich landlord. Many of the presumably antifeudal attacks on chateaux during the so-called Peasant Revolt of 1789 actually occurred in the course of organized searches for grain by town dwellers. More often, however, the rural food riot began with opposition to the shipment of grain out of the community and ended with the grain wagon emptied and smashed, the merchant manhandled, and the grain sold—once again publicly and at an agreed-upon just price.

Throughout the country and small towns of the Sarthe, for example, rumors spread in September 1839 that people were being starved to feed the English. (In fact considerable shipments of grain were going to England.) Other rumors said wheat shipped to Paris was being dumped into the Seine. Near Mamers, a crowd of men, women, and children seized an outbound wagon from an inn where the driver had stopped to refresh himself and carted the grain to the local market. They took other sacks of wheat from the storehouse of a local flour merchant, tearing down and smashing his sign in the process. At nearby Connéré "the people" stopped numerous grain wagons and sold their contents in the public square at the current price.

These disturbances were more or less rural, but that does not mean the people were peasants. Mamers and Connéré were centers of rural spinning and weaving. There is every likelihood that hungry, underemployed weavers played a large part in the food riots there, as they had in 1789–1793. In fact, anyone who is familiar with the map or rural textile activity in the West during the 1830's will notice striking similarities with the map of grain riots, not to mention the geography of counterrevolution then and forty years before. The large mass of workers in declining rural industries surely took a larger role in the rural disturbances of the 1830's and 1840's than our usual casual labeling of these disturbances as "peasant" suggests.

The food riot, then, had not only an established routine, but a fairly fixed geography. During years of acute subsistence crisis, such as 1829 or 1846, riots broke out with great regularity in a semicircular band of departments to the west and south of Paris. They were not France's poorest departments, or those most liable to crop failure. Instead, they were the areas which had to feed Paris when the capital's usual suppliers (especially the Beauce) suffered dearth. Indirectly or directly, local merchants felt the urgent demands of Paris and found it profitable to heed them. Thus they gave substance to the indignant complaint that famines were the work of hoarders and profiteers.

The ordinary people who rioted were not simply acting out their hunger; starvation is silent. Instead of gradually falling into disuse as the French food supply improved during the early nineteenth century, the food riot reached a great peak in 1846–1847, only to vanish during the next ten years. During each of the nineteenth-century crises up to that point, the rioters were outraged by profiteering, angry that the local authorities had not met their traditional responsibility to assure a supply of justly priced bread, soured on a regime which let such things happen, at least vaguely aware that collusion of local merchants with outsiders had helped produce their plight. When repeated over and over, the humble food riot took on local and national political significance. Demands from the center, rather than purely local misery, provided the incentive to riot.

The indignant response to pressure from the center shows up in the other forms of collective violence as well. In the case of direct resistance to exactions by the central government, the point is obvious; the recurrent resistance of winegrowers to the imposition of the metric system in 1840 and the widespread attacks on the census takers of 1841 all challenged the central government's right to intervene in local life.

I expect that when the histories of the food riot and the tax rebellion have been carefully examined, they will turn out to be closely intertwined. Just as the food riot came as counterpoint to the growth of hungry cities, the tax rebellion grew to an important degree from the exactions of an avid, expanding state. The expansion of the state and the growth of cities depended on each other. Both forms of protest became more serious and widespread with economic crisis—not because they were reactions to hardship as such, but because in times of hardship the pressure from the center increased exactly as the means to satisfy that pressure diminished. Before their abrupt disappearance, both swelled to a large scale during the prosperous nineteenth century, instead of gradually dwindling as the exactions of city and state became easier to bear.

The tax rebellion—at least of the sort which was to last into the nineteenth century—appears to have come into its own in France early in the seventeenth century. According to Jean Meuvret, it was only during the seventeenth century that the principle of royal taxation for the ordinary operation of government, rather than the extraordinary costs of war, began to gain acceptance. Some of the sharpest debate over the "crisis of the seventeenth century," indeed, centers on the place of tax rebellions in the larger political and economic transformations of the time. The triangular disagreement among Boris Porchnev, Roland Mousnier and Robert Mandrou about popular rebellion before the Fronde has to do especially with the extent to which the numerous tax protests of 1615 to 1645 grew out of deep misery, expressed popular opposition to the royal power, or resulted from the manipulations of self-interested elites. But all agree that attacks on tax collectors, bailiffs and the like were extraordinarily common and vigorous in the period, that in fact they became the standard form of rural rebellion, and that whatever their origins they constituted a direct and conscious challenge to the authority of the central power. Despite the famous slogan "vive le roy et sans gabelle" resistance to the tax collector was an act of political opposition.

That was still largely true in the eighteenth and nineteenth centuries. One sign of it was the tendency of tax rebellions to flourish immediately after the major French revolutions. August 1830, for example, produced attacks on tax collectors, toll gates, and fiscal records throughout France. Most of them resembled the little outbreak in St. Germain (Haute-Vienne) on the fourteenth of August, in which, after customs officials had stopped a wagoner to inspect his load of produce, a crowd of men, women, and children "armed with hoes and rocks" surrounded them, shouted complaints about the duty the officials were hoping to collect, and forcibly dragged away man, wagon, and produce.

As trivial as this sort of action was in itself, its multiplication effectively blocked the flow of tax revenue from large sections of the French provinces after the July Revolution. As the *procureur général* of Riom declared in his report to the Minister of Justice on 25 August 1830:

> The memorable events of the capital caught the enthusiasm of the population here as elsewhere; but the people, thinking that the revolution entailed the legal suppression of all the indirect taxes (that is, taxes on

production, consumption, and trade, as opposed to wealth), rushed to all the toll gates of the city on the evening of Sunday, 1 August, and broke them to bits. The impossibility of punishing all those involved kept me from taking any judicial action, and in any case it was simply a moment of excitement and error which it was more prudent to let calm down by itself. I hoped that mature reflection would bring people back to a sounder way of seeing things. However, all collection of taxes has been suspended up to the present and the administration, held back by the anger of the people, has not dared to set up the toll gates again, nor to start collecting the *octroi* or the indirect taxes again. That state of affairs harms the national treasury, the city, and public order, since the law is no longer respected.

Last Sunday, the twenty-second, two employees of the *octroi* were rather violently manhandled; and during the night, a National Guard patrol was attacked by a number of persons, and almost disarmed.

Elsewhere in France the attacks on revenue offices were so widespread and effective that the authorities began to talk in terms of a political conspiracy. Many towns in the hinterland of Montpellier saw crowds break into offices, smash the furniture, and burn the tax rolls. A mid-August report said that "some people went in turn to the places of the director and of the receivers of indirect taxes in Béziers, forced their way into the offices, pillaged all the papers belonging to the administration and afterwards made bonfires of them in a number of public squares." These scenes were reminiscent of 1789 and premonitory of 1848. They were like those other revolutionary disturbances in combining essentially personal or local resentments with a threat to the regime.

While tax rebellions sprouted in the shadows of revolution, they could also grow in the glare of political order. During the early nineteenth century the central government's attempts to establish new taxes, reestablish old ones, or simply to rearrange their administration quite regularly stirred collective violence. An outbreak at Libourne in 1833 illustrates the usual run of such events.

At the request of the city council of Libourne, two officials of the administration of indirect taxes came to the city last Saturday to help reestablish the beverage tax . . . these first attempts did not come off very well; the population gathered and displayed energetic opposition to the measures they proposed to take. Stones were thrown at the officials, who went away and pretended to desist at the request of the local authorities, who feared that the leisure of the next day (Sunday) would provide an opportunity for serious trouble.

Yesterday, Monday, they wanted to try again; but this time the opposition of the local residents was more threatening. In order to disperse the crowds, the National Guard was called three times, but in vain. The authorities sounded the general alarm, but the National Guard remained inactive. Only a few out of a force of 700 to 800 men actually turned out. Then the 14th cavalry regiment was given the order to mount, which it did at once. That order was the signal for grave disorders; stones were thrown at the troops and against the authorities; a number of soldiers were wounded. The cavalry charged a few times, but no one in the crowd was hurt.

Under military guard the tax officials inventoried the drink on hand, but even then they found many cafés locked up and their owners uncooperative. Later the prefect of Gironde officially disbanded the unreliable National Guard.

The little rebellion of Libourne was an isolated event. Even outside of major revolutions, however, tax rebellions commonly traveled in families. Like food riots, they had their own favorite territories. In nineteenth-century France the southwest quadrant in general and the Massif Central in particular repeatedly threw up attacks on revenue agents. Gabriel Ardant has an interesting interpretation of this geographic concentration: "The typical areas for fiscal revolts were evidently those parts of the Massif Central which tended to live in a closed economy. The tax authorities forcefully told them to enter the world of the market but the government did not give them the means to do so, with the result that for these provinces any exaction, however small, was painful." In other words, when the central government demanded cash payments from villages only slightly engaged in a cash economy, it forced them into the market; this in itself caused a good deal of distress, but when there was no market for whatever surplus the village might be able to accumulate, that was more distressing still. It led, in fact, to anger and revolt.

Tax revolts also grouped together in time, largely because the changes in national policy which commonly incited them affected many areas at more or less the same time. Over the period we are considering, the most emphatic burst of tax rebellions outside of a major revolution was the resistance to the special census of 1841. The new Minister of Finance, Georges Humann, planned the survey as a means of reforming the creaky, inequitable tax system inherited from the eighteenth century. However just his intention, Humann stirred up the dissident, secret political associations which were slowly coming to life throughout the provinces at the same time as he stumbled over the older and wider resistance to all the central government's attempts to taxation. As Félix Ponteil, the principal historian of the movement, puts it:

> The opposition parties made a considerable effort during the months of July, August and September. All regions were not equally contaminated. According to the documents we have been able to consult, the Southwest, the Center and the North were particularly involved in the melee. The trouble crystallized around four main points. Toulouse, Bordeaux, Clermont and Lille. These four names symbolize the most violent and feverish thrust of the parties hostile to the government.

His account gives pride of place to the section of France southwest of Clermont-Ferrand, which was, of course, the usual breeding ground for tax rebellion. Whatever success the opposition parties may have had in the region, they were building on a durable tendency of its people to resist the demands of the center. Ponteil himself speaks of the "federalism latent deep in the provinces." And he continues: "The struggle against the census was the form that the opposition of distant communes to the decisions of the central power took under Louis Philippe. The census was only the precipitant."

As with the food riot, the tax rebellion broke out in one last spectacular burst shortly before practically disappearing from the French countryside. The "Forty-Five Centime Revolt" of 1848 responded, like the 1841 tax riots, to changes in direct taxes: imposts on property. That was unusual; the indirect taxes usually bore the brunt of popular rebellion. But the Forty-Five Centimes was only the most spectacular feature of widespread resistance to taxes after the Revolution of 1848. Rémi Gossez has argued that "by particularly touching the winegrowers, the extraordinary tax crystallized discontent which had been created mainly by indirect taxation." "The latter," he continues, "in the form of octroi or of liquor tax, struck especially at a winegrowing industry made acutely sensitive to the least exaction in cash . . ." Later he adds that the poor mountaineers of France joined the protest as well.

Two features of Gossez's detailed analysis ought to attract our attention. First, regardless of the economic encitements to rebellion, the Forty-Five Centime Revolt frequently took on the tone of political opposition. The concerted (although relatively peaceful) resistance to the tax at the frontier of Gers and Hautes-Pyrénées produced its first confrontation with the authorities at Malabat (Gers), in April, when a retired soldier first refused to pay the surtax, then warned the collector not to try to get it from anyone else, and finally "at the market of Miélan publicly exhorted the inhabitants of city and country not to pay. He said that the taxes had been ordered without the participation of the legislature, and that no one should pay until they had been duly passed." The resistance grew, and eventually led, on the sixth of June, to a faceoff between a subprefect, a judge, three brigades of gendarmes and a crowd armed with "forks, hoes, scythes, sabers, daggers, bayonettes on poles, halberds, rods and clubs."

According to the procureur général: "They made mad and menacing remarks about the government, the people and the workers of Paris. 'Death! A thousand times Death!' they cried. 'Death rather than pay the 45 centimes. We are overwhelmed by misery. We have no goods, or we can't sell what we have.'" And the movement spread so rapidly through the region that by the eleventh of June the lieutenant of gendarmes was writing to his superior: "Resistance is organizing on a large scale. More than 100 communes of the Gers, Hautes-Pyrénées and Basses-Pyrénées have joined together. At the first sound of the tocsin they are all supposed to go wherever the agents of the government appear. Emissaries are on the move continuously to recruit followers, and it seems that their recruitment is easy. Anyway, those who don't sign up of their own free will are threatened with death or burning."

The massive rebellion never occurred. Yet it should be clear that in the revolutionary year of 1848 the numerous incidents of resistance to taxation knotted strands of political opposition and economic discontent into a knout threatening the government itself. As Gossez says, "In many parts of the country, when it came to open resistance, it had the character of popular opposition to the National Assembly . . ."

Gossez's analysis marks out one other striking feature of the revolt: its geographic distribution. For the tax rebellions of 1848 clustered very heavily in the triangle Bordeaux-Toulouse-Clermont—the area which had so regularly produced furious assaults on the agents of the central government. In short, despite their hints of increasing political organization and awareness, these last large revolts against taxation belonged, in form and locale, to the reactionary tradition of their predecessors.

This reactionary character, combining local grievances with resistance to changes promoted from the center and affecting the entire nation, also appeared in the other ordinary disturbances of the time. The innumerable incidents in which country people broke down fences and swarmed over fields or forests formerly used in common directly pitted the rural poor against the rural rich, but the incidents also expressed local resentment against a national forest code favoring private appropriation of public property and against the officials who enforced such a code. Even the men who smashed newly installed machines and sacked newly built factories in Lodève or Elbeuf sometimes shouted political slogans as they swung their clubs.

Despite their sharp differences in other respects, the predominant forms of collective violence during the first half of the century embodied, to an important degree, angry reactions to the growth of a centralized nation-state organized around free markets, factory production, and capitalistic property. The men who made the collective protests came largely from established classes being squeezed out by the big change. As forging, spinning, and weaving concentrated in industrial cities, a vast number of artisans remained, workless, in the old towns and the deindustrializing countryside. At this very time land and property rights were becoming increasingly concentrated. Thus small landholders and tenants of many regions came to feel their livelihoods threatened. Firmly embedded in local life, they were not the uprooted, atomized masses that theorists of modernization have taught us to look for. But it would not be too inaccurate to sum up their actions as negative responses to modernization.

The rarer urban rebellions of the time do not fall into place so neatly. They were too various. Nevertheless, several important lessons emerge from recent studies of their character. The rebellions, large and small, continued and extended peaceful political action in the cities; workers' rebellions in Paris or Lyon grew directly from a matrix of strikes, demonstrations, and nonviolent protests. Violence and nonviolence complemented each other. The largest, and politically most effective, rebellions brought out an alliance of bourgeois (as typified by the National Guard) and workers (as typified by the joiners, shoemakers, and stonemasons of 1830). In any case the most reliable recruits to rebellion were the established, ordinary craftsmen and shopkeepers of the city. The barricades sprang up in their own streets and were manned by men who worked, drank, and argued politics together every day.

The large urban disturbances often compounded several different types of collective violence while retaining the essential features of each of them. In Auxerre, in mid-October 1830, a crowd including a considerable number of winegrowers formed outside the gates of the city and tried to keep workers from going out to their jobs. They hooted the mayor and the National Guard and forced them back to the city hall. Several hundred persons then sounded the tocsin, marched on the market, and sold off the grain supply at 8 francs instead of the prevailing price of 11. After the sale the crowd rushed to the home of a local grain merchant, broke in, and sold his stock publicly. The National Guard of Auxerre and reinforcements from nearby towns finally put down the rioters, but within the next few days smaller groups broke into more houses, smashed toll gates, and destroyed tax rolls. The authorities restored order after three days, making twenty-one arrests in the process. Here we see a conjunction between the food riot and the tax rebellion, with little obvious political content, but important local political impact.

But the character of urban rebellion was changing in the decades before 1848. In the insurrections of Lyon and Paris in 1831, 1832, and 1834, there were increasing signs of durable, formal, politically active working-class organization. Students, printers, turners, and other urban, politically active groups began to transform such ancient institutions as the charivari into true political demonstrations. In 1839 the Insurrection of the Seasons saw a political association deliberately, if unsuccessfully, organize a popular rebellion. During the same period, in Lille, Lyon, Saint-Etiénne, and Paris, the violent strike began to take on the prominence it was to have through the last half of the century. Under the July Monarchy the forms of collective violence which were later to predominate throughout France were already taking shape in the largest industrial centers.

The new forms displaced the old with extraordinary speed. In 1845 the old forms of collective violence ruled almost everywhere. Ten years later they had virtually disappeared. And during those ten years, rather than petering out, the old forms broke out in one last furious burst before subsiding.

What happened from 1845 to 1855? Politically, of course, France went from monarchy to republic to empire through a revolution, several insurrections, and a coup d'état. Economically, it experienced a crisis, a depression, and a great spurt of growth. Demographically, it felt a distinct quickening of the movement of people to the cities and a sharp drop in the birthrate. Everything happened at once.

The year 1845 was calm. The year 1846 started the cascade of food

riots which rushed over the country in 1847. The year 1848 brought not only
a revolution and a series of urban insurrections directly linked to it, but also
a farrago of provincial disturbances: more food riots, anti-Semitic attacks in
Alsace, panics in the Vendée, forest invasions in the Southwest, machine-
smashing and attacks on the railroads through much of France, workers'
protests in Marseille, Lille, Lyon and elsewhere, election disorders in numerous small towns, and the resistance to the 45-centime surtax on property. The years 1849 and 1850 were like 1848, but much less turbulent. Very
little happened in 1851 until the December coup d'état, which set off an
enormous burst of rebellions in city and country alike. After Napoleon III had
put down the rebellions and his political opposition through a massive program of arrests and police control, the years 1852–1855 produced nothing but
a last (and greatly attenuated) scattering of food riots in the traditional departments during 1853 and 1854, a few violent strikes, and an abortive workers'
insurrection in Angers. By that time the old-style disturbances had virtually
expired.

The rest of the Second Empire saw very little collective violence of any
kind. But when violence revived at the end of the 1860's, its character had
greatly changed. The Paris Commune of 1871, to be sure, explicitly operated
on an anticentralist program and implicitly incorporated a reaction against
the scale of the modern industrial state. But it occurred at a time when the
central authority had virtually collapsed under the pummeling of the Germans, and the rest of France had in a sense seceded from Paris. From that
point on, with few lapses, the modern forms of disturbance predominated in
France.

Let us look more closely at the two most massive outbursts of violence
during the pivotal decade: the June days of 1848 and the resistance to the
coup d'état of 1851. The June days matter precisely because they have gained
the reputation of marking a great shift in France's revolutionary style, the
resistance to the coup d'état because it has so consistently been taken as evidence of the weakness of the republican and revolutionary forces outside of
Paris.

The June days brought a moderate but significant shift in the kinds of
people taking part in urban rebellion and an equally significant shift in the
organization of rebellion. Unfortunately, no one has so far uncovered the
crucial documents which could establish the degree of overlap between the
membership of the National Workshops established to contain the Parisian
unemployed and the actual participants in the June days. The government
compiled splendid dossiers on the 11,000-odd persons charged with joining the
insurrection, and they are available; the missing information once existed, and
may still exist, in censuses and rollbooks of the National Workshops. As long
as it is missing, the exact place in the June days of the National Workshops
will no doubt remain hotly disputed.

Still, no one denies that thousands of men from the workshops took part in the titanic rebellion, or that a series of mass meetings and demonstrations largely manned by workshops' members led directly to the first outbreaks of violence. To a considerable degree the organization of the workshops continued into the insurrection; one of the first barricades to go up bore the banner "Ateliers Nationaux, 4e Arrondissement, 5e Section." A police report of 23 June describes "A column of 1,500 to 2,000 workers from the National Workshops, banner flying, marching across Paris to shouts 'Vive Barbès! Vive Louis Blanc! A bàs l'assemblée! Allons à la Chambre!' "

Who were the rebels? In sheer numbers the largest contingents were the 2,000-plus construction workers and the more than 1,000 men from metalworking industries, mainly mechanics and locksmiths. In proportion to their place in the Parisian labor force of the time, the industries overrepresented in the June days were metals, construction, foods, leather, and printing, while textiles, clerical occupations and the innumerable knickknack industries of Paris contributed far less than their share. The quintessential cast of characters for the reenactment of the June days would feature a mason born in the Creuse rooming near the Hotel de Ville, a railroad worker from Reims living in La Chapelle, a turner from Lille (or maybe Brussels) settled in Quinze-Vingts, a laborer from Savoy living in la Villette, and a native Parisian printer lodged near the Sorbonne. The cast is a perfect combination of the old trades and the new.

The appearance of groups of workers new to urban rebellion, the apparently large role of political preparation in the National Workshops, the carrying over the organization of the workshops into the rebellion, and the preliminary sequence of relatively disciplined mass demonstrations all make the June days a considerable break with previous disturbances. In the short interval after the February Revolution, the coming of universal suffrage, the freeing of the press, the relaxation of restrictions on assembly, the proliferation of political clubs, the activity of workers' corporations, and the formation of the National Workshops provided the workers with an accelerated political education. Surely this rapid mobilization helped transform the character of collective violence.

If the June days somehow crystallized the newer type of rebellion, the insurrection of 1851 marked the disintegration of the old. The resistance to the coup d'état has been variously labeled a plot, a jacquerie, and a fiasco. In the more or less official history of the period, Charles Pouthas dismissed the insurrection with a sneer: "The resistance by force was even more pathetic than the resistance by legal means." To Marx, it offered a classic illustration of the incoherence of the peasantry and the immaturity of the proletariat.

Yet it was a huge rebellion. More than 100,000 men rose against the government. More than 500 died in the attempt. Armies of thousands went out to quell insurrections through large sections of France. In the aftermath, more than 26,000 people were charged and 20,000 convicted of participation in the rebellion. Though not so bloody as the June days or the Commune, the insurrection of 1851 ranks, by scale and geographic spread, among the great rebellions of the nineteenth century. Only the fact of its failure relegated it to obscurity.

In some places the rebellion even succeeded, at least in the short run. Some 6,000 rebels overran Digne on December 7, burned the tax rolls, established a governing Resistance Committee, and defeated the troops sent to quell them. In la Suze (Sarthe), 300 workers seized the town hall, captured the local officials, and threw up barricades for defense. Although Napoleon's men quickly put the rebellion down in Paris, they had to kill some 400 rebels, and then make 3,000 arrests.

The local insurrections took two basic forms, both of them involving an interesting interaction of city and country. In the first, a group of republicans seized control of a regional capital or market center, then appealed to their country cousins for aid. In Marmande 800 insurgents set up a provisional government and then broadcast a poorly heeded call for men from the hinterland to join them. In Clamécy the flotteurs de bois and other urban workers took the first steps toward the seizure of power and were successful in attracting thousands of rural supporters to the city, where urban and rural rebels alike faced a deathly fusillade.

The second pattern consisted of the descent on the capital or trading center of crowds from the surrounding rural communes. Around 2,000 countrymen swarmed into Crest and attempted to seize control of the town, only to be driven out with 50 casualties. Another 5,000 occupied Aups (Var) and fought a pitched battle in which 80 or 90 died. Some 800 republicans from the area around Montelimar (Drôme) tried to take the city on the 7th, but 100 men of the line were able to turn them back. In appearance the insurrection was another Vendée—only a Vendée more futile than the original.

In actuality the insurrection was not nearly so agrarian as our standard histories say. True, some of the departments most heavily involved—Basses-Alpes, Var, Vaucluse—were largely agricultural and had produced frequent forest disorders or rural tax protests over the previous few years. True, 7,000 of the 26,000 persons charged with taking part in the insurrection were agricultural workers. But another 7,000 came from the much smaller populations of merchants and free professionals. Considering their numbers in the general French population of 1851, the occupational groups contributing more than their share to the insurrection were the professions, commerce, metals, and "industries related to letters"—printing, journalism, and allied occupations. Proportionately speaking, agriculture contributed least. Furthermore, the two patterns of insurrection just described have a crucial common property: in both cases the initial call to action usually came from republican activists in the city and went to allies they had been recruiting in the countryside over the years of the Second Republic. The main difference was whether the urban insurgents were able to take over the city before the countrymen arrived.

The great rebellion of 1851 marked a transition in rural rebellion in something like the same way that the June days displayed the transition in urban rebellion. In Paris and dozens of smaller cities throughout France, the well-organized republican activists made a vigorous vain effort to prevent the coup. Being highly visible, they bore the brunt of the Napoleonic repression. Out in such departments as Pyrénées-Orientales and Basses-Alpes, thousands of peasants and rural craftsmen spilled out their anger in equally vain attacks on their local centers of government. The attacks were reminiscent of the tax riots of previous years, but they established a higher level of organization and a greater degree of rural-urban coordination than ever before. Then the countrymen were silent.

What happened? It is not just that France calmed down, although the country did subside into peace for close to twenty years. More happened than that. When collective violence returned at the end of the Empire, it was more highly organized, more regularly based on associations, more explicitly in pursuit or defense of a political program. It was modern. Rural rebellions eventually reappeared, but mainly in modern dress: as organized demonstrations or articulated criticisms of government policy. The old forms had ignored or resisted the influence of the center. The new forms took that influence for granted, but acted to change its character.

. . . The provincial disturbances of 1848 through 1851 brought out not only the dying peasantry, but also large numbers of people—semirural semi-industrial workers whom the deindustrialization of the countryside was driving into oblivion. After the failure of their last great protests, they gave up. From that point on, the surplus rural population turned to migration toward the big cities. More so than we have realized, the midcentury provincial disturbances recorded the final outraged cries of whole classes whom the growth of a centralized, capitalistic, industrial nation-state was stripping of political identity and means of existence. Those who held on longer, like the Poujadist *petits gens* of the 1950's, mounted their petty protests later. But most of them had voiced their rage and then expired by 1855.

At the same time, their very classes created by the growth of a centralized, capitalistic, industrial nation-state were acquiring political identity by means of collective violence, if not by that means alone. Like their basic conditions of existence, their forms of violence were shaped by their willy-nilly implication in such a nation-state. Hence the fundamental traits of the new forms of collective violence: complexity and durability of organization, growth from formal associations, crystallization around explicit programs and articulated ideologies.

Crime and Industrialization in Britain

J. J. TOBIAS

The history of crime has as yet only barely been sketched, so we cannot claim definite correlations between crime and modernization. Crime may go up as the strains of modernization increase—it seems to have risen generally in the twentieth century—but it also may go down, as it did in many areas in the nineteenth century. The nature of crime does change with modernization. Crimes of violence probably declined with urbanization in Europe. The tensions of life in small villages—tightly knit communities from which escape was not easy—and the absence of police were conducive to violence, particularly when supplemented by the pressures of population growth. The growth of more impersonal, better-policed cities reduced the rate of violent crimes, while encouraging new expectations that led to an increase in crimes against property. Thus the nature and motivations of criminals were changing. In this sense crime should be analyzed in the light of the broader modernization of lower-class outlook, for its motives may be seen as perverse expressions of more general new values.

This selection attempts a general survey of English crime patterns during the first stages of modernization. Tobias finds that crime reached a peak in the first half of the eighteenth century, just before the first signs of modernization emerged. Thereafter crime probably declined; violence certainly did. If these findings are accurate, they constitute an important contribution to our understanding of modernization, at least in Britain, for they suggest that urbanization and industrialization created more new constructive opportunities than they did tensions. They resolved more problems for the lower classes than they created.

The change in the nature of crime is also noteworthy. Not only did violence decrease—itself a development of major importance—but crimes became more subtle, and the old hero-criminal, the man of daring action, became a less common figure. Again, it does not seem far-fetched to suggest a major change in the outlook of criminals paralleling the broader process of modernization.

The passage also suggests the problem of public attitudes toward crime. In the early nineteenth century, when social unrest was severe and the strains of industrialization were particularly acute for upper-class traditionalists, crime was generally thought to be rising, whereas in fact it was probably declining.

Attractive as these judgments are, if only because they overturn any simplistic approach to crime in modern society, they must be subjected to critical scrutiny. The judgments bear on urban, not rural, society; yet the problem of crime may have been greater in the countryside. They derive almost solely from qualitative studies by contemporary observers; there are no hard statistics. Contemporary observers can be wrong, even when their impressions contradict more fashionable opinions by pointing to a decrease in crime.

One may wonder, then, if the crime pattern is as clear-cut as Tobias suggests. In particular, there must be some lingering uncertainty about the 1820s and 1830s, when material conditions in the cities seem to have been deteriorating. But the long-range trend Tobias projects seems hard to refute for Britain. By the second half of the nineteenth century crime was decreasing. The passage suggests a number of reasons for this, relating primarily to city organization and material conditions. One must ask if these are sufficient explanations. Broader changes in lower-class culture may have been involved as well. The decline of crime by children and the general drop in violence might, for example, point to new kinds of behavior in the family.

The lawlessness of London in the first half of the eighteenth century has often been described. Mrs. M. D. George, in her *London Life in the XVIIIth Century*, observes that at the beginning of the century "the forces of disorder and crime had the upper hand in London"; she quotes the City Marshal's remarks of 1718:

> Now it is the general complaint of the taverns, the coffee-houses, the shop-keepers and others, that their customers are afraid when it is dark to come to their houses and shops for fear that their hats and wigs should be snitched from their heads or their swords taken from their sides, or that they may be blinded, knocked down, cut or stabbed; nay, the coaches cannot secure them, but they are likewise cut and robbed in the public streets, &c. By which means the traffic of the City is much interrupted.

These remarks, moreover, apply to the area within the jurisdiction of the City, then better policed than the growing portion of the metropolis outside the City limits.

Over 30 years later, Henry Fielding, the pioneer Bow Street magistrate, took an equally gloomy view; his famous and often-quoted work, *An Enquiry into the Causes of the Late Increase of Robbers* . . . , leaves us in no doubt of his views about the crime of London in 1751, three years after his appointment. Fielding can be left to speak for himself:

> . . . The Innocent are put in Terror, affronted and alarmed with Threats and Execrations, endangered with loaded Pistols, beat with Bludgeons and hacked with Cutlasses, of which the Loss of Health, of Limbs, and often of Life, is the Consequence; and all this without any Respect to Age, or Dignity, or Sex. . . .

Street Robberies are generally committed in the dark, the Persons on whom they are committed are often in Chairs and Coaches, and if on Foot, the Attack is usually begun by knocking the Party down, and for the Time depriving him of his Sense. But if the Thief should be less barbarous, he is seldom so incautious as to omit taking every Method to prevent his being known, by flapping the Party's Hat over his Face, and by every other Method which he can invent to avoid Discovery. . . .

How long have we known Highwaymen reign in this Kingdom after they have been publicly known for such? Have not some of these committed Robberies in open Day-light, in the Sight of many People, and have afterward rode solemnly and triumphantly through the neighbouring Towns without any Danger or Molestation. . . . Great and numerous Gangs . . . have for a long time committed the most open Outrages in Defiance of the Law. . . .

There are at this Time a great Gang of Rogues, whose Number falls little short of a Hundred, who are incorporated in one Body, have Officers and a Treasury; and have reduced Theft and Robbery into a regular System. There are [members] of this Society of Men who appear in all Disguises, and mix in most Companies. Nor are they better versed in every Art of cheating, thieving, and robbing, than they are armed with every Method of evading the Law. . . . If they fail in rescuing the Prisoner, or (which seldom happens) in bribing or deterring the Prosecutor, they have for their last Resource some rotten Members of the Law to forge a Defence for them, and a great Number of false Witnesses ready to support it. . . .

It is possible that one or two of Fielding's remarks would not stand up to investigation, but that the substance of them is correct is not in doubt. Jonas Hanway in 1775 wrote:

I sup with my friend; I cannot return to my home, not even in my chariot, without danger of a pistol being clapt to my breast. I build an elegant villa, ten or twenty miles distant from the capital: I am obliged to provide an armed force to convey me thither, lest I should be attacked on the road with fire and ball.

There is much similar evidence, which has been described by other authors.

Indeed, so powerful were the criminals that parts of the town were wholly given over to them: it was not until well into the eighteenth century that the Alsatia, or area of sanctuary, disappeared from London. Such places, by the end of the seventeenth century,

in theory . . . had no existence, or existed on sufferance only to secure . . . the protection of the debtor against imprisonment for debt; in practice they were criminal quarters where the officers of justice were set at defiance, and where no man's life was safe unless he had the privilege of being an inhabitant.

They were a survival of the medieval sanctuaries, where criminals could take refuge prior to appearing before the coroner to admit their guilt and abjure the realm. The comment that the sanctuaries had in theory ceased to exist was justified . . . [but] sanctuaries continued to exist, and in the last decade of the seventeenth century there were several in London. . . .

Mrs. George, after taking stock of the crime situation in London in the early part of the eighteenth century, suggests that things were at their worst in the 1740s and 50s, and that thereafter an improvement took place. Though some contemporaries raised the "cry of national deterioration," she sides with Francis Place, the Radical tailor of Charing Cross, who claimed that the "crimes and vices" of the days of his youth greatly exceeded those of the early nineteenth century. "By the end of the [eighteenth] century," she sums up, "we are in a different world."

While Mrs. George quotes testimony to the good order in London at the end of the eighteenth century—a guidebook of 1802 claimed that "no city in proportion to its trade and luxury is more free from danger to those who pass the streets at all hours, or from depredations, open or concealed, on property"—other modern writers take a more pessimistic view. Dr. E. O'Brien quotes the Solicitor-General in 1785—"nobody could feel himself unapprehensive of danger to his person or property if he walked in the street after dark, nor could any man promise himself security in his bed." Professor A. G. L. Shaw quotes advice of 1790 to visitors to London "never to stop in a crowd or look at the windows of a print-shop, if you would not have your pocket picked." Patrick Colquhoun's well-known *Treatise on the Police of the Metropolis* . . . , which went through several editions between 1795 and 1806, has often been used to show the level of criminality that existed at the time he wrote. He spoke of "the outrages and acts of violence continually committed, more particularly in and near the Metropolis by lawless ravagers of property, and destroyers of lives, in disturbing the peaceful mansion, *the Castle of every Englishman*, and also in abridging the liberty of travelling upon the Public Highways." In Cheapside, he said,

> a multitude of thieves and pickpockets, exhibiting often in their dress and exterior, the appearance of gentlemen and men of business, assemble every evening in gangs, watching at the corners of every street, ready to *hustle and rob*, or to *trip up the heels* of the *warehouseporters and the servants of shopkeepers carrying goods;* or at the doors of warehouses, at dusk and at the time they are locked, to be ready to seize loose parcels when unperceived; by all which means, aided by a number of other tricks and fraudulent pretences, they are but too successful in obtaining considerable booty. In short, there is no device or artifice to which these vigilant plunderers do not resort: of which an example appeared in an instance, where almost in the twinkling of an eye, while the servants of an eminent silk-dyer had crossed a narrow street, his horse and cart, containing raw silk to the value of *twelve hundred*

pounds, were driven clear off. Many of these atrocious villains, are also constantly waiting at the inns, disguised in different ways, personating *travellers, coach-office clerks, porters and coachmen,* for the purpose of plundering every thing that is portable; which, with the assistance of two or three associates if necessary, is carried to a coach called for the purpose, and immediately conveyed to the receiver.

He described in great detail the various river thieves who preyed on the shipping in the Port of London, though he had the satisfaction in the later editions of the work of recording that the Marine Police—of which he was the originator—"may truly be said to have worked wonders in reforming the shocking abuses which prevailed."

There is thus a conflict of views. Those who consider conditions around the end of the eighteenth century are struck with the level of crime and violence then prevalent, while Mrs. George, surveying the century as a whole, sees an improvement. Others indeed have shared her opinion. Crime of course still abounded, and criminals were often violent; but things, it seems, were probably better than they had been earlier.

The changes appear to be associated with the Industrial Revolution. . . . In the last half of the eighteenth century and the first half of the nineteenth century, . . . society was in violent transition. The towns were growing rapidly, and the facilities available to their rulers were very limited and their knowledge of how to use them even more limited. Their population, ever increasing, was predominantly a young one, and the young town-dwellers were faced with a whole host of unfamiliar problems, problems for which their background and training provided them with no answer. The towns, and especially London, had always had a criminal problem different from and larger than that of other areas, and there were groups of people, living in distinctive areas, who had evolved a way of life of their own based on crime. Many young town-dwellers, faced with these problems and receiving no assistance from their families or their employers (if they had families or employers) or from the municipal authorities, found solutions by adopting the techniques, the habits and the attitudes of the criminals. There was thus, in London and the other large towns in the latter part of the eighteenth century and the earlier part of the nineteenth century, an upsurge of crime which was the fruit of a society in rapid transition.

We now return to the question of the course of crime at the end of the eighteenth century. It was seen earlier that the weight of evidence is in favour of the view that the level of crime about the year 1800 was lower than it had been earlier in the century. However, if the analysis just made were correct it would be expected that crime should by then have increased somewhat as a result of the first decades of the Industrial Revolution. The contradiction can, it seems, be resolved. First, it is necessary to make a distinction between qualitative change and quantitative change. There seems no reason to doubt the view that crime was becoming less violent in its nature in the eighteenth century—there is considerable evidence that such a trend existed throughout the nineteenth century. Such a change can be ascribed to the more civilised way of life and the reduction in the violence of life in general which is attested by historians of the eighteenth century. Mrs. George, for example, speaks of the

> change in the attitude towards social questions which was the outcome of the new spirit of humanity, the new command of material resources, and the new belief in environment rather than Providence as the cause of many human ills. . . . There had been a number of obscure reforms, whose cumulative effect was very great . . . an increasing realisation of evils and a growing intolerance of hardships. . . . The improvements in medicine and sanitation had bettered conditions . . . in London.

It is perhaps not irrelevant to note here that by the end of the century a much lower proportion of those condemned to death was actually being executed than had been the case earlier. For example, in the period 1749–58 two in three of the offenders sentenced to death in London and Middlesex were executed, but by the end of the century the ratio had dropped to less than one in three. There are thus grounds for accepting that there was a reduction in the amount of violent crime. However, such a reduction could very well have accompanied an increase in the amount of non-violent crime. Indeed, as violent crimes are the spectacular and eye-catching crimes, a decrease in their number could well have blinded contemporaries to an increase in the total amount of crime. Some contemporary observers were in the early nineteenth century able to insist that crime was increasing in quantity at the same time that they agreed that it was decreasing in violence; but a lesser increase in non-violent crime might well be masked from view. However, it is not necessary to adopt this line of reasoning, for it seems probable that other special factors were operating at the end of the eighteenth century.

A number of changes had taken place in the latter part of the eighteenth century which may well have offset the effects of the movement to the towns. Mrs. George attributes the reduction of crime which she notices, in part at any rate, to the various improvements in the lighting and policing of London, and she regards Henry Fielding's magistracy at Bow Street (1748–54) as "a turning-point in the social history of London." The street-lighting of London had indeed improved considerably during the eighteenth century. . . .

. . . The provision of better lighting would undoubtedly have made crime more difficult.

Equally certainly the life of the London criminals was made more difficult by improved machinery for enforcing the law. From the time of Henry Fielding's appointment, there was in London a magistrate who was both honest and zealous in the prosecution of crime. (Thomas de Veil has some claim to have anticipated Fielding: appointed a magistrate in 1729, he is described by Pringle as "the first London magistrate of the century to make a serious attempt to suppress crime" and as "the first of the Bow Street police-magistrates"; but unlike Fielding he did not live on his pay from government but took fees and other profits where he could.) After a time there was more than one magistrate at Bow Street, and in 1792 seven more police offices, each manned by three paid magistrates, were established. One of Henry Fielding's achievements was the establishment of a small group of detectives, "Mr. Fielding's People," who eventually became the Bow Street Runners; and when the seven police offices were established in 1792 each of them had a group of detective police officers of its own. There was also, from about 1782, a Foot Patrole of 68 men attached to the Bow Street Office and patrolling the streets at night. The changes thus made in the policing of London were to prove inadequate before long; but their impact might well have been sufficient to account for the improvement in the crime situation detected by some observers.

Together with these permanent changes there was in the years around the end of the eighteenth century a temporary change, an improvement in employment in London. The industrial expansion since 1760 had done something to increase the demand for labour, and in addition the generation-long war with France (1793–1815, with only brief intermissions) did much to stimulate industry and led to an increase in the chances of getting a job. Even Patrick Colquhoun thought that some of the decrease in crime on the river was due not to his Marine Police but to the employment possibilities created by the war—"the resource afforded by the present war, gives employment, for a time only, to many depraved characters and mischievous members of the community." It may well have been more important that employment was available more readily for youngsters who had not yet become "depraved" or —in the sense intended—"mischievous." . . .

. . . It is of course necessary to be very cautious before making pronouncements about changes in the nature or level of crime over any period of time, let alone one so remote as the nineteenth century. However, there are two propositions on this topic that can be put forward with some assurance.

The first of these is that there was a continuing trend to less violence in crime over the century. Such a trend probably existed in the eighteenth century; the evidence for its existence in the nineteenth century is even stronger. Throughout the century contemporaries accepted that criminals were becoming less violent, each generation seeing an improvement over the previous one.

The evidence before the Select Committee on Police of 1816–18 sets the tone. "Daring, desperate things seem to be worn out, except daring forgeries," said one police officer, and the question put to John Nares, a police magistrate of over 20 years' experience, and his reply will serve as a summary of the rest of the evidence: "The Committee have had in evidence, and indeed the observation of every one must have given him the information without that evidence, that atrocious crimes have of late years considerably diminished?—I have no doubt of that."

Blackwood's Magazine did indeed in 1818 write that "one strong feature of the times is the prevalence of atrocious crime. This is the common remark of every day." However, the Select Committee's reports leave no doubt that many people in the post-Waterloo period took the more optimistic view.

Street robberies in London increased dramatically in the early 1820s, and one writer in 1829 spoke of gangs being ready to "hustle, rob, or knock down" anyone carrying valuables; but he also said that "there have been few instances lately of forcing houses in the old-fashioned way, at the front, and taking possession by *coup de main*." Francis Place in 1831 was sure that crimes had decreased "in atrocity"; Edwin Chadwick too had no doubt about the matter. In 1829 he wrote: "It is acknowledged on every side, that crimes attended with acts of violence have diminished," and in 1839 the Report of the Royal Commission on a Constabulary Force, drafted by him, said that "Crimes of violence committed for the sake of obtaining property have diminished. . . . In the towns, burglaries and depredations in the streets are now rarely accompanied by violence." In 1832 a writer in *Fraser's Magazine* attempted an explanation:

> The character and feelings of the public thief, as of all other classes of society, have undergone a visible and marked change within the last thirty years. . . . Formerly, the heroes of their party were fellows conspicuous and famed for open and daring acts of plunder, in whom the whole body had a pride, and whom they all felt ambitious to imitate; failing only to do so for lack of the same quantum of courage. The more desperate and numerous the instances of robbery, the more were the parties lauded and admired. . . . All this kind of heroism has subsided; their leaders now are men rendered famous for scheming, subtlety, and astuteness. Formerly, the passport to enrolment under their banners was a name for boldness and monstrous acts of outrage; now a certificate must be brought of the man never having committed an indiscreet act in his calling.

Opinion remained the same at mid-century. Thus, despite outbreaks of violent crime over the whole country between 1850 and 1853, Frederic Hill, a former Inspector of Prisons, could write in the latter year that crimes were "taking a milder and milder form." Violent crimes continued to attract public attention on various occasions during the 1850s and 60s, particularly of course during the famous garrotting attacks in London in 1862. They caused much public alarm—perhaps more acute because of the relative safety of recent years—but belief that there had been an improvement over earlier years persisted. In 1862 the *Cornhill Magazine* wrote that the criminals' "character in respect of violence and cruelty has been much ameliorated during the last fifteen or twenty years. They do not like resorting to violence if it can possibly be avoided. . . . The modern thief depends upon his skill."

In the closing years of the nineteenth century the story was unchanged. Looking back over his long life a few days before his death in 1890, Edwin Chadwick summed up his views on this point in a letter to the Editor of the *Daily Chronicle* prepared for his signature but never signed:

> When the Police were first instituted [presumably the reference is to the establishment of the Metropolitan Police in 1829], men who were mechanics in good position were asked why they did not have a watch to mark the time. "Yes" was the reply "and get my head broken by thieves." They could hold in safety no personal property of any sort, and life would have been insecure. So with their families. They had no silver spoons, nor any other article of that kind. The possession of such property at that time endangered their lives.

It must be admitted that in 1891 the Rev. W. D. Morrison wrote that "offences against property with violence display a tendency to increase," but he was talking about the number of cases recorded in a particular statistical category rather than the quality of the acts themselves. Charles Booth in the 1890s found that violence was regarded by criminals and police alike as a breach of the "rules of the game, which provide the rough outlines of a code of what is regarded as fair or unfair." Thomas Holmes, surveying in 1908 his 21 years' experience as a police-court missionary, was satisfied that there were fewer crimes of violence.

Thus over the whole of the century there is evidence, much of it from sources entitled to our respect, that the use of violence in crime had decreased; and the conclusion that this is true seems irresistible.

A qualitative change in criminality can thus be established; what can we say about quantitative change? Here it is much more difficult to make definite statements. The difficulties of ascertaining changes in the level of crime are well known, and the people of the nineteenth century were not likely to have had any clearer idea of what was going on than we have of what is going on today. The evidence of what they thought was happening is, moreover, hard to interpret. What exactly do we understand when someone says that "the tranquillity . . . of the whole town is miraculous . . . very different from what I remember, even within a few years," but adds "we have a vast number of pickpockets occasionally, and frauds in abundance"? How far is he being contradicted by a witness who affirms that "the petty offences" and "the juvenile depredators" have increased? Does either of them mean the same thing as the witness who thought that there had been an increase but only in "simple larcenys, burglaries and so on, nothing very enormous" or the witness who agrees that crime is on the increase "in numbers certainly, but not in depravity by any means; we have . . . less serious offences"? Despite these difficulties, however, it is worth surveying the evidence, and for this purpose it is convenient to divide the century into two parts, the division occurring in the middle 1850s.

The phrases quoted in the previous paragraph show that it is easy to produce testimony to an increase in non-violent crime in the first of these two periods. Other evidence can be quoted. The Under-Sheriff of London and Middlesex said in 1817:

> As to the length of the Old Bailey sessions, it is within the memory of most persons who are now engaged in its business, that if a session continued from the Wednesday in one week to the Monday in the next (or five days) it was an extraordinary circumstance, whereas it has now become a common occurrence for a session to last a fortnight and three weeks. . . . I am persuaded that the actual increase of crime will alone explain the increased length of sessions and assizes.

The Rev. W. L. Clay, writing in 1861, had no doubt that in the early part of the century "the real increase of crime had been very serious, the apparent increase terrible," and though the comment quoted was made in relation to the 10 years from 1825 to 1834, it represents his view of the whole period from about 1810. Several witnesses before parliamentary committees of enquiry and others whose opinions are on record put forward similar views. On the other hand, the contrary view is well supported, and if the bulk of the evidence is for an increase, there are one or two powerful names in the opposing camp. Alderman Matthew Wood, M.P., who was a leading figure in the affairs of the City of London but who on this occasion can be regarded as a disinterested witness, as he was talking about London outside the City, said in 1828 that there were fewer offences but that more were being detected because of improved policing—"that is a fact I have no doubt about." Francis Place was of the same opinion.

Moreover, some observers of the criminal scene in the post-war years were not prepared to accept that any change had really taken place. In 1816 a witness had said that juvenile delinquencies had not increased "so much as is generally supposed; I apprehend that they are more known from being more investigated." He "hoped, and was inclined to think" that there had been an increase in police activity rather than a "real augmentation in the number of crimes." In 1828 the Superintendent of the Hulks said that "The increase of crime has not been much beyond the increased population of the country; I do not state that it has not increased, but not to that extent that seems to be the prevailing opinion." "Do not you think," he was asked, "that on the whole the general notion as to the great increase of crime is exaggerated, and not quite founded in fact?" and he replied: "Certainly." The Select Committee on Police before which he was speaking was the one which reversed the tenor of previous reports and recommended a change in the police of the metropolis, and thus gave Sir Robert Peel the opportunity to create the Metropolitan Police. However, even they did not go further than to say that they had obtained "no information which justifies them in reporting further, than that" the increase in commitments and convictions in the metropolis must be considered to emanate

> from a combination of causes. . . . A portion only of the accession to Criminal Commitments, is to be deemed indicative of a proportionate increase of Crime; and even of that portion, much may be accounted for in the more ready detection and trial of culprits, also in less disinclination to prosecute, in consequence of improved facilities afforded at the courts to prosecutors and witnesses, and of the increased allowance of costs.

Edwin Chadwick observed in 1829 that for the previous 6–8 years there had been a general belief that crime in the metropolis had been steadily increasing since before 1815 but that there was no evidence for this belief; all that had happened was that crime was more prosecuted and more exposed to view.

This game of matching quotation to quotation could go on for a long time; until the early 1850s the argument between the three points of view continued. Enough has been said, however, to show the difficulty of reaching any conclusion. It seems probable that the level of crime after about 1810 was higher than that of the previous two decades. Professor Radzinowicz has recorded the view that crime in the early nineteenth century was on the increase, but despite this powerful authority it is difficult to reach any firm conclusion about changes in the amount of crime in the period from Waterloo to the middle 1850s.

When we turn to the second part of the century, from the middle 1850s to its end, we reach the second point about which a reasonable degree of certainty is attainable. There was a marked drop in juvenile crime and in the number of juvenile criminals in the 1850s and 60s. In the 1850s some writers were still speaking of an increase of juvenile crime, but already opinion was beginning to change. The Rev. John Clay, the Chaplain of Preston Gaol, in his report for 1855–6 wrote:

> Any doubts which may have been entertained as to the successful issue of reformatory schools, when the great movement in their favour took place a few years ago, ought now to be set at rest, for it has been sufficiently proved that wherever they have been earnestly and judiciously worked, there criminality has received a check.

In 1859, T. B. L. Baker, a Gloucestershire magistrate and a prominent writer on criminal matters, claimed that a reduction in juvenile crime had commenced, and he later gave details of what he thought had happened. He regarded 1856 as the year in which the decisive change took place, that being the year in which it became the general practice to commit all qualified offenders to reformatory school on a second conviction, almost regardless of the actual offence. He thought that the progress was maintained despite a minor increase of crime in 1860–3. It must be admitted that he was relying, in part at any rate, on the criminal statistics, as indeed other people may have been; but some of the names on the list of those who shared his opinions are impressive. The Rev. John Clay has already been quoted; the others include the Rev. S. Turner, the Inspector of Reformatory Schools, in his 1859–60 Report, the Rev. W. L. Clay in 1861 and Miss Carpenter in 1861 and 1864. These are powerful authorities.

The case for saying that there was a marked reduction of crime in the 1850s does not rest merely on the testimony of those active at the time. Looking back over the perspective of a decade or two, people could see that the change was not merely quantitative but qualitative as well. The hardened juvenile thief, the hordes of criminal youngsters, had disappeared from English towns. There were few children left as bad as those of twenty years before, wrote C. B. Adderley in 1874. "It is almost impossible in these days," wrote the *Gloucestershire Chronicle* in 1886, "to realise the extent to which juvenile crime prevailed forty years ago." The Royal Commission on the Reformatories and Industrial Schools of 1884 accepted that the gangs of young criminals had been broken up, and an end put to the training of boys as professional thieves.

There were dissenting voices, of course. W. Hoyle, an ardent advocate of temperance, used the criminal statistics to show that an increase of crime had taken place. Rather more weight should perhaps be given to the Rev. W. D. Morrison, who in 1892 argued that crime had increased during the previous 30 years, i.e., from a period just after the reformatory schools had begun to have an effect. In his view "whatever the prisons have lost," the reformatory schools and the industrial schools have "more than gained." His argument was in part based on the number of juveniles in these three types of establishment taken together but, as Captain Anson, the Chief Constable of Staffordshire, pointed out, the increase was mainly in the number of those in industrial schools, not all of whom were offenders. Moreover, Morrison himself had the previous year said that "crime in England is not making more rapid strides than the growth of the population"; this is at any rate an acceptance that there was no increase in crime relative to the population.

It thus seems certain that a marked decline in the level of juvenile crime took place in the 1850s and 60s, and that at the end of the century the general level of crime was lower than it had been during most of its course. The Rev. J. W. Horsley felt that the last 20 years of the century had seen a real decrease in crime and a steady improvement in conduct in general. Sidney and Beatrice Webb wrote that "It is clear that the proved criminality of the eighteenth century was enormously in excess, both absolutely and relatively, of that which prevails at the opening of the twentieth century." It may fairly be claimed that it is only in the decades indicated that there is any sign of this "enormous" decrease taking place. R. F. Quinton just before the First World War wrote of the steady decrease of crime, and especially of serious crime, in the past 30 years. He too spoke of an "enormous" decline, this time of the number of professional criminals; he was quite sure there was an "actual decrease in crime." Mr. B. D. White, in his survey of the history of Liverpool, notices a fall in crime from 1875 to the end of the nineteenth century (and an increase in the first 14 years of the twentieth).

There is a further piece of evidence that a marked change had come over the criminal scene by the end of the nineteenth century. Charles Booth's survey of London in the 1890s affords an opportunity to compare conditions then with those earlier in the century; and one can only conclude that things had vastly improved. Booth gives details of specimen streets to illustrate his methods of classification, and the worst of these, St. Hubert Street, is described as

> An awful place; the worst street in the district. The families are mostly of the lowest class. . . . The children are rarely brought up to any kind of work, but loaf about, and no doubt form the nucleus for future generations of thieves and other bad characters. . . . A number of the rooms are occupied by prostitutes of the most pronounced order.

Yet, of the 58 heads of households in the street who are put into Booth's grading, only 12 fall into Class A—"the lowest class of occasional labourers, loafers and semi-criminals." The occupants of the street are listed tenement by tenement and family by family. In one case a member of the family is in prison, and in another the husband is just out of prison; two families have boys at industrial school (not, be it noted, reformatory school, where those convicted of the more serious offences were sent). All the people in Class A have some occupation listed, even if it is nearly always "casual labourer" or "hawker." It is true that Booth warns us that "Class A must not be confounded with the criminal classes," but he goes on to say that the lowest grade of criminals "mix freely with Class A, and are not to be distinguished from it." If, as we must assume, St. Hubert Street is a fair specimen of the worst types of street found by Booth and his investigators, the criminal scene had vastly improved. . . .

In general terms the pattern of crime in [the] provincial towns followed that of the country as a whole. In particular they participated in the decline in juvenile crime in and after the late 1850s. . . . One writer in particular paid attention to the provinces. T. B. L. Baker, the Gloucestershire magistrate, declared in 1860 that the regular, habitual, skilful boy-thief with half a dozen convictions or more had almost ceased to exist outside London. He had earlier spoken of reductions of crime in Liverpool, Bristol and Birmingham. His strongest claim was made in relation to his own county, and in particular Cheltenham, the area of operation of the Hardwicke Reformatory School of which he was a sponsor. The capture of "two young master-thieves" in 1856, coupled with the introduction in the same year of an automatic sentence to reformatory school on second conviction, led to a reduction by half or more of the number of juvenile criminals brought before the courts of Cheltenham; when the sentencing policy was altered in 1861 the number of juvenile offenders rose again, and a reversion to the automatic sentence brought it down once more. This enthusiast for the reformatory school is not a disinterested witness, but his views are broadly consistent with those of others. There seems good reason to accept that the crime of the provincial towns in the last 40 years or so of the century was at a lower level than it had earlier been.

A Criminal

JOSEPH KÜRPER,
as told to Arthur Griffiths

This selection covers the period between 1848 and 1874, when industrialization was taking hold in Germany after several decades of population growth and disruption in the countryside. It does not necessarily describe a typical case, but it is particularly valuable in that it comes directly from a criminal.

The author suggests the compulsion brought about by material need that contributed to a life of crime. Not surprisingly, an unusually troubled family background and the suggestion of continued difficulties in romance played important roles as well. Here, perhaps, is the reason that some members of the lower classes turned to crime while others, sharing similar material conditions, did not, though the question of what led a person out of normal lower-class behavior into a life of crime is not easy to resolve. Certainly, the link between a criminal with this kind of background and ordinary artisans was close in many ways. The attitude of the broader society, expressed specifically in treatment by employers and police, helped drive Kürper to crime, just as it would impel many artisans to protest. Kürper clearly suggests that no simple economic explanation, either in terms of sheer misery or in terms of rising material expectations, can explain his career.

There is in fact an ambiguity in Kürper's approach. On the one hand he suggests class antagonisms that seem rather modern. On the other, he seems fearful of the freedom that modern life has allowed, specifically mentioning the desirability of a guild structure that would keep people like himself in line. There is a similar ambiguity in his methods. Vagrancy was not new, though it may have been increasing in Germany in these decades; but from this traditional base Kürper becomes more and more sophisticated, and ends up more a swindler than a beggar—and all, it might be noted, without particular resort to violence, despite the violence used against him.

Germany has suffered grievously in recent years from the growth of vagrancy. The highroads are infested with tramps, and the prisons are perpetually full. Every good citizen is keenly desirous of reducing these scourges of society, but the progress of reform is slow. It is a difficult problem, but the first step toward solving it is to acquire a more accurate knowledge of the true

From Arthur Griffiths, *German and Austrian Prisons* (London, 1851).

spirit and character of these wrong-doers. One of the most unregenerate and irreclaimable has revealed the whole story of his life and transgressions, and some quotations from the account may throw light on the difficulties of the problem confronting the prison reformer.

"My name is Joseph Kürper and I was born at H. in the Palatinate on June 14, 1849. I was an illegitimate child and I spent my early years with my mother. When I was four years old, she went to service and I, thrown on my own resources, was forced to beg for broken victuals from door to door. Sometimes I was driven away with hard words or the dogs were set on me. I cannot remember ever having owned a pair of shoes, and as a child I had no bed to sleep in. I suffered all kinds of hardships. When the time came for me to go to school, my troubles increased. As I was dressed in evil smelling rags and tatters, I was kept apart, treated like a leper and an outcast, and if I played truant I was cruelly beaten. Nevertheless, I managed to evade instruction almost entirely and did not learn much more than the alphabet. My life was that of a poor waif forsaken by God and man.

"At first I bore no ill-will to the well-to-do, and I had no quarrel with those who had treated me so harshly. Gradually, however, I realised my grievance against society and began to wage war on it by acts of pilfering, the first of which I committed in the house of a small farmer where my mother was in service. Tormented by hunger, I got in through a window and stole a loaf of bread and a few kreutzers. This was my first theft and it had bad results for me, for, when taxed with it, I confessed and was cruelly flogged by the farmer. Out of revenge I killed one of his fowls every day. Presently my mother again gave birth to an illegitimate child, a girl, and when the little thing was just able to toddle, she sent us out to beg in company, preferring this mode of support to that of working herself. We were beaten if we returned empty-handed to our hovel, so I became an expert thief in order to avoid the stick. My mother applauded me and my success was my ruin.

"At last, in the continued practice of stealing, I committed a theft that brought me for the first time within reach of the law. In the spring of 1860, when in my eleventh year, I laid hands on a watch in an empty house in the village of Kottweiler. I broke it up into its different component parts, which I sold separately to the children of our own village for pieces of bread. Though the watch was missed, I was not suspected and, growing bolder still, I soon after audaciously possessed myself of another watch hanging in a bakehouse. This time I was caught red-handed, severely flogged, and then taken before the magistrate at Kusel. He put me through a cross-examination and I confessed everything. On my return home the village authorities vented their rage against me by beating me black and blue, and my little sister having let out the secret that I was also the thief of the watch at Kottweiler, I was again arrested and taken back by a police official to the magistrate at Kusel, who, on account of my youth, only sentenced me to two years' detention at the industrial school at Speier. I was allowed to go home with my mother before being sent there, and when the police came to convey me, I ran away and managed to get over the Prussian frontier to St. Wedel. Here I first begged and then worked for a small farmer in the neighbourhood. After a time I ran away again, taking with me the watch of this brutal man who had maltreated me. I now tried to live by carrying luggage at the railway station of the town. Here I found several opportunities for committing daring thefts and finally absconded, after helping myself to some money from the till of the refreshment room. After again intermittently working and stealing, I tried to set up as a highway robber, but without success, and was soon arrested by a police official who had a warrant out against me, and actually handed over to the authorities of the industrial school at Speier.

"Had this institution been the best in the world, I should not have felt at my ease in it, as I was like a young wild-cat or a bird of prey shut up behind iron bars. About one hundred Catholic children were confined there, all of them vicious and corrupt. Those who were unversed in criminal ways soon learned from the others. The majority, among whom I count myself, left the school worse than they entered. The system of education was perfectly worthless; we were constantly beaten and, being badly fed, we lost no opportunity of stealing broken victuals. I must acknowledge that I learned a great deal at school in regard to my trade, that of a shoemaker. But I had not been long in the place before I contrived to escape and reach the town of Lautern. Here I was taken into the house of a worthy tradesman, to whom I told my real name and origin; but I concealed the fact that I had run away from Speier. He became fond of me, and I noticed that he now and then put my honesty to the test, which induced me to resist every temptation bravely. As he was childless and wanted to train me up as a tradesman, a happy future might have been in store for me, had not fate decreed otherwise.

"One Sunday my master proposed taking me to see my mother, and we started on our drive. I was so afraid that the authorities of the village would send me back to Speier that when we halted somewhere to dine, and my master had dropped asleep, I ran away. I wandered about homeless for a time until at Kaiserslautern I was caught and returned to Speier. There I soon became aware that nothing good awaited me, and my fears were realised, for I was deprived of my supper the first night and on going to bed was cruelly flogged with a knout until the blood streamed down my back. But, though specially watched, I again escaped to Kaiserslautern, where I was employed by an upholsterer who taught me a great deal. Once more I was discovered and sent back to Speier, where I was a second time welcomed with the knout. I now made no further efforts to escape and for the rest of my time possessed my soul in patience. The days passed monotonously, the only variation being that sometimes I was flogged more than usual. We rose early, dressed, washed, prayed and did our school tasks, breakfasted on thin soup, in which there was never a scrap of fat, and worked in the various shops until eleven o'clock, when we dined. After that meal came gymnastic exercises and drill. Then school or working at our trades alternately occupied the time until supper at seven, and we went to bed at half past eight. Sundays were more entertaining. In the afternoon, after service, we went to walk outside the town. On these expeditions we stole what we could in the way of edibles and took our booty to bed with us to eat it during the week, though, of course, we were flogged if our thefts were discovered, which, however, did not deter us from further efforts at pilfering in the institution itself. When the two weary years were over, I had grown into a tall, likely lad. I possessed a fair amount of schooling and I believed myself to be qualified to take a place as assistant to a shoemaker, being expert at my trade. I had received no religious impressions; principles I had none. I only longed for freedom and to enjoy life.

"My dreams of golden liberty were not to be fulfilled as yet. On being dismissed from the school, I was provided with two suits of clothes and sent to Lautern, where I had to present myself to a certain Herr Meuth, the president of a reformatory society. He placed me with a shoemaker. I had hoped I should be paid wages but, when claiming them with the other journeymen, I was told I should get what I deserved, and my master proceeded to take down a dog-whip from a peg where it hung and flogged me unmercifully. On the following Sunday he informed me that I was only an apprentice and should have to serve him in that capacity two years longer and could not escape it. At the end of that time he offered to keep me and pay me regular wages, but I refused, as he had so often abused and maltreated me. He gave me my indenture, which was, at the same time, a certificate of good conduct. I packed my possessions and wandered out into the world.

"As happy as a king, I started on my journey to Mannheim. I carried a satchel on my back and my road lay through the Rhine district where the trees were in full bloom. Arriving at my destination, I found occupation with a shoemaker who, however, declared that my work was not of a very high character and paid me only one gulden a week, with insufficient food. In everything outside of my trade I was left to my own devices and consequently, being of an undisciplined nature, I led anything but a decent life. Looking back to these days, I recognise how very much better it would be if every apprentice, at the outset of his wage-earning life, were forced to belong to a guild, so that he would be protected by a strict corporation of this sort and obliged to obey its laws. In those days I thought otherwise, but now that I am under prison rule I regret the license I was allowed then. I remained a year at Mannheim but, as my master refused to raise my wages, I departed one fine day and walked to Karlsruhe, passing through Bruchsal and Heidelberg on my way.

"In Karlsruhe I likewise had the good fortune to find occupation without undue delay. The court shoemaker, Heim, took me into his house and gave me good wages and, as I did piece work, I sometimes earned from 12 to 15 guldens a week. On Sundays I used to dress myself in fashionable clothes, on which I spent my pay, and walk out with a glass in my eye and a cigar in my mouth, hoping to be taken for something far superior to a shoemaker's assistant. I was a good-looking lad, and on a fine Sunday in summer I walked into a beer garden, where I made the acquaintance of a pretty young lady who was sitting at a table with a party of respectable people. I represented myself as the son of a rich man from Munich and said that my name was Junker, that I held a position in Karlsruhe as a confectioner and lodged in the house of the shoemaker Heim. The girl and her family believed my statements, and I was received with kindness as a visitor at their house. Of course, courtship in the guise of a rich man costs money, and I was soon obliged to pawn my watch. A Sunday came round on which I was unable to call on my sweetheart; I had to sit on my stool and draw my cobbler's thread through shoeleather. My lady-love came to inquire for me, and saw me in my working garb. She turned and left the house, but I followed her and tried to excuse myself, whereupon she took out her purse and, pressing it into my hands, said, 'Keep it and amend your ways. I do not quarrel with you for being a cobbler, but I am grieved that you should have deceived me.' I returned to my room terribly ashamed and wrathful. I determined not to remain a moment longer in the town, so I paid my debts with the contents of my purse and took my departure. It was lucky for the respectable and decent girl that she discovered my swindling practices before it was too late."

After this the tramp wandered to and fro, from Baden to Offenburg, leading a precarious existence, working as a shoemaker when he could find employment and living royally when he had the funds, but begging for food and half-starved when out of luck. At last he reached Darmstadt where he joined an organisation of professional vagrants. Their headquarters were at a low tavern where false passports and "legitimation" papers were manufactured to help in confusing the police as to the true antecedents of this semi-criminal fraternity. He continues: "The day after my arrival at the inn, my new colleagues joined me at breakfast and a plan of campaign was fixed upon. I was to take off my shirt and leave it at the inn, wind a cloth around my neck and button up my coat to meet it; thus attired, I was to start out, accompanied by one of the vagrants dubbed in familiar parlance 'the Baron.' He was to point out to me the most likely houses for our purpose. I was to enter the first of these and beg for a shirt, and having obtained it, repeat the process at other houses. Thus by evening we should have collected from twenty to thirty shirts, which we were then to sell. By pursuing this line of business we should have money in abundance and live at our ease. This is a fair picture of the mode of existence of large numbers of journeymen lads in Germany, the children of respectable parents who go to perdition, body and soul. My first attempt turned out most successfully as the Baron had foretold, and I became very expert in my new calling. We worked as follows: The Baron pointed out a house where I might hope to obtain something in the way of a gift and indicated a place where he would wait for me to rejoin him. When the servant answered the door, I gave him the envelope containing my false 'legitimation,' and a begging letter describing my miserable condition, and asked him to take it to his mistress. He soon returned with my papers and a thaler, explaining that this was the best the lady could do for me. Flushed with victory, I ran to find the Baron, who slipped my papers into another envelope. He always carried a supply of envelopes to replace those that had to be torn open. We next went to the house of the Bavarian envoy, where I received a gulden and a good shirt. We continued our successful round until the evening, when we returned to the inn with our rich booty. Here every article was inspected, sorted, valued, and later, when the other habitués came in, the parlour was turned into an auction room. Among the buyers was a policeman and, as he had first choice, he selected the best of my shirts, some of which were quite new, for himself. Other purchasers followed, and at the end of the evening we had disposed of all our goods. Our ready money amounted to a good round sum and was divided into three portions. I had made more in this one day than I had ever been able to earn in a week.

"Our plans for the following day came to nought. I was arrested about four o'clock in the morning by four police officials who penetrated into my room, pinioned me when I offered resistance, and took me off to the police ward No. 2 on the charge of theft. Here I was interrogated as to what I had done with the articles I had stolen on the previous day. I denied indignantly that I had stolen anything at all, but I was next conducted across the market place to a jeweller's shop and identified by the owner as the rascal whom he suspected. I was quite puzzled at the unwarranted accusation against me, although I remembered having been in the shop on the previous day. From the police ward I was carried to the prison and locked up in a cell, where I remained for three whole days, until interrogated, and, as the jeweller persisted in his accusation, I was detained for eight days longer. Finally the jeweller, Scarth by name, appeared, full of apologies, and admitted that the knife he had believed to have been stolen had been found. The end of this incident was that Scarth compensated me handsomely for my long and unjust imprisonment. The next morning I packed my satchel and started for Frankfurt. I walked from Darmstadt to Frankfurt, and only remember that on my way I stopped at a farmhouse where, as I found no one about, I annexed a ham. Toward evening I reached the end of my journey and betook myself at once to a well-known 'inn father'—for so we called our landlords—in the Judengasse. It is needless to state that a real vagrant has a perfect knowledge of all the disreputable haunts and low public houses of the whole German Empire. Next day I went direct to Baron Rothschild's house, as he was the Bavarian consul, where I rang the bell, and, on being admitted to his presence, was told to produce my papers. I received two thalers and a free pass to the next place for which I said I was bound. This was all entered on my 'legitimation,' which was also impressed with an official seal, so that it became absolutely useless to me. As I now thoroughly understood the manufacture of these false documents, however, I made myself another one the same evening, entering myself as the sculptor Burkel from Messau and under this name and designation I spent ten months at Frankfurt without doing a stroke of work. I made out a plan of the town and pursued my trade of begging from wealthy families in the principal streets, with great success. It is true that I was arrested several times, and put under lock and key for a few days now and then. Though warned to leave the place or to find work, I did neither, but ran the chance of being caught and identified. . . .

"Soon after this I was arrested as a disorderly tramp and sentenced to a short imprisonment with an injunction to find work on pain of being expelled from the town. The yearly fair was being held at Frankfurt, and I obtained employment on my release with the proprietor of a menagerie. My business was to attract people to his show, but I soon left him, as the public refused to pay for the sight of the sorry and starved wild beasts he exhibited. Next I hired myself out to the manager of a puppet show where I developed a great aptitude in the art of manipulating the puppets. When the fair was over, I had got together quite a considerable sum of money and I resolved to leave Frankfurt and go on to Stuttgart.

"Stuttgart is a happy hunting ground for those of my sort. It contains many 'pietists,'—a sect made up of good and charitable souls who give freely. I remained there four weeks and did a wonderful business. I now figured in my papers as a compositor and on the strength of these documents even appeared before the Bavarian consul. I had collected a fine store of clothes and a lot of money when one day, toward the end of the fourth week of my stay, I was arrested in the Königstrasse by a man in civilian dress who told me to follow him. There was something in his looks which so impressed me that I dared not resist. I was condemned by the police actuary to fourteen days' imprisonment and then to be banished from the town. I was taken to the Stuttgart prison where the governor received me with harsh words; he was a Swabian and the Swabians are ruder than any other Germans; in other respects I had nothing to complain of.

"Several of my colleagues were sitting or lying about in a large room where we were detained, and at first they did not notice me. At last an old boy, who had evidently been through many vicissitudes, addressed me, and after some conversation, promised to wake me next morning to communicate something of importance. At three o'clock he poked me gently in the side and then led me to a corner of the room; there he told me that he was interested in me and wished to contribute to my success in the future, and that though he knew I was a member of the guilds, still I did not understand what most appealed to the public. At the present time, the war being just over, soldiers played first fiddle. He possessed an iron cross and a genuine 'legitimation' as the owner of it. This would suit me excellently, as it came from a Bavarian. He was old and had no more use for it and would sell it to me for three thalers. I was overjoyed at this offer which promised me large receipts, and I gladly paid the old man the three thalers.

"On my release I resolved to try my luck at Baden-Baden. I began by purchasing a newly published illustrated description of the French war, which I studied carefully, and tried to form an idea of those regions where I intended to lay the scene of my deeds of heroism. I bought a list of the visitors at this fashionable resort and selected my victims. I decided to present myself in person to German families of position, but to foreigners of distinction I would appeal in writing. At the end of two days I had purchased all the outfit I required from a dealer of old clothes, and on the third day I started out fully equipped. I had strapped my left arm to my naked body; the empty sleeve was pinned to my coat; on my breast I proudly wore the iron cross; in the pocket of my blouse I carried my 'legitimation,' and I had given my small moustache a martial twist. I began with a German baron, into whose presence I was admitted and who looked at me approvingly. 'Ah,' he exclaimed, when he had read my papers, 'one of our "Blue Devils"; you Bavarians must have given the French gentlemen a rare dressing.' 'We showed them,' I replied, 'that a Frenchman cannot wage war with Germans, Herr Baron.' I then told him, in answer to his further inquiries, what regiment I had served in, etc., and that I had lost my arm at the storming of the Fort Ivry. He said he would gladly assist a brave soldier who had bled for his country, and gave me two gold pieces. This gift filled me with joy and confidence.

"At a country house where the family of a Prussian count were spending the summer, I was likewise admitted. The ladies were drinking their coffee on the veranda. 'Look, mamma,' exclaimed the daughter, 'there comes a "knight of the iron cross," like Papa. And the poor man has suffered the loss of an arm in battle.' The young lady seemed to me rather over-enthusiastic, but that was all the better for my purpose, and I satisfied her curiosity with accounts of my prowess and deeds of daring and described how, when my heroism had resulted in my arm being shattered by a cannon ball during the storming of the village of Bazeilles, it had afterwards been sawed off in the hospital. I also told her in answer to her eager questions as to whether I was in want, that I had an aged mother to support and wished to buy a hand-organ. She gave me all the money in her cash box, and when I returned to my lodging I found a large parcel of clothes which she had directed a servant to leave for me. All my other visits were more or less profitable, and the foreign visitors whom I addressed by letter, two Russian princes, the Duchess of Hamilton and the Princess of Monaco, each sent me a handsome present in cash. Owing to the insufficiency of the police, I was able to carry on my frauds unmolested until I had almost exhausted the fashionable world at Baden-Baden. One morning whilst I was absent a police official called at my lodgings. Hearing of this on my return, I hastily packed my spoils and took train for Karlsruhe.

"The account of my criminal career would be incomplete without some mention of prisons. They play a larger part in the life of the budding convict than many people realise, and contribute materially to his development. While the state turns its chief attention to the larger gaols, the smaller prisons are often sadly neglected. If these were better administered, fewer large houses of correction would be required. Here the vagrants tarry, shaping their plans; here one thief learns from another various artifices and tricks; here young offenders are won over to the criminal life. The principal evils of these small prisons undoubtedly are the promiscuous congregating together of all offenders and the absence of occupation. It is not surprising, therefore, that the time is passed in idle talk, and that the man who can relate the largest number of rascally tricks he has played should be the hero of the company. Many an inexperienced lad listens to these anecdotes and acquires a taste for the life of a sharper. When to all this is added a brutal superintendent, open to bribery, then the prison becomes a real training school for criminals."

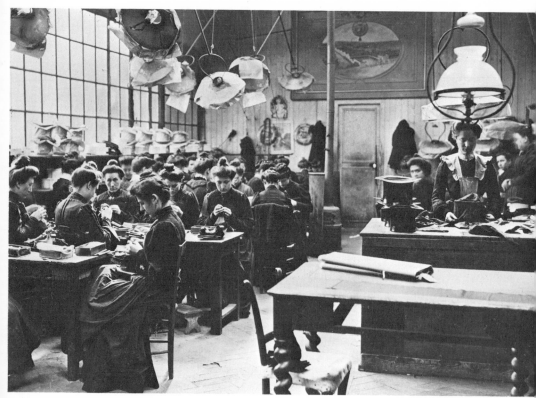

PART 3

Mature Industrial Society, 1850-1918

With industrialization well established in central and western Europe, some of the more dramatic social dislocations eased, if only because a smaller percentage of the population was moving from countryside to city —that is, from a traditional to a dynamic environment. Major problems of adaptation remained, however; the conversion of rural people to new values had just begun. Many workers were still new to the factory setting. Even some older workers, who had successfully preserved elements of a traditional approach to work during the early stages of industrialization, had major problems of adjustment as industrialization became more firmly entrenched.

And the nature of industrial society continued to change. For factory workers and artisans, the introduction of new techniques and the rise of big business organizations created obvious difficulties. Women in many social classes felt the impact of change more acutely in this period than ever before. In the early industrial revolution, middle-class women preserved many traditional goals: they worked closely with their husbands in business; they expected to have many children. Working-class women faced a less familiar situation, particularly when they worked outside the home, but again their outlook probably remained fairly traditional. They expected to marry, after which the vast majority would stop working outside the home, and service to their families would largely define their lives. In the later nineteenth century a declining birth rate gave women more free time, and rising levels of education produced new expectations. In some cases expectations outstripped opportunity, for the definition of a woman's "place" changed only slowly. In the middle class particularly, problems of adjustment became increasingly obvious. By the 1900s, one result, in many countries, was an intense feminist movement.

Many of the attitudes formed during this period of maturing industrialization proved quite durable. Although many workers were new to their situation and the nature of industrial life continued to change, a recognizable working-class culture began to emerge—one major outgrowth of the general modernization process that endures in most respects to the present day. Many of the new ambiguities in women's lives also persisted. At the same time, the broader popular culture was changing in directions that seem quite familiar to us today. It was in the later nineteenth century that a new interest in sports arose, soon to become a consuming passion for many people.

The outlines of modern society were becoming clearer. Most people in western Europe were now accustomed to change, so questions arising from the sheer confrontation between tradition and innovation now give way to more subtle issues. Was the new interest in sports, for example, an expression of modern man's alienation, his desire to escape monotonous labor and recover, if only vicariously, some of the aggression and passion of his primitive ancestors? Or was the rise of sports a more positive sign, an indication of growing affluence and leisure time and an expression of the desire to develop new fields of individual achievement? Similar questions apply to more familiar topics: Did the rise of socialism signify a growing belief in progress and an orderly political process on the part of working people, or the institutionalization of class warfare and periodic acts of violence? Was imperialism the product of a confident, dynamic society or of a society that translated its insecurity into aggression abroad? With change established as an inescapable part of modern life, the need to assess its meaning become paramount.

Bibliography

The history of women is beginning to receive considerable attention, but completed work remains scanty. J. A. Banks has written *Property and Parenthood: A Study of Family Planning Among the Victorian Middle Classes* (New York, 1954). A good general introduction to recent writing on the history of women is Martha Vicinus, ed., *Suffer and Be Still: Women in the Victorian Age* (Bloomington, Ind., 1972). Another recent study is Duncan Craw, *The Victorian Woman* (London, 1971). Older studies by C. Willett Cunnington remain valuable: *Feminine Attitudes in the Nineteenth Century* (London, 1936) and *The Perfect Lady* (London, 1948). Some key trends among working-class women are discussed in Margaret Hewitt, *Wives and Mothers in Victorian Industry* (New York, 1958). William L. O'Neill, *Woman Movement: Feminism in the United States and England* (Chicago, 1969), is a good brief survey of this important movement at the turn of the century.

Studies that deal with workers, as opposed to formal protest movements by labor, are not overabundant. For Britain, E. P. Thompson, *The Making of the English Working Class* (New York, 1964), and Eric J. Hobsbawm, *Labouring Men: Studies in the History of Labour* (New York, 1964), are works of major importance. On Germany, Guenther Roth, *Social Democrats in Imperial Germany: A Study in Working-Class Isolation and National Integration* (Totowa, N.J., 1963), relates the rise of socialism to the situation of the working classes. See also Harvey Mitchell and Peter N. Stearns, *Workers and Protest: The European Labor Movement, the Working-Classes,* and the Origins of Social Democracy, 1890–1914 (Itasca, Ill., 1971). To follow continuities in working-class culture into our own time, see John H. Goldthorpe et al., The Affluent Worker in the Class Structure (New York, 1969). See also Robert Blauner, Alienation and Freedom: The Factory Worker and His Industry (Chicago, 1964).

Carlo M. Cipolla, Literacy and Development in the West (Baltimore, 1969), and Geoffrey H. Bantock, Culture, Industrialization and Education (New York, 1968), provide a general background for the modern history of education. There are no overall surveys in English on the development of the French educational systems. Michalina Vaughan and Margaret S. Archer, Social Conflict and Educational Change in England and France, 1798–1848 (New York, 1971), is good on the early period. E. H. Reisner, Nationalism and Education since 1789 (New York, 1923), deals with another important theme, the inculcation of nationalist values through the schools. F. Ponteil, Histoire de l'enseignement en France (Paris, 1966), is a fine French survey. English education has been extensively studied: see B. Simon, Studies in the History of Education, 1780–1920 (London, 1960), and Howard C. Barnard, A Short History of English Education (New York, 1955). R. D. Altick, The English Common Reader: A Social History of the Mass Reading Public, 1800–1900 (Chicago, 1957), deals with the uses of growing literacy.

The history of sport is another of the important subjects that has not been given much attention by serious historians. Johan Huizinga, Homo Ludens: A Study of the Play Element in Culture (New York, 1970), provides an interesting general interpretation, stressing the decline of a real interest in play in modern society. Peter C. McIntosh, Sport in Society (New York, 1963), and Physical Education in England Since 1800 (London, 1969), are useful. Eugen Weber, "Gymnastics and Sports in Fin de Siecle France: Opium of the Classes?" (American Historical Review [1971], pp. 70–98), sees the rise of sports as an aid to political conservatism.

The Dilemma of Middle-Class Women

J. A. BANKS

The situation of women should have been improving in the later nineteenth century, at least outside the working classes. More wealth, more education, fewer children—all these were potentially liberating factors. Women's health undoubtedly improved, and they began to outlive men by a substantial margin. But the impact of a new material environment and new opportunities is hard to calculate. For people accustomed to traditional roles, change can come as a profound shock.

Furthermore, women were not free to adapt on their own. Their lives were still defined in great part by men, as tradition dictated, and middle-class men in the nineteenth century were bent on glorifying women in a peculiar fashion. Businessmen, fiercely competitive and devoted to making money, found it soothing to idealize their wives and daughters as guardians of beauty and moral purity. The pedestal image developed, and women were accordingly expected to be decorative, frail, and pure.

These trends were most pronounced in Victorian England. The following selection discusses the impact of changes in women's traditional functions against the distinctive background of the pedestal image.

There is much still to learn about the history of women. We do not, for example, know how far down in society the pedestal image really describes the lives of married women. It was widely known, but did it really apply to the ordinary middle-class woman struggling to manage a complex household with the help of at most one servant? The real middle-class woman undoubtedly knew that she was supposed to be gentle and respectable. Her education was consistent with this ideal, being largely decorative. But this left her all the more likely to be overwhelmed by growing responsibilities as rising wealth made the maintenance of a household an increasingly elaborate job. At the same time, many middle-class women were undoubtedly confused by the declining birth rate and other challenges to traditional functions. Thus, instead of living the narrow and rarefied lives suggested by proponents of the pedestal image, many women had to deal with a bewildering variety of problems. But many probably had enjoyments that the pedestal image does not convey: for example, while the pedestal notion dictated that women be passive and reluctant sexual partners, the women's literature read, and surely often approved, by the middle classes urged an active sexual role. It seems clear that the impact of modernization on women must be considered in its own right, for the process may have developed in somewhat different stages and caused different stresses from those that affected men.

In the 1830's and 1840's . . . a host of books [appeared], produced by both male and female writers, who professed to establish the precise place of women in society and who sought to set out in very vigorous terms the duties of the wife and mother of a family. "The sphere of Domestic Life is the sphere in which female excellence is best displayed," was the general line taken by this school of thought; in the home a woman was certain of being useful; domestic comfort was "the greatest benefit she confers upon society." In attempting to assess the changes which occurred in the position of the middle-class married woman during the second half of the nineteenth century, we cannot do better than to begin with an appreciation of her role in the family as it was seen by such writers; for they most clearly reflect what members of their class believed she ought to do and be, even if individual middle-class women did not always match precept with practice.

According to this school of thought it was fundamentally the woman's task to create a home—and such a home that would provide an environment of emotional stability for her husband and children.

> Not only must the house be neat and clean, but it must be so ordered as to suit the tastes of all, as far as may be, without annoyance or offence to any. Not only must a constant system of activity be established, but peace must be preserved, or happiness will be destroyed. Not only must elegance be called in, to adorn and beautify the whole, but strict integrity must be maintained by the minutest calculation as to lawful means, and self, and self-gratification, must be made the yielding point in every disputed case. Not only must an appearance of outward order and comfort be kept up, but around every domestic scene there must be a strong wall of confidence, which no internal suspicion can undermine, no external enemy break through.

This passage provides us with the key to understand why so much emphasis was laid on the sanctity of family and home. It was a place of refuge from "those eager pecuniary speculations" and "that fierce conflict of worldly interests, by which men are so deeply occupied as to be in a manner compelled to stifle their best feelings." It was a sanctuary in which the husband could recover from the trials of his business life and over which his wife reigned as guardian angel. Alternatively, it could be thought of as "a walled garden" with her as its queen. As Ruskin put it:

> the man . . . must encounter all peril and trial; to him, therefore, must be the failure, the offence, the inevitable error; often he must be wounded, or subdued; often misled, and *always* hardened. But he guards the woman from all this; within his house, as ruled by her, unless she herself

From J. A. Banks, *Feminism and Family Planning in Victorian England* (Liverpool: Liverpool University Press, 1964), pp. 58–70. Reprinted by permission of Liverpool University Press.

has sougth it, need enter no danger, no temptation, no cause of error or offence. This is the true nature of home—it is the place of Peace; the shelter, not only from all injury, but from all terror, doubt, and division.

It is this contrast between the harsh competitiveness of the outside world of industry and commerce, and the seclusion of the home which most appealed to the Victorians, and explains their emphasis on the feminine virtues of gentleness and sympathy. Women might fall short in their practice of these graces but the ideal was always kept before them in the form of a home that would be "a bright, serene, restful, joyful nook of heaven in an unheavenly world."

The contemporary theory of woman's biological nature, combined with traditional religious teaching, reinforced this concept of the wife's essentially domestic role. Her position, as the "helpmeet" of man, was inevitably a subordinate one, and it was her task, above all, to please her husband.

> With grace to bear even warmth and peevishness, she must learn and adopt his tastes, study his disposition, and submit, in short, to all his desires with that graceful compliance, which in a wife is the surest sign of a sound understanding.

In the same year as Mills' *Subjection of Women* Mrs. Sewell could still argue, in a book dedicated to her husband, that:

> it is a man's place to rule, and a woman's to yield. He must be held up as the head of the house, and it is her duty to bend so unmurmuringly to his wishes, that the rest of the household will follow her example, and treat him with the due respect his sex demands.

Yet this did not mean that the husband for his part was freed from all obligation. He was exhorted, for example, to pass over his wife's errors with indulgence, attributing "her follies to her weakness, her imprudence to her inadvertency." All his care and industry should be "employed for her welfare; all his strength and power . . . exerted for her support and protection." It was his duty to provide a comfortable maintenance for her while he lived and to take steps to ensure that she was safeguarded after his death in case he should die first. There was thus a clearly defined division of labour, "the prudent management" of the wife being as necessary as the honest toil of the husband; and while he was away from home she was exhorted to "think on him for one moment labouring with busy hand, with anxious eye and thoughtful brow, for your support and comfort, and say, 'Does he not deserve a happy home?' "

The duties of the perfect wife, moreover, were not confined to her obligations to her husband. Inevitably they were widened to include her duties as a mother since this was regarded as "the consummation of the world's joy to a true woman. She has gone through the last ordeal that is required to place her in that responsible position of life which nature demands all women should attain . . ." In this position she was expected to fulfill special obligations to her children. "No one can understand so well the wants of a child as a mother—no one is so ready to meet these wants as she; and, therefore, to none but a mother, under ordinary circumstances, should the entire charge of a child be committed." Indeed, in the eyes of many, the noblest aim of her existence was "to generate beings who, as women, may tread the footsteps of their mothers, or, as men may excel in the higher virtues which these, to them softer and sweeter occupations, render it impossible that they themselves should attain." In infancy, it was argued, the mother was the best nurse, in childhood the best guardian and instructress.

It was for this reason that "a woman when she becomes a mother should withdraw herself from the world, and devote herself to her child." An anonymous writer in 1835 pointed out the "impropriety" of women, when they are mothers, "aiming at mere wordly pleasures and distinction." Instead, "the highest honour of a virtuous woman consists in a rational seclusion." When we find the doctrines that a woman's place was in the home pressed to so literal a conclusion it is no wonder that the claims of such early feminists as Harriet and John Stuart Mill were received with consternation and alarm. . . .

It must not be supposed, however, that the wife and mother was, in consequence of these doctrines, expected to be simply a household drudge. Increasingly throughout the nineteenth century manual labour in the middle-class home became the province of domestic servants recruited from the working-classes, and by the 1850's and 1860's their mistress had become "for ever elevated above the still-room and the kitchen." Indeed, the middle-class mother was expressly enjoined to avoid all routine domestic chores in order to devote herself to the moral development of her family.

> But how can she be adequate to this if the whole attention to the personal comfort of several young children devolves upon her? If she is to make and mend their articles of dress, bear them in her arms during their period of helplessness, and exhaust herself by toils throughout the day and watchings by night, how can she have leisure to study their various shades of disposition, and adapt to each the fitting mode of discipline, as the skilful gardener suits the seed to the soil? . . . The remedy is for the mother to provide herself with competent assistance in the spheres of manual labour, that she may be enabled to become the constant directress of her children, and have leisure to be happy in their companionship. This would seem to be a rational economy.

The amount of actual domestic labour which, it was believed a woman ought to perform with her own hands, was dependent upon her position in society, and, as a necessary corollary, on the number of servants she kept. While a wife should not presume to live above her rank, neither should she forget, in the words of Mrs. Ellis, "the loss of character and influence occasioned by living below our station." While she should always be ready and able to lend assistance herself on "extraordinary occasions" it was necessary, in general, to observe the correct mean between "doing too much, and too little, in domestic affairs. . . . It can never be said that the atmosphere of the kitchen is an element in which a refined and intellectual woman ought to live; though the department itself is one which no sensible woman would think it a degradation to overlook." Her true position was that of "administratrix, mainspring, guiding star of the home."

What this implied in practice is more difficult to discover but fortunately Mrs. Beeton has provided us with a detailed description of "how to manage house, servants, and children." Her account of the housewife's day is concerned mostly with how to pay calls, to receive visitors, and to entertain generally, but it includes certain duties of a more purely domestic character. Before breakfast she must see that the chlidren "have received their proper ablutions." Her next task, after breakfast, is to make the "round of the kitchen and other offices, to see that all are in order, and that the morning's work has been properly performed by the various domestics. The orders for the day should then be given; and any questions which the domestics desire to ask, respecting their several departments, should be answered, and any special articles they may require handed to them from the store-closet." While this ends her own purely domestic administration, even these tasks were not required by the wealthier housewife for Mrs. Beeton adds that "in those establishments where there is a housekeeper, it will not be necessary for the mistress, personally, to perform the above-named duties."

In the ordinary middle-class household there would, however, be no housekeeper and "after this general superintendence of her servants, the mistress, or the mother of a young family may devote herself to the instruction of some of its younger members, or to the examination of the state of their wardrobe, leaving the latter portion of the morning for reading, or for some amusing recreation." Only where the means of the mistress "be very circumscribed" will she be "obliged to devote a great deal of her time to the making of her children's clothes." Luncheon was normally taken by the family at the same time and from the same joint, but not necessarily together.

> The usual plan is for the lady of the house to have the joint brought to her table, and afterwards carried to the nursery. But, if circumstances are not strongly against the arrangement, the children of the house may take their dinner with the mistress. It is highly conducive to the good behaviour of children to have their principal meal in the company of their mother and other members of the family, as soon as they are able to feed themselves. Many little vulgar habits and faults of speech and manner are avoided by this companionship . . . The nurse, likewise, by this plan is released, for a

short period, from the care of her little charges, and, while she enjoys her dinner with her fellow-servants, the "waiting on nurse," a great obligation with many housemaids, is avoided.

While the time taken to perform these duties would clearly vary with the efficiency of the mistress and the number of her servants it is clear that for all whose means were not, as Mrs. Beeton suggests, "very circumscribed," it would not take up a woman's whole day, or even, in many cases, a whole morning. Indeed the following semi-humorous account of what *Punch* calls the mother's Saturday review, seems hardly more onerous, in spite of its author's attempt to make it sound so:

> To examine the linen when it comes home from the wash and take care that the same is properly aired and mended before distributed to its respective owners; to take the circuit of the tradesmen, and pay all the weekly bills; to take stock of the larder, and see what is wanted in the house for the ensuing week; to make a rigorous journey of inspection round the kitchen, and examine whether the cook keeps her pots and pans in a proper state of cleanliness, and if the copper kettle is as bright as it can be made; to look into the scullery and satisfy oneself that no undue quantity of rubbish is allowed to accumulate in the sink or elsewhere; to give out clean towels and sheets and table-cloths and dusters to housemaids and servants; to count over the plate with the footman . . . ; to have the parlour thoroughly cleaned, and the mahogany table properly oiled and rubbed in anticipation of the morrow's dinner; to make liberal preparation for the same . . . ; to get out best bonnet for church the following day; to collect all accounts and make up house-keeping book before submitting it, properly vouched and balanced, to one's lord and master; to go into the nursery after dinner, and observe with one's own maternal eyes that the young olive-branches in the tub have their usual scrubbing and small tooth-combing once every seven days; to drill the younger children in their catechism before kissing them, and tucking them up in bed; to see that the house is closed, and everyone between the sheets, before twelve o'clock; and to do all this in the gentlest, kindliest, most methodical, and yet dignified and matronly manner, exacting obedience, and yet winning respect from all.

Indeed the modern housewife contemplating her own daily tasks, might well agree with the feminists and their sympathizers who argued that there were

> few things more simple than the management of an English household . . . of the daily supervision and management required, giving orders, controlling servants, etc., an hour or two in the morning is, perhaps, the utmost that anyone can spend in such business.

Yet the emancipation of the English housewife of the middle and upper classes from actual domestic labour was only possible because of a cheap and plentiful supply of servants, and it is no coincidence that this pattern of living which prohibited the mistress of a family from interfering in the "minutia of household occupation" was developed and extended at a time when servants were rapidly increasing in numbers.

No middle-class household was complete in all its functions at this time unless it employed the basic minimum of three domestics, cook, parlourmaid and housemaid, or cook, parlourmaid and nursemaid. Members of the lower middle classes, of course, could not normally afford so many, and frequently were obliged to make do with a general servant or maid-of-all-work, assisted occasionally by a young girl; but as they rose up the income scale they added first a housemaid or, if there were children, a nursemaid, then a cook. Beyond this point extensions were merely variations on the basic theme. The cook was provided with a kitchen maid, and later a scullery maid. Housemaids were increased in number and the whole body of servants put in charge of a housekeeper. It is not surprising, therefore, to find during this period of middle-class expansion, that whereas the number of general servants increased no faster than that of house-occupiers, the number of cooks, housemaids and nursemaids grew more than three times as fast and housekeepers nearly six times. The greatest growth, that is to say, took place amongst the more specialized classes of domestic labour; and the middle-class housewife who aspired to a household of "gentility" was accordingly relieved of routine work herself. In consequence, she was able to give "that necessary touch to personal toilet and to the lay-out of the meal table." However necessary it might be for the spinster and the widow to find employment, the middle-class married woman was rapidly becoming a lady of leisure.

The consequence of this development was that increasingly the women of the middle as well as the upper classes devoted little of their time to the organization of their household and spent most of the day in "visiting, dressing, light reading," and other activities of conspicuous leisure. The non-productiveness which had for long been the hall-mark of the lady was spreading down into all but the lowest ranks of the middle class. The *Saturday Review* commented acidly in 1868:

> It is strange to see into what unreasonable disrepute active housekeeping —woman's first natural duty—has fallen in England. Take a family with four or five hundred a year—and we know how small that is for "genteel humanity" in these days—the wife who will be an active housekeeper, even with such an income will be an exception to the rule . . . the snobbish half of the middle classes holds housewifely work degrading save in the trumpery pretentiousness of "giving orders." Novel-reading, fancy work, visiting, letter writing, sum up her ordinary occupations and she considers them more to the point than practical housekeeping. In fact it becomes a serious question what women think themselves sent into the world for. . . .

It was indeed on this point that the feminists were most in agreement with their opponents. They, too, were critical of the frivolity of girls and young women and their ignorance of domestic affairs, and they looked to a change in the quality of education to provide a solution to this problem. For many of them an improvement in this respect would not only provide middle-class girls with better jobs if they remained single; it might also make them better wives and mothers if they married.

> Whilst marriage is held to be the only credible destiny for women above the poorest class, the general opinion and custom of society prevent their receiving any such training, as might fit them to form and manage healthy, moral, and happy homes; and places before them instead a life of frivolity, vulgar display, and helplessness, as what they ought to aim at.

It would seem, therefore, that by the 1870's the daily round of the middle-class wife involved many activities far removed from household tasks as such. Although she remained "administratrix, mainspring, guiding star of the home" she performed very few of the actual labours necessary for its maintenance. Nor was she withdrawn from the world into a purely domestic seclusion. It is true that her outside activities, in the great majority of cases, brought her no pecuniary reward or political notoriety, yet her morning calls, her tea and whist parties, her balls and receptions often took her out of her home. In so far as this gave woman more freedom of movement it is sometimes regarded as a phase in their emancipation but there is no evidence that their position had become any less subordinate. The man was still the head of the family whose decisions had legal as well as moral authority over all its members and whose word had the ultimate sanction of physical force. Indeed, it might even be argued that as middle-class women became less productive, as they spent their time increasingly in conspicuous leisure, they became more dependent on their husbands, whose labour in business or profession made their genteel idleness a possibility.

There remains to consider how far this new pattern of behaviour, because it marked a change in the outlook of the middle classes, and irrespective of whether it may legitimately be regarded as emancipation or not, was a causal factor in the decline of family size. Certainly, the new interests and new pleasures of the middle-class wife made demands upon her which were incompatible with her personally fulfilling the duties of the nursery, but for a long time there is evidence that those mothers who could afford it had handed over the care of their small children to nursemaids. Mrs. Ellis, in 1843, had criticized those women who found time for morning calls, when they had none for the nursery or the schoolroom. By the 1870's the number of such women had increased. The "richly appointed nursery" with its staff of nursemaids had become the *sine qua non* of any fashionable household and a woman was considered to have done her duty by her children if she saw that they were fed, clothed and well-supplied with toys while she followed her own enjoyment elsewhere. So far, indeed, did women carry their desire for freedom from the constraints of the nursery that they resorted increasingly to the wet-nurse. Some of them were genuinely unable to suckle their own infants, but there is no doubt that others, often with the approval of their doctors, acted for reasons of convenience rather than necessity.

This raises the question of why family planning amongst the Victorian middle classes should not have been the next step in a simple logical sequence from the employment of nursemaid and wet-nurse. Undoubtedly there had always been women who, like Queen Victoria in 1841, wished they could be relieved from what she referred to as "the hardship and inconvenience" of child-birth, especially if it occurred too frequently. Now that a growing number of married women had become emancipated from the traditional duties of child-rearing—why should they not go on to claim emancipation from their traditional duty of childbearing, or at least from some part of it? Of course, we cannot tell whether in the period 1850–70 there might not have been a growing desire on their part to shake off a little of this burden. There is some evidence that abortions among middle-class married women became more common, but on the whole such a desire could not have resulted in family planning as this was a later development. All that we can say is that the transition from the perfect wife to the perfect lady in these years predisposed middle-class wives to the acceptance of birth-control once it was acceptable *on other grounds*. It remains, therefore, to consider what these other grounds might be.

It is easy to see that if the circumstances of the perfect lady were to change in such a way as to threaten the new pattern of life to which she was now accustomed, she might be induced to adopt family planning as a defensive measure. A decline in the supply of domestic servants, for example, might have presented her with the choice between having fewer children or returning to the nursery or kitchen herself. In point of fact, however, she was never faced with such a choice during this period. There was no slackening off in the employment of servants generally, or of nursemaids in particular, until well after birth-control was firmly established. So far as we can tell, there were no changes in the circumstances of the middle classes in the 1870's and after which did not affect husband and wife equally. There were no special problems facing wives as such.

We may put this differently by asserting that there is no evidence to support the view that emancipation from the traditional pattern of domesticity for middle-class women was carried through in the teeth of opposition from their husbands. On the contrary, all the evidence we have suggests that in the transition to the perfect lady they were assisted and, if anything, encouraged by the men. This indicates that the same may well have been true of the decision to practise some form of family planning, which, far from being a revolt of wives, could have been a joint decision on the part of the married couple acting together. Indeed, in the absence of any evidence that women were successful *at this time* in achieving a greater independence in decision making and in the light of their financial dependence on their husbands, it might well have been the case that the resolve to adopt birth-control was determined by the man alone, and that in this, as in other matters, his wife merely acquiesced. A more plausible approach to the problem, therefore, would seem to be to consider an alternative explanation for the flight from parenthood which might also be regarded as responsible for the changes in the concept of the perfect wife. We can hardly do better at this point than reintroduce the issue of the relationship between the middle-class standard of living and family size, which has been dealt with in detail elsewhere, and which must now be reconsidered in terms of its bearing on the position of women.

The Adaptation of Workers

PETER N. STEARNS

This essay examines various forms of adaptation or alienation found among German workers in the late nineteenth century. Despite the fact that industrialization had begun many decades before, many German workers were still in an early stage of adjustment. A significant minority maintained traditionalist views. Another group had picked up almost middle-class values with regard to individualism and mobility aspirations. A large middle group stood in between. These workers found traditional goals inappropriate and were groping toward new values, but they found the transition exceedingly painful.

In broad outline, the values that developed among German workers prevailed among workers elsewhere, and they have shown great durability. Workers in Britain in the 1960s, although far more affluent and less often fervently socialistic, maintained a similar culture. They too expressed expectations for themselves and for their children that they could not really follow up; they too found factory work distasteful; they too had difficulty planning rationally for the future. They had, of course, made a more complete transition to a consumer ethic, so that they were willing to endure boring labor for the rising wages that resulted; this trade-off was only beginning to develop among German workers around 1900. And there have been changes in family structure and residence patterns that reflect new trends in adaptation to modern life. But many elements of the culture workers developed in response to industrialization have persisted, and they continue to set workers off from other social groups in modern society.

. . . Social history seems to me dreadfully badly developed for Germany at least for the century and a half since industrialization began. In labor history the preoccupation with socialism has left even trade unions inadequately studied, not to mention actual workers. My purpose in this essay is somewhat broader than gap-filling, however. German industrialization was about fifty years old in 1900. The modern working class was still quite new. Thanks to the sociologists and the socialists we have qualitative information about the workers that does not exist for, say, English workers at a comparable stage.

From Peter N. Stearns, "Adaptation to Industrialization: German Workers as a Test Case," reprinted, with permission, from *Central European History*, III, No. 4 (December 1970), pp. 303–31.

We can answer some questions about adaptation to industry using the German materials, or at least phrase the questions far more precisely.

I am not, then, interested in what is distinctively German about the German working class between 1890 and 1914. I recognize of course that points about Germany cannot automatically be transferred to other countries in comparable stages of industrialization. German socialism was certainly an unusual phenomenon compared to patterns either to the west or to the east; it influenced workers' adaptation, though not too greatly. German industry was more advanced in organization and mechanization than industry had been in Britain at an otherwise comparable stage; this would tend, I think, to make adaptation more difficult. German peasants were traditionally far poorer, German artisans far more guild-oriented than their western counterparts as they came into the factories. This too would leave a distinctive mark on adaptation. Admitting all this, I nevertheless believe that information about German workers at least suggests lines of inquiry that can be applied to other instances of industrialization.

The issue that has dominated historical consideration of working classes —material conditions and their trend—need not delay the student of German workers too long. Real wages rose fairly steadily for factory workers from the beginning of industrialization. They certainly were rising between 1890 and 1914, despite rapid inflation, though the rate of their increase diminished. Conditions were still bad, far worse than in France or Britain. Housing was cramped, diet still rather meager. Yet there was improvement in most consumption items. This being reasonably well established for the 1890–1914 period, we can more readily turn to questions of adaptation to industrial life which many historians, in their preoccupation with material conditions, have only touched in passing. We must in fact broaden the scope of "material conditions" to include pace of work or transportation time from home to job. For material conditions were obviously part and parcel of adaptation. German workers' adaptation may have been facilitated, vis-à-vis Britain at least, by the improvement in living standards over accustomed levels; but we must be sure that the quality of material life did in fact improve, that modest gains in consumption do in fact allow us to judge this quality.

Many aspects of Greman manufacturing suggest the transitional character of the labor force even after 1900. Of course, given the constant change which industrialization imposes, a social group is always in transition. And a comparative framework for the German economy needs to be more carefully worked out than has been done heretofore. Nevertheless, it can be suggested that from the standpoint of the working class the German economy was not so uniformly advanced as national production figures imply and that some categories of workers were touched by traditions that had long been forgotten not only in Britain but also in France. . . .

The majority of factory workers were first- or second-generation even in 1914. Census figures reveal this clearly. Between 1895 and 1907 the mining labor force almost doubled, as did that in metallurgy. Textiles grew more slowly and chemicals advanced only 60 per cent, but the machine-building industry almost tripled its employment. More specific studies confirm this pattern. In the wool hat industry in Luckewalde, where the industry began in the 1870's and grew only modestly, only 30 per cent of the workers had had fathers in the textile industry and only 24 per cent had had grandfathers who were factory workers of any sort. Of the fathers 23 per cent had been artisans, 9 per cent peasants, 11 per cent members of the higher professions; of the grandfathers 38 per cent had been peasants. In the Ruhr mines in the mid-nineties only 37 per cent of the workers were children of miners, and a few years later only 40 per cent of the miners' children of working age were in the the mines—and this in an industry where stability was usually high aside from outright increments to the labor force. In one Mönchen-Gladbach textile firm only 14 per cent of the workers had peasant fathers, though in the city as a whole large numbers of the new semiskilled workers came directly from the countryside. In clearer contrast, a Berlin machine-building giant had only a small core of workers whose fathers had been in the industry; a large number of the new workers were from East Prussia while many of the unskilled had previously been handworkers in textile or shoe manufacturing, many of the skilled former smiths. Everywhere machine building, including automobile production, drew in massive numbers of locksmiths from the villages and small towns.

Despite Germany's ranking as an industrial power, industrialization in the literal sense was new to most of its workers around the turn of the century. It was drawing in peasants. It attracted servant girls, following a common pattern in relatively early industrialization in which servant status constituted a transition from rural life to factory life. It attracted many small-town artisans, even though none of the large artisanal groupings was declining in size. This, too, reminds us of an important aspect of early industrialization which had largely ceased in Britain.

We can, then, learn something about the nature of adaptation to new artisanal forms and to factory industry by studying German workers. Adaptation to new residence and to new work is a massive subject, and I cannot pretend that what follows is an exhaustive treatment. The role of religion, for example, is not directly examined. Some questions that are germane to earlier industrial situations cannot be followed up for Germany at this point. There was little overt resistance to machines. When a Bremen shipbuilding company introduced riveting machines, manned by semiskilled labor, older workers angrily curtailed their production, but in general the reaction to machines was subtle. Obviously machines were too well entrenched for Luddism to be conceivable, nor was this the truly brand-new industrial labor force from which Luddism stems.

The most basic subject to raise is whether the work itself was found pleasant or unpleasant. A study of the modern British working class bases its claim that a distinctive class exists primarily on workers' distaste for their jobs. Can this be applied to an earlier industrial situation? Immediately after this we must ask what the wage meant and the extent to which consumption was viewed as a compensation for unpleasant work. The big question here is the extent to which a traditional view of both work and the wage gave way to a market or progressive view that related production to wage incentives and insisted on steady improvements in living standards off the job. Changes in family structure were naturally forced by industrialization; what did they mean to workers? What was the workers' general outlook? Insofar as adaptation involved stress, what remedies did they seek? Finally, in all these questions, to what extent were workers united in their reaction? Were they developing, as E. P. Thompson suggests for British workers as early as 1832, not only common institutions but a common structure of feeling and a collective culture?

Unskilled workers who came into the factories from the countryside worked hard without complaint. There is overwhelming evidence on this point. Silesian miners who came to the Ruhr thought it was evil to miss a shift. Amazed at the laxness of the Ruhr miners, they thought, "We Silesians are better than this crummy crew." In metallurgical factories in Hanover Poles and Germans of rural origin were noted as zealous workers. In a Mönchen-Gladbach textile plant workers from small towns and the countryside earned up to 12 per cent above the company's average because of their high production. Key groups of workers were loath to strike for a reduction of hours. Dockers did not mount the pressure for a limitation of their long workday that their counterparts in French ports began in the 1890's. Many were proud of their ability to work around the clock periodically, if only because their extra earnings contributed to their family's well-being. German miners rarely raised questions of hours of work in their strikes, though their working day was two hours longer than that in France and Britain. Their docility in this matter was due to the fact that over half of them were freshly in from the countryside.

There were several reasons for the new arrivals' zeal for work. They were grateful for regular employment. German unemployment rates were quite low for unskilled workers according to official figures, but there was substantial seasonal unemployment, at the least, in the countryside and the small towns. Satisfaction with what seemed to them high pay was another obvious factor. Miners from eastern Germany thought that pay in the Ruhr was splendid. They delighted in daily meat and butter and were happy to be allowed to work hard, accepting overtime on top of their long shifts. Accustomed to hard work anyway, many of them found nonmaterial satisfactions in working with machines. Some were entranced by the sheer power of machines. Others were lured by the prestige of a big company; a worker took pride when it could be said of him. "He is with Daimler." Perhaps most important, they found factory work exciting or at least not boring. Women were particularly pleased with the bustle and camaraderie of factory work, when contrasted to their rural traditions or their work as servants.

How much did the ardor for work mean beyond the willingness to put in long hours? In the one study of the Mönchen-Gladbach textile factory, the above average production of workers from the countryside contrasted with the up to 30 per cent below average production of city-bred workers. Rural masons and bricklayers also seem to have outproduced their urban counterparts. But in general it seems likely that the rural workers accepted long hours in part because their pace was rather leisurely. They were not usually highly skilled and therefore were not subjected to the most intense pressure to produce at maximum. Comparative studies revealed that German workers despite their longer hours were less productive than British; textile workers, for example, handled only a half to two-thirds the machinery per worker that their British counterparts managed. There is some indication that German workers took more breaks during the day than workers in France and Britain. The unusually high ratio of foremen to workers in Germany reflects the leisurely pace that many workers sought to adopt. Production fluctuated more during the week in Germany than was common elsewhere, with productivity on Mondays particularly low. And workers, including some of rural origin, had habits of job-changing that reduced both their productivity and the work they actually put in during a given year. Much of this evidence admittedly is hard to apply to the newly arrived workers specifically. But it does suggest that the zeal for work had yet to be harnessed to an industrial pace, that it consisted mainly of plodding through a long day.

German workers generally had a different view. Some of the contrast has already been suggested. Big-city workers and miners established in the Ruhr did not seem to work as hard as the new arrivals. Skilled workers found the *Arbeitsfreude* of the unskilled proof of their unintelligence. Adolf Levenstein's survey gives us a statistical picture of sorts. In textiles, 75 per cent of the workers found no joy in their work; 60 per cent of the miners agreed, while 15 per cent enjoyed the work if the pay was good, and 18 per cent professed indifference. Of the metal workers surveyed, 57 per cent found no pleasure in their work. Levenstein probably had a biased sample, for he elicited responses from an unusual number of convinced socialists. A survey of workers in Mönchen-Gladbach textile plants, while not focusing on attitudes toward work specifically, revealed that 44 to 50 per cent of the workers were "satisfied" with their position, though only 29 per cent said that they really wanted to be textile workers.

There were workers, then, who enjoyed their work. A weaver wrote that he could get through the day quite pleasantly thinking about other things, particularly astronomy. A miner said, "There is no work so interesting as that of the miner." Many skilled workers remained proud of their work, even when new machines were introduced. Printers who switched to the new composing machines resisted any return to manual labor, partly because this involved longer hours but partly because, though the skill required on the machines was reduced, they were able to read more manuscripts. Still other workers took pleasure in working for a piece rate, because it increased their freedom and made the job more interesting. This was particularly true of the highly skilled, including some who had been artisanally trained in small towns.

But majority sentiment was against these positions, even if some groups of workers, in metals particularly, had to surrender their opposition to piece work. Textile workers complained of exhaustion: "My eyes burn so—if I could only sleep." Metal workers worried more explicitly about their health. Both complained of noise and boredom, one noting that his work was so dull that "wild longings" tormented him. A miner in the Ruhr, Max Lotz, wrote an impassioned lament about the dangers and hardships of his work, which he found beneath human dignity. Even in the mines he found that "The work is becoming increasingly mechanical. No more incentive, no more haste, we muddle along wearily, we are worn out and mindless."

The outlook of the majority of German workers, particularly among the skilled, was revealed in strikes and in the trends of per capita productivity. Construction workers cut their production dramatically as more and more construction shifted to the big cities, perhaps by as much as 50 per cent. In 1913 Berlin masons set 300 stones a day, compared to 600 in Göttingen. Their production had begun to drop in the 1890's and by 1912 had reached British levels—suggesting that urban construction workers could catch up to the patterns of advanced industrial countries rather quickly, a point to which we shall return. In mining, productivity which had more than doubled in the second half of the nineteenth century fell slightly between 1900 and 1913; in one Silesian company it dropped from 368 tons per worker in the 1890's to 340 tons between 1901 and 1910. Technical factors undoubtedly contributed to these developments, particularly in mining as shafts deepened, but there is evidence here of genuine worker reaction. Both mining and construction were of course loosely supervised industries in which workers could indulge their resistance to hard work with some freedom.

Thirty-two per cent of all German strikes between 1899 and 1914 raised demands concerning hours of work. This contrasts vividly with the situation in France, where only 15 per cent of the strikes involved hours of work. To this should be added many of the 21 per cent of German strikes directed against foremen or other workers, though this rate was not so unusual. Many German strikes that seemed to stem from other issues actually concerned the intensity of work. Miners in Barsinghausen, for example, struck for a raise because this seemed a safe demand, but the real cause of their strike was a new foreman who was driving them to work harder. Construction workers and metal workers pushed hard for an eight-hour day—far harder than their counterparts in France or even in Britain. And the strikes for hours reduction were justified in different ways in Germany. In France, workers who struck for shorter hours generally talked of the desirability of cutting unemployment; some also wanted to seize the opportunity for more overtime pay. These factors were present in Germany. Unemployment rates among skilled workers ranged around 5 per cent in normal years—much higher than the rates among urban unskilled, ironically—and this undoubtedly encouraged strikes for shorter hours. But workers also talked directly about the need to curtail their fatigue and the dangers to their health. The key grievance in the great Crimmitschau strike was chronic fatigue. Shoemakers in Pirmasens struck for nine hours because new machines had made the work more intensive. Doubtless socialist influence helped workers articulate their resistance to intense work, but labor movements in France and Britain tried the same arguments with far less success among their constituents. Finally, skilled workers in Germany began to seek annual vacations. Far more strikes—though still only a handful—involved this issue than was true in other countries, and far more workers won the point. In 1908, 75,591 metal workers (particularly in machine building) had gained regular vacations; in 1912 the figure had risen to 233,029.

The German strike movement was not, as a whole, nearly as sophisticated as that in France or Britain. Strikes were smaller, longer, and for the most part raised less advanced demands. So the attention to relieving the intensity of work stands out strongly.

The reaction to factory work was unquestionably intensified by the speed-up devices manufacturers everywhere were introducing around 1900— such as the *Kalkulationsbüros* which appraised piece rates—and by the relatively advanced technology. Even so, the German workers' reaction may tell us something of the difficulties new workers experienced in comparable stages of industrialization elsewhere. We can speculate about English workers' first exposure to the din and pace of factory labor, but we know that many German workers were appalled. It took a generation for unskilled workers to shake off their rural-bred resignation, but the workers born in the cities and the large contingent of artisans entering factories or larger craft units for the first time had real problems of adjustment. Their vigorous resistance may have alleviated the problems, of course, as hours of work declined and in some cases as productivity itself leveled off. At the same time it can be suggested that this stage in the adjustment to industrialization was just that, that contentment with work might grow as experience increased and job conditions improved. A survey of German workers in the 1920's revealed that 67 per cent of the skilled workers and 44 per cent of the unskilled felt more pleasure than distaste for work.

Even before 1914 the labor force was deeply divided in its reactions to work. Probably very few felt as strongly as Max Lotz. How many, at the other extreme, agreed with the miner who thought his work the most interesting in the world? We cannot know precisely, but the existence of strong minority enthusiasm for work and the piece rate is undeniable. Differences in personality and health from one worker to the next make any generalization suspect. One can discern certain industrial patterns. Variations in discontent with work among textiles, mining, and metals were considerable even in Levenstein's poll. Textile workers, at least males, were least happy with their work because they were physically weak—their rate of military rejections was extremely high—and because their pay was low. Metal workers worried about the intensity of their labor but they found some interest in it. And they were better-fed and healthier to begin with. Metallurgical workers were more satisfied still, despite the fact they worked twelve-hour shifts. Their piece rates were rarely altered, partly because labor costs were a low percentage of the total, and so they could earn more as they worked harder or more skillfully. In machine building piece rates fluctuated, if only because the nature of the work changed so often; this created a tension in which the worker could easily feel unfairly paid and therefore overworked.

Variations of this sort could be endlessly refined. I think that, for general purposes, three sets of reactions to industrial labor can be marked off. The first is of course the traditionalist approach brought in by the unskilled, to work long hours but not usually very intensely; traditionalism was sometimes abetted, particularly among women, by a sense that the factory was a diverting place. The second reaction was one of shock and resistance, as with male textile workers. The third embraced workers who found some genuine interest in their job, or whose resistance paid off sufficiently, in shorter hours for example, to remove any fundamental grievance, or who learned to compensate for unpleasant work by other enjoyments. The second group set much of the tone for the period, as was reflected in the polls that were taken. But we cannot determine the importance of each group by reaction to work alone. The outlook toward wages varied widely also, exacerbating the despair of some of those who detested their work—like Max Lotz, who could scarcely imagine being paid enough to compensate for his arduous labor—but aiding the adjustment of others to new methods and a new pace.

The outlook of the new, unskilled workers toward the wage has already been suggested. They seemed content, even delighted with the pay and living standards they won in the factories. As a skilled worker noted scornfully, they were "satisfied when they are able to buy cigarettes." They concentrated particularly on improving their diets, recalling a rural childhood of potatoes and milk. Silesian workers in the Ruhr, particularly the women, adopted local styles, but in most factories a hierarchy of dress persisted in that the unskilled wore simple garb. In Stuttgart factories the unskilled wore no overcoats and professed to find this appropriate. Perhaps the key was the attitude of the women, who were used to plain clothes and did much of the family sewing. Housing—which was quite exiguous in the cities—seemed satisfactory. The unskilled complained of rents but not of housing directly. Here, obviously, the bad quality of rural housing set low expectations. The unskilled were generally satisfied with two rooms. They were not the ones who pressed out to surrounding villages to seek their housing; what they found in the cities sufficed. There was little interest in other items of expense. Medical care was feared. As one East Prussian woman said, "God is the best doctor. If he wishes, I'm healthy; otherwise not . . . I would rather die than let them cut." It is, I admit, always presumptuous to talk of satisfaction among poor people, but this seems to be accurate here. Traditionally low standards which factory work exceeded in terms both of pay and of regularity of work, plus the hope of some that factory life was only temporary, a basis for a return to the countryside with enough money to buy land, make this outlook understandable.

The traditionalists were a large group, but probably not a majority of the labor force. What of the rest: the textile workers and others who hated their work, the skilled workers in factories and shops who faced changing conditions on the job?

To what extent were German workers eager to improve their wages? As the outlook of the traditionalists indicates, such eagerness cannot automatically be assumed. The question can be further refined. To what extent did workers become aware of the wage as a market item, as an incentive which should be increased when production increased? Did they transfer some of their dissatisfaction with their work to the wage? Or did they view the wage more as consumers, in which case the question is less involved in the work situation, more in the degree to which improvements in the standard of living were sought? Both of these approaches are useful, but I find the latter more applicable to the situation of most German workers in this period.

Again, even aside from the traditionalists, German workers were divided in wage matters, but let us begin with some general points. Compared to workers in older industrial countries, German workers were not avid for wage gains. It is true that their real wages continued to increase, though slowly, in contrast to trends in Britain and France after 1900. It is also true that one must not exaggerate French and British eagerness for material progress. But there is a difference, clearly related to the stage of industrialization.

If German workers were able to transfer their grievances about changing work conditions to wage demands, one would expect a massive wave of strikes in this period. Such was not the case. Despite Germany's much larger labor force, fewer German than French workers went on strike between 1899 and 1914—25 per cent fewer in absolute terms, over 100 per cent fewer per capita of the manufacturing labor force. Relatedly, the average strike—with 119 workers—was unusually small. Wage strikes were still smaller than this average, the reverse of the pattern in more advanced industrial countries. Few German workers could be roused over this issue, and often those who were found themselves a minority among their immediate colleagues. Hence a French manufacturing worker was almost two and a half times more likely to strike over wage issues than his German counterpart.

It is true that 71 per cent of all German strikes did raise pay demands, a percentage higher than that in France (where the figure was under 65 per cent) and much higher than that in Britain. Without doubt, a minority of workers were capable of seeking wage gains. But a surprising number of major wage strikes were actually defensive, against a reduction of pay. Unfortunately it is difficult to be very precise in comparisons. Between 1899 and 1914, 8 per cent of all German wage strikes were listed as defensive—about the same figure as in France. Even here, it is noteworthy that the French defensive strikes were much smaller than average and that they were bunched around the 1901–1902 slump, declining sharply thereafter. In contrast German defensive strikes were of about average size and their rate increased. Furthermore, the official figures underrepresented defensive wage strikes. Metal workers had to strike repeatedly against piece-rate reductions that cut their take-home pay. So did shoe workers and textile workers—like the Cunewalde weavers who struck against an 18 per cent cut in 1901. Again, essentially defensive strikes were far more important in other countries than official figures convey, but they were less common than in Germany and usually less direct reactions to a pay cut. In many of their wage strikes, German workers argued simply in terms of poverty. Masons in Gelsenkirchen asked for a raise so that they could earn enough "that we can regularly feed our families." Arguments of this sort almost never appeared among workers in older industrial countries. They suggest that many German wage strikes and the high rate of wage strikes overall reflected no new attitude toward the wage but rather the marginal conditions in which many German workers lived.

Miners in France and Britain were in the forefront in the development of progressive material expectations. There were hints of a similar evolution in Germany, as in the Barsinghausen strike where miners asked for a raise to compensate for the rising pace of work. But the great Mansfeld strike stemmed simply from misery. Miners in the Ruhr in 1905 ultimately asked for a raise, but the strike initially broke out in pits where pay had been falling, and miners in the whole basin had for two years been subjected to periodic losses of earnings—and great physical discomfort—during hospitalizations for the worm disease. The strike actually illustrates the amazingly elaborate set of causes necessary to rouse large numbers of German miners and to produce even limited wage demands.

Working-class budgets confirm the judgment that German workers found it difficult to envisage major improvements in their living standards. Overall, German workers spent a low percentage of their income on rents and recreation—the two items most revealing of rapidly rising material expectations. This, of course, is partly a statement of their relative poverty. More important for our purposes is the fact that when incomes went up, workers did not alter their budget allocations greatly. Metal workers earning under 1200 marks a year spent 56 per cent of their budget on food and drink; those with incomes of 1200 to 1600 marks dropped this only to 55 per cent; those with incomes of 1600 to 2000 marks dropped it yet another two percentage points; those with incomes of 2000 to 2500 marks dropped it to 52 per cent. Conversely the percentage spent on rent rose from 12 to 14 to 15 per cent in both the higher income groups. All this suggests a desire to use higher earnings mainly to improve existing levels slightly, with particular stress on a better diet including more meat; yet metal workers had more advanced expectations than most German workers. Textile workers actually increased their percentage expenditure on food with higher earnings, while cutting the rent percentage. Recreation and health expenditures were very low generally.

Only in clothing were there signs of hopes for rather rapid improvement, as Ruhr miners and others awakened to possibilities of new fashions. Correspondingly this was the only nonfood budget category where German workers led those of the older industrial countries. The interest in clothing is characteristic of workers in many early industrial situations. Possession of respectable clothing for walking about the city on Sundays was extremely important. Along with some improvements in diet it seems to be the first new consumption interest to emerge. Why? Obviously clothes are cheap; perhaps an interest in them is naturally human, an extension of the skin as Marshall McLuhan would have it. But students of consumption habits can beware of calling anything "natural." Only by indirection were many workers led to want better housing; as we shall see, changes in family life rather than a virgin birth of the modern economic man were often involved. The early interest in clothing was a reaction to change, a desire to prove one's place in fairly well known terms, for even in the countryside differences in dress were known marks of status. For some of the small-town artisans and others who had status anxieties as well as a general sense of uneasiness in the factories stylish clothes may have been particularly important. By the same token the interest in clothes was not immediately part of a desire for more material goods generally. Workers could be satisfied with better dress. And clothing was cheap enough that it did not prompt elaborate wage demands.

Three factors add to this impression of limited expectations; at least two of them, like the limited expectations themselves, flowed naturally from the early industrial setting. German workers were filled with a longing for the countryside. "I believe that every city resident, as soon as time permits, should go to the countryside, go to nature, and fill his lungs with pure, unspoiled air." Workers acted on this sentiment. An overwhelming majority listed walks in the country and gardening as their favorite recreations; pastimes that cost more money and might have induced higher expectations—including books and education—could not compete. Miners and then textile workers particularly relied on nature and gardening, but the interest was general. Longing for nature reflected the rural origins of many workers and the grievances about work that many felt. One may speculate that the walks and gardening not only inhibited material expectations but also, for the millions of workers who still could enjoy them, provided some genuine satisfaction.

Drink was another carry-over from tradition that was also fed by discontent with work while inhibiting higher expectations. Many German workers were frequently drunk. They spent 6 to 11 per cent of their budget on alcohol—an allocation that was not matched by higher segments of German society until the level of university professors. Articulate miners deplored their fellows' penchant for drink, which retarded their education and limited their goals. When polled, a fifth of the miners admitted their dependence on drink. Less than a tenth of textile and metal workers made a similar admission, but their budgets too revealed high rates of spending on alcohol which tended to rise as incomes went up.

Skilled German workers showed a marked interest in cleanliness. (The unskilled did not, so I think we can dismiss sheer Germanness as a cause of the characteristic.) They carefully washed and changed clothes before leaving the worksite and they often struck for improved wash facilities. Their concern stands out among workers of other industrial countries. It suggests some of the tension and status anxieties of workers from small-town and craft environments. It is related, obviously, to the interest in clothing. It may also have distracted workers from more elaborate consumption expectations because so many German companies provided excellent wash facilities and because agitation for further improvements took up eneriges that might otherwise have been used for wage gains. As one group of Ruhr workers noted when they won new rules on bathroom conditions in their factory, "These rules are worth much more to us than a pay raise."

In contrast to the general hesitancy about advancing wages, a minority of workers were committed to expanding prosperity. Some were in factories, like the metallurgical workers who shunned company housing and moved into towns distant from concentrations of lower-paid workers. Far more were still in the crafts. At an extreme, artisans like printers adopted an essentially bourgeois consumption pattern, even though their wages might be in the middling range. They cut the percentage they devoted to food—down to 39 per cent in one case. They drank little and sometimes had their wives make their clothes. But they valued housing, spending up to 28 per cent on rent, and they saved for the education of their children. Still more workers kept a rather proletarian expenditure pattern but strove for steadily advancing wages. Skilled construction workers led the way. Their wage strikes resembled those in France and Britain in frequency and in the arguments used, which means they sharply departed from the norm in Germany. They conducted 32 per cent of all strikes between 1899 and 1914, though they numbered only 18 per cent of the manufacturing labor force, and their offensive wage strikes were almost 30 per cent more frequent among all their strikes than the rate for strikes in general with construction strikes excepted. They led the way also in wage movements that did not result in strikes; in 1905, for example, masons conducted 507 such movements affecting 106,761 workers. These workers, along with printers, brewers, and others, had a "modern" idea of the wage and of advancing living standards. They were not for the most part new to their trade. Though many of them faced radical changes in business organization and substantial changes in working methods in this period, they could adjust through the wage. And, minority though they were, their numbers were not small.

Examination of adjustment to work and the wage yields three groups of workers—an assortment that is not surprising but one that is decidedly hard to unify. At one end were the traditionalists in work habits and consumption expectations. At the other end craftsmen and metallurgical workers either found enjoyment in their work—remember the printers on the composing machines—or compensated by seeking higher wages, or, most commonly, both. This leaves the group in the middle, the reasonably skilled factory workers, many from small-town craft backgrounds. Most of them had not made a full transition to a progressive view of the wage and consumption. Some of them were content with their work—the middle group of the work-aggrieved was smaller than the middle group of consumption-conservatives. But there was a mass of workers, in textiles, mining, machine building, and shoe manufacture, who disliked their work without finding full compensation in a new view of the wage. These workers were not yet capable of making the basic bargain that industrialization required, to admit new work methods, sometimes unpleasant ones, in return for advancing earnings.

Were these workers bereft of hope? Did they find other compensations? Some undoubtedly were extremely unhappy. Some of the most convinced socialists whose voices have reached us, apart from formal socialist leaders, fit this category. Hear Max Lotz: "What is my meaning in this great world plan where brutal physical and psychological forces feast themselves in orgies? Nothing! . . . Only Social Democratic activities could give me goals and offer me economic security too, so that I may attempt my plans. I therefore adhere to socialism with every fiber of courage and idealism." Moritz Bromme was perhaps even more typical of the ardent socialist. Self-taught like Lotz, he desperately wanted to be an artisan but was blocked by his lack of money for apprenticeship. His life became increasingly hard, if only because his lack of knowledge of birth control methods burdened himself with too many children and an increasingly shrewish wife. Socialism may have had its deepest meaning for men like this who were still close to traditional ways of doing things but with frustrated hopes for a better lot. There is evidence for this on a broader scale. Levenstein's polls showed that textile workers—those archetypically discontented workers in this transitional period—rated socialism as a goal over earning more money. For metal workers the situation was reversed. Eighteen per cent of textile workers thought about politics and union matters while at work, like the man who said, "I build a new world while I work."

Here, I think, is the key to the special hold socialism had in Germany at this point. It fit exactly the mood of those workers who hated their work but could not easily find personal compensations. These workers were in a minority except among male textile workers. Most socialist workers took their doctrines less seriously—as witness the fact that over 80 per cent of the books taken out of party libraries had nothing to do with social issues. A socialist machine builder stated the more normal qualified position:

> You know, I never read a Social Democratic book and rarely a newspaper. I used not to occupy myself with politics at all. But since I got married and have five eaters at home I have to do it. But I think my own thoughts. I do not go in for red ties, big round hats, and other similar things. All that does not amount to much. We really do not want to become like the rich and refined people. There will always have to be rich and poor. We would not think of altering that. But we want better and more organization at the factory and in the state. I openly express what I think about that, even though it might not be pleasant. But I do nothing illegal.

Still, there was a large enough minority of desperate workers to give German socialism an unusual role. Did socialism in the long run help allay the desperation of these workers or did it perpetuate their alienation? Did it tend to delay their conversion to new personal expectations?

W̱ell-organized socialism had not been present in a comparable stage of workers' developments in France or Britain, of course. A second aspect of the German workers' survival effort, oddly but closely related to socialism, has more general applicability. The workers formed elaborate expectations for themselves and, to a degree, for their children. Some, the unskilled particularly, could not answer questions about what they would most like to be; their goal was simply to get through life. The wool hat makers in Luckewalde, of heavily peasant origin, could not articulate goals. Most simply said they wanted a happy old age, though the young males talked of hopes for their own business or land. In general textile workers had more trouble forming a personal dream world than metal workers, partly because such hopes were far less realistic. But in a Mönchen-Gladbach textile factory, where only 29 per cent of the workers said they wanted to be in textiles, 27 per cent wanted to be artisans and 22 per cent yearned for the higher professions. Skilled automobile workers in Stuttgart—many trained in small-town crafts—talked of wanting to be artisan masters or, with almost equal frequency, state officials. In a Berlin precision-tool factory, the order of popularity of major goals was as follows: 1. a secure old age; 2. one's own business; 3. foreman; 4. freedom from capitalism; 5. possession of savings; 6. obtaining postal or railroad work. Here, I think is a common mixture: some sheer traditionalism (secure old age), a bit of socialism, and a good bit of longing for independent business or the dignity and security of state employment.

Obviously these latter goals were realistic for some workers. We must again refer to a minority, particularly in the crafts, who were decidedly upwardly mobile. Some skilled metal workers or their children did get their own bicycle repair shops. Many metallurgical workers advanced steadily from unskilled to skilled in a generational process; this was the clear pattern at Krupp, where even the unskilled planned their families with care to assure future advance. Printers were generally upwardly mobile. In one large survey only 7 per cent of all printers were children of printers, while 40 per cent came from the ranks of journeymen and the unskilled; in contrast 30 per cent of their children of job age were printers while 35 per cent were teachers, booksellers, technicians, bureaucrats, or professional people. This mobility is exceptionally important, but it does not describe the majority of workers who harbored hopes for their future. The workers themselves sensed that their goals were hopeless. They talked almost in the same breath of God's will determining what would happen or of ending "where the wind blows me." Did such goals nonetheless offer occasional comfort, as pleasant dreams, or was their hopelessness a nightmare that exacerbated despair? There is evidence that the trait continues among workers, who talk of bright futures for their children while doing little to further them.

Workers were able to make some adjustments to their lot, apart from their dreams and apart from work and the wage. They altered their family relationships. Again, we cannot talk of workers as a whole. The unskilled from the countryside tried to preserve the traditional family pattern. Many of them delayed the marriage age until twenty-eight or so. Many got their wives pregnant before marriage, peasant fashion, to be sure they were not "buying a pig in the poke." They let their wives work only if severely pressed; in Berlin they brought their wives back home as soon as their income reached 1200 marks a year. Many of them had large families and were ignorant of contraceptive devices. Bromme describes how experienced factory workers increasingly talked of contraception, many claiming that *coitus interruptus* was best, others swearing by "Parisian articles" (condoms); but it took time to get new arrivals in the plant to adopt any "artificial" method. At the other extreme craftsmen, who also had traditions of late marriage age, maintained essentially middle-class family size, a key element in their generational mobility. They, too, were loath to have their wives work, though the wives often took care of boarders (which could add 300 marks a year to the family income).

But what of the workers in between? They were limiting their birth rates rapidly, particularly in the textile cities (compared to mining and metallurgy) where incomes were low. The birth rate among these groups of workers dropped 25 per cent between 1900 and 1913. Relatedly, their wives were working in increasing numbers. Again, textiles led the way, but metal workers and others followed close behind. In Berlin 17 per cent of the skilled factory workers' wives were employed, compared to 23 per cent of the much poorer unskilled workers; the cutoff income for the skilled was about 1500 marks a year. What does this mean? Obviously, a taste for a higher living standard. Perhaps the desire to raise the living standard by these means preceded (in part by necessity) a coherent effort to improve the wage by collective action.

Obviously also, since the women's work (aside from some of it in textiles) was not a strict economic necessity, it meant a recognition of greater independence for the woman. Women often wanted to work. Furthermore, the reason behind the hope for higher income is intriguing, at least in the case of the Berlin machine builders: they wanted a two-bedroom apartment so that their children would sleep apart from them.

Add all this up: reduced birth rate by "artificial" means, new attitude toward wives, separate bedroom for the children. There is suggested here a new sentiment within the family, the possibility of greater affection for the children, who were not underfoot all the time, and greater sensuality and equality in the relationship between man and wife. All this, I admit, is tentative. It certainly reflects the absence, in Germany, of some of the worst pressures on the family that prevailed in early English industrialization. It suggests the beginnings of working-class family relationships that have been examined by contemporary sociologists. I think these relationships may have begun to develop rather early in industrialization, even before decisively new attitudes to the wage can be found. They were at once the product of earnings above the subsistence level and the need for an emotional balm for increasing tension at work. They may have been an important solace indeed.

I can be far more definite about the last reaction to industrialization, though here too it is not easy to interpret the role it played for workers. Workers changed jobs with incredible frequency. Not all workers. The unskilled tended to be much more stable, in their gratitude for regular employment. Many firms, particularly the big ones, had a nucleus of old-time skilled workers who did not quit; a few paternalistic firms, like Krupp, managed to stablize most of their workers. But this was not the norm. In Upper Silesia 76 per cent of the workers left the company in the first year, though those who did not quit the first two years were unlikely to and so 40 per cent of workers in the average firm had been there over five years. Many Ruhr miners shunned company housing so that they could switch jobs easily, and their shifts were frequent. In one company for each one hundred workers 63 were in, 51 out in 1899; by 1907 these rates were up to 63 and 58; by 1911 to 69 and 61. This was the common pattern. In textiles the rate was lower, but still up to a third of the workers changed companies each year. Many changed professions as well; several studies revealed that over half the male textile workers had had two to four different professions. Metallurgical workers stayed in their profession, but they changed jobs more frequently even than miners; in 1906 163 per cent of Düsseldorf blast-furnace workers changed jobs—that is, a large number changed jobs more than once.

What does this extraordinary fluctuation mean, aside from a reduction of worker efficiency? We have one precise poll, of skilled precision mechanics in Berlin who had changed jobs. Twenty-five per cent of them did so to better themselves; an almost equal number did so because of lack of work;

18 per cent left because of a pay cut; 15 per cent because of a clash with the foreman; 8 per cent because of a speedup of work; 6 per cent because of wanderlust; the remainder for more scattered reasons. Motivations varied with the industry. Metallurgical workers changed jobs above all to seek higher pay. Machine-shop workers changed jobs much less often than foundry workers, because the latter were subjected to a much more rigorous pace of work. We obviously have to see job-changing as a direct reaction to discontent with the work—it must often have given workers a needed brief vacation. There is a correlation also between job-changing and workers' vague dreams for a better lot. Male spinners had much higher personal goals than weavers; they could not realize these goals but they could change jobs, which they did far more frequently than weavers did. Workers from the small-town craft background were particularly prone to job-changing in all industries. How many felt like the turner who said, "I didn't feel really at home in the big hall," or like the slightly more industrialized type who changed jobs until he felt able to "feel with the machine"?

Massive job-changing was common in the early stages of other industrializations, as in France. It reflected motives that were more common still. There was a stable group in the factories, composed partly of the traditionalist-unskilled but partly also of those skilled workers who found their work pleasant. The two groups together were near a majority, as in Silesian mining. In the unstable group was an important minority of upwardly mobile workers or workers who sought steadily advancing pay—this was actually a majority in metallurgy. These workers had made a full adjustment to industrialization. Another minority changed jobs because of lack of work or out of the traditional reaction to a cut in pay. This leaves the largest group, who changed jobs to seek relief from work or work situations they did not like, and to prove their independence, and to make some vague gesture at fulfilling their thwarted aspirations. The question remains: how much did job-changing provide at least temporary solace and make factory life endurable? My guess is, quite a bit. I think it did give workers a sense of freedom, a chance to thumb their noses at their supervisors. Certainly it inhibited collective protest. But possibly it too proved just a delusion, particularly as workers grew older and could not afford to indulge in it so frequently.

Workers did have some sense of choosing their occupation, even if they did not like it. This was possibly the most concrete result of job-changing. Even in textiles only 40 per cent of the workers polled said they did not know why they were textile workers or that they had simply obeyed their parents' wishes. Again, we cannot say whether the sense of making a decision was of much comfort. But it does demonstrate how far these workers had moved from peasant traditionalism, in their ability to think of themselves as individual agents in the economy.

I need not belabor the point, in conclusion, that I find no unified working class in this mixture of traditionalists (really peasants at heart), artisans, skilled factory workers who could adjust to a new work and wage, and skilled factory workers who could not. All, it might be added, except the traditionalists, could be loyal socialists. For if we find the greatest fervor among the maladjusted factory workers, we find large numbers of socialist voters among all the nontraditionalists.

Nor do I need more than mention the implications of this study for the history of protest. Artisans aside, workers in this stage of their development were not likely sources of massive direct-action protest unless material conditions were deteriorating or the rural milieu from which many came was already troubled. Neither of these factors applied to German workers at this point. German workers were also spared major disruption of their family life by outside forces, which further differentiates them from British workers earlier in the nineteenth century. The grievances workers felt most keenly were hard to articulate. Even the high rate of strikes for reduction of hours of work only palely reflects the anxiety that the pace and strain of factory labor produced. The traditions of lower-class protest—in Germany as elsewhere—directed attention to problems faced as consumers, to the prices of goods. They were of little help in expressing problems in the work situation itself. Well after 1914, and not only in Germany, workers had trouble translating work grievances into protest. Before 1914 in Germany, as in western Europe earlier, too few workers had been converted to new material expectations to produce massive protest on this basis. Some of their efforts at adjustment actively inhibited collective protest; individualistic job-changing was a more important inhibition than that familiar villain, drink.

For what must be stressed above all in this stage of industrialization is the extent to which workers other than traditionalists had been won to individualism (which is not meant to be incompatible with being a convinced socialist). We know that much loneliness was forced upon early industrial workers, as they encountered strangers and impersonality—like the German workers' wives who endlessly wrangled in their crowded tenements or the metallurgical workers who, conscious of others' opinions and the complex hierarchy in their own ranks, carefully ate lunch in separate corners so that no one would see what they ate. Much violent protest was individual as well. Many workers in Germany fought among themselves, particularly when foreign workers were present, and general crime rates in the industrial areas rose rapidly. More important was the adjustment which even most discontented workers made to their situation. They formed dreams of individual advancement. They changed jobs according to their individual needs, more often psychic than material. A majority had some sense of consciously choosing their occupation even if it fell short of their hopes. They developed new ties—more individualistic but probably more intense as well—with their immediate families. This was the first step in the modernization of their outlook. It was in part forced upon them. It was often small comfort for the hardships industrial work imposed. But it did reflect a positive adjustment by people who were not simply cogs in an industrial machine. It suggests that —not surprisingly—immense changes in popular outlook accompanied the first generations of industrialization. Some of the changes have been overlooked in the historian's search for protest movements and some of them have proved much more durable.

Popular Education

ROGER THABAULT

The following sketch of the development of formal education, in a French village near Angers, covers three periods: the formation of the school and the resistance and apathy it encountered; the awakening of new interest by the 1860s; and the development of a strong, secular school tradition after 1880.

Not surprisingly, peasants adapted to modern values and institutions more slowly than any other social group, and French peasants may have been unusually resistant. Peasants maintained contact with many traditions, including religion. Their adaptability was further limited by the exodus of many younger, enterprising peasants to the cities.

Yet peasants were pressed to change their outlook and way of life, and the national education systems that developed in the later nineteenth century played a major role in this change. Many peasants who long refused to send their children to school finally did yield. Their understanding of the possible value of education reflected their changing circumstances. Small-town artisans quickly seized on education as a means of social mobility, often seeking new skills to compensate for the diminishing utility of traditional craft training. Peasants, however, had to undergo a more fundamental shift in values to make a similar transition. The intense economic problems in agriculture from the 1870s onward helped expedite this shift.

As education was accepted, further changes were inevitable. Everywhere the state and the upper classes sought to use education to shape the lower classes into obedient and productive citizens. They preached national loyalty. But they also emphasized the value of science and technology, and in France after the 1870s they actively attacked religion. Most teachers eagerly supported these positions, for their own prestige was enhanced by associating themselves with progressive forces such as science and by attacking traditionalism. So peasants were exposed to many new ideas. In a real sense education brought them, at least in France, into contact with the ideas of the Enlightenment. Although they did not necessarily accept all they learned, they could hardly avoid considerable questioning of traditional ideas, and for some, education did prove to be a truly radical force.

The following account is less a formal history than a memoir by a man who went through the village school and studied its past with care and affection; hence the author's many references to his own research and experiences.

Under the Empire . . . there were very few schools. Most probably there were no more during the reigns of Louis XVIII and Charles X. Nevertheless, when a public school was about to be opened in Mazières a certain number of the people did know how to sign their names.

In 1835, the very year the school opened, among 119 people, ranging from 25 to 78 years of age, who were summoned to witness the registration of births, deaths and marriages, 22 could write their names.

The general custom at that time was to teach reading before giving the least instruction in writing. It may be assumed that people could read more or less fluently and it is reasonably certain that they could count as well. In my childhood I knew many completely illiterate old men who were perfectly able to count.

Doubtless many of the signatures were extremely crude, which shows that their authors were little used to writing. Probably, too, the witnesses were deliberately chosen from among those who knew how to write. Be this as it may, in 1835, before any school had been opened, nearly 18 per cent of the male population was not completely illiterate.

It would be surprising if the more wealthy landowners of the commune whose names appear in the registers had received no schooling at all. At Parthenay and Niort there were public secondary schools and at Niort a private boarding school.

It is not surprising, either, that the village constable and the sacristan could sign their names: they had probably been appointed for that very reason.

But how and where had the peasants, the weaver, the flour-merchant, the artisan whose signatures appear on the registers, acquired the rudiments of education that they possessed?

One can only guess at the answer. . . .

The results must have been quite unsatisfactory since the urgency of having a public school had been recognized and that, to obtain it, the commune agreed to extra public expense in the same resolution.

The Influence of Guizot

The resolution was passed at an extraordinary meeting called to consider a circular from the Prefect, dated 17 May 1832.

The Prefect had issued the circular only in obedience to orders from Guizot who was preparing his famous Law, promulgated in 1833, for the organization of primary education in France.

It is very doubtful that the Municipal Council would have taken the initiative of asking for a public teacher and of paying for him. The sum offered of 60 francs was minimal in the light of the normal salary of 200 francs. And Mazières' commune was the only one of the whole canton which "warmly welcomed the school." Three others were "agreeable"; five were "indifferent"; one "disagreed." Another asked that its pupils should join those of a neighbouring commune. Verruyes commune, indeed, offered to repair the priest's woodshed to act as school room, once the priest had agreed to give it up temporarily.

The few notabilities of Mazières who signed the resolution of 10 June 1832 and who, in the Mayor's absence, were administering the commune, were thus the exception.

It is unlikely that their views were, in general, very different from those of the councillors of other communes. Their eagerness to start a school—while keeping its cost to themselves to the minimum—can only be explained by special motives. Perhaps M. de la Laurencie, or one or two important people, were interested in the mental development of the peasants; perhaps the priest at Mazières saw in the opening of a public school—which would naturally be under his control—another means of spreading the faith and also a means of recruiting a most useful helper who would bring children to the church to sing at services. Perhaps, again, the Council thought it would be useful to have men who could read and write.

Lastly, perhaps a few leaders of this poor little township, which chance had made the chief place of the canton, had children of their own of school age. In any case, as will shortly be seen, the Council speedily lost all interest in the school once it had been established.

The reasons which led Guizot to take the initiative in organizing public primary education throughout France are better known. His memoirs are explicit in the matter.

The 1832 Ministry of which he was a member had limited itself to completing plans of which the outline had been drawn by all previous governments. "It cannot be said," he wrote, "that from 1814 to 1830 primary education was free from political influence but it did not perish from this dangerous contact; either from a sense of equity or from prudence, the very powers who worried over its claims thought it best to treat it with kindness and support its development." The government of Louis Philippe was forced politically to organize a system of popular education.

Guizot saw clearly, moreover, that the evolution of ideas rendered such an organization necessary:

> Family feeling and duty is of great influence today: the political and legal bonds of the family have weakened; the natural and moral bonds have strengthened . . . a new idea has joined forces with these sentiments and given them greater effect—the idea that personal merit is today the greatest force and prime condition for success in life and that without it nothing

can be done. It is to this feeling of ambitious foresight in families that the Ministry of Education owes its popularity. Now a matter of great public interest has taken its place beside this powerful domestic interest. Necessary as it is for the family, the Ministry of Education, it is no less necessary for the State . . . The great problem of modern society is the government of men's minds.

Guizot counted on the development of reason as a means of controlling minds. His letter of 16 July 1833 accompanying the text of the Law of 1833 announced to all teachers:

> Make no mistake, even if a primary school teacher's career lacks glamour, even if the daily round of duty is performed within the bounds of a commune, his work is of moment to the whole of society and his profession shares in the importance of public affairs. It is not for the commune alone nor for the purely local interest that the law desires that all Frenchmen should acquire, if it is at all possible, that knowledge which is indispensable for social life and without which intelligence languishes and may decay; it is also on behalf of the State and public interest, it is because liberty becomes firmly established only among a people sufficiently enlightened to hear the voice of reason. Universal primary education from henceforth will be a guarantee of order and stability in society. Since everything, in the principles of our government, is true and rational, to develop intelligence and to propagate enlightenment will be to ensure the continued reign of constitutional monarchy.

Thus it was above all to buttress a stable social order that Guizot developed primary education, because it seemed impossible to him that a man could be intelligent and educated and not share his views, and not recognize that the principles of constitutional monarchy were completely true and rational.

In 1860 in his memoirs he declared that "the Church formerly was the sole governor of minds" and he added: "This is no longer so; intelligence and knowledge have become secularized and in so doing have claimed more freedom for themselves. But precisely because they are now more secular, more powerful and more free than before, intelligence and knowledge cannot remain out of the hands of the government of the society."

But he insisted on the absolute necessity of associating Church and State in all that pertained to primary education. Only higher education could be permitted to enjoy a degree of freedom: the primary school must be profoundly religious:

> While the co-operation of State and Church is essential for the wide establishment of popular education on a solid basis, it is also necessary if that education is to have true social value that it should be deeply religious. By that I do not mean only that religious instruction should have its place

and religious customs observed in school. A people is not brought up in religion by such petty and mechanical means. Popular education must be given and received in the midst of a truly religious atmosphere permeated from all sides by religious attitudes and habits. Religion is not a study or exercise to which one can assign its time and place; it is a faith and a law which must make itself constantly felt everywhere: only in this way can it exert all its beneficent influence on the soul and life itself.

This means that the religious influence must always be present in the primary school. If the priest mistrusts or shuns the teacher; if the teacher looks on himself as the independent rival and not the trusty aid of the priest, then the moral value of the school is lost and it is near to becoming a danger. . . .

. . . How were the central government's intentions interpreted in Mazières? What opportunities for education did they offer to the people we know so much about? What kind of welcome did they receive?

The school was opened in a building rented by the commune which was considered satisfactory by the primary schools inspector for the department of Deux-Sèvres. The statistical table "The State of the Communes concerning School Buildings" compiled on 15 August 1836 by this official shows, indeed, these premises as "sufficiently large" and suitable accommodation for fifty boys and twenty girls. A certain amount of repairs were, however, needed and 2,400 francs would be required for purchase and repairs. The supply of school furniture was sufficient but it did not belong to the commune. The only things lacking were a crucifix and a bust of the king. The municipal council was well disposed and would do its best to find the necessary funds.

The teacher was M. Michel. From school returns for the year 1835–6 we learn that he enrolled fifty boys and ten girls during the winter. In the summer only twenty boys were left. The textbooks used were *Simon de Nantua*, Fénelon's *Télémaque* and the Catechism. School fees brought in 400 francs and so he had a total of 600 francs a year to live on. His character, ability, enthusiasm and his standing in the community all appeared to be good. Nevertheless, by 1838, M. Michel was no longer teaching at the commune school. He conducted a private school in Mazières with a roll of sixteen pupils in summer and eight in winter. The inspector reported on him: "This teacher was formerly the commune teacher: he has lost the confidence of the people."

This severe judgment must have been correct, since the District Committee at its meeting on 2 May 1840 recommended that he be charged in court with misconduct and immorality and he be subject, if found guilty, to the sanctions of Article 7 of the Primary Education Act of 28 June 1833.

By that date the commune teacher was a certain Thébeau, who was a property owner in the village of La Touche near Mazières as well as being a teacher. He held the elementary Diploma, but it is clear from the documents published by M. Dauthuile, Academy Inspector, in his work on primary education in Deux-Sèvres district from its origin to the present day, that the elementary Diploma was the equivalent, in academic standard, only of our elementary Certificate.

M. Jacques Texier, who was a teacher at an independent school at Teillé until 1875, tells how he passed his Brevet examination at Niort in 1850: "The tests," he says, "were limited to a short dictation, two simple problems, a grammatical analysis of no difficulty, a few questions on grammar, religious history and arithmetic." This is what we should require, except for religious history, for our elementary Certificate today.

M. Dauthuile adds: "A study that we undertook of the reports of the examining boards of Niort and Parthenay revealed no marks nor any question papers but merely vague notes on the capability and moral character of the candidates."

Teacher Thébeau appears to have used teaching methods which would be strange to us today. According to an old man whose father attended the school for two years without learning to read, the teacher did not make use of the spelling book. He would read out a sentence from the reading book and have the children repeat it. This method, however, does not make him a precursor of the Sentence Method in honour today: it is the same procedure as that used by the *Fquih* in the Koranic schools. The children were not required to make any effort to understand the words or to attempt to associate the shapes with sounds and meaning. They merely repeated what had been said to them and gradually discovered, thanks to those clever on-the-spot "tricks of the trade" known to all teachers who care for their pupils, by the place on the page or the approximate shape of what they were given to read, the sounds they were required to emit to avoid being beaten.

The few children who did learn to read would read religious books or various school readers. Old men whom I knew as a child remember particularly vividly *Simon de Nantua* and the *Story of the Four Sons of Aymon*.

The teaching of arithmetic, an easier and more immediately useful skill, bore more fruit. Many illiterate old men could count perfectly well.

Furthermore, the teacher was required to teach reading before writing, as he himself had learnt, instead of teaching both together as is done nowadays.

M. Thébeau was a teacher of adequate competence who came to neglect his pupils. . . .

M. Thébeau must have been very like the people of the commune in his habits and his way of thought and action. He was to end his days as a farmer at La Touche.

There is every reason to believe that he followed closely the recommendations of the Mayor and the priest and that—as was required by the school regulation of the Parthenay district, dated 1835—every lesson opened and closed with prayer. He certainly would have led his pupils to mass on

Sundays and Saints' days. And he must have taught them in class religious history and the Old and New Testaments. It was probably because he conformed to these strict requirements that the municipal council allowed him to carry on his work with a slackness that the inspector could not always condone and which seems to have increased over the years. . . .

Thus practically all the pupils attended school for a few months only, chiefly in winter and on average for three or four months, although it is true that they would go on attending until they were 15 up to 18 years old.

This was long enough to learn the elements of reading, arithmetic and to be able to write their names. While in 1833 only 22 out of the 119 inhabitants of the commune who were summoned to sign their names knew how to write, there had been 35 out of 94 in 1813 and 37 out of 69 in 1853. But the amount of knowledge that most of them had acquired did not make them very different from the completely illiterate.

It should be noted—and this is important—that of the three pupils who regularly attended school, two came from the township—the sons of the smith and the inn-keeper. The third was the son of an independent farmer at La Coutancière. Similarly all those who in 1852 were at school for more than four months were the children of poor craftsmen in the township.

Thus by the years 1850–2 the school placed at the service of the people of Mazières by virtue of the law of 1833 had achieved only a relatively small success.

Reasons for This Lack of Success

The reasons for this are fairly easily found. They derive in the first place from the personality of the teacher. It would have needed an apostle to attract to and hold at school children who must have preferred wandering about in the fields to working shut up in an uncomfortable room and who, moreover, were put to work at a very early age by their parents. And Teacher Thébeau, although very probably a good-hearted, rather gentle man, had nothing of the apostle about him.

Lack of success derives, also, from the indifference of the local authorities towards education. This is clearly seen in their lack of action when the teacher stayed away from his school. This attitude is echoed in the following letter from the Mayor of Mazières to the Sub-Prefect at Parthenay on 18 February 1851:

> The majority of the municipal council is unwilling to accept the resolution contained in Circular No. 12 from the Ministry of Education in the sense that they will not vote any salary increment to the teacher above his 200 francs plus the product of school fees. Being unable to reconcile the two views it has been agreed to refer the matter to you before recording the resolution in the minutes.

School fees amounted to 263 francs and the sum which would have to be added to the budget, already in deficit, is rather too much.

This was a precaution which the mayor, as a prudent man, took *vis-à-vis* the central government. Here, in fact, is the resolution carried on 16 February 1851 as recorded in the council minutes: "The Municipal Council records here that it is expressly agreed to place nothing to the charge of the commune and, even if the budget were not in deficit, it would not consent, under any pretext, to add any sum whatever as an increase to this salary. If forced to do so, the Council would prefer to have an independent teacher."

In point of fact the teacher did get his increment but it was under pressure from the government. The local Education Committee did not concern itself as much as it should have with the teacher's attention to his duties: and the Municipal Council refused to improve the teacher's material lot, as it was required to do by law.

Finally, I discovered in a letter written in September 1848 by M. Pouzet to M. de Grandenay (*counseilleur général*), informing him of the commune's needs, proof of the little importance he attached to the school and particularly to its buildings. After speaking of the need to maintain the road-work depôts and the value of classifying at least one road as departmental, he emphasized the question of repairs to the presbytery: "Our presbytery is in the worst possible state: it has been occupied for more than forty years by the Venerable Abbé Pressac who has had practically nothing done to it and it is now in great need of repair. . . .

"Another very great need would be the establishemnt at Mazières of a registry office." And he ends by saying: "These, my dear Sir, are the most pressing requirements. As regards a school house, we will bring this up later, since repairs to the presbytery will completely absorb all our few resources."

I must again point out that Dr. Pouzet was a remarkably good administrator who loved the people among whom he lived, devoting himself to their service. But he loved them as they were. It was not possible for him to imagine that they should or could change or evolve as a whole.

And finally the school's lack of success stems from the people's indifference. This is not to say that the mass were completely indifferent to education: they could not be for already the red tape of the administration had begun to enmesh individuals, illiterate and literate alike. One had to sign leases or make one's mark at the bottom of important contracts that one could not read. Forms had to be filled for conscription and for marriage: and there were the court cases. When loans of money were made, the written word was a precious piece of evidence. Thus it was useful not only to know how to count—which everyone could do more or less well—but also to read and to write.

Also education was respected for its own sake. I have already mentioned how proud the old men were in knowing how to read, write and figure. But there is more than that. In many peasant houses you will still find, religiously preserved in some corner, exercise books in which some learned ancestor kept his accounts and wrote notes. The care with which these books have been kept shows the respect given to knowledge. I have looked at many and they are all alike. They contain accounts, fragmentary and haphazard, drafts of letters, receipts, models of contracts and agreements and recipes, all written higgledy-piggledy with no thought of making a methodical collection of useful information. Many even give the impression of having been written by their authors more as a means of maintaining their pride in writing than with a thought of practical use. Take, for example, the book of the owner of a large farm in a neighbouring commune to Mazières—Saint-Marc-la-Lande. This book was started in 1836 when the author must have just left school. It was kept up until 1860. It contains estimates, probably relating to the farm he was working:

The grey mare is valued at	450 fr.
The black mare is valued at	350 fr.
The pony is valued at	100 fr.

It also contains many rough workings of sums (he must have used the book to work out all his bargains); recipes for tisanes, models of contracts or family and business letters but also the correct way to address petitions:

"When one speaks or presents a petition either to a great dignitary of the State, or to a Minister or to a Prefect or to any other person belonging to the constitutional authorities of the first degree, one must use the title appropriate to him; for example, to a Prince of France or a Princess the title of Royal Highness, to the high dignitaries of the Realm, that of Most Serene Highness," etc. Then there is an unexpected copy of a letter, truly moving in its piety and resignation, from a priest of the neighbourhood—the Curé Bastard—who had had to flee to Spain during the Revolution.

So, in this book, one can discern not only the practical use of education to a peasant in 1850 but also the scope of his imagination and the matters which affected him most deeply. It is remarkable that, in this document which was so honoured that it had been preserved for more than a century, one finds side by side with matters which are purely utilitarian, other matters which are there purely because they are worthy of veneration.

There existed, therefore, a widespread respect for knowledge which derived not only nor even especially from its utility but because it is in itself worthy of honour and because it permits a man to raise himself up and maintain himself through thought and memory to a higher mental level.

And yet, as we have seen, the peasants did not send their children to school.

The first argument that comes to mind to explain this abstention is the length of the journeys to be undertaken and the bad state of the roads. This may have played a certain part but it was not an important part. To go four kilometres on foot over difficult ground seems to us today a considerable undertaking. This was not the case in those days. . . .

In actual fact those peasants who wanted to send their children to school did so. In 1852 a boy from La Coutancière attended school for the whole year. Now La Coutancière is nearly four kilometres from the town, which was reached only over particularly bad roads. Moreover, the roads to Mazières were stone-surfaced between 1848 and 1855 and completed in 1855, but school attendance hardly changed from 1851 to 1855, the year in which M. Thébeau, was replaced by another teacher, M. Bertout, or even during the two years that the latter remained there. Here are the figures:

1851	69 pupils (in August)
1852	87 pupils (in August)
1853	83 pupils (in August)
1854	87 pupils (in August)
1855	67 pupils (in August)
1856	80 pupils (in August)
1857	92 pupils (in August)
1858	83 pupils (in August)

Thus, it is not because they lived far from the school that the peasants in 1850 did not send their children there.

School fees might have been a burden: 1 fr. 50 per month in 1850 constituted no negligible sum. But here again this is not a fundamental reason: indigent children, whose fees were remitted, did not attend school regularly.

Furthermore, if school fees had been considered burdensome by those involved, one would have found traces in the archives of demands either for their abolition or for an increase in the number of pupils receiving free schooling. Quite to the contrary, the Mayor of Mazières, writing to the Sub-Prefect at Parthenay on 20 February 1850, stated categorically that there was no knowledge in the commune or even in the canton of a petition circulating in the neighbourhood—probably in the lowlands—which called for free schooling.

In fact, the widespread respect for knowledge among the people, however real it may have been, was not sufficiently strong in 1850 to shake the peasants out of their normal way of life and lead them to give up their children's labour and subject them, at the cost of continual nagging, to the discipline necessary for regular attendance.

The illiterate were too many to feel shame at their lack of knowledge, and the state of isolation in which the commune lived forbade the development of any deep intellectual curiosity. Moreover, the semi-closed economy and the narrow horizons of the world in which they lived did not require a constant use of the symbols taught at school.

They needed to know how to count. Most of them could do so, thanks either to the school or the help of their parents or friends and many achieved great facility in mental calculations of the simple matters they most often had to deal with. There was, moreover, more than one ingenious device to supplement the use of written symbols. For example, the *coches*, which were still used in bakers' shops twenty years ago, were current custom in 1850 among millers, etc. For the rest, they had no letters to write or read—or very seldom. They had no accounts to keep, for their money expenditure was kept to a minimum. Important official statements which should be known by all were announced by the town crier. People existed without much consciousness of their ignorance of symbols and it must be recognized that what was taught at school did not fit the needs of the peasants—as far as they could see. In the commune only the local patois was spoken: at school the teacher taught children to read in French, that is to say, in a learned language which one needed to use only on very rare occasions. People measured length in *toises*, *ligues* and *pouces*; firewood was charged by the *corde*; area was measured in *boisselées:* and things were valued only in *pistoles* and *écus*. At school the metric system was taught, even if only the bright pupils really learnt it.

The main reason for the poor attendance at school, therefore, is found much less in external causes such as the length and difficulty of the journeys to reach it, or in school fees, but rather in deeper causes relating to the state of mind of the people and the kind of life they lived. No one compelled them to send their children regularly to school. They had respect for learning but rather as a luxury of little use to a peasant. Neither from the point of view of personal dignity nor for daily practical use could they see the necessity of learning to read or write. So they would not undertake the effort to send their children regularly to school.

But roads were being built from 1848 onward: they were completed in 1855. At the same time the system of agriculture was changing and the country becoming more wealthy. It was entering a cycle where economic exchange became both necessary and possible. The way of life and state of mind changed as communications became easier and trade expanded. We shall see how parallel with this development, the enrolment at school increased and the peasants themselves became more demanding for the education of their children. . . . What had happened to the school during these thirty years? What effect had all these events had on it to assist or slow down its progress? What part had it been able to take in them?

In 1848 the mayor of Mazières considered, as we have seen, that the most urgent work to be undertaken was the construction of roads and the repair of the presbytery: the school could wait. However, in 1853, when the Emperor had made available a grant of two million francs as an encouragement for the communes to undertake schemes in aid of the unemployed, there was talk of builidng a school at Mazières. Plans and estimates were drawn up and on 8 January 1854 the council in consideration of the fact that it is absolutely essential to build a school at Mazières as promptly as possible because the building in use at the moment as a school and which the commune rents at high cost is most inconvenient, quite inadequate in accommodation and that there is no possibility of finding alternative accommodation,

And considering that the commune owns land suitable for the building of a school, approved unanimously the plan and provisional estimate of 9,000 fr. presented by the Department Architect dated 19 December.

On 14 March 1854 the council requested financial aid towards the cost of building the school. In this way it would be able to offer work for the needy on preliminary operations pending the final formalities of approval. A list of their earlier efforts was provided:

2,500 fr. for the presbytery
12,000 fr. for the church
400 fr. for the clock
1,800 fr. as assistance to the poor during the winter.

6,000 francs was voted for the school. Construction began during 1855. A resolution of 16 October 1855 states that it was almost completed. A further resolution of 25 October 1857 considers that the work has been well and truly done and that the building offers every guarantee of permanence and solidity. The vote had been overspent by 2,500 francs but this excess was considered justifiable.

This school still exists. It stands half-way up the slope on the road to Parthenay. The school house consists of two large rooms on the ground floor, one of which serves as a kitchen/dining-room: there is a bedroom on the first floor. The teacher also had the use of a large woodshed and an immense garden. Today all this seems very small and ill-arranged: in 1856 the peasants must have looked on it as almost a palace. The school itself comprised a small playground and one classroom which the pupils reached (and still reach) only by passing in front of the teacher's house.

Teacher Thébeau occupied it for only one year, because he left in 1856.

The Enrolment: Its Geographical and Social Distribution

The year 1856–7 will serve us as a convenient starting-point. The material progress that we have been noting had not yet begun; only the roads had been built. The teacher was a village man and we know about him.

In 1856 there were 48 pupils on the school register, attending for periods varying from two months to a year.

17 were children of artisans or shopkeepers in the town;
1 the son of a carter living in a village;
6 sons of day labourers;
3 sons of millers;
1 son of a weaver;
20 sons of farmers, all from villages in the north of the commune or from the borders of the town.

Now, in the commune there were 174 children of school age (94 boys and 80 girls); only 42 attended school—more or less—34 boys, 8 girls. Thus 132 had never set foot inside the school—60 boys, 72 girls. A certain amount of importance was therefore attached to the education of boys since a good proportion of them had attended school, even if for only a couple of months. Little importance was given to girls' education. The eight little girls who did go to school may be listed as follows:

1 daughter of a baker in the town;
1 daughter of a ropemaker in the town;
1 daughter of a blacksmith in the town;
1 daughter of a poor day labourer from Beugnon village;
1 daughter of a farmer living in a place called Petite Ville;
2 daughters of a miller;
1 daughter of a roadman living at Ternant village.

Thus only one daughter from among the farmers.

We will now make a closer study of the distribution of the boys according to the places where they lived and the work of their parents.

In the town there were 16 boys of school age. Two were not enrolled at the school: they were the sons of the justice of the peace and a wealthy landowner and must have been brought up in Niort or Parthenay. The 14 others were all enrolled and attended very regularly for the whole year. They were all children of artisans or small shopkeepers, except for two from very poor families and who were admitted to school without fees. Thus, the attendance of boys from the town was excellent.

In the villages to the north of the commune there were 35 boys: 11 attended school, 24 did not. Of the 11 at school three were admitted free (two were sons of day labourers, one of a wheelwright); one was the son of a carpenter/farmer; the rest were the sons of peasant farmers. The registration was, therefore, over 30 per cent but most of them attended very irregularly and then only during the winter months.

In the villages and farms in the south-west of the commune there were 43 boys of school age: only nine went to school. Of these nine, one was the son of a well-to-do landowner, two were sons of road-workers (at Ternant) and one the son of a carpenter. The remaining five came from peasant families.

Admittedly the southern villages and farms were a little further from the town than the northern villages but I have already pointed out that we need to bear in mind the concept of distance at that time. Moreover, from the villages nearest to the school, like Roulières, only one boy (out of three) was enrolled.

Also, it can be shown that this contrast in school attendance, as between children from the town or northern villages and those from the south, depended on the attitude of the parents rather than on economic position. . . .

Nevertheless . . . new economic and social forces were about to transform this old countryside in the 1860s.

A farm school was in operation at Petit-Chêne. It only accepted youths with some education. . . . What went on there and what was spoken about was not for poor peasants. And yet Masse from La Jaunelière and others went to see what went on and to hear what was said about it. A small, new wind coming from afar was beginning to blow over the country.

Land clearance was beginning. But it is not enough just to clear land: one must work out whether the clearance brings in a good return. New farm implements were being bought and they were costly. In the end it would perhaps be an economy but how could one be certain if one did not know how to reason things out and do one's sums? The most ignorant, that is to say the majority, evidently relied on the experience of the more prosperous and better educated. They copied them full of wonder at their knowledge and began to think that, even in their own sphere of activity, it would be a good thing to be able to think things over, pen in hand. Some of them, still very few—those who could read—obtained employment as postmen, or road-workers and, among large families, this meant more room for the children.

Also, since that terrible year of 1855 when there had been almost complete destitution, people began to hope, despite a mediocre harvest in 1859, that they would be able one day to rise out of their poverty. They had more things to sell. The markets at Champdeniers and Parthenay from whence produce was sent to Paris by the railway at Niort and Saint-Maixent were very busy. The roads were good. People travelled often to market where they met many folk and could chat with them. Those who could read the notices were much admired: those who could read the almanach and books on agriculture which gave good advice were envied. Little by little, everyone came to accept the idea that it would be useful to know how to read and count and also that it is a good thing in itself. After all, it might not be impossible, if a little trouble was taken, for the children to gain these benefits.

All this might have remained a vain hope or, at least, have come about only very slowly, despite the fine new school, if there had not been a change of teacher. But the authorities were beginning to be worried at the slackness of M. Thébeau. The report on the schools in the Parthenay arrondissement for 1855 notes: "The teacher at Mazières is a man of little energy; the local authority requests his transfer."

In 1856 M. Thébeau was moved to Saint-Georges-de-Noisne and was replaced by a young teacher named Bertout who had just qualified from the Ecole Normale at Parthenay. He was not to stay long at Maziéres—for barely eighteen months—at the end of which time he resigned. He must have found, in common with many other teachers, more lucrative employment.

A Good Schoolmaster

On 29 April 1858 the mayor of Mazières was advised that "by a Departmental Minute dated 28 of this month, M. le Préfet de Deux-Sèvres had appointed as schoolmaster for the commune of Mazières-en-Gâtine le sieur Popineau (Jean-Victor), schoolmaster in the commune of Marigny."

On 4 May M. Popineau came to Mazières, where he "swore obedience to the constitution and loyalty to the Emperor" and was installed as teacher for the commune. He was to remain at Mazières until 1876 and all his pupils would remember him with gratitude, admiration and affection. It can be said that, thanks to him, the latent forces then ripening in the area which would sooner or later have compelled the establishment of an efficient school came into full bloom at once, at the right moment.

He was born in 1831, the son of an artisan at Saint-Maixent named Isaac Popineau. He was a student at the Parthenay *école normale* from 1847 to 1850, and this is a point which should be noted. The *Loi Guizot* in 1833 had made provision, together with primary schools in the communes, for teacher training institutions in each *département*. We have seen that this provision had had no noticeable effect as far as the school at Mazières was concerned. But in 1835 the *département* of Deux-Sèvres had established an *école normale* at the only suitable place—Parthenay—and now this training college was about to permit, in 1858, the realization at Mazières of the intentions of the law of 1833.

Furthermore, M. Popineau was born at Saint-Maixent, that is to say, in a small town in the plain of Deux-Sèvres where the presence of a certain number of Protestants among a majority of Catholics had, because of the controversies to which this led, maintained a certain activity of mind and often a certain moderation in belief.

It happened, too, that he was a student at the training college from 1847 to 1850, that is, during a revolutionary period when staff and students were in a kind of ferment. In particular there had been difficulty in maintaining morning and evening prayers and it was only because they were compelled to that the students continued to repeat their Paternoster.

It seems, therefore, highly probable that, together with the professional competence which would soon show itself and the intellectual and moral qualities which would win him the esteem of the whole population and particularly that of the mayor, M. Popineau brought to Mazières a certain independence of mind. Remember that M. de Tusseau was to cause him to leave in 1876.

He performed his duties meticulously. I have found in the school log-book, which he kept most carefully, many references to religious education. He took his pupils to church on Sundays: he sang mass. He would never have inspired confidence in the parents if he had done otherwise: and his success was complete.

Eighty pupils had been enrolled in 1856 under M. Thébeau. In 1857 the number rose to 98 with M. Bertout, and fell to 83 in 1858 with M. Bertout and M. Popineau. But it became 105 in 1859, 135 in 1860 and remained around that level until 1870. The following are the figures of school enrolment for these ten years:

1860	135 including 10 indigent
1861	128 including 12 indigent
1862	137 including 17 indigent
1863	140 including 18 indigent
1864	125 including 14 indigent
1865	126 including 17 indigent
1866	129 including 17 indigent
1867	137 including 17 indigent
1868	133 including 19 indigent
1869	140 including 23 indigent

The efforts made by Duruy at the Ministry of Education this time had immediate and direct effect at Mazières. The teaching of history and geography was introduced: I have found records of marks given to pupils in history and geography from 1867 onwards. . . .

. . . Nevertheless the number of pupils at the school after 1870 increased continually:

1869	140	1873	209
1870	151	1874	221
1871	160	1875	234
1872	189	1876	250

The fee revenue from this kind of enrolment, modest though it was, gave the schoolmaster a reasonable salary. Already in 1860 M. Popineau received 1,123 francs: by 1875 this had risen to 2,325 francs. The regard in which he was held in the countryside must have contained something of the respect paid to success, to those who have managed to make money and find themselves a really good job. This is the tone, it seems to me, of the resolution passed on 21 October 1866 confirming the continuing success of M. Popineau's school "which is thriving." He was a shopkeeper whose trade was of a rather special nature, something like a chemist, who had done well in his business.

A Sharp Increase in Numbers After 1870

We will now try to explain why the enrolment increased rapidly after 1870. First, material prosperity, the causes and first signs of which we noticed between 1860 and 1870, showed itself in a more marked fashion. Through the consequences of this material prosperity, through the development of trade, through the effect of more frequent visits to market, people's attitudes changed and became more favourable to the school. I have attempted to show this in explanation of the success of M. Popineau's school between 1860 and 1870.

From 1872 compulsory military service, by removing many young men from their homes, by obliging the illiterate—both parents and soldiers—to correspond with each other only through a third party who could write and read their letters, drew everyone's attention to the value of education.

The increase in the number of minor jobs and the possibility for anyone who had successfully completed primary education to obtain them, the practical use made by some of the knowledge gained at school, on the spot and in their own trade, in improving their circumstances carried a good deal of weight in this sudden increase in school enrolment.

We have just seen the significance of the fact that from 1858 on all the town children went to school and that children from the countryside attended only rarely. Here is something even more significant: the children from town families who attended a school were all able to use what they had learnt in earning a living.

One son of the rope-maker remained a rope-maker like his father; but, towards 1880, he added to his earnings as an artisan the income from an insurance agency which he took on. The other son left the village between 1872 and 1875 to join the railways and returned to die in Mazières in the house inherited from his father.

Of the two sons of the village *marchand*, one stayed a dealer like his father; but he added to his trade a small tinsmith workshop; the other was killed fighting in the Jura as a lieutenant in the *gardes mobiles*.

The grocer's son carried on the grocery business, but there is no need to emphasize that a shopkeeper, no matter how small his shop may be, must be able to read and keep accounts, especially as his trade develops and if he finds he needs to extend credit to his customers. The innkeeper's son became a captain in the army. Young Guichard (Eusèbe) from La Mimaudière who went to school in 1858 became [an] estate agent. . . .

On the other hand, none of the children from prosperous farming families in the south of the commune who did not go to school or, if they did, attended very irregularly, changed their situation. Only one, one of those who attended regularly, did stay on in the army where he finished his career as warrant officer.

If now we pass from the list of names of those who made gifts of bread to the list of unfortunates who received them, we find a number of children, some of whom came to school as paupers who did not pay fees. One of them, one of the poorest (his name was Det and he was called Champagne, why I don't know), was to become a railway employee at Paris, like the son of the prosperous rope-maker who had subscribed forty livres of bread—and at the same time as he.

And so, this humble village school at Mazières was making it possible for the most impoverished, as well as the more prosperous, to obtain some of those many minor posts of employment which the economic, social and political development of France was causing to multiply and, what is more, to take their place in them on terms of equality. This double take-off must have been the subject of conversation for many years in the village and in the farms of Mazières. Its effect could only have been to add to the prestige of the school in the township: the peasants' indifference was broken down.

Furthermore, the frequent elections held between 1870 and 1880 and the burning political debates of the time which had their echo in Mazières certainly aroused among the electors whose votes were now being solicited a greater sense of their dignity. Those who could read were listened to with close attention.

M. de Tusseau's council does not seem to have discouraged this enthusiasm for the school—quite to the contrary, for the number of pupils admitted without fee rose from 23 in 1870 (Dr. Pouzet's council) to 24 in 1871, 30 in 1872, 33 in 1873, 43 in 1874 (de Tusseau's council). It is true that it returned to 39 in 1875 and to 30 in 1876 at the time when the *République des Ducs* was threatened and was on the defensive. I have been unable to discover the number of pupils not paying fees who were admitted in 1877 at the moment of acute crisis, the new teacher's arrival being accompanied by some disorder in the school records.

The impetus had been given and, with education being more widespread, it became a matter of shame not to be educated.

In 1863 of 69 persons called upon to sign as witnesses at the registry of births, marriages and deaths, 37 could write their name i.e. 58 per cent. In 1873 the figure was 56 in 81 i.e. 69 per cent: in 1883 63 out of 88 i.e. 70 per cent.

In 1853 out of eight conscripts, five were classed as completely illiterate; in 1863 out of 11 conscripts, five were classed as completely illiterate; in 1873 out of 11 conscripts, one was classed as completely illiterate; in 1883 out of nine conscripts, one was classed as completely illiterate and four who could not read.

Parents began slowly to feel guilty if they did not see that their children went regularly to school. All of which goes to explain why, in 1876, M. Popineau had 250 pupils on his school register.

Teaching Methods

We may ask how he—the only teacher—could possibly teach so many pupils at one time. In fact, he had as assistant his wife who, under his supervision, looked after the girls while he gave his close and personal attention to the boys. The teaching he gave was very mechanical: it could not have been otherwise since his class usually contained more than 100 pupils, taking into account the absentees owing to such an irregular attendance. He used Noel and Chapsal's grammar which, like a catechism, consisted of a series of rules to be learnt by heart, the only exercises it contained being in the form of question and answer. In geography the pupils had to learn by heart the names of the principal countries with their capitals and chief towns: an old man who was once his pupil could still, a few years ago, recite to me what he had learnt in this way 70 years earlier. It was the same method for history and religious education. In addition he set many problems and gave much dictation and, for the brighter children, plenty of French composition. Thus, a very mechanical kind of teaching. Nevertheless, because it was given regularly and carefully supervised, clever pupils who attended regularly and, after leaving school, continued in the adult classes, reached a standard of knowledge and culture equal to that of the *Brevet Elémentaire*.

M. Popineau does not seem to have bothered to adapt his teaching to the environment, that is to say, to give an agricultural bias. In this matter he limited himself to giving his pupils, as a reading book, a work on agriculture edited for the Départment of Deux-Sèvres by M. Guillemot, departmental professor of agriculture. In 1845 Jacques Bugeaud had wanted farmers to learn to read so that they might be able to read such works and thereby be led to improve their farming methods. In actual fact, it does not seem that the reading of M. Guillemot's book at school had any remarkable, or even noticeable, effect. Not one of the old peasants whom I interrogated on this point had preserved any precise memory of what they had read. It must be remembered that the most regular attenders at the school were the sons of artisans or shopkeepers in the town: agriculture did not interest them directly. And I cannot imagine that the farmers sent their children to school to learn how to farm better than they themselves. All that has been said earlier leads one to the conclusion that, on the contrary, they sent them because gradually they began to see the importance that words and figures held, and necessarily held, even in a half-closed society like their own and because education allowed man's dignity to rise: but more because to be ignorant became a mark of inferiority. . . .

. . . M. August Bouet was born in 1858 at Vausseroux, a tiny commune in Gâtine, about fifteen kilometres from Mazières. He was the only son of a peasant farmer. He was a brilliant pupil at his village school, so much so that, when he was twelve, his teacher entered him for the scholarship examination for the Lycée. He failed on account of a grammatical error due to his peasant origin (for him at that time the word *vipère* was masculine and not feminine in gender because country folk said: "*un grou (gros) vipère*"). If he had passed he would most certainly have had a brilliant university career. In spite of this disappointment he continued to attend school until he was sixteen when, without ever having left his village, he went to the *Ecole Normale* at Parthenay. In 1878 he passed out top of his class with the full Certificate (*Brevet complet*) which is equivalent to the present Higher Certificate (*Brevet supérieur*) but which was rarely awarded at that time even among students at the *Ecole Normale*. For a few months he taught at Secondigny-en-Gâtine; for a year at Saint-Marc-la-Lande, five kilometres from Mazières. In 1881 he came to Mazières as headmaster. He married a girl from the township and remained there for the rest of his teaching career. In 1925 he became mayor of the commune.

The simplicity of this career, confined to a single appointment, is extremely significant. It indicates, first of all, that throughout his life M. Bouet had more the feeling of being a member of the commune—or, rather, the whole district—in which he exercised his profession than of being a member of a special, outside, body: the teaching force of the *département*. His ambition was to be one of the respected leading citizens among the people with whom he had integrated himself and not one of the most highly regarded public servants in his profession.

This view of life very probably derived from his peasant origins, from a childhood spent in the midst of the countryside with no thought of the possibility of travelling or moving away from it. It would even have allowed him to be content to remain in the rural commune to which fate had sent him, since there he found peasant folk he could understand and love; where he could rediscover the pleasures of his childhood—fishing and gardening. He would even have felt—and with every justification—that he had achieved a good social success. The girl he married was well-off: she was the only daughter of a tradesman in the town who owned several houses. In a sense, this marriage was symbolical of the social transformation which was happening in Mazières, of the increase in wealth and the transference of influence which was taking place. Here was the only son of poor peasants coming, because he was intelligent and industrious, to take up employment as a Government servant and consolidating his situation and movement upward in the social scale by marrying the only daughter of a small shopkeeper in the township who had been able to gain a certain amount of money by reason of the development of trade and an economic revolution in the region.

Because he was known to have money, as much as because he was a good teacher, everyone respected him. He consorted as an equal with the town officials of a higher rank than his own: the justice of peace, the tax inspector, the surveyor. Dressed like them, often superior to them in knowledge and

culture, always in his intimate knowledge of country matters, he went shoot-
ing with them—a sport in which he excelled.

He was secretary to the mayor. He enjoyed M. Proust's friendly confidence—something of which he was very proud. Among the people of the
town he formed strong, if respectful, friendships. And so, throughout his
career, he had that feeling of stability and that deep inner contentment which
are indispensable to active happiness. The very fact that he showed himself
so completely attached to the soil on which he lived and to the customs of
the country gives a clear idea of the kind of influence he was to exercise.

As we have said, he was an excellent student at the *Ecole Normale* at
Parthenay. He had acquired a broad and solid education much more oriented,
it seems to me, towards history and science than to philosophy and literature.
In history itself he was much more interested in facts than in ideas; and the
curiosity of his mind was directed more to the observation of local things than
to more general study. The only writings he has left are a local monograph and
a course in agriculture, and a few articles on local history.

At the *Ecole Normale* he had had lessons in the methods and principles of education which are to be found in some notebooks I have been able
to consult. The following is an important passage:

> Finally, in the fifth place, we shall consider the qualities and, especially,
> the duties of the teacher. These duties are concerned with the following
> points: first, with his private conduct as a man. The teacher must be sin-
> cerely religious; he must, as much by his attitude as by his words, inspire
> respect for the established government, for the law and for the magistrates
> charged with its execution. Also his home must be a model of concord
> and good behavior: he must be prompt in paying his bills and he must
> avoid that sorry mania of wishing to raise himself above his station. Besides
> these general duties, the teacher has special duties towards those placed in
> charge of the direction and inspection of primary education: to these au-
> thorities he owes respect, deference and affection.

This was the course given at the Parthenay *Ecole Normale* by M.
Brothier, Principal of the college in 1877. M. Bouet was a hard worker and
could not understand how anyone could not enjoy work: no one was more
severe than he on tramps and idlers. He was thrifty and could not understand
how anyone could expect to become well-off other than by hard work and
thrift. He would never have that "sorry mania of wishing to raise himself
above his station." Nevertheless, he was not religious in the sense intended by
his Principal, that is, he was not a practising Catholic. He believed, on the
contrary, very deeply and very religiously in the existence of a secular morality,
independent of any religion. The essential elements of this religion were,
moreover, the same as those which were growing spontaneously among the
people and which we have noted: faith in progress, belief in the Republic,
love of country.

As regards human progress, M. Bouet had *la foi du charbonnier*. This can be seen in the local monograph from which I have quoted several significant examples. After speaking of the farm workers who, from fear of unemployment, tried to put threshing machines out of action by mixing stones with the sheaves of wheat, he compares them with the Weser boatmen breaking up Papin's steamboat. He adds: "Clearly these happenings cannot last long: but these gross mistakes to which the common people fall prey demonstrate excellently to the government how important it is to educate people, to enlighten them and destroy the prejudices of days gone by." No shadow of doubt crosses his mind: machines manifest a striking victory of human ingenuity and the power of reason over matter. It would be a sin against reason not to make use of them; they cannot but lighten man's burden and hasten progress: anything that stands against this march forward can be only superstition and prejudice which education will chase from the scene.

He was an ardent republican but in no way a democrat. He would most certainly have been shocked if the mayor of Mazières were a peasant or a tradesman and not a bourgeois like M. Proust. He never envisaged that his best pupils could aspire to a future different from his own, to a career superior to that of a teacher. It was certainly not he who gave Pascal Chaignon, the postman, the idea of sending his son to the secondary school. On the contrary, he supported in good faith and with all his power the conservative views of M. Proust. Later on he was to oppose in the *canton* socialist propaganda whose egalitarian arguments he detested.

He was a true patriot. He belonged to a generation when teachers were not called upon to do military service and so he had never been a soldier. But he gave his daughter in marriage to an officer and, throughout his career, he was continually repeating to himself, to raise in his own eyes his modest but noble profession, "that in 1870 it was the Prussian teachers who defeated France." He would never ask himself if the progress in which he believed imposed on him any different duty: he did his utmost to inspire his pupils with a love for their country.

Such, then, was this man who believed in Reason and in Progress, in the nobility of his task but whose thoughts moved only among things that he knew well within a narrow physical field, among men he respected. . . .

The virtues extolled by our teacher, both in his formal lessons and in the trend of all his teaching, were, moreover, the same as those I have referred to earlier. Respect for grandparents and parents, love of one's brothers (a brother, he said, is a friend provided by nature), pity for the weak, neighbourliness—all these were taught in a way we could understand with examples taken from life. As regards one's duty towards oneself, he emphasized temperance and thrift and he even used arithmetic lessons to show how necessary it was to be sober and thrifty. I remember working many problems on how much a workman could save if he did not smoke or drink: by the end of his life, thanks only to his economies, he would be able to buy himself a little house. These lessons were not without effect in an area in the grip of full social mobility where people are thrifty by nature.

In this way he taught us to control our desires and instincts in line with our own well-understood interests. But he also strove to develop in us that part of every individual's personality which must form the base of any moral code worthy of the name: in his teaching he gave cardinal importance to love of one's country.

The French Republic, daughter of the Great Revolution, mother of all progress, was in his eyes worthy of every sacrifice. He read to us and gave us for dictation famous writings which glorified France. Among many others, the passage where Michelet, comparing France with other nations, declares that she had done much more for mankind than any other, seemed to us to be indisputably true and filled us with joy and pride. One day he dictated to us a text on a postage stamp representing France the Sower which moved him to tears: "In this picture the whole spirit of France can be seen." Every year he would read to us a passage from an author whose name I forget which described two enemy soldiers, French and Russian, dying on the battlefield. In the morning the survivor awakes surprised to find himself warm: the other, before dying, had covered him with his cloak. "Little Frenchmen, guess who had died and who it was who had made this sublime gesture. I can see you hope it was the Frenchman. Well then, be happy, it was the Frenchman." And indeed we were happy.

We learnt to recite poems by Eugène Manuel, Déroulède, and Victor Hugo. We learnt military songs:

> Où t'en vas-tu, soldat de France,
> Tout équipé, prêt au combat,
> Plein de courage, et d'espérance,
> Où t'en, vas-tu, petit soldat?

Our reading book was entitled *Tour de France*. M. Daniel Halévy . . . made a close, but rather cruel, analysis of this little book. He brings out all the implications of renunciation it contains. We, for our part, could see only one thing: two orphans driven out from their land by Germany who discover France and do their utmost every day to improve themselves and become more worthy of being French. The last sentence of the book uttered by little Julien when he has at last found himself a home, a corner of French soil where he may live, was:

> "I love France!" "I love France! . . . France! . . . France!" came the clear echo from the hillside and was taken up again within the ruined farmhouse.
> Julien stopped in surprise.
> "All the echoes answer you one after another, Julien," said André gaily.
> "All the better," cried the boy, "I wish the whole world answered me and that every nation on earth said: 'I love France.'"

"For that to be," said Uncle Volden, "there is only one thing to be done: let every child of the Fatherland strive to do the best he can; then France will be loved as much as she is admired throughout the whole world."

Such an ending, read to us time after time, could not help moving us and engraving itself on our memory.

The Rise of Sports

PHILIP GOODHART

CHRISTOPHER CHATAWAY

The British middle class, which is widely known for its sponsorship of the work ethic, also pioneered a new leisure ethic. By the later nineteenth century, members of the middle class no longer had to work so hard to increase their wealth. They began to relax, at first with some feelings of guilt. The most persuasive early arguments for sports and recreation stressed their importance in improving performance at work. Calm nerves and strong, healthy bodies would incease output. Using this rationale, the middle class began to preach the virtues of sports as it had earlier urged work alone. One of the questions about the new recreational patterns is the extent to which they have, at least for the middle class, escaped this role as an adjunct to work.

The middle class helped change the nature of sports. With its rationalizing outlook it began to standardize rules in sports such as cricket and soccer football. It applied new technology to sports, so that new kinds of games constantly appeared. It helped commercialize sports too, for where there was a dollar to be made, the middle class would not be far behind.

Sports soon caught the fancy of the lower classes, and in the major sports the interests of the masses quickly predominated. Sports came to express many related aspects of modern behavior: the fascination with speed, an interest in individual self-expression and achievement, the consumption of one fad after another. By the mid-twentieth century, as the following passage suggests, sports had become a major focus for loyalty and violent partisanship.

Do sports also represent a major change in the "modern" mentality? The emphasis on individual achievement and competition may suggest that sports extended the mentality that the middle class had begun to create in the eighteenth and nineteenth centuries. But sports can also be seen as a flight from modernity: they stress action over thought; they involve mass passion and reaction; often they involve violence, not only on the playing field but also in the stands. Without question, movements such as Nazism that have protested the nature of modern man, particularly his claim to rationality, have correspondingly emphasized sports.

Goodhart and Chataway see sports as a tragic alternative to an empty existence. But sports can be seen as immensely liberating as well. The spread of sports among the middle class in the nineteenth century encouraged a variety of new forms of behavior. The bicycle craze at the end of the century illustrates this vividly. Women had to wear more informal costumes in order to bicycle, and traditional chaperoning practices declined as would-be chaperons found they could not keep up with a pedaling courtship. So the situation of women changed significantly. Middle-class religious interest waned as people found new things to do on Sunday.

The rise of sports thus introduces a complex element to the history of modern man. It may be seen as a vital supplement to other aspects of modernization; or as a sign of old impulses seeking new outlets, suggesting that modernization has not proceeded as far as is often imagined; or as an explicit rebellion against modern life.

At 3:45 P.M. on 4th July, 1954, the Hungarian defence half cleared the ball from their goalmouth, but it bounced awkwardly to Rahn, the German inside left. From a range of 15 yards Rahn hammered the ball into the net as Groscis, the Hungarian goalkeeper, clawed vainly at the air to his right.

Five minutes later the game was over. For the first time in four years those masters of modern soccer, the Hungarian national team, had been defeated. Western Germany had won the World Cup, and the thousands of Germans in the crowd at Berne's Wankdorf Stadium went berserk with joy.

A fortnight later in the Olympic Stadium at Berlin, President Heuss presented silver laurel wreaths to the victorious German team. "We can all rejoice about this German victory," President Heuss told a cheering crowd of 80,000, "but nobody should believe that good kicking is good politics."

There were not many German leaders who took such a detached view of their team's success. The Chief Minister of Bavaria had proclaimed that the victorious footballers had shown that Germany once again held "equal partnership in the society of nations." The Chief Minister was only one of many commentators who saw this victory as a symbolic climax to the post-war period of moral and physical reconstruction.

Some foreign observers were alarmed by the intensity of German reaction to victory in the World Cup and the homecoming speech of Dr. Peco Bauwens, the President of the German Football Association, gave particular offence. As The Times' Bonn correspondent wrote: "He exhumed Feuhrerprinzip and other such words. He addressed the eleven innocent footballers as if they had routed a national enemy on a field of battle." But, The Times' correspondent reminded his readers, "A foreign observer has to make allowance for the apparent excess of rejoicing. Germans collectively have felt starved of successes in the last ten years."

While the Germans rejoiced, the Hungarians wept and rioted. The Deputy Minister of Sport had accompanied the team to Switzerland; the windows of his home were smashed by an angry crowd. Thousands of angry Hungarians damaged the main offices of Toto, the Hungarian state-run football pool.

From Philip Goodhart and Christopher Chataway, War Without Weapons (London: W. H. Allen & Co. Ltd., 1968). Reprinted by permission of Winant, Towers Limited.

It was the largest hostile demonstration seen in Budapest since the arrival of the Red Army ten years before. *The Times* reported: "Some observers connect the demonstrations and the failure of the police to deal with them with the sudden dismissal announced on Tuesday night, of Mr. Gero, the Minister of the Interior."

While President Heuss was greeting the victorious German footballers, the Soviet Union was celebrating Physical Culture Day. In the Dynamo Stadium, Malenkov and Khrushchev joined a crowd of 90,000 to hear Mr. Romanov, the chairman of the Central Soviet Sports Committee, salute the performance of Soviet sportsmen in foreign competition—including victories in three major events at the Henley Regatta. These successes, said Mr. Romanov, had been gained "by putting into practice the instructions of the Communist Party."

In any other age it would have seemed odd indeed that the leaders of great nations should talk in these terms about mere games. But then the whole twentieth-century concept of representative sport would have been strange to them. The jousters in a mediaeval tournament might have recognised the social function of a modern international sportsman, but they, like the Roman gladiators, were essentially warriors, and their sports were simply modified techniques of combat. It was the emergence in the nineteenth century of games with accepted rules and universal appeal which paved the way for modern representative sport. The country in which most of these games evolved, and in which the rules were quite suddenly standardized, was Britain.

As the scene of the first industrial revolution, Britain had, by the nineteenth century, a prosperous middle class and good communications. These basic conditions allowed seven schools and two universities—Rugby, Eton, Harrow, Charterhouse, Westminster, Winchester, Shrewsbury, Oxford, and Cambridge—to exercise a considerable influence in Britain, on the continent of Europe, and throughout an expanding empire. In these schools and universities international sport was born. Most of the games that are now played across the world and which command such earnest attention from kings and presidents, were invented by a few hundred wealthy young Victorian Englishmen. Football, which, in its various forms, is far and away the world's most popular game, was their greatest innovation.

One of these founders of modern sport was a Rugby schoolboy, William Webb Ellis. The record of his career is worthy but unremarkable. The Rugby school register shows that he entered Rugby as a day-boy at the age of nine in 1816. He went up to Brasenose College, Oxford, in 1825, and played for his university at cricket in 1827. He became rector of St. Clement Danes and died at Menton on the French Riviera in 1872. The exploit that assured his place in history came one autumn afternoon in 1823. Then, as the memorial tablet in Rugby Close records, William Webb Ellis "with a fine disregard for the rules of football as played in his time, first took the ball in his arms and ran with it, thus originating the distinctive feature of the Rugby game."

As a local day-boy Ellis was a member of a despised minority, and there are some who interpret this memorable "disregard for the rules" as an act of social defiance. Certainly, his innovation did not win quick acceptance. A young contemporary of Ellis, the Rev. Thomas Harris, recalled that, "Our Hero [Ellis] was generally regarded as inclined to take unfair advantages at football," and it is plain that Webb Ellis' initiative was disimssed by many of his contemporaries as the sort of conduct one might expect from a day-boy. Thomas Hughes, the author of *Tom Brown's Schooldays* and a passionate football enthusiast, had this to say:

> In my first year, 1834, running with the ball to get a try by touching down within goal was not absolutely forbidden, but a jury of Rugby boys of that day would almost certainly have found a verdict of "justifiable homicide" if a boy had been killed in running in.

The fame of the football played at Rugby spread widely. When Queen Adelaide, the widow of William IV, visited Rugby on 19th October, 1839, she unexpectedly announced that she would like to see a game of football. The boys promptly removed their coats and waistcoats and played in their best shirts and trousers. . . .

By the early 1860's, in fact, games had become a dominant influence in public school life. In answer to a questionnaire sent by the Clarendon Commission in 1864, it was revealed that a keen cricketer fighting for a place in the Eton XI would be expected to play 21 hours a week during the season. At other public schools the time consumed was, in some cases, even greater.

The new influence of the muscular schoolmasters was powerfully supported and expanded by a muscular novelist, Thomas Hughes. The publication in April 1857 of Hughes' *Tom Brown's Schooldays* was the most spectacular publishing success of the year. Eleven thousand copies were sold during 1857, and the author made more than £1,000 in royalties in less than six months.

There are stirring descriptions of a football match, a fight, and a cricket match, and the author extols the values of games in the building of character. As Tom Brown's young friend Arthur puts it, cricket is "the birthright of British boys old and young, as habeas corpus and trial by jury are of British men."

Until the publication of *Tom Brown's Schooldays*, it could be argued that the most profound literary influence on the development of British sport was the club betting book at White's. Indeed, the whole concept of modern record-setting, of competing against time rather than opponents, can be traced back to the successful wager made by John Lefton of Keswick in 1606 that he could ride between London and York five times in one week not counting the Lord's Day. In the eighteenth and early nineteenth centuries, a gambling mania washed over all sections of the country.

Rich and poor alike would bet on anything from cock-fighting to cricket. There was a vogue for walking or running matches in which some professional runners would have to carry midget jockeys on their backs. Outlandish contests between little girls or one-legged men were popular, and in 1808 Captain Barclay Allardice, a wealthy Scottish landowner, won fame with a wager of a thousand guineas that he would walk one mile in every hour for a thousand hours.

But although races between men aroused the excitment of some gamblers, nothing could match the popularity of horse racing, which was the first British sport to be organised on lines that have survived unchanged to this day. In 1727 meetings were held in 112 English towns. By 1760 the Jockey Club had established its powers to control racing and was soon able and willing to warn off offenders, from the Prince Regent downwards. Between the outbreak of the American revolution in 1776 and the surrender of General Cornwallis in 1787, the St. Leger, the Oaks, and the Derby were established.

Cricket, too, owed much of its early development to gambling. Betting on cricket seems to have started in the late seventeenth century, and by the 1750's as much as £20,000 would be staked on a single match. Of course, there were abuses: races were fixed, prize fights were "arranged," cricket matches were sold—a tavern called the Green Man in Oxford Street was known to be the main meeting ground for both cricketers and gamblers—but in the main, the British love of gambling had provided a stimulus of vital importance in the development of certain sports—notably cricket, boxing, and horse racing. But gamblers do not need an elaborate or sophisticated sporting organisation in order to find an opportunity to bet, and by the beginning of the nineteenth century the importance of gambling as a sporting stimulus had passed its peak. Indeed, the strong connection between gambling and sport in the eighteenth and early nineteenth centuries was a positive affront to the stern moral principles embraced by so many members of the emerging middle classes.

A new image was needed and was soon provided. The new breed of muscular schoolmasters and the notion popularised by *Tom Brown's Schooldays* that sport nourished virtue now embellished games-playing with a new respectability, and the advent of respectability meant that the enormous organising ability of the solid Victorian middle classes could now be applied to sport. . . .

It is a remarkable record. In one brief period the rules of association football, rugby football, and hockey had evolved. Boxing had been dressed in respectable clothes. Athletic and swimming competitions were first organised in their modern form. Lawn tennis was introduced to the world, and polo was reintroduced. Competitive golf was launched. Minor sports, such as badminton, court tennis, squash rackets, fives, and croquet, all went through a new phase of organisation or reorganisation. The unscaled peaks in the Alps were climbed by the first wave of British mountaineers and international athletic competition had begun. It was a sporting revolution, and the revolutionaries were young graduates of English public schools and universities.

The seeds sown by these eager young enthusiasts fell onto fertile ground. Before 1850 William Clarke and his "All England" eleven of cricket professionals had bumped from one end of England to the other in embryonic railway carriages and badly sprung stage coaches playing scratch matches in small towns. But if organised sport was to thrive there must be good communications, people with the leisure to play games and to watch them, and a considerable degree of urbanisation.

The sporting revolution of 1860–75 came at the right moment. Communications had been vastly improved in the 1850's and 1860's. By 1860 the new industrial towns of the North and the Midlands were thrusting forward as the spearhead of a more general urbanisation of Britain.

But if many of their inhabitants of the new towns were to have an opportunity to play and watch the new games, the working population needed more free time than they could normally command in the middle of the nineteenth century. Sunday, of course, was already a whole holiday, but sport on Sunday in England had always been hemmed in with restrictions. During the seventeenth century under the Stuarts, sport on Sunday had even become a major political issue. James I had taken a liberal approach, and wrote in his "Book of Sports" that:

> Our pleasure likewise is, That, after the end of Divine Service, Our good-people be not disturbed, letted or discouraged from any lawful recreation, Such as dancing, either of men or women, Archery for men, leaping, vaulting, or any other such harmlesse Recreation . . . But withall we doe here account still as prohibited all unlawful games to bee used on Sundays onely, as Bears and Bull-baitings, Interludes, and at all times, in the meaner sort of people, by Law prohibited, Bowling.

Charles I reissued this Royal declaration on Sunday sport in 1633, with the full backing of Archbishop Laud. Meanwhile, Parliament had forbidden Sunday sport, and many clergymen read the declaration from their pulpits under protest. There were some contemporaries of Archbishop Laud who believed that this controversy hastened Laud's downfall and execution.

All sports were, of course, banned on Sunday by Oliver Cromwell's Puritan colleagues—who also tried to suppress race meetings as habitual underground gathering places for royalist supporters. The Stuart restoration brought a sharp liberal reaction in attitudes towards Sunday sports, but by the nineteenth century the general tide was again in the direction of more restriction. Indeed, the explosion of the sporting revolution coincided with the flowering of the full rigours of the English Sunday. If working men were going to have a chance to participate in these new sports, it would have to be on a Saturday afternoon, and the move for a Saturday half-holiday was already under way.

By 1848 the building trades in some towns had already won the right to stop work at 4 P.M. on Saturdays. When in the early 1860's George Cadbury, the founder of the chocolate firm, closed his Birmingham factory on Saturday afternoons, "people told us it would mean ruin," but by the 1870's millions of workers began to enjoy a weekly half-holiday—and the number of sports clubs mushroomed.

By September 1893, exactly thirty years after the break between the rugby and association football codes, 481 clubs were members of the Rugby Football Union. The association football game had grown even faster—by 1880 there were more than 300 clubs in the Birmingham area alone.

The attendance records of Football Association Cup Final matches are as fair a guide as any to the growth of interest in sport. The first F.A. Cup competition in 1872 drew fifteen entries and the final was watched by 2,000 people. In 1889, one year after the formation of a professional football league had consolidated the growth of football, 22,000 watched Preston North End complete the double by winning both the Cup and the new League Championship. In 1897 65,891 people watched Aston Villa beat Everton. In 1910 no less than 110,000 watched Tottenham Hotspur draw 2–2 with Sheffield United at Crystal Palace. In less than forty years football had become a national mania in Great Britain. The era of mass, representative sport had arrived.

Fortuitously, then, the major period of creativity in the organisation of sport coincided with the improvement of communications, the growth of leisure, and the rush from the countryside to the towns that was necessary for the development of sport on its modern, massive scale.

The Twentieth Century, 1918-Present

Contemporary Europe began to emerge in the horror of the First World War. The war severely damaged Europe's morale. Its staggering death totals distorted the population structure. The economic dislocations that resulted from it induced, or at least intensified, two decades of economic insecurity, culminating in the Great Depression. It set other disturbing trends in motion. Crime rates in Britain, for example, began to rise in the early 1920s and have continued to mount to the present, although they have not reached the levels of the late eighteenth century. It is not hard to portray twentieth-century European history in gloomy terms, compared with the nineteenth century. Certainly any history that focuses on the two decades between the world wars must stress the extreme social and political chaos that prevailed throughout most of the continent.

But Europe recovered after the Second World War and entered a new stage of affluence and industrial growth. Some observers believe that the society that has emerged since the 1940s is a radically new one, calling it "postindustrial" or "postmodern." Has the basic process of modernization given way to some new set of values and institutions? My own belief is that the modernization process is still continuing, despite admittedly great changes in many areas ranging from technology to the world's diplomatic structure. But the question deserves serious consideration, particularly with regard to the lives and outlooks of the major segments of European society.

What is certain is that Europe continues to change rapidly and that, within a recognizably common framework, it is developing a blend of the old and the new that differs from other advanced industrial countries such as the United States. Compared with our own country, Europe is less violent. Its family life is more stable, despite important changes in family values. At the same time it is much less religious. Its politics tend toward greater diversity and extremes. Social mobility is about as common in Europe as it is in the United States, but Europeans tend to place less emphasis on it, so that European society at least appears to be more stratified. Similarly, the position of women may seem more rigidly controlled, and in some countries it is demonstrably inferior in law; but how great are the real differences between Europe and North America in this area?

It is not easy to determine major trends in the very recent past, and the essays that follow cover only a few of many possible topics. We do, however, have something of a head start in interpreting key features in the development of contemporary European society. We know some of the basic responses to earlier modernization. We can compare recent patterns with these responses, to see if ordinary Europeans are reinforcing values established earlier or creating new ones. We can even try to assess the strengths and weaknesses of the society Europeans have developed.

Bibliography

There are many studies of Nazism, but most deal purely with the movement itself. Alan L. Bullock, *Hitler, a Study in Tyranny*, rev. ed. (New York, 1964), goes well beyond the confines of biography and is an excellent survey. Karl D. Bracher, *The German Dictatorship: The Origins, Structure and Effects of National Socialism*, trans. by Jean Steinberg (New York, 1970), deals extensively with the bases of Nazi strength. Ernst Nolte, *The Three Faces of Fascism* (New York, 1966), is an ambitious interpretation, but it is written mainly from the standpoint of intellectual history. A valuable specific study of Nazism's causes and impact in a small German town is W. L. Allen, *The Nazi Seizure of Power* (Chicago, 1955). For a recent interpretation of Nazism's effect on German society see Ralf Dahrendorf, *Society and Democracy in Germany* (New York, 1969).

Seymour Lipset, *Political Man, the Social Bases of Politics* (New York, 1959), studies the variety of modern political attitudes from a liberal point of view. John E. Goldthorpe et al., *The Affluent Worker: Political Attitudes and Behaviour* (New York, 1968), based on data from a recent study of the British working class, offers a different interpretation of workers' political values. For the political background, see Francis Boyd, *British Politics in Transition, 1945–1963* (New York, 1964), and Judith Ryder and Harold Silver, *Modern English Society* (New York, 1970).

Recent studies of sports include Richard Mandell, *The Nazi Olympics* (New York, 1971), and R. L. Quercetani, *A World History of Track and Field Athletics, 1864–1964* (New York, 1964).

Probably the most sensitive study of modern women, with careful attention to historical background, is Simone De Beauvoir, *The Second Sex*, trans. by H. M. Parshley (New York, 1953). See also Betty Friedan, *The Feminine Mystique* (New York, 1963). A vigorous recent survey is Evelyne Sullerot, *Woman, Society and Change* (New York, 1971).

On the twentieth-century family, Colin Rosser and Christopher Harris, *The Family and Social Change* (New York, 1965), is an excellent detailed survey, based on a study of a Welsh city. See also P. Willmott and M.

Young, *Family and Class in a London Suburb* (New York, 1960). Michael Anderson, *Family Structure in Nineteenth Century Lancashire* (New York, 1971), offers valuable background material. Richard Sennett, *Families Against the City* (Cambridge, Mass., 1970), presents a pessimistic view of modern family trends, based on a study of a Chicago neighborhood that deserves comparison with the European studies. Kent H. Geiger, "The Family and Social Change," in Cyril E. Black, ed., *The Transformation of Russian Society: Aspects of Social Change Since 1861* (Cambridge, Mass., 1960), surveys recent developments in Russian family structure and offers something of a model of the modernization of the family. J. R. Pitts, "Continuity and Change in Bourgeois France," in Stanley Hoffman, ed., *In Search of France* (Cambridge, Mass., 1963), and John Ardagh, *The New French Revolution* (New York, 1969), comment on changes in the middle-class family. J. H. Goldthorpe et al., *The Affluent Worker in the Class Structure* (New York, 1969), specifically contests Ferdynand Zweig's thesis of growing working-class contentment, but the study barely touches on family relationships.

The Social Bases of Nazism

DAVID SCHOENBAUM

The rise of Nazism in Germany, and of similar movements in other countries, is the outstanding characteristic of the two decades between the world wars. How could such a movement take shape and win substantial support? Social scientists have developed a number of approaches in trying to deal with the phenomenon. Some see Nazism and other totalitarian movements as endemic in the condition of modern man. Robbed of traditional values, such as religion, and close community ties, modern man stands alone and fearful; he easily yields to the solidarity and discipline of movements such as Nazism. Others view Nazism as a specifically German phenomenon, seeking in the German past an acceptance of authority and militarism. Still others emphasize more temporary factors, maintaining that Nazism was the product of a massive and unexpected defeat in war and of a variety of severe economic pressures, all of which had much greater impact in Germany than elsewhere. Even amid unprecedented social and political stress Nazism did not really gain popularity until the Great Depression.

Interpretation of support for Nazism is further complicated by the sheer opportunism of the movement, which tried to appeal to almost all groups and was quite capable of switching stands to win support. Relatedly, the reasons Nazism won popularity differ considerably from the results of Nazism in practice. No one has yet clearly assessed the extent to which Nazi anti-Semitism and aggressive nationalism won support; all we know for sure is that they did not deter the Nazi voters. But Nazism's promises of support for small business and small farmers and its suggestion of a return to a more traditional Germany were directly contradicted by the actions of the regime once in power. It has even been argued that, horrible as it was, the Nazi movement ultimately helped make Germany more genuinely modern and thus less susceptible to similar movements—after Nazism itself was defeated in war.

The following selection seeks to explain the varied social bases of Nazism, dealing both with the immediate problems and the longer-range grievances that led people to embrace the movement. It emphasizes the persistence of anxieties about modernization. Were these anxieties, or at least the intensity with which they were experienced, peculiarly German? Are war and depression sufficient explanations for the way in which these anxieties were expressed? Questions like these must be faced, for in understanding Nazism's appeal we must try to estimate the chances of its recurrence, in Germany or elsewhere. This in turn leads us to ask what has happened to the social groups and values that supported Nazism. Have they changed or disappeared with further modernization? The passage stresses not only social but also generational tension during the period of Nazism's rise. Young people were disproportionately enthusiastic about the Nazi movement. Again we must try to determine whether this is because of peculiar circumstances in the period, or German characteristics, or perhaps more enduring problems of youth in modern society.

The concept of a sick society causes problems if only because no one knows exactly what constitutes social health. But to the extent that the concept has meaning, Germany after 1918 was an appropriate place for its application. The most spectacular symptoms—the propensity to physical violence, the hyperbolic inflation of 1923, and the near-overnight disintegration of the economy in 1929–30—had their equivalents elsewhere. But elsewhere they led to crises and convalescence recognizably within the limits of previous historical experience and the status quo. In Germany, however, the permanent disaffection of major social groups, the alienation of those groups who presumably support a liberal republic, was reflected in the progressive and total collapse of all liberal parties, and in the discrepancy between social reality and its political interpretation. They testify to a latent malaise whose consequences, even without Adolf Hitler, would have led to major social and political transformation. This need not have led to war and Auschwitz. But with high probability, it would have been fatal to the Weimar Republic in the form envisaged by the authors of its constitution.

National Socialism was not the cause of the malaise, nor was its ultimate totalitarian, imperialist form the inevitable consequence. Its programmatic demands were neither original nor peculiar to Hitler's Party. The Nazis came to power by miscalculation rather than by some exclusive popular demand focusing on the person of Hitler or his Party. The mandate with which Hitler took office was a conglomerate of disparities and contradictions long apparent to anyone interested in politics, both outside the party and in it. The common denominator of Nazi appeal was as remote as the smile of the Cheshire cat. In its negative form, it was a promise to make things different, in its positive form, a promise to make things better. But as far removed as it was from the unitary political will Hitler claimed to see in the uniform columns of the SA (Sturmabteilung—Storm Troopers, "brown shirts") or the ecstatic acclamation of a mass audience, there was in it nonetheless a homogeneity great enough to cover the yawning cracks in the Party program with ballot papers. This was the homogeneity of common disaffection.

The disaffection was structural, endemic in all Western industrial societies, but intensified in Germany by special historical factors: a non-competitive, highly concentrated, high-priced industrial economy, the disproportionate influence of a small class of large landowners, a high birthrate until

World War I, too many rural smallholders, an inflated urban petite bourgeoisie. All of these had been built into Bismarck's Reich. Carried along on the winds of economic expansion, they formed a fair-weather constellation whose stability was virtually identical with the success of its political leadership in balancing the conflicting demands and requirements of industry and agriculture, labor and capital, West and East, centralism and particularism, Catholic and Protestant, rich and poor. Success created a clientele that included even the nominal enemies of the established order. Their own vested interest in this order was certainly an important factor in the SPD (Social Democrat) decision to vote war credits in 1914. But the compromises of the old order failed to solve, even precluded solving, the problems of an industrial society. The collapse of the monarchy in 1918 with its chaotic "return to normalcy" only reintroduced the problems of the prewar era after four uneasy years of civil truce. But they were now complicated by the by-products of defeat: a "lost generation" of demobilized soldiers; a floating population of eastern refugees, many of them aristocrats; the liquidation of millions of war loans floated with middle-class savings; and a large disproportion in the demographic relationship of women to men. Finally, there were the economic consequences of the war: reparations, loss of export markets, exhaustion of both plant and raw materials, and inflation. The latent social problems of the prewar era were further complicated by a crisis of legitimacy in the political order coinciding with economic disintegration. The results were paradoxical; on the one hand, consistent and uninterrupted extension of the social tendencies of the prewar era, on the other, an ideologized misinterpretation of these tendencies that effectively prevented the solution of the maladjustments they caused.

A statistical résumé leaves no doubt about the unambiguous course of social development (see Table 1).

Table 1
German Occupational Distribution in % of Population

Year	Agriculture	Industry and handicrafts	Services
1882	42	36	22
1895	36	39	25
1907	34	40	26
1925	30	42	28
1933	29	41	30

This was the classical pattern of industrialization, urban growth, industrial rationalization, and the development of distribution and service industries.

While only 5 per cent of the German population had lived in cities of over 100,000 in 1871, the proportion had grown by 1925 to 27 per cent. Equally striking was the relative redistribution of ownership and economic status (see Table 2).

Table 2
German Occupational Status in % of Population

In %	1882	1895	1907	1925	1933
Independent	38	35	27	21	20
Their employed dependents	4	4	8	10	11
White collar including civil service	8	11	14	19	18
Workers	50	50	51	50	52

While the figures were neutral as economic indicators—pointing only to advancing industrialization and relative only to success in feeding, housing, and clothing an industrial population—they were full of implications as a reflection of social and political tendencies. The loss of economic independence, the employment of family members, the ballooning white-collar population characteristic both of the big city and the bureaucratic state and economy all affected the self-respect of the people they touched—or at least were capable of doing so as soon as they seemed to coincide with a decline in the standard of living. If the processes themselves were characteristic of capitalism, it stood to reason that those affected by them would come to consider themselves anti-capitalistic, without, however, accepting the theoretical Marxian implications of their misery and disappearing in the traditional proletariat. Theodor Geiger estimated, on the basis of the 1925 census, that 25,000,000 Germans could be classed, socially, as proletarians. But 45,000,000, roughly three quarters of the population, were living—during a period of increasing prosperity nearly five years before the depression—on proletarian incomes.

Particularly characteristic of this tendency were the retail traders, a bumper crop sown by the imperial order and in constant fear of being mowed down by the economics of the Republic. Between 1882 and 1907, the number of small retail traders had grown faster than both population and the national product as people sought to exploit urban growth and a rising living standard in tobacco shops, groceries, drugstores (Drogerien), and delicatessens (Feinkosgeschäfte). Even before the war, existing statistics pointed to a decline in professional quality. A survey of Brunswick grocers (Kolonialwarenhändler) in 1901 established that only 34 per cent had had any vocational training compared with 67 per cent in 1887. Even before the depression, the economic consequences of the peace had revealed the weaknesses of the small shop-keeper, exposed to the business cycle, unresponsive to shifting population, and inadequately trained for either successful competition or other employment. Added to his problem on the one hand were the price-sinking creations of advancing technology and concentrated capital, the chain and department stores, and on the other, the vast overaccumulation of non-competitive man-power in retail trade. Between 1907 and 1925, the number of retail outlets rose from 695,800 to 847,900, an increase of about 21 per cent. Between 1924 and 1929 it increased another 3 per cent. Geiger estimated that in 1925 nearly 45 per cent of those engaged in retail trade were already living on pro-letarian incomes.

Meanwhile the number of department store subsidiaries rose from 101 in 1925 to 176 in 1929. While their absolute share of retail turnover was still small enough, their relative share by 1928 was growing 22 per cent faster than the total volume of retail trade. Between 1925 and 1931 so-called "specialty" shops lost 5 per cent of their share of retail volume, a relatively small figure but one magnified by higher operating costs, lively imaginations, and then by the depression. A 1929 tax study showed that the department stores had, in fact, taken over only 4 per cent, the chain stores at most 1.1 per cent of retail trade. This included, however up to 6 per cent of the turnover in cloth-ing and 20 per cent in household goods and furniture. By 1928 retail pressure groups were pressing for increased taxes on department stores, a goal achieved by 1929 in Munich and Frankfurt, Main. In 1932, the Brüning government declared a limit on further department store expansion, followed before the year was out by a similar ban on chain stores. Whether his misery was caused by his own inefficiency, his aversion to co-operatives, to the methods, eco-nomics, or good advertising of larger units within his own line, or by the department stores was a matter of indifference to the retail merchant whose effective desire was a self-contradiction: free enterprise minus its attendant risks.

But while the economic implications of retail trade seemed to point in the direction of the Marxist prognosis, toward concentration, intensified com-petition, and the strangulation of the small, independent proprietor, another development pointed in the opposite direction. This was the rapid growth of the white-collar population, "sociologically perhaps the most significant de-velopment of the last decades," as Ferdinand Fried called it in 1931. It was indeed characteristic of the period that the white-collar workers formed one of the best-observed of all social groups, their origins, attitudes, and habits becoming a subject of considerable public interest. Siegfried Kracauer's Marx-ist phenomenology of the white-collar worker ran for weeks in a daily news-paper in 1929 while the white-collar "little man" became in 1932 the hero of a fictional best seller, Hans Fallada's *Little Man, What Now?*

Coming as they did both from the ranks of the traditional bourgeoisie and from the proletariat, it was nonetheless clear that the white-collar workers were neither workers nor middle class in the traditional sense. Contemporary social science begged the problem of categorization rather than solved it by calling the entire group, from shop clerks to graduate engineers, "the new middle class." But this was hardly a guide to their behavior, which was, from the Marxist point of view from which they were most often observed, a collection of anomalies.

The white-collar worker was usually employed in a big city and by a big employer. He—or still more likely, she—was often of working-class origins, even before the war. Hans Speier quoted a number of surveys (see Table 3).

Table 3

Year	Job classification	Working class origins
1906	Berlin saleswomen	33.6%
1909–11	Young Munich saleswomen	66.9
1932	Cologne saleswomen	51.5
1929	Apprentices of Gewerk-schaft der Angestellten (clerical union):	
	Male	33.6
	Female	42.9

White-collar workers showed a progressive tendency to organize, and in a relatively militant organization from which employers were excluded. But both the form and the objectives differed from the traditional union pattern, corresponding in part to the different social origins of the membership, in part to the nature of their employment. While Geiger estimated that less than 4 per cent of the working-class population was skilled (qualifiziert), he estimated that 70 per cent of the white-collar population had some professional qualifications. This alone might have led them away from the traditional union demands. While 80 per cent of the workers were organized in the so-called "free" socialist unions in 1931, only 25 per cent of the white-collar workers were organized in the socialist Gewerkschaft der Angestellten (clerical union), while 22.6 per cent were in the national-liberal Hirsch-Duncker unions and 34.1 per cent in the so-called "Christian-National" organizations like the Deutschnationaler-Handlungsgehilfenverband (German National Sales Clerks Association) (DHGV), perhaps the only economic-interest organization in Weimar Germany that combined a racist-nationalist (völkisch) program with mass membership. It is also of interest that 39 per cent of the DHGV membership came from working-class origins.

While the white-collar union was a tough negotiator and the pressure of economic circumstances could bring about a professional solidarity great enough to overcome the ideological divisions separating the white-collar groups, white-collar consciousness made itself felt in a preoccupation with salaries instead of wages, long-term contracts, and pensions; reflections of a concern with security—including the security of social status—that distinguished it from the blue-collar unions. Weimar legislation continued to distinguish white collar (Angestellten) from blue collar (Arbeiter), granting the former special job security, separate status in wage contracts, and a separate insurance fund.

Both Schumpeter and Lederer-Marschak claimed to see the line between blue collar and white collar fading, Schumpeter because the workers were coming to live like petits bourgeois, Lederer and Marschak because the white-collar workers were coming to behave like other workers. The depression proved the contrary. Unemployment hit blue collar and white collar alike, but psychologically it hit the white-collar worker harder. Speier quotes an unemployed white-collar worker: ". . . . one is immediately ostracized, one is déclassé, without means of support, unemployed—that's equal to being a Communist." Déclassé is clearly the important word, reflecting a sensitivity of self-esteem different from that of the traditional working class. The increased employment of women—between 1913 and 1921 the proportion of women in the white-collar organizations had grown from 7.7 to 23.8 per cent—tended to increase the tension by making higher paid male jobs more vulnerable and compounding class war with sex war.

A key group in the white-collar population was an academically trained class, multiplied by postwar circumstances beyond its prewar numbers and increasingly absorbed in salaried employment in an economy that placed growing demands on technically trained manpower. The economic crises of the first Weimar years fell with particular weight on them, a group already sensitive to its exclusion, in part real, in part apparent, from traditional careers in the Army and civil service. While the social structure of Germany's political leadership changed significantly, the structure of the university population changed little except to the extent to which it grew and suffered. The 1922 Who's Who revealed that 20.3 per cent of the political entries came from the working class and 30.8 per cent from lower-income groups while only 40.8 per cent came from the old upper classes (Oberschicht). But the universities were peopled by the sons of the groups most conscious of the loss this revolution had caused them. The relative frequency of sons from the families of professional men went up in proportion to the restrictions imposed on business and the military. But while the sons of lawyers cautiously chose to make their ways in other areas, considerable numbers in medicine, pharmacy, and the natural sciences, the law faculties were filled with the sons of the petite bourgeoisie seeking the traditional prewar way to the top. In 1929, 23.4 per cent of all students were from the families of university graduates, 11.5 per cent from the homes of the rich—big landowners, company directors, etc. But 64.2 per cent came from the middle class intent on making their way in a world whose political direction was increasingly dominated, as they would tend to see it, either by the discredited representatives of the old order or by their social and cultural inferiors.

"The age of the self-made man is past," Robert Michels claimed. The only career open to the talented working-class boy was political. At the same time there was every evidence of dissatisfaction in a university graduate population of 840,000 while the student population tended to grow by 10 per cent a year. Since the routes to the top narrowed, and the traffic increased, the result appeared to be fewer and fewer rewards for higher and higher qualifications. Fried, who clearly felt himself a victim of the process, was eloquent in his description of its consequences: four to six years of university study, costing from five to nine thousand marks, rewarded with starting salaries ranging from two to four hundred marks monthly and advancing to a level commensurate with family obligations and social status only when its re-cipient reached the age of forty or fifty. The university graduate, Fried declared, felt as he had once felt during his first weeks of military service: spiritually and physically exploited. But while he might once have become a reserve officer for his pains, his civilian occupation under present circum-stances offered him the chance of one day becoming—with the best of luck—a prokurist, a kind of economic sergeant. "The way to the top is blocked off," he concluded, including among the obstacles the oligarchy of age. Reichstag deputies were, on the average, fifty-six years old, the two hundred leading economic figures, sixty-one years old—"rigid, dead, outdated and reactionary like the SPD."

One other major social group, the farmers, shared the general disaffec-tion. Geiger estimated that nearly 60 per cent of them were living on pro-letarian incomes. The intensity and quality of their disaffection varied accord-ing to region and market conditions but was ultimately reducible to the classic problem of agriculture in an industrial society: the farmer's inability to con-trol prices and production in an otherwise manipulable economy. The result was a curious dilemma. Massive economic disintegration might bring him short-term advantages, as it did during the 1923 inflation which liquidated his debts and brought him the short-term benefits of a barter economy and a sellers' market. But in the long run, the farmer suffered as the general econ-omy suffered. On the other hand, prosperity, even as it brought him higher prices, tended to increase the lag between farm and industrial income on one side and farm and industrial prices on the other. His efforts to overcome this gap resulted in overproduction with a consequent decline in prices. . . .

None of these problems was new or unique to Germany. In one form or another they had been, since the middle of the nineteenth century, not only the raw material of German politics but in varying degrees of the politics of all industrial and industrializing countries. In America similar phenomena had fueled political controversy since at least the election of Jackson in 1828 and formed the bases of the mass Populist and Progressive movements before World War I and later the basis of the New Deal.

What complicated solution in Germany was not a failure to recognize the structural inadequacies of industrial society, but rather a failure to find an alternative social model adequate to correct them. Advancing literacy, urbanization, industrialization, and the development of overseas agriculture all pointed to the liberal society envisaged by the Weimar Convention. But the main currents of social thought since at least the constitution of the Reich pointed away from it. They aimed instead at what René König calls "the two revolutions that didn't occur." One of these was Marxist. The other was what Fritz Stern has called "the politics of cultural despair," a kind of Peter Pan ideology for a society that didn't want to grow up. As aware as the Marxists of the evils of industrialization, the cultural pessimists saw their correction not so much in a redistribution of ownership as in the elimination of industrial society itself. They waged war against the city, turned rural emigration into the pejorative "Landflucht" as though it were a form of desertion, created a distinction between Gemeinschaft, the Arcadian community of the rural village, and Gesellschaft, the soulless rat race of urban society, and turned the sociological discussion of the period into an exhaustive analysis of "class" and "estate." The homestead act of 1919 and the economic parliament foreseen by the Weimar Constitution were testimony to their influence even during the brief honeymoon of popular support for the liberal Republic. In the form of land reform and conventions of estates (Ständekammern) and supplemented with demands for industrial profit sharing, nationalization of trusts, and redistribution of department store properties to small business, both measures found their echo only a few months later in the "inalterable" Nazi program of 24 February 1920.

This was less evidence of Nazi originality than of the Zeitgeist. The infant Party was obliged to climb on the bandwagon to remain in the race. What subsequently turned the NSDAP into a mass organization with a voter potential of fourteen million, and finally into Germany's governing Party, was at no point its programmatic command of the issues or pseudo-issues, but its manipulation of them. It was the mobilization of disaffection.

A form of this general disaffection had created National Socialism even before Hitler discovered it. In its original form, National Socialism was a phenomenon of the South German border areas, an organization of "little men," frequently handicraftsmen, frequently of small-town origin, all of them hungry for the respect of their German-National social betters. An outline of its general premises can be found in the unassuming autobiographical essay of Anton Drexler, the chairman of the little German Workers Party Hitler discovered in Munich in 1919. Drexler described with horror his youthful experiences in Berlin, his ostracism for unstated reasons by Socialist unionists, and the humiliation of having to play the zither in a restaurant. With the querulousness of the born crank, he was quick to find a Jewish-capitalist-Masonic conspiracy at the root of all problems, to appreciate its diabolical exploitation of existing class differences to plunge Germany unprepared into World War I and then to secure its defeat. While addressing himself to the working class, he was careful to avoid offense, to declare the worker a Bürger, and the officer and civil servant non-bourgeois. He declared himself in favor of capitalism but "healthy" capitalism, and drew a line between the Bürger, the farmer, the worker, and the soldier, on one side, and their common enemy, the capitalist Jew, on the other.

In industrially underdeveloped Munich at the end of the war and after the left-wing putsch that followed it, this was an ideology with a certain appeal. The following it attracted was not limited as Hitler later tried to suggest. Hitler, who joined with membership card No. 555, found both a rudimentary party program and a potentially expansive membership. The ideology was the work of a kind of Central European William Jennings Bryan, the engineer Gottfried Feder, whose specialty was inflationary fiscal policy and who had previously tried without success to sell his schemes to Kurt Eisner, the Socialist leader of the 1918 Bavarian revolution. The membership was mixed, in part a combination of desperate small shopkeepers, professional men, and workers like the machinist Drexler and his friends from the railroad, in part of demobilized soldiers like Hitler himself, at loose ends and unable to find their way back into civilian life. There being potentially large reserves in both the "civilian" and the "military" groups, this was a combination with a political future, provided that it found leadership capable of holding it together, and that economic and political stabilization did not undermine its attractiveness. . . .

While the Nazi vote for the Reichstag fell in 1928 to 810,000, or ninth in order of representation, the creation and combination of ideological clienteles—Feder's petite burgeoisie, Rosenberg's cultural pessimists, Goebbels' and the Strassers' young activists—and, above all, the charisma of Hitler, sustained both a base and an image. Radical, youthful, anti-Communist, sympathetic to small business, not necessarily hostile to big business, and ferociously nationalistic, the Party, like its program, was potentially acceptable in one way or another to nearly every large social group. Even while the vote fell, membership rose steadily—from 27,000 in 1925 to 178,000 in 1929. National Socialism had its hard core, a sociological base more diversified than that of any other party except the Catholic Center (Zentrum), variously maintained by fear of the department store, fear of communism, fear of the Poles, fear of further decline in the price of farm commodities, and "the politics of cultural despair." The numbers were small but tenacious; the cadres were there.

On the eve of its first great election victory on 14 September 1930, the Party consisted of:

workers	26.3%
white collar	24.0
independent	18.9
civil servants	7.7
farmers	13.2
miscellaneous	9.9

Still more revealing of its sources of support was its age distribution:

18–20	0.4%
21–30	36.4
31–40	31.4
41–50	17.6
51–60	9.7
61–	4.5

In the Party groups in Berlin, Halle-Merseburg, Mecklenburg-Lübeck, the Palatinate, and Württemberg-Hohenzollern, the 21 to 30 year-olds were more than 40 per cent of the total membership. In comparison to the average for the Reich, the underdeveloped areas of South Germany, Lower Bavaria, Franconia, the Palatinate, and Schleswig-Holstein with its chronic agricultural crisis were overrepresented.

The Nazi deputies elected to the Reichstag in September 1930—who, under Weimar's proportional electoral system, were men who had distinguished themselves in the Party apparatus rather than men with direct public appeal—included, by their own identification, 16 in crafts, trade, or industry; 25 employees, both blue- and white-collar workers; 13 teachers; 12 career civil servants; 9 editors and 6 Party employees, together 15 full-time Party functionaries; 8 military officers; a Protestant clergyman; and a druggist, Gregor Strasser; as well as 12 engaged in agriculture. Of the 107, 12 were under 30 (compared with 8 of the 77 KPD deputies), 59 between 30 and 40 (compared with 45 of the 77 KPD deputies, 17 of the 143 SPD deputies). Roughly 60 per cent of the Nazi (and KPD) deputies were under 40, compared with scarcely more than 10 per cent from the SPD.

Hitler's course from here to the Machtergreifung (seizure of power) was, even more than before, tactically rather than ideologically defined. As Weimar's social and political supports collapsed under the impact of the depression, his object, as before, was effectively negative: to do nothing that might antagonize potential support. This went so far, as Theodor Heuss noted, as to exclude Jews as the favored target. Hitler had nothing against "decent" Jews, he is supposed to have told a foreign visitor after the September election, and Heuss had the impression that Goebbels' characterization of bourgeois opponents as a "stinking dung heap" caused him genuine embarrassment. Even before the election, Otto Strasser—a "utopian socialist," as he considered himself—left the Party, antagonized by a series of what he felt to be officially sanctioned harassments and outraged, he reported, by Hitler's evident opportunism. There was no such thing as social or economic revolution, Hitler is supposed to have told him, redistribution of ownership was a Marxist chimera, the economy in its existing form was inviolable, and socialism meant nothing more than State intervention to assure the prevention of conflict. He even rejected autarky. "Do you think we can isolate ourselves from the world economy?" he asked. Nazis were forbidden to join a strike in Saxony in April 1930, another of Strasser's sore points. In October 1930 when the dimensions of a metalworkers' strike in Berlin made this impossible, the Party dispatched its economic advisor, the retired major Otto Wagener, to persuade Saxon industrialists that the alternative was a mass migration to the SPD. Officially Hitler announced in the *Völkische Beobachter* that participation in the strike was intended to teach German industry a lesson in the consequences of observing the conditions of the Versailles Treaty.

At the same time, the Party permitted itself occasional displays of its old radicalism. On 14 October 1930, the newly elected Reichstag deputation presented a bill demanding confiscation of all bank and brokerage fortunes, of the property of all East European Jews who had arrived in Germany since 1914 and of all profits accruing from the war or speculation, as well as nationalization of the larger banks and a maximum interest rate of 4 per cent. But they withdrew it in the face of the SPD and KPD who threatened to support it, knowing this would frighten Hitler's financial supporters, and equally in the face of Germany's economists who bought newspaper space to testify to the bill's impracticability. In early 1931 a bill in the budget committee of the Reichstag forbidding the acquisition of any further public debts and the financing of all public works with interest-free Reich credit bills testified to the survival of Feder's influence and the old populist spirit. So, in May 1932, did Strasser's famous proclamation of the antikapitalistische Sehnsucht (anticapitalist yearning), with its demands that Germany go off the gold standard, increase its farm productivity, break up its urban concentrations, create a rural labor service, control farm prices and wages, finance cheap credits, and lower interest rates.

But Hitler's course led away from specific demands rather than toward them, even at the risk of offending potential radical support like the SA, which was already susceptible to mutiny, or like the young Reichswehr lieutenant Richard Scheringer whose indignation about the Party's apparently anti-revolutionary course led him in 1931 to make a public switch to the KPD. The Party was becoming respectable, and Hitler, concerned very much with votes and financial support and very little with ideological consistency, did his best to ease and hasten the process. Fritz Thyssen reported later that Hitler had given him the impression that he intended to clear the way for a restoration of the monarchy, while the young and foolish Prince of Schaumburg-Lippe told of Hitler's assurance that his movement had room for monarchists and republicans alike. Thyssen agreed to underwrite the Party. Schaumburg-Lippe volunteered to campaign actively in its support and noted by 1931–32 that his relatives—one of the Kaiser's sons among them—already had not only accepted "high and highest" positions in the party and SA but had been sent ahead as Landtag and Reichstag deputies. Krebs, at the same time, noted that the later Hamburg Gauleiter Karl Kaufmann, then close to the Strasserite wing of the Hamburg Party, had been censured from Munich for his critique of Hitler's "Harzburg Front" with Alfred Hugenberg and the Stahlhelm, and that he himself was being edged out of his position as press secretary of the Party by a man with the "best connections" to the Hamburg merchant bourgeoisie.

Still presented in their "inviolability," the twenty-five points of the Party program were meanwhile subjected to a creeping violation intended to reduce any remaining resistance in yet untapped electoral reservoirs. As early as 1928 Hitler had replied to a challenge from the farmers' organizations by declaring that the land reform envisaged in the Party program would not lead to expropriations. The phrase "uncompensated expropriation," he stated, referred only to Jewish speculators. The Party stood firmly in support of private property. In its practical activity, the Party went still further. When the SPD in Brunswick presented a bill granting the state automatic priority of purchase right in sales of land, a bill whose language was copied directly from Rosenberg's official exposition of the land-reform paragraph in the Party program, eight of the nine Nazi deputies voted against it. As early as 1928, this combination of tactical accommodation with falling prices resulted in a steep climb in rural support, particularly in hitherto untapped North and East German Protestant areas.

Appealing to the middle class, Feder confined the problem of profit-sharing to the very largest industrial concentrations like the I. G. Farben, then redefined it as simple price-reduction, which would bring its benefits to everyone, rather than confining it to employees of the firm concerned. He also distinguished between "moral" industrialists and "anonymous, depersonalized" corporations. Rosenberg left the problem to the future. Still more important than ideological concessions was political organization in the form of the Kampfbund für den gewerblichen Mittelstand (Small Business Action League), another fellow-traveler group, under the leadership of Theodor Ardian von Renteln, earlier the Party's first youth leader. The organizing of fellow travelers was meanwhile extended to every other possible interest group—to lawyers, doctors, teachers, schoolboys, and to women whose organizers were instructed to avoid titles, uniforms, and class appeals, and to concentrate instead on Christianity, motherhood, and the family as the basis of the future Reich. Hung above each subappeal—fixed prices for the farmers, jobs for the unemployed, liberation from competition with big competitors for small business, and careers open to talent for the young—was the general appeal of "Rescue Germany," an idealized form of "sauve qui peut," as Geiger said, directed at a population that had lost the selfconfidence of 1848 and 1870 and was now prepared to throw itself into the arms of its own desperation. Underpinning it was a style composed equally of radical activism, military hierarchy, and the grandiose hocus-pocus of a fraternal lodge, embellished with stars, stripes, oak leaves, medals, and badges. Hitler's Party had become a revolutionary mass organization whose members addressed one another with the formal, plural "Sie" rather than the familiar "Du." . . .

Seen against its social background, National Socialism is far too complicated a phenomenon to be derived from any single source or reduce to any single common denominator, whether it be the depression or the course of German history. Its very dynamism precluded easy generalizations. If, before 1930, the NSDAP tended to be a Party of völkisch true believers, like the Göttingen Nazis who saw their mission in the compilation of a directory of Jews in German academic life, it tended after 1930 to be an organization of the economically desperate with a considerable admixture of opportunism. "When I joined the NSDAP," Fritzsche testified at Nuremberg, "I did not have the impression of joining a Party in the conventional sense since this was a Party without a theory. . . . All the Party theoreticians were under fire. . . . There were already whole groups of former DNVP members in the NSDAP or of former Communists. . . ."

"The formula, 'National Socialism is exclusively that which So-and-so says or does,' whereby the particular proponent was referring to himself, replaced the Party program . . . ," Hans Frank declared in his memoirs. "Any number of names filled the formula at the start: Hitler, Goering, Strasser, Röhm, Goebbels, Hess, Rosenberg, and more. There were as many National Socialisms as there were leaders."

The most general theory—that National Socialism was a revolution of the lower middle class—is defensible but inadequate. National Socialism had a striking appeal for the Auslandsdeutsche, Germans who had spent the impressionable years of their lives in a German community abroad. Whether at the microcosmic level of the Göttingen Party or in important positions in Munich, like Rosenberg or Darré, there was an impressive number of them. National Socialism was no less a revolt of the young against the old. While a theory of National Socialism as a lower middle-class phenomenon applies very well to voter behavior, it fails to account for important sectors of Party leadership with their violent animosity toward the social forms for which their voters yearned. Himmler's contempt for the bourgeois self-indulgence of railway dining cars was no more a lower middle-class attitude than the longing for action, power, nights of the long knives, or a radical reorganization of society, shared by the Party's leaders. National Socialism drew unmistakably on the historical reserves of liberal support, but its leaders were unequivocally sworn to the destruction of liberal values and liberal society.

This hard core of revolutionary destructiveness existed before the depression in quantities too great to be dismissed as simple personal idiosyncrasy.

The longing for security that it exploited existed before the depression as well, but sought its objectives elsewhere in unrevolutionary places. What brought them together, leaders and followers, was a common hostility to the status quo at a moment of unique desperation, a desperation only two parties, the KPD and the NSDAP were fully prepared to exploit. In promising everything to everybody, the Nazis promised nothing to anybody. The tactical pursuit of power obviated any immediate urgency in the discussion of what was to be done once it was attained. As it was to Frank and Fritzsche this was clear to the farmer who told Heberle ". . . we believe that in the Third Reich, we, the farmers, will be so strong a power that we can shape it as we desire." From a contemporary standpoint, National Socialism was wide open, its disparity not a handicap but a positive advantage. What united it ultimately was not a mandate for war and Auschwitz, but a universal desire for change.

Working Class Politics

ROBERT McKENZIE

ALLAN SILVER

Politicization is one of the leading features of modernization. Before modernization, the common people had a political system of their own. Peasant assemblies, for example, were often lively gatherings, making decisions on a variety of issues important to the village. And peasants were aware of wider political relationships, notably those that bound them to a manorial lord. But peasant politics were highly personalized. Peasants lacked an ability to grapple with abstract issues, and there is no doubt that the attitude of the common people toward the central government was not politicized in the modern sense. Peasants and city dwellers might have expected the central government to do some things for them—help out in famines, for example. They had a loyalty to the traditional monarch, but they did not see government as something in which they could or should participate. When they rioted they did not do so to challenge a political structure that excluded them. Indeed, they often explicitly declared their allegiance to the king, even as he sent his troops against them, claiming that he was misled by bad advisers.

We have already seen stages of the transition to a modern political outlook. The nature of modern protest, as Charles Tilly sees it emerging in the mid-nineteenth century, was in large measure based on political demands. Socialism served as a vehicle for voicing political as well as economic demands. Socialist politics became central to the lives of many workers, in Germany and elsewhere. Nazism was politicization of another sort, drawing some types of people into the political process for the first time. These examples alone show how complex politicization has been and how difficult it is to predict its results.

Each nation has something of its own political style. Elements of the English lower classes began to be politicized in the mid-eighteenth century. They participated in a number of radical political movements until 1848. Since then, their politics have been rather moderate by European standards. A labor party developed late, rising to importance only after 1900, and its socialism was mild and undogmatic. Nevertheless, as the party grew, British politics seemed to polarize around class interests and to express class antagonisms in the same way, if in more muted form, as in France or Germany. The Labour Party, like many Marxist parties, claimed to be the party of the workers. Yet in no country did political lines ever coincide more than roughly with class lines. Hence the following passage, though based on a British study, has wider applicability in its comments on the different forms politicization can take.

The selection assesses the different kinds of self-images that lead to distinctive voting as well as the various kinds of broader loyalties that find expression in politics. In this sense it explores the ways in which workers have participated in some of the larger movements of modern times—not only socialism, but nationalism as well. Basic differences have developed about what the political process itself is, with a major question being not only what party is selected, but whether workers will bother to vote at all. European workers have voted with decreasing frequency since the Second World War; in the United States, where politicization developed sooner, voting rates began to drop even earlier in the twentieth century. Is politicization receding? Did modern political ideas ever thoroughly replace traditional views? Or is a disgruntled segment of the population struggling to find new expression for an intense but frustrated political consciousness?

. . . Conservative and Labour working class voters are in many respects similar sorts of people. But we have dealt so far almost entirely with certain of their social characteristics. This chapter explores differences and similarities in the realm of ideas between voters for the two parties. It is not primarily concerned with attitudes to current political issues. Its aim is rather to investigate some of the broad perspectives of working class voters which may dispose them to support one or the other of the major parties over long periods of time.

Conservative spokesmen never tire of explaining that Conservatism is not a doctrine or an explicit blueprint for society; it is fundamentally a set of attitudes towards life itself, towards the nature of society and social change, towards the nation and one's place in it. To what extent are the basic assumptions of Conservatism reflected in the social thought, however rudimentary, of working class Conservative voters? And how different are working class voters for the two major parties in their broad and fundamental outlooks on these matters?

For this purpose, it is essential to have some measure of the degree to which voters are committed to the parties. We divided Labour and Conservative voters into two groups, called *constants* and *changers*. *Constants* are those who both voted for a particular party at the previous general election and expressed a clear intention to do so again at the next. *Changers* are those who did not express an intention to vote again for the party they supported in the last general election. (In almost all cases, changers said they "did not know" which party they would support. Since all informants in the sample had voted at the last general election, it is unlikely that the changers include a significant number of habitual non-voters.)

The distinction between constants and changers is intended to measure degrees of party commitment during a period between elections. Although most changers doubtless ended by voting in the subsequent election for the same party they had supported in the last, they can as a group be seen as less committed to a party than are the constants. That the Conservatives were relatively unpopular at the time of interviewing, according to opinion polls, means that Conservative constants are fairly hard-core Conservative voters.

Images of the Parties

We wanted voters to describe their images of the two major parties in their own terms, unprompted by terms or phrases suggested by the interview itself. Almost at the start of the interview, therefore, we asked a series of "open-ended" questions, which encouraged them to talk at length and in their own words, about their general perception of the Labour and Conservative parties. Only later in the interview did we ask informants to evaluate the parties with respect to specific matters, using "closed-ended" questions which they could answer by choosing among alternatives supplied by the interviewer. Thus, we hoped to obtain informants' spontaneous descriptions of the parties.

For this purpose, we asked the following questions: "Suppose you had a friend or relative from Canada who was visiting this country, and he asked you what the Conservative and Labour parties are like. How would you answer him? First, what would you tell him the Conservative party is like? Would you tell him anything else about the Conservative party? What would you tell him the Labour party is like? Would you tell him anything else about the Labour party?" This wording was intended to avoid giving the working class informants any impression that the interviewer, as a person with more education and of higher social status, was investigating the extent of their political knowledge. It also left completely open the way in which they could describe the parties (for example, neutrally or evaluatively), and which aspects of the parties they might choose to describe (for example their leadership, policies, general philosophy). The replies were recorded verbatim.

To deal with these replies, some framework of analysis is required. Inevitably, this involves a process of condensation and abstraction, for such a framework is designed not to take into account every variation in response but to illuminate some major themes contained in them. On analysing the response to this series of questions we found that four such major themes could be identified. The great majority of informants perceived the parties primarily in terms of one or other of the following considerations:

1. The extent to which the respective parties served the interests of particular social classes.
2. The extent to which they did or did not serve the national interest.
3. The intrinsic personal characteristics of the party's leaders and members.
4. Substantive party policies.

The replies were further classified in terms of favourable or unfavourable references to particular parties (Chart 1).

When working class Labour voters were asked what the parties are "like," they tended overwhelmingly to reply in terms of class and, rather less frequently, in terms of policy (usually with reference to welfare policy). Working class Conservatives, on the other hand, most frequently described the parties in terms of their policies. But in addition, two other themes emerge in their replies which are only very rarely mentioned by Labour voters. The Conservatives frequently described the parties in terms of the extent to which they serve the national interest. And they placed much stress on the personal qualities of the leaders of the respective parties. Indeed, if these two themes are considered together, they are mentioned even more frequently than the policy differences between the parties. (It will also be noted in Chart 1 that the Conservatives very rarely describe their own party in class terms.)

This unprompted stress by working class Conservatives on the national interest and on personal qualities of leadership is of great importance. The first of these themes is perhaps the most insistent in the whole literature of Conservatism and the second, although offered now in rather more muted form than in earlier periods, is an almost equally fundamental Conservative assumption: that they are *intrinsically* better qualified, in personal terms, to lead the nation.

The following are verbatim replies in which working class Conservatives explain what the party they support is like.

> [The Conservative party] more or less gets its name because it's quiet and stable. They don't uphold nationalization. They have some of the best brains in the country. They are altogether more successful and brainy than the Labour, and they have a great deal of experience behind them. They've a tradition of governing and leadership behind them for generations.

> They are businessmen who know what they are doing. They have been brought up to rule, to take over leadership. They have been educated to a certain extent to take over. They have no axe to grind for themselves. They look out for other people . . . all types and the country as a whole, really.

> The Tory people are the brains of the country. They know how to get things done. Everyone of them is a man you can look up to and respect.

> They are for England; well, for the country. They know what they are doing for the country.

Clearly, for some of their supporters, the Conservatives transcend the narrow concerns of partisanship; they are the unique custodians of the national interest. Their experience is intrinsic and inimitable; their intelligence and capacity to govern is of an unmatchable order. Conservatives who are also business leaders are clothed in the robes of traditional aristocracy; older

Chart 1
Evaluations of Political Parties
by Conservative and Labour Voters

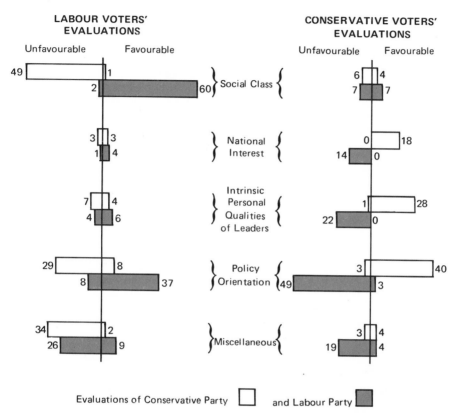

LABOUR VOTERS'
EVALUATIONS

CONSERVATIVE VOTERS'
EVALUATIONS

Unfavourable   Favourable

Unfavourable   Favourable

49 | 1 } Social Class { 6 | 4
2 | 60 7 | 7

3 | 3 } National { 0 | 18
1 | 4 } Interest { 14 | 0

7 | 4 Intrinsic 1 | 28
4 | 6 } Personal { 22 | 0
Qualities
of Leaders

29 | 8 } Policy { 3 | 40
8 | 37 } Orientation { 49 | 3

34 | 2 } Miscellaneous { 3 | 4
26 | 9 19 | 4

Evaluations of Conservative Party ☐   and Labour Party ■

Summary. This chart was based on a series of open-ended questions: "Suppose you had a friend or relative from Canada who was visiting this country, and he asked you what the Conservative and Labour parties are like; how would you answer him? First, what would you tell him the Conservative party is like? Would you tell him anything else about the Conservative party? What would you tell him the Labour party is like? Would you tell him anything else about the Labour party?" Percentages do not total 100 since some informants did not volunteer favourable or unfavourable evaluations or replied in terms of more than one of the categories used to classify evaluations. The uppermost bar in the left half of the chart may be used to illustrate how to read it: It shows that 49 per cent of Labour voters referred unfavourably and 1 per cent favourably, to the Conservative party in terms of social class criteria. In general, Labour voters were more likely to describe the parties in social class terms; Conservative voters, in policy terms. Conservatives were also more likely to use the rhetoric of national interest and to mention personal characteristics of leaders.

and newer elites are fused. Indeed, for many working class Conservatives the very fact that many of the party's leaders are wealthy is in itself a special recommendation:

> I always go by money. If you haven't got money it's no good, so you have got to go to the party with capital. It is a good party. I think that covers everything. When you say capital, that means everything, because without it you can't do anything, and the Conservatives have the money.

> If you vote for Conservatives—the motto I was taught when I was a boy was if you mix with money you can gain some. I feel the same. When the Labour got in, the Conservatives froze the money. It makes unemployment.

> The Conservatives are very good and have done a lot for the working people since they were in power. I've always had a good opinion of them. Without them there wouldn't be any money in the country. They are the people with the knowledge and they know how to use it.

Some of these voters appear to make little distinction between the public treasury and the private wealth of Conservatives. For others, the power of money is incontestable and definitive; before it, the working class has no choice but to acquiesce, whether in respect or in helplessness. Both views are reminiscent of themes in older Conservative propaganda directed to the working class: the solicitous concern of the traditional elite for the common man, and the unique support due the business elite because of its control over financial resources.

Working class Conservatives' unfavourable evaluations of Labour are similarly patterned. In policy terms they condemn Labour for its support of nationalization, its wastefulness, and its hindering of initiative and enterprise. But they also judge Labour unfavourably in terms of the national interest and the personal qualities of the party's leaders. Labour is frequently seen as selfish and greedy, incompetent, uneducated, and moneyless and as lacking the inherent virtues of a traditional elite.

> Most of them who are in the Labour party are out to see what they can gain for themselves and friends financially. They haven't the brains to run the country.

> They are a poorer class and they might not fully understand how to rule, as it is so difficult for people who are not educated and most of them are not. They are undoubtedly for the poorer group of people.

> The Labour party muffed up the health service. I think to a certain extent they mean well but they overstep the mark. They try to do things for us but in the end we are worse off. The health service is exorbitant.

> Labour is a good party but what they tell you they are going to do, it is impossible. Financially, if the revenue isn't coming in they can't give the

pensions. They have been in twice in the last twenty-five years and each time they have come out the country has been financially flopped.

There is so much trouble and gossip between them. They're unreliable. They don't seem to know where they are going. They don't agree with one another. Really they are all talk and they don't seem to get anywhere. They are always arguing among themselves.

Thus, even where Labour is credited with good intentions towards the common man, it is seen as hampered by incompetence and confusion, as though Labour were more solicitous than efficacious. The Conservatives, though perhaps less solicitous, are more efficacious and therefore can do more for ordinary people. But Conservatives also point to the superiority of their party's policies:

The Conservatives have the right idea. You've got to get down to competitive prices—their policy of trying to make things cheaper, of keeping prices down. They are out to manufacture things cheaper to compete with overseas. . . .

I'm . . . quite satisfied with [the Conservatives'] policy—quite satisfied with the health service and cost of living. The wages are quite good—they maintain a high standard. All their pensions schemes are good. When they feel they can do something for us, they do. Things are not left to stagnate; they are progressive. Regards the H-bomb, Labour wants to give it up; I don't agree with that—Britain should hold her own, like the Conservatives say.

I would say that the Conservatives have done well as regards housing, labour, and schools. There is more of a headway as regards work—if you start a business, there is more opportunity. . . .

These replies are expressed in far more pragmatic terms than those which refer to the national interest or to the intrinsic virtues of the party's leaders. The Conservatives are credited with the promotion of wise policies which have encouraged both private initiative and the general well-being of the community; they are in this sense judged on their record rather than on the basis of an intrinsic superiority attributed to their elite background or their wealth. There are clearly two rather different perspectives from which working class Conservatives view the parties.

In this respect, working class Labour replies were much more homogeneous; they almost never spoke in terms of the national interest or of the qualities of the party leaders but stressed with overwhelming frequency the differing class bases of the parties and the relative merits of their policies, especially with regard to social welfare and employment.

Labour stands for the working man, the other lot [the Conservatives] are no use to us.

> They're [Labour] the working man's party, aren't they? They give us better pensions.

> Labour does more for the poor. They care more for ordinary people.

> We've always been with Labour; it runs in the family I guess. They try to do more for people like me.

> The Labour try to help the old folks; that's all I can think about them.

> Labour are for the ordinary people; Conservatives back the rich.

> I guess there's not much difference [between the parties], but I've always been Labour. Why should I change?

In these representative descriptions by Labour voters of the party they support, there is an almost complete absence of any reference to "socialism" or a "new social order." That section of the working class which supports Labour appears to do so almost entirely through class loyalty and the expectation of greater social benefits from a Labour government.

> It's not politics that make me vote Labour—it's a case of the one that helps you most. Only wish I was in the position to vote Conservative.

> . . . I've got to study my own self first, but if I had a well-paid job I should vote Conservative.

> The Conservatives are all for themselves. They would give you a ride in a car on the day of the election and run you over the next.

Even some of Labour's own supporters seem to feel that the party's good intentions are flawed by its inability or powerlessness, as these comments by Labour voters suggest:

> They have the right ideas, but don't go the right way about them.

> Some very big ideas, but not the money to carry them out. The wrong kind of men in the party. Their ideas are good, if only they had the backing to carry them out.

Another Labour voter, an elderly lower-working class woman, said with some excitement:

> Labour could do as well as the Conservatives, if only they could keep the capital in the country. How you're going to get round that I don't know, but that's the trouble. As soon as they're in, out goes the big money and they don't know what to do about it.

In summary, Conservative and Labour voters' images of the parties are expressed in different terms. Although both frequently see the parties in terms of their policies, the Labour voters are much more likely to describe or evaluate the parties in terms of social class issues and themes. Conservative voters are more likely to speak in terms of party leaders' personal characteristics (disparaging those of Labour and praising Conservative leaders' unique and intrinsic qualifiations to govern) and to use the rhetoric of "national interest." Thus, the fundamental framework in which the parties are viewed differs markedly between working class Labour and Conservative voters, with many of the latter echoing some of the classic themes of Conservative philosophy. . . . [Are] Conservatives in any sense alienated from the political process and therefore less able to locate their "true" political interests within it? One measure of this is informants' sense of "political self-confidence"—their feeling that they and other ordinary people can influence political decisions. We asked, "Do you think that people like yourself have any say in how the country is run?" And after the informant answered, a further question was asked, "Why do you say that?" The answers were recorded verbatim and subsequently rated as indicating "high," "intermediate," or "low" degrees of political self-confidence.

Conservatives had a generally higher degree of political self-confidence (Chart 2). Indeed, Conservative constants were the most politically confident of all groups. Working class Conservatives, then, seem more politically confident than Labour voters. In this sense, they can hardly be described as less adequately linked to the political process.

Politically self-confident voters for both parties, for example, mentioned the vote as the basis of popular influence with equal frequency; and they tended to speak in much the same terms about the possibility of ordinary people's influencing the course of events.

We can force an issue by petitions. . . .

It's up to us if we have an interest. You could if you had the time.

We have the right to reverse any unsavoury decision by united action.

If you feel strongly about it, you could get yourself heard—I think you could get things done.

The people are the homes and the children that come out of them. You help run the country by your opinions and the things you do.

Those among the self-confident who speak in these terms seem to have in mind either the possibility that the active individual can "get things done" or that a form (usually undefined) of collective action will produce results. But the less confident, whether Labour or Conservative, speak of the powerlessness of the individual in the face of huge organisations such as trade unions, the political parties, and the organs of government.

Chart 2
Conservative Voters Are Less Likely To Feel
That They Have No Influence over Government

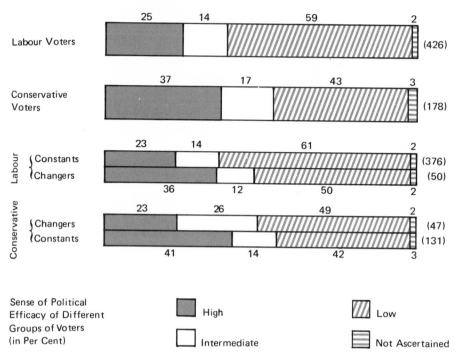

Summary. Of Conservative voters, 43 per cent were classified as low in sense of political efficacy, compared with 59 per cent of Labour voters. Labour constants are lowest in sense of political efficacy (61 per cent), and Labour and Conservative changers are nearly the same. The results for those high in sense of political efficacy are not so clear cut.

Not in Labour unless you go and join the trade unions and fight to get to the top. And you can't get on in the Conservative party without a lot of money.

I can vote, but it's no use, they are overruled by unions. We need stronger action to control [unions]; they have too much influence over our M.P.'s.

It is Labour against Conservatives. It is one party against another. I don't think we can have any say in it.

If you want to get any satisfaction at your town hall, you can go in front and pass from one to another till you are out at the back. You can never get in touch with them.

The individual is lost.

The outright defeatism of the last remark frequently recurred and was often expressed in terms of social class:

> The likes of us don't get a chance.

> It's only the upper class who have any say—because they have the money.

> The working class people are at the bottom and haven't a big say.

> Working class have no say in the country's affairs; what we'd say would stand for nothing.

> Simple reason is that the ordinary working class person has no say at all in anything.

Very few respondents seemed to share the conception of collective working class strength drawn by one informant:

> To some extent working class opinion goes a long way. We are a big majority, and strong public opinion always does have an effect on anything.

Among those of both parties who were classified as "high" or "intermediate" in political self-confidence, only 5 per cent mentioned trade unions as vehicles which enabled people like themselves to exercise influence. Where the ordinary person is seen as politically efficacious, it is almost always through the polling booth and not through working class political or industrial organisations. And many of those who lack confidence are so pessimistic about the powerlessness of the working class that they seem to view the electoral process as a futile exercise.

> No matter how many times we vote it makes no difference. We working class are always out numbered by the other class, and there are more of them.

Labour voters speak much more frequently of the powerlessness of the working class; and it is the Conservatives who more often see themselves as able to influence those who govern.

These findings, taken together, appear to undermine any conception of working class Conservatives as the non-involved, ill-informed and uninterested members of the working class who acquiesce in the rule of the traditionally dominant upper class party largely through apathy and indifference. On this evidence, the working class Conservatives, compared with their Labour counterparts, are somewhat better informed about politics and more often convinced that people like themselves have some voice in how the affairs of the country are managed.

European Sports Today

ROBERT DALEY

Here is another, more recent view of European sports by an American, a reporter for the *New York Times*. The article makes some suggestions that a decade later seem rather shortsighted and self-satisfied—America the friendly and secure—which shows the danger of making hasty comparisons with one's own country. Daley relies here on notions of American national character that were not solidly researched, even by distinguished social scientists at the time. He also assumes, somewhat dangerously, a unity in important aspects of European character, regardless of the different areas involved.

But the comments on European sports have real merit. Sport in Europe does differ in important ways from sport in the United States. Soccer riots, for example, do not have many recent American counterparts, if only because Americans have been busy rioting elsewhere. The suggestion, then, that sports are a manifestation of, and sometimes fail to sublimate, violent mass impulses in Europe deserves attention. So does the analysis of European fascination with heroic individualism. The preoccupation with speed, not only in sports but in ordinary driving, is not easy to analyze, but it too continues to be an important part of modern European life that cannot simply be explained by the valid claim that cars are somewhat newer to most Europeans than they are to Americans.

On its eighteenth day, when most of the men were already exhausted, the Tour de France bike race pedaled up and over Restefond Pass, nearly 9,300 feet high, the highest road in the Alps. That day's stage started at Antibes—sea level—and as soon as the road began to climb a Belgian named Eddy Pauwels sprinted out ahead of the pack.

Up and up hurried Pauwels, pedaling hard, and as he neared the pass he was minutes ahead of the pack. The race was above the clouds now, the air so fine a man could scarcely breathe, much less pedal a bike. As Pauwels crossed the pass, sweat was streaming off him, he was gasping for breath and his eyes were glazed by fatigue.

Down into the valley he plunged, sometimes at speeds of sixty miles per hour or more, the frail bike shivering with strain as he wrenched it around turns; then up, up again, over other passes. He was still ahead, but so tired

From Robert Daley, *The Bizarre World of European Sports* (New York: William Morrow, 1963), pp. 1–9, 83–87, 156–60. Copyright © 1963 by Robert Daley. Reprinted by permission of William Morrow and Company, Inc., and the Sterling Lord Agency, Inc.

now he began to crash. Three times in simple bends he was thrown to the road. Also, the road tore his tires to bits. He got five flats, fixing them himself, frantically, his fingers fumbling with valves, pumps, spokes, half-crazed with haste and exhaustion. Each time he remounted, wiped the blood from his face, and pedaled on.

The flats and the crashes took all that was left out of Eddy Pauwels. After leading the race over the highest part of the Alps, he was caught up and passed by the pack in the final few miles before the night's finish line. For nearly nine hours he had led the race; in the end he got nothing.

Except that he was the hero of all Europe, loved for "attacking" Restefond Pass, loved for the flats, loved for the crashes, loved for the way he sobbed so bitterly at the finish. Newspaper stories called him "valiant," as "magnificent" as the mountains themselves. TV cameras closed up on him; "What I have done, no beast would have done," he said, and the tears rolled down, streaking the sweat, dust, and blood on his face. Europe wanted to hold him in her arms.

Literally and emotionally, that day was the high point of the 1962 Tour de France, and also of sports in Europe for the year. It was a day of terrible effort, of suffering and pain, of raw danger, of man tiny and lost amid the towering mountains, yet conquering them with his heart and his will. It was a day of grandeur.

For what is really admired in sports in Europe is individual exploit: one man against some sort of terrible adversary. This does not mean another man. To be really exciting to a European the adversary should be partly brute nature at its most fearsome: the sheer wall of a mountain, the sea, a wild beast, tremendous distance, the speed of a race car hurtling past walls and trees; and secondly, the adversary should be partly man himself, his weaknesses as a man: fear and fatigue.

There is violence in sport everywhere, even if only the limited violence of the home run; but in Europe it is a different kind of violence, and there is much more of it. There are reasons why this is so.

Firstly, there is more sport to begin with because there are so many countries so close together, all of them engaging in certain common sports such as car racing and soccer, but all guarding also sports out of their own past: bullfighting in Spain; bareknuckle boxing bouts still fought clandestinely in Britain; bareback horse races round the cobblestone piazzas of Italian towns.

And secondly, there is more violence because Europe is a continent of still smoldering passions; yet it is an orderly place, too. If there were little order (as in Black Africa and parts of Asia and South America) there would be little sport or none at all. And if the people of Europe were as friendly and secure as most Americans, there would be less violence. But the people of Europe are not friendly and secure. On the whole they are suspicious. They keep expecting something to erupt. They have lived with violence a long time. They are used to it.

And so they find violence in their sport—or put it there. With one exception, games do not really interest them. Too tame. The exception is soccer, a diversion akin to baseball in that there is no violence, no body contact at all, in either game when properly played.

That is, in soccer there is no violence on the playing field. There is often plenty, too much, even, in the grandstand. Three or four times a year in countries as widely different in temperament as Poland, Italy, Austria, and Spain fans go beserk at soccer matches. Players have been shot from the grandstand, or kayoed by rocks, although this is less usual than general riots. Some riots are colossal in size. In a towering rage fans tear out seats to fling at players and officials—and also at each other. The fixtures of entire stadiums have been uprooted, destroyed, and while the riots last, players barricaded themselves in dressing rooms in fear and trembling. One team in Italy keeps a chauffeur and car, engine running, under the grandstand, ready to hustle the referee out of town the instant a riot starts.

Soccer riots and "incidents" are front page news in Europe. Fans read of them avidly. It has always seemed to me that the possibility of a riot, or at least a good fist fight in the grandstand, is one of the appeals of soccer. Certainly soccer stars, while well-paid and well-known in all the countries, are not nearly so rich and famous as an ace bike racer, car racer, bullfighter. And if soccer matches draw big crowds, it is partly because there are so many of them, and because they are so much cheaper and more accessible than the heroic, violent sports.

For Europeans cannot wholeheartedly admire team spirit, team play, or team victory. Only Britain is strong on the *team;* teamwork is taught in the schools there during daily recreation periods, and many team games flourish. But for centuries in schools on the Continent boys have been given all work and no play. School often started at 8:00 A.M. and lasted till five or later in the afternoon. No recreation was organized. Boys, being boys, found ways to play, nonetheless, but mostly this meant running, jumping, climbing, something a boy could do on his own, or at least without any need for special equipment, special play areas or adult referees. Teams rarely existed, and boys learned nothing about teamwork. It was every man for himself. This became the national attitude, and carried over into national taste in sport. Sport must be individual, and if possible, terribly challenging.

Put a man, or two men roped together, on the north face of the Eiger Mountain in a storm, and Europe will wait anxiously to know what happens to them. If they are killed, no one will say, "They were asking for it." Instead the whole continent will be saddened, and the feeling will be that man (not just those two men) has been defeated again.

Recently a man named José Meiffret, aged fifty, pedaled a bicycle behind a Mercedes acting as windbreak at 128 miles per hour. This is insanely dangerous, of course. The record Meiffret broke was his own, for no one else is crazy enough to try such pedaling. There was no prize, monetary or otherwise, to be won. He did it because, he said, he was sure he could do it; therefore he had to.

The attempt, which took place on an autobahn in Germany, cost Meiffret, a Frenchman, about one thousand dollars. There is small chance he will get any of this back. All he has earned is fame, via television and news-reels, and the sympathy and admiration of nearly all Europeans.

Or take the case of Louis Lourmais, a swimmer who stroked his way fifty-three miles from Sein Island off the coast of Brittany, up the estuary of the Odet River to Quimper. There is no comprehensible reason why anyone should want to swim this route; it is not even a straight line. But Lourmais wanted to badly enough to stay in the water for three days. When finally he dragged himself onto the quai at Quimper an excited crowd applauded tumultuously. Lourmais could not have been too thrilled by this as he was trembling uncontrollably from fatigue, and could not even talk.

All over Europe individuals, on their own, constantly attempt feats which are bizarre, incredibly difficult and completely without significance. A fifty-six-year-old English lady hikes from the Scottish border to Land's End in twenty-three days. A Frenchman drives his motor scooter virtually nonstop from Rheims to Jerusalem and back during fifteen straight days.

Each time Europe watches avidly. Indeed, it is certainly the interest of the Continent, the receptions, flowers, speeches at the end which perpetuate such attempts at "exploits."

Most likely, America would be amused by some of these people, though not by many. All would be considered some kind of nut. The fifty-six-year-old English lady, Dr. Barbara Moore, hiking from Scotland south, drew such crowds that they trod on her feet; she held the front pages of Europe for weeks. Later, expecting a similar triumph, she marched from San Francisco to New York—to the massive indifference of the United States. This confused the old girl mightily, for her much shorter hike in Britain had made her the heroine of eighteen countries. When she got home, she began tramping about making petulant speeches, avowing her complete distaste for the New World.

On the organized level, sport in Europe still leans heavily on the individual, and on exploit. Europe is not so much interested in watching skill as in watching heroes cope with epic suffering, epic danger, epic fatigue.

The bike race is all of these things. The bike race came into prominence in an era when everyone pedaled to work. Today the bicycle as transportation is ceasing to exist in Western Europe. Each year more cars and fewer bikes are sold, and hardly anyone rides bikes except the very young. Nonetheless, bike racing remains the queen of European sport, precisely because it satisfies all that a European demands of sport: it is individual, it is heroic in concept, grandiose in scale. Just to finish one is an exploit, meaning that at every finish line the fan has fifty or seventy or a hundred heroes to applaud.

The twenty-two-day, 2,600-mile Tour de France bike race is world fa-mous. But there are dozens of other Tours nearly as long: the Tour of Italy,

Tour of Spain, Tour of Yugoslavia, Tour of Switzerland, Tour of Luxembourg, and so on. The Communists run a Tour from East Berlin to Prague to Warsaw, but call it the Peace Race.

Bike races last so long, involve so many racers (sometimes more than a hundred fifty start a major Tour) and spend so many days high in the mountains that drama, violence—in short, *exploit*—are virtually inevitable.

Consider the most recent Tour of Italy. Three weeks in length, it was to pedal over Alps, Apennines and Dolomites for twelve days; often the route would be dirt roads high up and soaked by spring thaws.

For two weeks nothing much happened, beyond a few crashes, a few fights, a few accusations of collusion, doping and the like. There was no blistering heat on the plain, and the mountains were high but docile enough. Then, in the Dolomites, a blizzard struck the race.

For seven hours the race pedaled up through wind and storm. Snow fell steadily. It was bitterly cold. Shivering riders begged sweaters, pants, gloves from coaches, officials, and journalists following in cars. There were not enough to go round. Hour after hour the storm beat down on the race, the thin wheels running ever deeper, ever more slowly in the snow.

Riders abandoned by the dozens. The world champion, Rik Van Looy, led twenty men into a farmhouse, where they huddled around a fire drinking all the wine and grapa they could find. The great Charly Gaul of Luxembourg stumbled up the mountain on foot, two Italian peasants trying to talk to him. One pushed Charly's bike, the other held an umbrella over his head.

Riders were taken away suffering from frostbitten fingers and toes. Peasants walked up and down the road collecting abandoned bikes. In all, fifty-five men abandoned the race during the one hallucinating stage, refusing to pedal anymore under the driving blizzard.

Europeans, reading about this the next day, were moved, excited, thrilled. To them, this was sport. This was the kind of emotion which no game, played according to rules under perfect conditions in some stadium somewhere, could ever give.

The prosaic sports do exist. There are international competitions every year in soccer, rugby, basketball, volley ball, water polo . . .

But in none of these sports does a man really risk anything. Not only do men not risk their lives, they do not even risk defeat or glory, both of which accrue only to the team. The European wants to cheer (or revile) a man like himself, one man, not a mass, not a team. And so some Europeans are interested in one or more team sports, but Europe as a whole is not.

To draw any kind of crowd for such events, it must seem nation against nation, rather than team against team. Let flags wave and anthems play, and Europe then will watch. If it cannot be man against exploit, then let it be one nation's team (youth) against another nation's team (youth), and all can watch and cheer in a spirit of patriotism. This is true even in soccer, where the biggest matches by far are international matches, and where there are now about thirty major international tournaments per year.

I do not mean to give the impression that Europe as a whole is blood-thirsty. I do not think it is. Few, if any, Europeans attend the blood sports (so-called) hoping to see blood. They have seen enough of that in their own towns, on their own doorsteps in other years. No, the audience is there to watch man cope. Cope with the brute enemy, with his own nerves, with fatigue. Cope with being a man.

Europe does not admire daredevils. The car racer is a big man in Europe, but this is because the European sees him as an individual trying to make a living in the most dangerous of all sports; if he were truly a daredevil (the European feels) he would have been dead long ago. Ski racers are considered much more foolhardy and are much less highly regarded. The skier is known to be a very young man probably of peasant stock who is stronger in the legs than the head. However, the skier is credited with great skill, because merely to get to the bottom in one piece is an achievement. The tracks in Europe (man against the mountain again) are bulldozed sheer and treeless so that the skiers often exceed sixty miles per hour standing on their own two feet. On one track in Italy, Adrien Duvillard of France averaged fifty-nine miles per hour winning, and at the steepest part of the track was clocked at eighty-three.

The European is fascinated by speed, understanding the lure; and by weight lifting too, understanding that under the ponderous load thick-thighed man is at his most frail, for his tendency to overreach himself is ultimately irresistible.

Most of all, the European is fascinated by suffering, especially if it is colossal enough; most years in the spring there is a walking race, 285 miles from Strasbourg to Paris, nonstop, during three days and nights, up and over the "wall of sleep" that third night into Paris while Europe watches baffled, yet full of wonder: how can men do it? Each summer hordes of people swim, or fail to swim, the English Channel; in the East they are hauled shivering and exhausted out of the Bosporus and the Caspian Sea just about as often. There used to be a three-day bike race nonstop (Paris-Brest-Paris) and there still is one which lasts about sixteen hours, leaving Bordeaux at two o'clock in the morning and reaching Paris late the next afternoon. There is an eight-day car race (the Auto Tour of France) which is contested virtually nonstop, the men finishing dirty, unshaven, and half-blind with the need to sleep. In the Alps nearly every expedition lasts two days or more. Once an Italian, Walter Bonatti, scaled the Aiguille du Dru alone. It took him seven days. For most of six nights he slept standing up in a sleeping bag hanging by a rope over the black void. Each day he inched a little closer. The skin was gone from his hands, he was numb with cold, tortured by thirst. Terror and exhaustion fought for control of his soul. On the seventh day he clawed his way over the peak—and was joyously pummeled and embraced by a group of his friends, who had come up the "easy" way.

Skill and competition are admired by the European. But it is exploit that he loves.

In Europe, car racing (and to a lesser extent motorcycle racing) is the most serious sport. Scientific genius, money, national pride, and exquisite personal risk are all in it in equal amounts. At each Grand Prix or major sports car race, the investment by the nation, the factory, the organizer and the driver is tremendous. In American oval track racing in the past the machines were slapped together by mechanics. They were skilled mechanics, but still just mechanics. The nation had no stake in the matter, nor did even a major factory. The organizer had no great task, for an oval is easy to sell tickets to, and easy to police. The drivers still risked their lives, but only as individuals, not as standard-bearers; they were, except to a few devotees, nameless, faceless men. Dead today, forgotten tomorrow.

In Europe, at its simplest, a Belgian contract driver for an Italian factory wins, say, the British Grand Prize. At its most tragic, the Spanish driver of a German machine hurtles off the road to slaughter French spectators, and the entire continent goes into mourning. But the next year, almost certainly, the race will be run again. It is a showcase for the nation's industry, genius, and brave young men, and must not be allowed to lapse.

In France, guys and girls—and hundreds of tired business men, too—flock to the 132 Go-Kart tracks that now litter the country. They seek a little fun and relaxation at speed.

And in England, a traffic officer observes that fans returning to London after motor races at Silverstone "seem to think they are all Stirling Moss. You get people doing 100 to 130 miles an hour on the M-1 Highway." The points to be made are that France's 132d Kart track will not be her last; and that the English traffic officer, E. S. Turton, is nonetheless against speed limits on public highways. Highways don't have limits in England, anyway.

"I think that how a man drives a car is his own business," says Turton.

All this may be incomprehensible to the American mind, conditioned as it is to rigidly controlled traffic, severely limited speeds, and huge comfortable cars that can easily seat four abreast and are so softly sprung they could cross a golf course at forty miles an hour without jostling a passenger.

In the United States, there is a minority that has discovered the sports car, and an even smaller group that has begun to be interested in Karting.

But the mass of the population persists in considering sports car owners as eccentric, and devotees of speed in any form as sick.

Indeed, speed is seen as an outlet for a titanic inferiority complex.

The one explanation that apparently has not been considered in America is the one that all of Europe long ago accepted as true: Men drive fast because it is fun. France's 132 Kart tracks have all been built in the last year or two. It is impossible to suppose that every Frenchman who frequents them is sick.

America pioneered the fat, comfortable car, which heels so drastically in a turn that the driver glides sideways in the seat and has no notion whatsoever how much tire adhesion he has left or how near the car is to flipping or skidding off the road.

In fairness to Detroit, all of Europe is gradually coming to this same type of machine. Comfort is on the ascendancy in Europe. Most of the new cars are more comfortable and thus less sporty than the old ones.

Formerly, however, the European car was small, tightly sprung, and equipped with bucket seats. It couldn't do more than sixty miles an hour flat out. No one was afraid of it and there was no publicity campaign, such as the American "Speed Kills" to worry the country.

The European car did not heel in tight bends. The driver did not slide across the seat in turns because the bucket seat held him fast.

Stirling Moss, generally regarded as the fastest race driver of the world, has said of racing cars, "I love the way they hold me."

But Dauphines, Volkswagens, Fiats—everything held a man in the old days. In a turn that the driver had entered a bit too fast, the car did not heel or skid. The tail sort of skittered in short jumps, two or three of them, outwards, in what racing drivers call "oversteer." This was accompanied by a slight squeal of tires and pressure on the driver's back and hips from the seat. If he accelerated, the skittering stopped.

It was fun.

If it sounds dangerous to drivers of American cars, this is because such sensations cannot be had safely in a big, soft Detroit machine. They can't be had in many of the big new European cars, either.

Not only are the tightly sprung cars disappearing here, but so are the winding roads (as new highways are built) on which it used to be so much fun to drive them.

This is perhaps the reason Karting is becoming so popular. Karts are tiny four-wheeled platforms powered by motorcycle or lawn mower engines. A Kart holds a man so he can feel—and enjoy— frustrating centrifugal forces.

As for highway driving, speed limits were not necessary here when few cars could exceed sixty. They are becoming more necessary now and, in fact, do exist on some roads during some periods.

Most traffic officials, Turton among them, want to hold off speed limits as long as possible. Turton stations two or three times as many police cars along the M-1 after motor races than normal. This "sobers" drivers, he says.

He and most of his colleagues, however, don't believe in arbitrary limits, nor that speed kills, in itself. They do believe that driving a car is sport, or can be, and that drivers should be smart enough to watch their mirrors and to adjust their speeds to the conditions and circumstances of the moment.

Europe agrees with this thinking, and nearly everyone drives as fast as seems safe at all times, slides around bends whenever possible, and often refuses to let other cars pass until their drivers prove conclusively over several kilometers that they are faster.

In Europe the automobile is still regarded primarily as a contraption built for sport. It is romantic, glamorous. Sports car and Grand Prix races draw enormous crowds. Annually there are a quarter of a million people at Le Mans and the Nürburgring for races. The Grand Prix de Monaco draws more than 50,000, two and a half times the population of the place. In many countries the results of car races are not even printed on the sports pages of newspapers; they go on the front page, or on a news page, together with accounts of riding to hounds, horse shows, and other aristocratic pursuits.

There are also an enormous number of rallies which can be entered by anyone in any type of car. Basically, a rally is run in several stages of prescribed distances at prescribed speeds. A driver may neither undershoot nor overshoot his average without losing points. Points are also lost for dented fenders, for failure to get tanks sealed and route cards stamped at various controls, for not having correct licenses and/or passports, or for getting lost. The rule book for a rally may be forty pages long in complicated legal language; the winner is never known for at least twelve hours after the finish, and sometimes not for days. But Europe loves rallies too. Some draw 125 entries, some over 300.

In the capitals of Europe automobile shows draw tremendous crowds. Hundreds of perfectly ordinary cars are displayed, nothing more, but the public rushes to swarm around them. Newspapers devote pages and pages of space, prime ministers make official visits lasting an hour or more, and in the city itself hotels are filled and it is difficult to find a table at choice restaurants. Rome during the Olympics was not nearly so crowded as Paris (or Geneva, Turin, London) during the annual automobile show.

Cars have raced on public roads in Europe since 1894. The men who drove them were and are heroes to be talked about in hushed tones. Only in the last few years has possession of a car been within reach of the average European. Previously his only contact was in watching races or reading about them. In Europe the automobile has an exotic aura about it which has not existed in the United States for decades.

The Le Mans car race lasts twenty-four straight hours. Two drivers switch off every two hours or so. This relieves incipient cramps perhaps, but is not nearly time enough to relax, to sleep. Round and round the cars go, all night at 115 miles per hour or more with tired men trying to hold their eyes open behind the wheel, trying to hold that absolute pitch of concentration which is a man's only security at such speeds, knowing in their fatigue that any error could be fatal.

The major bike races last three weeks or more, seven hours a day, day after day. Chafed backsides are only one of the riders' problems. Saddlesores erupt, and under constant chafing from the seats, infections start. Some harden to boils. Riders tie raw steaks to the seats, hoping it will help. It rarely does. Even the one-day races are more often tests of stamina than speed. One, Paris-Bordeaux, starts at 2:00 A.M. in the darkest part of the night, the riders pedaling for 350 miles, sixteen straight hours to reach Paris.

The Automobile Tour of France is an eight-day, 5,000-mile disguised Grand Prix. Each year a hundred or more cars start. Twenty-five or so finish, no one in them having slept more than catnaps in a week.

Three nights of the Tour are set aside for "repose," but neither drivers nor mechanics go to bed for more than a few hours. There is too much to do to make sure the cars are fit to roll the following dawn.

In theory the mechanics drive all night, leaving the drivers fresh to drive the hill climbs and closed-circuit races schedule for the following day. But in fact they share even the night driving, for the next day the mechanic has to be awake enough to flash signals from the pits, to oversee hundreds of other details.

Each year there are those who manage to run out of gas in the middle of the night on some desolate back country road with no hope of being rescued till morning.

There are those who try to make up time by sailing through predawn fog but end up ramming other cars which had been proceeding more prudently. There are crashes galore, more than twenty of them, usually.

One year on a single stage of the race, one man lost a wheel, another his wife (she said she had had enough of this nonsense and was going home), and a third lost all of his illusions together with his brakes while plunging down a precipitous mountainside.

But the saddest fate of all is that of the ten or so cars which fail the very last day with the finish in sight.

One driver recently was so tired that he lost control trying to enter a narrow bridge at about fifteen miles per hour. The car climbed slowly up the embankment and fell into the river, which at this time of year was only a few feet deep. The driver could not react fast enough to do anything about it. The next car also went out of control but stuck on top of the embankment. The two men in the river climbed up and helped push the car free so that it could reach the finish even if there was no further hope for victory.

In 1956, the year the Marquis de Portago won the Tour, it drew fourteen pro drivers of the front rank. Nowadays there are only two or three and the Tour attracts little international interest.

Most pro drivers say it is too much work and avoid it. It is loved only by those who consider exhaustion a pretty thing and simple ability to endure the most winning quality in sports.

A man named Pierre Marie, a garage mechanic from Rheims, France, recently returned from his two-week vacation. No loafer, Pierre. Instead of lying in the sun, he hopped on his motor scooter and drove to Jerusalem and back, a mere 7,000 miles in fifteen days.

The trip out took six days and ten hours. The scenery included Switzerland, Trieste, Salonika, Istanbul, the Syrian Desert, Damascus, and Amman as well as some Alps, part of the Balkan chain, and the Taurus Mountains of the Middle East.

Coming back, Pierre, who is forty years old, attempted to go nonstop from Trieste to Rheims (more than 1,000 miles), but he collapsed from bounding up and down in his saddle, from lack of sleep, and lack of food. He finally had to stop at a hotel. Otherwise, he would have made the trip in only fourteen days.

In Rheims now, they are talking about submitting Pierre's performance as a world record. The only trouble is, no one knows whom to submit it to.

Exhaustion Spanish-Style

As final evidence of the European fan's fascination with exhaustion, take the case of Jaime Ostos at Toulouse. Ostos, then twenty-five years old, is a bullfighter, and that year was the second most active matador in Spain and southern France. He is an earnest, steady young man, but not a great star. If he fought often it was mostly because promoters used him to fill cards on which the top names—Antonio Ordonez and Luis Miguel Dominguin—were appearing.

In most of his fights, Ostos killed two of six bulls on the program, working about forty minutes. The work was, of course, dangerous. It was also exhausting, demanding constant movement and intense concentration.

At Toulouse there were six bulls, as usual. But this time there was only one matador—Ostos. He was going to try to play and kill all six himself. A second matador was standing by, just in case. But it was Ostos's show if he could do it.

One-man corridas have been tried before, thought not often, and almost always with unhappy results. Dominguin himself had failed miserably eight years before in that same arena.

A two-hour corrida simply demands too much from the body and spirit of one man. Matadors have been known to faint from exhaustion, sometimes falling toward the horns in the process.

As the matador becomes more and more tired his morale sags to insupportable depths. No sooner is one bull dispatched than a fresh one takes its place. As the afternoon drags on, each succeeding bull seems bigger, stronger, and wilder to the dazed man who must kill it.

Ostos's first triumph was to attract 8,000 persons to the arena. Dominguin had drawn only 5,000 eight years before.

These spectators had not come to see art because Ostos is not an artistic bullfighter. He is valiant and hard-working. His repertoire is moderate.

No, the crowd had come to see exhaustion, to watch a man suffer, to watch two kinds of courage. Fearlessness of the horns was expected of him. Did Ostos also have the kind of courage that can make a man go on and on when there is nothing left inside him but the will to do so?

With his first bull Ostos worked hard but killed badly, and the crowd hooted and whistled derisively. The second bull was small but strong. Ostos gave everything he had, burying his sword to the hilt at the end and winning both ears and the tail.

The third bull was apathetic. Ostos was competent but tired. The crowd was behind him now and gave both ears to him. The fourth beast was a hooker and unworkable. Ostos, leaden with fatigue, dispatched it at length. The crowd was silent.

The fifth bull was one of the biggest and wildest ever seen in Toulouse. The combat was a riot of danger and swirling color, the arena rocked by the noise of the crowd and the air electric with fear for the risks Ostos was taking.

Where Ostos got the strength, no one knew. On and on the fight went, pass after pass without a pause or a moment's respite from tension.

Finally the bull, mesmerized by the cloth and gasping for breath, broke off the fight and Ostos swooped in with the sword. The bull dropped like a stone.

The delirious crowd awarded two ears, the tail, and a hoof to the matador. Ostos, nearly unconscious on his feet, hung on the barrier, gasping and retching.

The last bull raced out. The crowd was roaring for more, more, more. Ostos tried to give it, though now he had nothing left. Sometimes he tottered and nearly fell as the bull charged. Then, near collapse, he started to vomit. He hung two minutes gagging on the fence, then staggered back and killed the bull.

The crowd awarded one final ear, making the day's score seven ears, two tails and one hoof. The crowd carried the exhausted matador back to the hotel on its shoulders, his arms filled with flowers.

Modern Families

FERDYNAND ZWEIG

Most evaluations of modern life require at least passing reference to the family, and the more critical ones usually dwell on the subject. The decline of the family has been a constant theme in European history since at least the early nineteenth century. Indeed, its collapse has been suggested so often that it is a wonder there is anything left still to decay. Clearly, many who have found modern life distasteful have exaggerated their laments about the breakup of the family. But this does not mean that they have not correctly identified trends, for no one denies that great changes have taken place in family structure.

There are several key problems in dealing with modern family history, aside from the difficulty of obtaining adequate information. First, any valid judgment requires an evaluation of the quality of family life before the modern age. Most assessments of the modern family reflect, if only implicitly, deeply held beliefs about the premodern family. Those who find family life deteriorating and modern man bereft of the solidarity he needs to function point to the strength and the diverse functions of the premodern family. Yet we have seen that the premodern family may have had serious inadequacies, so that changes in family structure may conceivably have been good, not bad.

There are related disagreements about the facts of change. The modern family may be seen as a total contrast to its predecessors or as a modification only. Take, for example, the extended family. We have long imagined that premodern families united uncles, aunts, cousins, and grandparents with parents and children. This was a unit that could provide for itself and give guidance and support to all its members. Recent work, however, suggests that the extended family was not united quite so literally as has been assumed. It did not, in western and central Europe, live under the same roof, and it regularly sent members to work for other families; yet there is little doubt that fairly close relationships existed. What happened, then, with modernization? A common assumption is that the extended family disappeared, and many observers believe this was a great loss. Yet studies of twentieth-century European workers reveal that their social life is centered almost entirely within the extended family circle. Great interest is taken in the doings of distant relatives. It is true that the extended family is sometimes (though not always) spread out geographically, but it has not literally disappeared. The question of the stability of marriage raises another set of factual problems. Without doubt, divorce has increased in Europe over the past hundred years. Yet family breakups may conceivably have declined, for we have no way of knowing the rate of desertions before legal divorce became widespread. Add to this the fact that before 1850 the early death of one marriage partner would frequently dissolve the marriage within a decade or so, and one may wonder how decisive the institution of divorce is in the history of the family. There is broad agreement on many trends in family history, but the facts are by no means entirely clear.

Family structure varies with social class and with region. Some historians write of the premodern family as though it were essentially the same everywhere. Other observers claim that family structure has become more homogeneous with modernization. The two views can be partially reconciled. It is possible that in the early stages of modernization families were differentiated by class. The middle class, for example, brought up its children distinctively; the working-class husband released the tensions and frustrations built up at his job by browbeating his wife. In the twentieth century, behavioral differences began to break down once again. Greater equality between marriage partners is now more common at all levels of society, as is reduction of family size, although the reduction has proceeded at different rates at different social levels. Yet important variations remain. The working class still marries younger than the middle class. It cares for its children differently—toilet training is begun earlier, for example, and physical discipline is stricter. These differences are not in all cases the same as those that could be found in the nineteenth century, but it does seem obvious that distinctive family patterns boh reflect and cause key distinctions in social structure. This has to modify any overall generalizations about family evolution. Regional variations are important also. French parent-child relations are stricter than English, and far stricter than American. Divorce rates vary, in part of course because of law.

Finally, after one does the best possible job of getting the facts and making the necessary qualifications, there remains the question of interpretation. We can easily agree that although its importance as a unit of consumption has increased, the family is no longer a key production unit. But what does this mean for the family? For some observers it suggests decay, a loosening of ties, since many family members now work outside the home. For others it suggests a reduction of the tensions and bitterness that family economic relations once involved. No longer, for example, are twenty-five-year-olds normally in their father's economic control, unable to marry before the old man retires or dies. With this kind of family function reduced, the family can become a closer emotional unit, with more affectionate ties between husband and wife and between parents and children. Adolescence has become a part of family structure. There was no clearly defined adolescence in the premodern family, at least in the lower classes; even among the middle class, it did not become a recognized reality until around 1900. The recognition and acceptance of adolescence reflected the decline in the age of puberty and the increased period of schooling to which middle-class children were subjected. Some observers claim that a defined period of adolescence has improved parent-child relationships by giving teenagers a peer group to identify with, thus modifying the authoritarian image of parents. Others find adolescence a symptom of the decline of family closeness resulting from the abandonment of teenagers as they face the problems of puberty and leading to an outright clash between adolescent and parent. Issues of this sort are factual in part, but facts alone are not enough. Evaluations of the modern family are usually highly moralistic. They reflect what the analyst thinks a proper life should be—how much independence people should have, what the proper role of women is, what kind of care children deserve and need, and so on. The following passage is based on sociologist Ferdynand Zweig's elaborate inquiry into working-class life in a number of British factories and manufacturing cities (particularly the Mullard Radio Valve Company in Mitcham) in the late 1950s. Zweig's findings were optimistic, and later observers have taken issue with him on many points. For example, his claim that strains at work have decreased is not universally accepted. But his judgments about family life *per se* have not been directly challenged. They depend heavily on what workers *say* about their families, which is important but not necessarily conclusive.

Zweig's conclusion stresses the importance of very recent changes in workers' family relationships. He suggests a protracted dominance of the authoritarian family. Workers may have a tradition of early marriage, but the satisfactions they now derive from their marriage are new; previously, the family seems to have been an outlet for the frustrations of the adult male. Now the family, far from decaying, has taken on new importance as an emotional unit. But, as in other social classes, an increase in affection can have unpredictable consequences. Zweig discusses the ambiguous effect on children of greater love and attention, and the conflicts that can result within the working class.

One of my standard questions for married men with children concerned their interest in the upbringing and education of their children, and from the answers I could gather that the overwhelming majority took an intense, sometimes passionate interest. The standard phrases which came up again and again, were: "We want to give them a better chance than we had," or "That is the finest thing—to give them every opportunity," or "The children—that's my life," or "We did our best," or "I help them in every shape and form," or "They come first," or "They have everything they want," or "We gave them everything we could."

Fathers of babies often push the pram, give them baths, see them to bed; fathers of toddlers often read them stories, play with them, take them for a walk at weekends; fathers of school-children often go to the school for progress reports and supervise their homework; fathers of adolescents try to apprentice them or find them suitable jobs: "I got a good job for the lad." Time and again I heard instances of considerable sacrifice for the benefit of the children, such as the following:

> A skilled man of forty-four with two children—fourteen and twelve— both in grammar schools: "Last summer I spent £25 for the girl's trip to Switzerland with the school."
> A rubber worker of fifty-one with a boy of fifteen: "Last year I bought him a bicycle for £27 from overtime money."
> Again and again: "I bought her a typewriter," or "I bought him a tape-recorder because he is very musical," or "I bought him an expensive encyclopaedia because he is very clever."

From Ferdynand Zweig, *The Worker in an Affluent Society* (New York: The Free Press, 1962). Reprinted by permission of Heinemann Educational Books Ltd.

A very widespread wish is to keep the children at school "as long as they can make it." To quote a few examples:

A skilled man of thirty-nine with four children, fifteen, ten, nine and one: "If they do well at school I will keep them there as long as I can."

A moulder of thirty-seven with four children, twin boys of nine and two girls, eight and three: "I would like them to keep in school as long as it is good for them. I insured the boys for £300 each at fifteen and the girls for £100 each at fifteen for their later education."

A skilled man of fifty-five with a girl of fifteen in a grammar school: "We want her to go to college if she can make it. We are prepared to make the sacrifice."

A skilled man of forty-four with a boy of fourteen: "I would like him to go to college if he is good enough, anyway to stay at school up to eighteen."

A man of sixty-four with a son of thirty-one, a sanitary inspector: "I spent on my son £300 during his two years at the Royal Technical College in Manchester."

Men rarely had ambitions for themselves, but a great deal of ambition for their children. ("Of course it is all up to them but personally I would like him to be . . .") The ambitions were mostly for professional or staff jobs or for skilled trades. In Vauxhall out of twenty-six men whose ambition for their children were recorded eighteen wanted a professional or staff job, saying: "I want him to be a doctor," or "A lawyer," or "To work in a laboratory," or "On electronics" (a very popular profession), or "To be a teacher," or "I would like him to have a profession and security, unlike myself," or "I would like to push him out of the manual class." Eight men wanted a trade for their sons.

In Workington, of twenty-eight fathers whose ambitions for their sons were recorded, thirteen men wanted professional or staff jobs, often saying: "I would like them to make some sort of a grade," or "I would like them to get into a profession," or "I would like to guide them into some sort of profession" or "I wanted him to become a professional man but he wanted to be a fitter." Thirteen other men wanted to give them a trade, and still two others wanted better jobs for their children than they had themselves. In Dunlop, out of twenty-three fathers, fourteen wanted a professional or staff job and nine wanted a trade for their children. In Mullard, out of seventeen fathers nine wanted professional or staff jobs and seven wanted a trade.

The level of aspiration for the children depended very much on the social position the parents themselves occupied. Those who were semi-skilled or labourers often wanted a skilled trade for their children, while those who were skilled or were supervisors had a higher level of aspiration. (In these four works, out of fifty-four men with professional or staff ambitions for their children twenty-two were skilled and four supervisors, while out of thirty-seven men with trade ambitions nine were skilled and three supervisors.)

Those who had children in grammar schools were proud of mentioning the achievements of their children, often adding: "Oh, she is very clever," or "She is above the average type, not like her father." And those whose children had failed the 11-plus examinations could not hide their disappointment, saying: "We wanted it, but unfortunately he failed," or "I am not worried, he will try again," or "I sent him to a private school," or "It was because of her nerves that she failed."

In Vauxhall out of forty-three children in the age group twelve to seventeen inclusive, eight were in grammar schools, two in high schools and two in technical schools; in Dunlop out of fifty-eight such children, nine were in grammar schools, one in high school and three in technical schools; in Mullard out of forty such children, three were in grammar schools and three in technical schools. The figures seem to suggest a higher proportion of grammar-school children among supervisors and skilled men than amongst semi-skilled or unskilled. Out of twenty children in grammar schools in these three works, twelve had fathers who were skilled or supervisors (actually five skilled and seven supervisors), much above the average for the whole sample.

The ambitions of fathers for their children are often one of the reasons why most young men do not like working with their fathers in the same shop. In Workington where a large percentage of young men worked with their fathers in the same firm, the overwhelming majority preferred working with other men than with their own fathers. Fathers are too critical. As one father suggested, "Fathers want perfection for their sons. We are less patient with our children than with others. Therefore you can understand someone else's children better than your own." And his advice was, "You have to make allowances; if not, they drift away from you."

Are the fathers still strict with their children? I often heard, when I asked this question: "I don't boss them," or "I am not bossy, I try to be friendly," or "I never use force," or "I am like a big brother to them," or "I am like a mother to my children," or "I am not forcing them in anything," or "I guide them but I don't push them."

Is there a social change involved in this attitude? I have no figures to offer here, but from the large qualitative material I would have no hesitation in answering the question in the affirmative. Men often referred to this, saying: "My father had power over us; I can't boss them," or "My father never bothered with us," or "I suppose I am a better father than my own," or "I never saw, in my younger days, a man pushing a pram; he would have been a laughing stock." Women in Mullard also referred to this, comparing their husbands' interest in children with that of their fathers.

There is little doubt that the image of the stern, bullying, dominating and self-assertive father or of the absent father who took no interest in the children, leaving them to the mother, is fast disappearing, and the new image of a benevolent, friendly and brotherly father is emerging. The Oedipus complex, for all I know, might have been a myth with the middle classes, but from my previous enquiries I gained the impression that it had been a stern reality with the working-class males. The man whose life oscillated between the works and the public house, or who came home only for his meals, or the man whose authority was used as a bogey to frighten the children, while the mother slaved around the clock, used not to be exceptional. And this was the background for the frequently distorted image of the father in the working-class man's mind. The "Mum" was the most powerful figure in the mind of the working-class child as, in many cases, she was the only parent who gave full care and full devotion to the child. Now the powerful figure of the "Mum" is receding and the father assumes a nearly equal place.

There are three main factors responsible for this change: First, the fact that many mothers go out to work, and take greater interest in the world around them, not only in the children; second, the part which the nursery school and the school play in a child's life, which is much greater than a generation ago; third, the growing interest of the fathers themselves in the children, which, in most cases, does not fall behind that of the mother.

More specifically I asked both men and women in Mullard whether the men took an equal share with their wives in the upbringing and education. Of sixty-one men, fifty-two contended that they took an equal share, saying: "I share fully," or "Fifty-fifty," or "Between us," or "I do more with the boy, the wife more with the girl," or "I am very keen." Six men said that they took the lead, or "I lay down the law," or "I look after them." Only three said that they "Leave it to the wife."

Out of forty-two women who were asked the same question, thirty-six stated that their husbands shared fully, while only six contended that the children were left more to them.

Another question which I explored in Mullard was the measure of devotion to parents, both as regards their relations to their own parents and their children. Out of sixty-four women in Mullard to whom I submitted the statement, "Our greatest devotion goes to our mother," asking for comments, thirty-nine agreed with this, stating: "My father didn't take an interest," or "It's 'Mum' all the time," or "When I have a problem, Mum will sort it out," or "Just that little bit more." Eleven women professed an equal devotion to both parents, while eight preferred the father ("I envied those who had such a mother, but my mother was not worthy of devotion.") Six others did not remember one or both parents or had neither father nor mother, being brought up in an orphanage. ("I never had the love of parents and that is still going on in me.")

Now for the devotion of their own children as the mothers saw it. Out of thirty-five mothers for whom the information is available, twenty contended that the children care more for them ("Just that little bit extra"); ten professed equal devotion or said, "Girls more for the father, boys more for the mother." Six others said that the children preferred the father. In the latter category there was an interesting disclosure: "Before I went to work, equal devotion; now he goes more to his father."

It was clear that the attachment to parents was thought to differ not only in terms of magnitude but in quality. It was "a different sort of relationship," or as one woman said, there were "different kinds of love for different persons." However, comparing the attachment for each parent only in quantitative terms for two generations, it is clear that the measure of devotion is moving towards a greater balance as between parents. The young man gets more friendship and affection from his father than the latter had from his own. This may often lead to conflicts in adolescence, as the father may be too anxious or too ambitious or too critical. I met a number of disappointed fathers, whose "do well!" or "do better!" was not heeded by the children. "I wanted him to have a trade but he was not interested," or "I apprenticed him but he packed up," or "I wanted him to be a technical man but he did not respond," or "I wanted them all to go to grammar schools but out of seven children only one succeeded," or "She hasn't done her best," were some of the remarks I heard.

This brings us to an interesting question: do the parents understand their children? My material is too fragmentary to answer this one way or the other. The question whenever it was asked was not whether they understood or not, only whether they felt they understood. Fathers of teenagers often felt they did not understand their children, saying: "I can't fathom them," or "They are a surprise." However, one man gave me an interesting reply: "I don't bother to understand them. I want to live with them. They all have their own troubles."

More specifically, forty-one mothers in Mullard were asked whether they felt that they understood their older children. Out of these, twenty-one answered this question in the affirmative, saying: "At this young age I think I still do," or "I have grown up with them," or "I think they are open-minded," or "I can always tell what is going on in their heads," or "We talk a lot, everything is talked out," or "He is an artist, but I understand him all the same," or "That depends how you bring them up. If you keep up with them and let them bring their friends into the home you understand them."

Twenty mothers felt they did not understand their children, or not quite, saying: "They surprise you as they grow older," or "It is a job to understand them really," or "They pass through an age when it is difficult to understand them," or "Father understands him better," or "Granny understands him better," or "Since he married I don't understand him any more," or "The boy has funny ways; he played truant for a fortnight and we didn't know a thing about it and still don't know why." Out of those twenty, twelve were mothers of children in the age bracket of fourteen to twenty. Two mothers were highly critical of their children ("A selfish lot," and "difficult to satisfy, we never had the privileges they have, they take everything for granted and ask for more. No thankfulness.").

Two mothers had the privilege of having children who "outclassed them." A mother of fifty-three said, "When they get education and a good job they get ideas. Whenever I speak they try to correct me. They must have it right. I feel that low." A mother of fifty-six: "He is a scholarship boy and he corrects me frequently, he doesn't like my way of speaking. I have to look up to him but I don't really mind." I believe all the same that many, if not most fathers and mothers, want to be "outclassed," although they may have mixed feelings about it later on. . . .

. . . Here we are concerned only with the normal family—which is a functional unit of the first order in workers' lives.

The husband–wife relationships were described by the overwhelming majority as happy. The upsets were reported only in odd cases. To my question, "Are you happy at home?," the scale of answers ran as follows: "Very happy"; "Happy"; "We have a good carry on"; "Nothing better to wish for"; "No worries"; "Good life"; "Nothing to grumble about." Very few men referred to tiffs of any consequence, perhaps one in twenty or less. Of course one realizes that such accounts may not be accurate, but I had the impression that they were truthful.

I probed a little deeper into the husband–wife relationship in Mullard where I introduced several provocative statements, asking for comments based on personal experience. One of these was: "Love is the sweetest thing in life." Out of seventy-four men, fifty-one agreed most readily, some very outspokenly, but most of them added that they meant by this home and children. "It's the finest thing; something to work for, to look to and to look after." "Everything I do is for my wife and children," said a young man of twenty-five. "It is an essential thing. Happiness is a mixture of love, contentment and good living" —said a man of twenty-eight. A man of thirty: "That's my life, wife and children." A man of thirty-six: "My love, that is my wife and children." A man of thirty-one: "All my life is centred around the home." A man of thirty-nine: "My children and my home, that is my love." A man of forty: "One of the three essentials, work, health and love." A man of forty-four: "Children and home, that's my life." A man of forty-six: "Love is the sweetest thing but not confined to age." A man of fifty: "My wife proved herself, she never grumbles." A man of fifty-six: "We get on tops." A man of fifty-nine: "Something to live for. If you have no-one to love you live like a rabbit in your hole." A man of sixty-five: "There is life in the old man yet."

Six or seven others agreed with this statement but qualified it in this way: "Not exclusive love," or "In the broadest sense, for everything, that is the only way to beat the Devil," or "Love not only for a woman but for birds and plants," or "Love with freedom."

"It's companionship more than love," or "It's more mutual understanding," or "Love, but not of a sexual kind"—contended ten men, mostly in the over-forties, adding often: "Love at first, then more companionship," or "The process of cooling off is a natural thing," or "Not the same thing as when you are young."

Six or seven others contended that love is rather a bitter sweet, saying: "It tastes rather sour," or "bitter," or that it was all right "If you have the right partner," or "If you have a proper bank account."

So it is obvious from these reactions that the overwhelming majority enjoyed a loving relationship or a relationship based on good companionship with their wives.

In the same firm thirty-nine women were presented with a similar question; "Is love the sweetest thing, or is it a bitter sweet?" Thirty of them subscribed whole-heartedly to the statement that love is the sweetest thing, amplifying it with "Home and children." I heard: "We are all happy together," or "We are very happy," or "Without love you are lost"—and from the older women: "It goes on all the time," or "Not confined to youth." Five other women, mostly in their late thirties or older, contended that companionship, or mutual understanding, or friendship counts more later on. Only four regarded love rather as a bitter sweet.

Some men in the same firm were asked about nagging: "Is nagging the greatest curse? What is your experience?" Most agreed, but out of fifteen only one said: "I have been nagged a bit," and another, "In one period of my life that was true"; but all the others said: "Not in my experience," or "Not in my home," or "I have never been nagged personally." Some referred to friends, sisters or mothers or in-laws ("Mother started nagging when father walked out," or "My mother-in-law was a great nagger").

"When we are married all the company we need is at home": fifty-nine men in Mullard were asked to comment on this statement. Twenty-four men agreed, saying: "We are quite happy at home, just the two of us," or "Just the three of us," or "We rarely go out, we prefer to stay at home," or "There is no need to go out nowadays." Many repeated the familiar phrase "We keep ourselves to ourselves."

The remainder, i.e. thirty-five, objected to this statement, often very emphatically, saying: "It's silly," or "You stagnate and become stale," or "You get into a rut," or "We always arrange holidays with another couple," or "You have to go out and meet other people." But out of those only three referred to something suggestive of an unhappy experience at home, saying: "You are fed up at home," or "Things I am interested in my wife is not," or "It is too dull at home." All the others, although they needed outside company, appreciated home and family life.

The same statement was presented to sixty women in Mullard for their comments. Out of these twenty-two women agreed with it, saying: "We are complete in ourselves," or "Homely types," or "Happy at home with husband

and children," or "I prefer my husband's company to anyone else's," or "Why go out if you have everything at home you need," or "When you are happy you don't need anyone else," and many again reiterated the phrase "We keep ourselves to ourselves." The remainder, thirty-eight, did not agree with this statement, saying: "You need outside company," or "It's nice to have friends," or "It's right for the first three years of married life but not afterwards," or "If you have children it is all right." But only four out of those who did not agree with the saying expressed their view in such a way as to suggest a not very satisfactory relationship: "I like to be out," or "You are fed up," or "You need a break from each other." Again it was clear that the overwhelming majority had satisfactory relations with their husbands.

Does the relationship tend to be, on the whole, more satisfactory now than it used to be a generation ago? I have no quantitative material to go by but from the qualitative material I would answer this question in the affirmative, and I would give the following reasons for this change, to which many referred in one way or another.

A marriage without conflicts is as inconceivable as a man's mind without conflicts, so I often asked about "tiffs" and their nature. It came out that most tiffs occur about children, money, about getting things done at home to make the home more comfortable, or when one of the partners is tense or tired, or about relations. The children nowadays are fewer, so tiffs on their account should be on the decline. The home is nicer, more comfortable: that, too, should provide less material for conflict. The money position is easier, the wife is not so hard up, so this, too, should account for less conflict. Upsets at work are, on the whole, on the decline as the work is not as heavy as it used to be and the worker is treated much better by his foreman than a generation ago, so this again should account for less tenseness. On the other hand the wife often goes out to work, and this may make for greater tenseness: but there may be some truth in the pronouncement of working women that they are too busy to develop arguments. T.V. fills most of the time at home, which means less opportunity for argument. Cars take the family out, and away from home tiffs are most rare. But the single and most potent reason for more satisfactory relationships is the decline in heavy drinking, and many women referred to this as the most important factor.

Is the husband–wife relationship still under the dominance of the male, or is the relationship moving towards greater equality of sexes? A manager with whom I discussed this subject put his view in a most pungent way, linking this with the social change in the factory: "The age of authority and its abuse has passed. Men were bullied at work and they bullied back their wives and children. Now you cannot order your men about, you have rather to coax and humour them. You cannot say: do this, or do that. You have to ask: would you like to do that, or could you do this, or what about doing this or that. The same change is reflected at home. There is not the same authority at home as there used to be."

There is, of course, nothing new in this idea of linking authority in the workshop with authority at home. It reminded me of the French social thinker of the last century, Frédéric Le Play, who linked the authority of the master in the *atelier* with that of the father in the household at home. The link between the two kinds of authority has a deep psychological foundation as the attitude in one sphere is often transferred to the other: instances of this could be seen most clearly in the attitudes of foremen. But in fact both attitudes have a deeper background in the general decline of authoritarian behaviour. Ours is not the age of authority, the age of absolute values. There are also other reasons for the decline of the authority of the *pater familias*. The husband is not the paymaster who can call the tune, to the same extent as he used to be. His wife may be working, or may have been out to work at one time or another, contributing to the family income. The Welfare State, with children's allowances, Welfare Services, and Assistance Board in case he fails to support his family, also supplements a man's wages. The phrase describing housekeeping money as "Wages for the Missus" is very rarely used nowadays.

Sixty-three married men in Mullard were asked more specifically about this aspect of male dominance in their relationship with their wives. They were presented with the statement: "Man is master in his own house" and asked for comments. Out of these thirty professed equal status with their wives and expressed this in such terms as: "Old-fashioned idea of being a master," or "We share responsibility," or "Fifty-fifty," or "Full partners: we must agree together in everything," or "Equal when the wife goes out to work," or "Combined operation," or "Two heads are better than one," or "One leg of trousers for each of us," or "Share the burden." Out of the thirty, two men said that their wives made them think they were masters but in fact they were not.

There were seven others who stated that they were equal but in big decisions the man had the final word. Again seven others claimed a status which can be best described as *primus inter pares*, saying: "A little bit over," or "One up," or "To a certain extent," or "Wife is a junior partner otherwise we wouldn't get anywhere."

A substantial minority, i.e. eighteen, still claimed definite superiority of the male, in such terms as: "I am the master," or "There must be only one master in the house," or "You are the leading hand by virtue of greater intelligence, greater strength and greater contribution," or "It's natural there should be one head in a family," or "Man is more conversant with the world," or "The last word is with me," or "When I say yes, it stays yes," or "It is recognized that I am the master." One man acknowledged the superiority of his wife who "wore the trousers."

So in fact three-quarters of the sample claimed absolute equality or near equality; only one in four claimed absolute superiority of the male.

Among those men who professed a full equality of status, half, i.e., fifteen out of thirty, had wives going out to work, while among those men who professed superiority of their status in absolute or relative terms, less than one in three, i.e., nine out of thirty, had working wives. My sample, here, is too small to prove the point, but it was certainly my impression that there was some correlation between working wives and feelings of equal status; and also the profession of full equality was a more prevalent attitude amongst the under-forties than the older couples. The frequent reference to: "Victorian," or "Old-fashioned ideas," of those who professed equality was a characteristic feature, pointing to social change.

Similar results were obtained in interviews with married women in Mullard, with even stronger emphasis on equality of status.

It seems to me that we are witnessing a considerable social change in husband–wife relationships in the working classes, and that this has a bearing on the world of man's values. The more he accepts his wife as an equal partner, the more he acquires, mostly unconsciously, her values and standards. He is no longer contemptuous of women's ideas as he used to be. They may differ from his, placing greater value on domesticity for example, but are more frequently nearer to his own. Once his was the specifically masculine world standing for self assertion, sturdiness, force and pungency. Now he tends to find room for softer and more feminine values.

There is a conflict in every man's mind between the desire to dominate and master and the desire to serve and please. But in this conflict the desire to serve and please seems to be on the ascendant in the working man's life.

La Rochefoucauld's saying: "There are some good marriages but no perfect ones" is often quoted with approval. But since I made this enquiry I am not quite sure whether there are not some perfect marriages too, as some men depicted their relationships in the brightest and warmest colours. . . .

"Home and work don't mix." This is a phrase which often circulates among working men. It means that "You should leave home at home, and work at work," or "Once you leave work, forget it." As one man said: "When you clock out, clock out your mind." Others said: "It is a mistake to carry your work home"; "Enough time is spent in work without taking it home"; or "I try to keep home and work separate."

Work matters are rarely mentioned at home. Men would say when I asked about it: "My wife never asks me and I never tell her," or "I never talk shop at home," or "My wife asks when I come home, 'Have you had a good day?' and I answer, 'All right' and that's all," or "Only if something extraordinary happens I mention it," or "My wife doesn't pretend to know about my job so she doesn't ask."

Work means tension, and home is for relaxation. Men would say: "I never mention work at home otherwise I would never relax," or "Home is entirely different, it's for relaxing," or "You have to refresh and renew yourself. Home should give you strength for the next day."

Only a small minority carry their work home, mostly those who have a leading position or do a very skilled job. A foreman would say: "It is impossible not to carry your work home although I try not to," or "I carry the usual foreman's worries with me." That is one of the reasons why some men do not care for promotion.

Whenever the wife is conversant with the kind of work her husband does, if for instance she was on similar work during the war, or she has a similar job, as was often the case in Mullard, or when the wife is especially affectionate and concerned about her husband, talking shop occurs more frequently. In these cases men would say: "My wife is very interested in what I am doing," or "My wife takes an intelligent interest; she knows all about the job," or "When I have a bad day, she knows at once and I have to tell her."

In Sheffield when the works were opened to the families of the work-people during the so-called "Open Week," one in three wives visited the work-place. The remainder did not avail themselves of this opportunity. One of the characteristic answers came to one husband who asked his wife whether she would like to visit the works: "Don't you think it's enough if you have to go to that place?"

Although "home and work don't mix" in the normative sense, they do in fact influence each other in more than one way. A man cannot help comparing his home and his factory, the two places where most of his time is spent. Men with clean homes demand clean and tidy work-places, and men working in clean and tidy factories demand also a higher standard at home. There is a subconscious connection between the standards in each place. At one time standards in both places were not very high, but now they are rising rapidly.

Formerly, the men who were bullied at work bullied their wives and children in turn. The authoritarian system at work was linked with the authoritarian system at home—I have already referred to this in another context. The type of discipline which is imposed at work may not be directly transferable in full measure to the home, but has a definite bearing on the type of discipline which a man tries to impose on those under his authority. This is most clearly seen in the case of foremen who are often reminded by their wives: "You're not in the factory; you can't be a foreman to your children." Some foremen, when asked about this, denied this transfer: "I have enough men at work to order about. I don't need to order my children about."

Work and home intermingle also under the head of worries, troubles and upsets. A good home background makes a good worker while a bad home is the root cause of many difficulties at work. Many foremen stated this as an undeniable fact: "Whenever the quality of work deteriorates I come up and ask the man what is the matter, and in most cases it's a family upset which causes it." Or as another foreman put it: "When they have troubles with their wives, they are embittered, they lose interest in their job. They don't do a clean piece of work and don't seem to pull with their mates."

Speaking about home and work upsets, we can distinguish three basic situations:

(1) A man has troubles at home as well as at work. This is, of course, the worst situation, as one aggravates the other. Troubles at work do not necessarily mean upsets, but they may lead to situations which impose a great deal of strain and worry. Foremen, charge-hands or leading-hands in responsible positions often find themselves in such situations. I came across cases where foremen or potential foremen had to give up their positions as they could not stand the combined weight of worries at home and at work. In typical cases a wife had to have an operation, or was suffering from heart attacks, or a child was dangerously ill, or there was an emotional upset with the wife and the foreman felt that he was heading for a break-down.

(2) A man has home upsets while the work is straightforward, not presenting special strain or worry. We have to distinguish here between major upsets such as those caused by estrangement from a wife or separation, or by the death of relatives . . . or ill-health in the family on one hand, and minor troubles and worries on the other. The first kind finds expression in loss of shifts and inability to concentrate. "The work becomes harder, your hands are not steady," men with such experience would say. Or as one man put it: "If a man cannot sleep and relax at home, of course it affects his work. Many accidents happen through home worry. A man's mind is not there."

A man of fifty-seven said: "My daughter was partly paralysed and ill for many years. For eight years I lost practically ten to twelve weeks in shifts yearly, and in one year twenty-two shifts. I contracted many illnesses, all through worry." Several years previously his daughter had recovered, and so had he. It is little realized that illnesses may not only be psycho-somatic but they may also have a social dimension. One illness in a family may bring in its wake other illnesses.

A man of fifty-two, a widower who had married again, had a wife with a weak heart, who had suffered two strokes and partial paralysis over several years. He lost many shifts and could not concentrate on his work. He lost a job on the machine where he was working. "You can't be a good workman if you have lost a good home, if your mind is not at rest."

A man of fifty-three had a wife who had suffered a nervous break-down after her last baby and, on the advice of her doctor, had left home for a while to join her mother. "It was very hard to get on with my job during that time —although you can't afford to let your mind run away with you."

In the case of small troubles and worries at home, work is more often a help, providing a balancing factor. Men often referred to this and women even more frequently. Out of sixty-two women operatives in Mullard, to whom I submitted the statement: "Those unhappy at home cannot be happy at work," for their comments, twenty-four contended that they often forget their troubles and worries while at work if they were not too great. These women said: "Little things are forgotten at work, they come back when you get home"; "You can keep your mind off your troubles"; "I forget myself, I lose myself here"; "When my son was stationed in Cyprus it helped me to forget"; "Better off at work with small worries"; "You can forget if your worry is not too great"; "Here, I get away from my troubles"; "When I had a nervous break-down, following a series of deaths at home, I went on short time; the doctor did not let me stop working and I felt better for it"; "Instead of nagging the husband we let off steam at work"; and even "I am happier at work than at home."

These women often referred to the possibility of confiding in their workmates as the main factor in bringing relief. "I confide and I feel better for it," they said, or "I am one of those who cannot keep their troubles to themselves," or "Women confide more than men, they relieve their mind." On the other hand there were those who said: "I don't confide," or "I don't display my feelings; those who can are better for it."

(3) Some men have upsets at work while their home life is normal. This affects their home life to a certain degree but to a much smaller extent than home upsets affect their work life. One man put it in the following way, comparing home upsets with work upsets: "While I cannot help bringing my troubles from home to work, I don't take my work troubles home. You can't switch your mind completely from your home because it is so much deeper than the work." Another man said, "It is easier to leave work at work than home at home." Most men would deny that upsets at work have an effect on their home life to any extent, unless they are very bad. However, a number of men confided: "When I have a bad day, naturally it affects my mood and behaviour. We are all flesh and blood"; or "After nights I am irritable"; or "If you are not careful it can affect your home"; or "If I have a bad day at work I feel niggly and snappy at home"; or "It does happen at times that I feel grumpy after a bad day."

As for social change, I believe the separation between work and home is in fact greater now than formerly in the sense that the home is now more insulated against the adverse effects of factory life. Previously a man used to bring work home in the form of dirt in his clothes; now more often he has a bath provided by the firm. He used to bring work home in the form of anxiety, perhaps as to whether he would be able to hold his job; now security of employment is much more general. He also used to have more frequent conflicts with his workmates with whom he was competing, or with his foreman who told him "to get on or get out." He used to be more tired, working longer hours under more strenuous conditions than now. Now when he gets home he not only wants to forget about his work but is also more able to do so as the job rarely carries a great load of frustrations, anxieties and conflicts. He is rarely pushed and driven, he is rarely offended in a way which could involve his self-respect. He does not need to keep his resentment or grievances, he can voice them freely, and can lodge his complaints. He still, so to speak, wears a mask while at work, but wearing it is not such a strain as it used to be. He feels better adjusted all round, so when he comes home he is not so "bottled up" as he used to be.

Modern Women

HELGE PROSS

The following survey of the situation of women in West Germany, written in the 1960s, raises above all the question of how much has changed during the last seventy-five years. The inferior position of women in jobs and in the family may have diminished, but the problem remains acute. The frustration of women, caught between an abandonment of traditional resignation and resultant new expectations on the one hand, and a denial of full equality on the other, has been a familiar aspect of life in western Europe and North America at least since the later nineteenth century.

Hence the selection should obviously be compared with Banks' discussion of Victorian women. The comparison, however, has some obvious flaws. The position of women in Germany undoubtedly changed more slowly than it did in Britain, so the similarity with British conditions several generations ago is not completely surprising. In this sense comparison should also be made with Zweig's study of contemporary British workers, in which rather different implications about women's roles emerged. Helge Pross is discussing a variety of social classes, not the middle class alone. It is probable that the transition to more modern values occurred later in worker and especially peasant households than in the middle class, again creating some unsurprising similarities with the nineteenth-century middle class. The author's viewpoint must be assessed, as in any study of human society; in this case the author has rather clear notions of what women's position should be. But with all the qualifications, the special problems of interpreting the impact of modernization on women remain. Athough women's lives in all major social classes may have changed more than those of men, their frustrations may be no greater, but simply different. It does seem likely, however, that the full implications of the modernization of women have yet to be worked out.

West Germany today is a modern society indeed. Highly industrialized, about 85 per cent of her population of 53 million live in smaller or larger towns, and only 15 per cent reside in villages and semirural communities. Little more than one tenth of all gainfully employed do agricultural work while approximately nine tenths are occupied in industry, private and public administration, handicraft, commerce, cultural institutions, or other non-agricultural jobs. During the last three or four decades the German social structure has undergone fundamental changes resulting in a society chiefly middle class in character. After World War II, the landed aristocracy, powerful for many a century, disappeared, while the industrial proletariat, exploited and underprivileged in the past, achieved a greatly improved economic position. Since the turn of the century a large and still growing new middle class of white-collar workers and civil servants emerged. To be sure, class distinctions have not been leveled out. They are marked, as far as property, income, social prestige, and educational opportunities are concerned. There is a small upper stratum consisting of a few extremely wealthy capitalists, the top executives of large industrial firms, high government officials, and the decision makers in the major political parties and pressure groups. However, this upper class, strong as its influence may be, has ceased to be a homogeneous ruling caste. On the other hand, no class of paupers is left at the bottom of the social pyramid. Working in an economy which for nearly a decade and a half has known no unemployment; enjoying a large measure of leisure (the workweek has been reduced to forty to forty-two hours); protected by an elaborate system of social security against the financial pitfalls of illness and age; and supplied with numerous opportunities for education and amusement, most Germans are citizens of quite an "affluent society" indeed.

Modern as the Federal Republic may be in her economic and social structure, she has not as yet broken with all traditions of an authoritarian and patriarchal past. The democratization of the state after World War II has not made for an egalitarian society. Although all men are equal before the law, society does not offer all of them equal opportunities. Some groups are still underprivileged in various ways. This holds true particularly for women. Remnants of age-old traditions regarding them as the intellectually weaker sex, less able to shoulder responsibilities in politics or the professions, stand in the way of true equality. Although the struggle for emancipation has been won, women are still discriminated against in the world outside the family and the home. Generally speaking, women in West Germany are confronted with social and psychological problems that, to a large degree, arise out of the disharmony between a demanding present and an unmastered past, and the conflict between preindustrial roles and the demands of modern life.

The Legal Position

Women in West Germany have nothing to complain about in regard to their legal position. The Basic Law, the Federal Republic's constitution, adopted in 1949, endows both sexes with equal rights. Women have the franchise, and enjoy the right of equal pay for equal performance. In 1957, the Federal Parliament took the last and decisive step towards the implementation of full legal equality. By a special bill all civil law was adapted to the constitutional principle. Among the many provisions of the new law, most important are those revising property and inheritance rights of husband and wife.

Under the old civil law, formulated at the end of the nineteenth century, the husband had remarkable privileges: he had the usufruct of his wife's estate and acted as her trustee. He managed their common property, and could dispose of it even against her will. At his death, the wife inherited only one quarter of his estate unless the couple had concluded a special contract in her favor.

All this has now been changed. The management and disposition of the wife's property is solely her affair. The husband is no longer allowed to handle their common estate without her consent. All decisions about common goods must be made by both. If the husband dies, the wife inherits one half of the property. In case of divorce, regardless of which of them is the guilty party, she not only retains what she brought into marriage, but receives in addition half of the possessions acquired by the couple while married. Even if the husband accumulated a fortune from his earnings, while the wife had no income of her own, she gets 50 per cent. This provision is meant to protect the housewife whose work the law considers indispensable for the creation and preservation of the estate. Formerly, if divorced, she had no legal claim to her husband's savings, [but] she now suffers no financial loss if, instead of seeking gainful employment, she devotes herself to the family and the home.

In addition to the provisions mentioned, the new law parts in all other respects as well from the old principle of the husband's right to decide in controversial family affairs. Formerly the decision about the children's education—whether they should or should not be sent to a *gymnasium* (academic high school), or to a university—was left to him, now both parents must agree. Also, the wife now has legal claim to regular payments of household expenses and pocket money for her personal needs.

The implementation of the principle of equality also affects the wife's claim to maintenance after divorce. According to the marriage law the guilty partner has to maintain the other one if the latter is unable to do so "adequately." The definition of what is adequate support varies, and is left to the courts. A woman with children is usually deemed incapable of earning an adequate living. If the woman is not guilty, yet able to take a job, she cannot claim regular payments. On the other hand, if she is guilty, and her husband is unable to support himself, she must make payments to him. This regulation, though sometimes criticized, is perfectly in keeping with the doctrine of equality. Based on the assumption that both partners have equal responsibilities for each other, it protects the institution of marriage as such. The husband cannot get rid of his wife without financial loss, nor is the wife allowed to sell her consent for the price of large alimony payments. On the whole, divorce against the will of the innocent party has become a rather difficult affair.

Finally, one more outcome of the doctrine of equality is worth mentioning. A woman marrying a foreigner used to lose her German citizenship on the day of marriage. The new regulations allow her to keep it.

Town and Country

In many respects West German agriculture lags behind the urban and industrial sectors of society. While some villages have taken great steps toward the modernization of their economic and social life, in others people still cling to more traditional patterns. Generally speaking, the rural population is also passing through a period of transition. Struggling to adapt to the requirements of a market economy, a large number of farmers surrendered and took up industrial jobs. In fact, from 1949 to 1959 about 50 per cent of the agricultural laborers, and one third (1.5 million) of the independent peasants quit agriculture. Many, if not most, of those who stayed cannot keep up economically with the urban population. Though all of them, male and female alike, work harder than the average city dweller, their standard of living is lower. So is their level of education. Of course, there are no illiterates in the rural regions, and much is being done to improve the farmers' general and vocational training. Many villages have centers for adult education or community houses offering regular lectures on agricultural techniques, home economics, baby care and sociopolitical subjects. Since these community houses frequently provide certain facilities, such as washing machines or deep freezers, for common use, they act as agencies of modernization also for those who could not be reached by mere theoretical instruction. In addition, radio and television, popular all over the country, are links to the non-rural world. Nevertheless, the average villager still seems to be less informed on national events. Nor is information about modern child-rearing techniques disseminated among them. In many places, children are looked after only until they are four years old. Afterwards, mothers leave them to themselves, rarely having the time to supervise and to guide them. Child labor is widespread, almost all village youngsters being obliged to help in the home, to look after cattle and poultry, or assist their parents in the fields.

Within the last two or three decades the rural family too has undergone some change. As to size, it does not differ much from its urban counterpart. Since the end of World War II the nuclear family has emerged as the representative and most widespread rural type. The number of children is small, almost never larger than two. This change indicates that the rural population has also turned to a more rational, calculating attitude toward life. The internal family structure is, however, somewhat different from the urban one.

With respect to the position of mother and wife, roughly three types can be distinguished, each representing a different stage of adaptation to more democratic ways.

First, there is the traditional patriarchal family, dominated by the father, with wife and children still subordinates rather than partners. In these families, practically all decisions are left to the oldest male. He manages the family budget, decides matters concerning the farm, and has the final word in controversies about the children. It is interesting that the patriarchal family's economic behavior also follows more traditional lines. Rarely are economic ends and means linked in a rational way. Neither do such families adopt a sensible scheme of division of labor, nor are there conscious efforts at better management. One result is an overload of work for the women. Responsible for the house, the poultry and the garden, they also work in the fields and have to step in wherever and whenever additional hands are needed.

In general, the working hours of peasant women in all types of families are long, from 60 to 80 hours per week. In spite of this heavy contribution, women are little respected. Most villagers show only a modest appreciation of female work, and the women themselves are too much resigned to their lot to object. Being overworked, they often are in a poor state of health and thus lack the physical energy as well as the time to search for improvements.

While according to the estimates of some sociologists a decade ago this traditional patriarchal family was the most widespread type in rural regions, more recently a different type has developed, the so-called partnership family (*Partnerschaftsfamilie*). In it, economic and personal matters are discussed between husband and wife, and decisions reached by mutual agreement. Again, family pattern and economic behavior are intimately linked, both evincing a certain open-mindedness and a more enlightened philosophy of life. On the whole, the partnership family seems to be quite efficient, oriented toward the market, and eager to introduce modern methods in production, work, organization and financial administration.

Finally, there is the family in transition, apparently the most unhappy one. Wives in such families, though they no longer unquestioningly accept the authority of the males, have not yet entirely emancipated themselves from their traditional role of subordination. Being the dominated party, they resent their responsibilities, and are as unable to collaborate reasonably as are the husbands. In these families (but not only in these) the conflict between traditional and modern norms makes itself felt also in the relation between older and younger generation. Regular pay and regular leisure, and even the claim to both, being denied to them, the hard-working boys and girls often leave family and village, though they may be heirs to the farm. Girls in particular want to get away so that they need not lead the miserable life of their mothers.

On the whole, the lot of rural women is difficult, particularly on medium-size and small farms (that is, in the majority of all farms): too much work, bad health, insufficient education, and too little help from outside. What is needed is a large-scale effort of government and private groups to educate both husband and wife, and teach the women how to better organize their work, recognize and defend their rights. (Further mechanization, still badly needed in the household, will not lead to the expected results unless rural women become more efficient in the organization and planning of their jobs.) However, the improvement of village life depends not only on education and individual intelligence. In the long run education, even when coupled with much needed mechanization, can bear fruit only if also the property structure of the entire rural sector is thoroughly reorganized.

Working Women

As in most industrial countries, the life of women in West Germany is influenced above all by the necessity to combine what is usually referred to as "women's two roles." One role is that of wife and mother, and the other that of the working woman employed outside of her home. A young girl who leaves school or finishes her vocational training has to find a job, but most girls also want to get married and a good many of them do. However, in the older age groups there are some exceptions to this general rule. There are those women who devote their lives solely to the traditional female tasks. They belong exclusively to the older generation (from fifty-five years upward), in which there are still quite a few, particularly among the bourgeois women, who have never been anything but housewives and mothers. On the other hand, there is a large group of about two million women, now roughly between thirty-eight and fifty years of age, who never have been and never will be anything but working women. They too would certainly like to marry, but have no chance to do so as a result of the fact that their potential husbands were slain during the war or died in Nazi concentration camps. In 1965 there were 27.9 million men and 30.9 million women in the Federal Republic, a surplus of 3 million women.

While many women give up their jobs after getting married, or, more frequently, after the birth of their first child, quite a number of wives and mothers continue to work. To do so has become more popular in recent years, particularly among young wives. Although in 1950 only 28 per cent of all married women from twenty to twenty-five years retained their jobs, the percentage rose to approximately 50 in 1957. In 1962 nearly one third (4.7 million) of all married women, and a little less than one third of those married mothers who lived together with husband and children (mothers in complete families) were working. In addition, there were in 1957 nearly 1.8 million working mothers of incomplete families, that is wives separated from their husbands, widows, divorced women, and mothers of illegitimate children, all with children living with them in the same house.

Large as the number of working mothers was, of all mothers who lived (1957) in complete families only a minority of 12 per cent (or one million) worked outside of the home. The majority, about 18 per cent (1.45 million) were occupied mostly in small family enterprises in or next to the home. These women, the wives of peasants, independent artisans or small business men, did not need to leave their children alone while at work. Though frequently overburdened, they can move freely between workshop and home. Neither of the two worlds these mothers live in, the family and their business world, is antagonistic to the other, and rarely do the tasks in the first conflict heavily with the duties in the second.

As compared with this group (the so-called *Mithelfende Familienangehörige*), the 1.2 million married and unmarried mothers who worked (1957) in factory or office, and whose children (under eighteen years) lived with them, had a more difficult time. These constituted 16 per cent of all mothers (married and unmarried) with children under eighteen years. It is these women who have to leave the children alone or under the supervision of somebody else, usually a relative and very rarely a neighbor.

The demands on working mothers being high, why do they consent to the twofold task? The motives vary chiefly according to social class, and change with time. A decade ago almost any German family still suffered from the damages of war, having lost home, furniture and clothing, or being refugees from the eastern provinces of the former German Reich. Very often, families could be founded and the household rebuilt only with supplementary income produced by the mother and wife. Once this emergency passed, the motives changed. Today, it is primarily, though not solely, the desire to improve the household equipment, to buy an apartment, or to build a house which makes mothers seek employment. This is true particularly of women in the lower-income classes. While the wages of industrial workers and of the rank and file in civil service and private offices are usually sufficient to cover current expenses, they very often do not allow for additional expenditure. If the family wants to maintain what is nowadays considered a decent standard of living, the mother must step in.

It would be too simple to call these women (as is often done) materialistic. Normally, it is not for luxury that they work. Of course, the definition of luxury varies. According to present standards in West Germany, a private car, an electric refrigerator, perhaps also a television set, but certainly not a radio, are deemed by many families to be luxuries. On the other hand, the working women, like practically everybody else, are victims of the "hidden persuaders" of advertising. In this context, moral criticism is not only useless but unjust as well. It usually overlooks the fact that many industrial workers and small business men can rise above the level of mere subsistence only by the additional labor of the wife. For the first time in German history these classes have a chance to keep up with the bourgeois families, and thus become more self-assured. They believe that it is more important to get ahead and to secure for their children a materially better life than for the mother to be present in the home all day during the early phases of her child's life. Psychoanalytic theory not being popular with Germans, and practically unknown among workers and in the lower-middle class, mothers think it more essential to stay at home when the children reach school age than to be available for the babies.

There is a small fraction of mothers who go on working primarily for the sake of personal independence or because they just love their jobs. Almost exclusively they are wives who went to college, women physicians, lawyers, economists, high school and university teachers. While the majority of working mothers would prefer to remain at home, and while many are likely to do so as soon as the family can afford it, quite a number of the women university graduates would not voluntarily withdraw.

The German public, being conservative in many respects, is ambiguous about working mothers. Among their most ardent opponents are the women themselves: two thirds advocate a law forbidding mothers with children under ten years to accept gainful employment. In general, however, the agitation against working mothers is of no avail. Manpower being in extremely short supply in Germany, wives and mothers are the only labor reserve left. Barring a recession in the near future, more and more mothers will be absorbed in the productive process. Society could and should help the mothers and their children in counteracting this trend not by outlawing work for them, but by a revision of the tax and wage system in favor of low-income groups. If special rebates were given to large families, making it more attractive for mothers to stay at home, probably quite a number would do so. It was the working mothers and their families who, by shouldering additional burdens, made a large contribution to the so-called "economic miracle" in West Germany. The country having been rebuilt, with the wealth of the nation greater than ever before, it is now time for society to repay them in such a manner that no mother with small children need seek employment solely because otherwise the family could not rise above the level of mere subsistence.

The Women in the Family

Surprisingly little is known about family structure in the Federal Republic. Aside from some sociological studies carried out soon after the war, almost no empirical research was done in the field. Relevant questions as to the internal structure of the family, the balance of power between husband and wife, the relations of parents and children, and the emotional climate of the group, have not yet found satisfactory answers.

Even without adequate research it is evident that the authoritarian family, long representative in Germany, has vanished. No longer is the urban family ruled by a powerful father, and no longer are wife and children willing just to obey. Although it is clear that the traditional structure is broken, and that especially in families of the younger generation hardly any trait of it is left, there is no reliable information as to what has taken its place. While according to some authors the relationship between husband and wife is now more that of partners who arrive at decisions by discussion and compromise, others insist that no such democratic family pattern has evolved, and that an atmosphere of indifference prevails in which neither authoritarianism nor individualistic attitudes can thrive.

Generally speaking, the family in Germany shows all the traits characteristic of fully developed industrial societies. Girls and boys decide themselves, almost without exception, whom they are going to marry and get married at the average age of 23.7 and 26 years respectively. Arranged marriages are entirely unknown. The future partners meet on the job, in the youth groups, or at parties. They want to marry chiefly for love. There are other motives, too, for instance, to escape the sense of loneliness and to gain security. Also, quite a number of them feel obliged to legalize an actual relationship because the first child is on its way.

To what degree women are content in marriage is generally unknown. A study carried out as far back as 1949 does not give too rosy a picture. At that time only half of a representative sample of wives thought it necessary for a woman's happiness for her to be married, thus pointing indirectly to some sort of dissatisfaction with their own marriages. One in six confessed frankly to being unhappy, and one in four did not believe their sex life harmonious. On the other hand, men gave the impression of being emotionally and sexually more contented, thinking marriage more rewarding than did the wives.

The habit of having but two children is a novelty, and to some degree an amazing one. This is not so much because in the past children used to be numerous, particularly in the lower social strata, and now it is exactly these strata which adhere to the new pattern (while in the upper classes there is a slight tendency towards larger numbers of children). Rather, the almost universal adoption of planned parenthood and of having few children is surprising for another reason. From its advent to power until its collapse in 1945, the Nazi government strongly favored a population increase. By propaganda, by prohibiting the sale of contraceptives, and by making special allowances for large families, it tried to induce parents to have many children. The result was a relatively high birth rate in the 1930's. However, after the war a change set in without ever having been publicly recommended. On the contrary, since 1949 all national governments have been formed by the Christian Democratic Union, the majority party which was strongly influenced by Catholics. Also Protestants had, until very recently, reservations about birth control. Nor were there powerful private agencies spreading information. In fact, the Planned Parenthood Association is little known, and the subject of family planning is seldom discussed in public. Yet people do plan—primarily for economic reasons. Realizing that at present they cannot have both large families and a high standard of living, they cut down on the number of off-spring. This might change again, if material conditions continue to improve. Then Germany may witness a baby boom. Whether this would be desirable for women is open to question. It could easily lead to a revival of concepts defining the family as the only legitimate domain of women, and to public agitation to confine them to it once again.

How stable marriages are in this country is difficult to assess. Figures on divorce—83 per 1000 marriages in 1960 as against 75 in 1938—reveal little as long as other data, such as the number of couples living separately, remains unknown. It may well be that under the strain of war, and in the misery of the postwar period, families proved more stable than might have been expected. However, with the return to normality since the 1950's, this may have changed. Whatever the case may be, German experiences of the last three decades allow for the hypothesis that a national crisis does not necessarily become also a familial crisis, while, on the other hand, stability of broader social structures does not inevitably make for the internal stability of the family. Rather, it can be suspected that in the present relatively stable social order destructive impulses of the individual, having few outlets, turn against the family, upsetting its peace, without, however, destroying the unit.

Sex Mores

Aside from the few data about marital happiness and unhappiness, there is practically no reliable information available on sex mores, and one can only speculate. Casual observations seem to indicate that German young people follow liberal patterns, though not in excess. Nearly half of all first-born children were conceived before their parents were married. Furthermore, abortion seems to be resorted to very frequently, in spite of the Catholic-inspired laws prohibiting it.

While these facts indicate the prevalence of premarital sexual experience among young people, they do not reveal how frequently boys and girls change partners before they settle down to marriage. We may safely conclude that girls tend to disregard the traditional rules which insist on premarital virginity and to experiment sexually with their fiancés and probably with other men as well. The men accept this practice readily, no longer demanding chastity of their future wives.

Although nowadays young men as well as young women are strongly inclined to idealize the family and marriage as an escape from loneliness and lack of parental understanding, there is no doubt that adultery has become rather a common practice, particularly for men after several years of marriage. For men over thirty or so, there are abundant opportunities, since many women between thirty-five and forty-five are unmarried and quite willing to consent to a love affair with a married man. Prostitution is well established in all of the larger cities. Thus, the conditions prevailing since the end of World War II invite adultery and extramarital relations on the part of men, while women, both married and unmarried, are in a vulnerable position, and must compete with each other because of their larger numbers.

The Home Routine

From mere observation it seems that young wives with children are not too satisfied. Though probably all of them wanted to get married and to have babies, some find it difficult to adjust to the traditional roles. In the first place, they are frequently overburdened. Maids and cleaning women are in extremely short supply, and usually there are no relatives around so that housework is entirely left to them. Of course, technical facilities ease the job. However, many of the labor-saving devices, like dishwashers, washing machines, automatic electric stoves, and so forth, are still too expensive to afford. So far the average German household is far from being as well equipped with major and minor appliances as is the American one. Furthermore, German husbands are not yet quite used to helping their wives in the home. Thus, mothers are continuously busy, and do not always like their work. Some of them feel lonely, too. Used to working in the company of adults, to having more leisure and money of their own, they resent their isolation during the day.

This dissatisfaction, evinced especially by young women, has its roots not just in individual failure or simply in egotism. It is the result partly of the necessity to combine women's two roles, partly of inadequate preparation. The conflict between the new demands and the traditional attitude makes for trouble also among those who need not take a job after marriage.

Education

However, many of those who resent matrimonial life could easily spare more time for activities linking them closer to the outer world if they only knew better how to organize their work. Lacking adequate training either for the homemaking job or for her other tasks, the average woman is unable to find her way out of drudgery and isolation.

A definite deficiency in the principles of education makes itself felt here. While schools at all levels provide rather thorough training in many fields, they fail as far as social and psychological preparation for the future task of women is concerned. First, schools do not supply the information about women's position in modern society needed to make girls more aware of what lies ahead. Discussions in class about the changes in family structure and the female role in the family are rare indeed. Also, instruction in child psychology is entirely neglected. Consequently, many young women, not properly prepared by their parents either, underrate the importance of their duties as the prime socializing agent of their children and of their responsibility for the home. Such misapprehension might be one cause of frustration, of the woman feeling cut off from the stream of life. Obviously, abstract ideological tribute which is abundantly paid to mothers by the public at large will not do. Rather, the future mothers need to be prepared more realistically for their job, gain more self-confidence and pride in it.

Moreover, while at school girls are not sufficiently made aware that they themselves will be responsible for their lives, and that they have to take the initiative in introducing desired changes. Thus after marriage they rarely seize the opportunities to improve their condition. Neither the school nor the average parent imparts that rational attitude toward everyday problems which is a a precondition of mastering them. The capacity to plan and to organize one's work is also insufficiently developed, as is the ability to grasp the limits of such endeavors. What women ought to learn, and schools to teach, is, therefore, a better awareness of ends, and the faculty to select means accordingly.

Once again it is evident that women in Germany are in a state of transition, confronted with new tasks while still searching more or less unsuccessfully for exemplars to guide them. For those married women who could manage to find spare time it would be helpful if some of their energies were channeled into voluntary work with political and social associations. More active participation of such women in local government, school administration, adult education and the like would certainly be to great advantage. However, such activities have so far gained little popularity, partly because the public is not used to them, and partly because the women themselves either do not recognize the opportunities or shy away from responsibility. This reluctance is not confined to women. Rather, it is a consequence of the specifically German political atmosphere. In contrast to the British and American tradition, the participation of individual citizens in local affairs and private initiative in public matters were never encouraged. Getting away from such patterns is more difficult for women. However, most men too still have to learn that lesson.

Women's Occupations

In 1962, West Germany had a female labor force of 9.4 million, roughly one third of all gainfully employed. Seventy per cent (6.7 million) were salary and wage earners, the remaining 2.7 million either independent business women, themselves owners and managers of small or medium-size firms, or assistants in some family enterprise. Two fifths of the wage and salary earners work in industry; one fifth in commerce, banking, and insurance companies;

the rest in agriculture, traffic, and construction. Female labor is of course nothing new in Germany. Common among farmers, and in the handicrafts of preindustrial times, modern industry made use of it almost from its very beginning. Since the 1840's, proletarian women have entered the shops, and later on, also, bourgeois women came to the fore, chiefly in lower clerical and teaching posts. Ever since, a large army of females has been on paid jobs— some 15 million during World War I, and somewhat fewer during World War II. After 1945 many withdrew, only to return in the 1950's. Under the pressure of an extreme shortage of labor, the trend is towards further increase, which, however, may have reached its natural limits by now.

In West Germany, as in any industrial country, female labor is no transitory phenomenon. Women have entered the productive process to stay. Even the most conservative minds realize that without female cooperation practically no branch of the economy could function efficiently. If all working women went on strike, a national catastrophe would result. Thus the public debate about women's rights to gainful employment, carried on for many a decade, has come to an end.

Though entirely indispensable, working women are somewhat under-privileged in several ways. Subtle discrimination begins early with the selection of future training and job. In 1960, twice as many boys as girls of the lower and lower-middle classes, upon leaving school at the age of fourteen or fifteen, began vocational training. Young girls of the same strata have a narrower choice as far as training and vocation are concerned. In industry, there are some three hundred categories of skilled jobs, yet most girls, on the advice of parents or teachers, stick to only half a dozen, which are traditionally considered better suited for them. Others take a job without special training, attending, in addition, schools for home economics until they are eighteen. These unskilled or semiskilled women make up 90 per cent of all the female labor in industry as against 10 per cent who went through apprenticeships. On the other hand, among men, the ratio of skilled to unskilled or semiskilled workers is 50:50.

To be sure, the majority of girls would prefer to receive further education after high school. Formerly, almost all unskilled women hoped to enter a qualified trade, yet were refused the opportunity by their parents. Many parents, particularly in the lower strata, consider additional schooling for daughters a mere luxury. Trusting the girl will marry, they want her to earn money immediately after finishing school and to acquire a trousseau. Rarely are they aware that additional training would open better jobs to her, let alone that she has the right to have her talents awakened and developed. The girls themselves, being too young to stand up against parents and relatives, after a brief period on the job become indifferent, and profoundly resigned. Realizing that without additional training they have no chance to get ahead, they now cherish the dream of marriage, expecting it to bring salvation from factory life. In recent years, however, there has been some improvement. In

1960 twice as many girls became apprentices in qualified trades as in 1950. Also, the number of lower-class girl students in vocational schools has increased.

Girls of the upper-middle and upper classes who want to attend a university are also confronted with special problems unknown to boys. However, their number has risen too. While in 1951 girls constituted only one fifth of the student body, the percentage rose to 23 in 1964. Nevertheless, the fact remains that in universities and *Hochschulen* women cluster in the so-called typically female disciplines such as teaching and medicine. Only a few dare enter the fields traditionally reserved for men. In law only 5.5 per cent, and in economics and social sciences only 7.8 per cent of the students are girls.

Adult women too, are at a disadvantage in several respects. First, some of them still do not get equal pay for equal performance. While this situation might change in the near future under the pressure of the (not too energetic) trade unions and some sections of the general public, optimism is less justified with regard to women's careers and their chances of promotion in industry, public administration, and the professions. Among top executives of private corporations there are almost no women, with the exception of those whose inherited property gave them access to positions of control. Nor can they easily rise to the middle-managerial level. According to sociological studies carried out in recent years, the vast majority of female white-collar workers in business concerns is employed in the lowest ranks. Thus, in the administrative sector of corporations, women are, so to speak, privates led by an almost exclusively male officer corps. Or, as a group of sociolgists has put it: "With regard to norms and stereotypes, the entire white-collar sector is dominated by conservative attitudes. To have a woman in a leading or otherwise highly qualified position seems in many places to be as revolutionary a thought as it was decades ago."

Also in the academic ranks of public or semi-public bureaucracies it is difficult for women to get ahead. While studying in the universities girls enjoy practically full equality with men, but upon graduation their situation becomes different. In the higher echelons of the German civil service, exclusively manned by university graduates, the proportion of women is between 2 and 3 per cent. Of all judges in the Federal Republic somewhat less than 3 per cent are females. One woman is a member of the Federal Supreme Court. The percentage of female university teachers is also low, not more than three. In the academic year of 1958–1959, of 2,328 full professors in the universities and technical universities of West Germany and Berlin, only eight were women. In the lower faculty ranks there were 3,558 men as against 111 women. There are almost no women among engineers, only a few in the diplomatic service (none of whom has achieved ambassadorial rank), and certainly not many in the legal profession. On the other hand, women are numerous in professions traditionally considered female. Thus they constitute roughly one third of the teachers in high schools (*Gymnasium*), two thirds of the teachers in elementary and secondary schools, and slightly less than one fifth of the physicians.

In politics, the picture is not much different. Of all adults entitled to vote some 55 per cent are women, and about one quarter of all members of political parties; but in state assemblies they are represented by only 6 to 8 per cent, and in the Federal Parliament by no more than 9 to 10. In 1961, for the first time in German history, a woman became the head of a national ministry, that of health.

Several factors explain why the number of women in higher and highest ranks is, and perhaps always will be, smaller than that of men. Many women do not really seek a career. Some of them, particularly young girls and married women, prefer to stay in lower positions with little or no responsibility involved. Many quit the job after marriage or after the birth of the first child. A further explanation is to be found in the fact, already mentioned, that on all levels the number of trained females is comparatively low. Some women work only temporarily to help out in a family emergency or to earn money for some other purpose. Finally, in a number of jobs such as civil service and teaching, it is difficult to promote married women, because promotion would demand that they move to another city. Since their husbands are usually tied to the place by their jobs, wives often turn down offers of promotion. It follows that even if they enjoyed fully equal opportunities, women would not be as numerous in the advanced positions as men.

All these factors, however, do not explain why the percentage of women in responsible ranks is so extremely small. The ultimate reason must be sought, not in the women themselves, but in the resistance of the environment. In conformity with the general ideological and intellectual conditions prevailing in Germany today, employers' attitudes and thinking are frequently dominated by old-fashioned prejudice, a general dislike of change, and possibly also by some fear of disturbance. Therefore, with rare exceptions, they hesitate to promote women. Many men in positions of authority are convinced that to remain in subordinate posts is to the good of the women themselves and of the community at large.

Generally speaking, the female role in Germany is still defined along traditional lines. The majority of men, and many women as well, hold with the old concept according to which the nature of women disqualifies them from shouldering responsibility outside of the home, acting as superiors, or performing intellectual tasks, let alone scholarly work. All the elements of the traditional definition of female character are still there: women are believed to be passive and emotional, and, due to their innate and unalterable disposition, incapable of abstract thinking. Nature, it can still be heard over and over again, has created them to serve in the family and the home, not in the world of men. Such arguments serve a twofold purpose: on the one hand, they restrain female ambition, on the other, they provide men with a justification for acting as they do.

When questioned as to their opinion about the promotion of women in business firms, employers usually point to these so-called innate deficiencies of women and to what they believe is woman's natural lack of technical interest, stamina, and psychological stability. On the other hand, they are believed to have an inborn talent for monotonous, dependent work, and should therefore be kept in dependence. It is interesting to note that those entrepreneurs who, in spite of widespread disapproval, promoted their women employees, gave excellent reports. Also, those women who did make their way up did not confirm the stereotyped expectation that they would not be accepted by subordinates.

To deem women principally incapable of qualified work is, however, not confined to businessmen. Leaders of institutions of higher learning cling to the same belief. University professors, usually considered more enlightened, would not like to have women on the faculties, either. First, so the learned men argue, women can have no authority with students, and second, they are mentally and physically unsuited for scholarly work. As one of them put it: "Intellectual creativity is a privilege of men," meaning that it should remain a male privilege. Ironically enough, none of those who were strongly opposed to having women on the teaching staff—and such is the attitude of the vast majority of those questioned—deemed the performance of girl students inferior to that of the men. The fact remains that the overwhelming majority of the men who hold the power of decision either hesitate or altogether refuse to let women get ahead. At best they do not encourage them.

The question arises why the considerable minority of women who want a career do not fight more energetically for it, and why in general women in and out of jobs do not strive more energetically for their rights. In many instances, such endeavors are likely to succeed, since the shortage of labor on all levels, including schools and universities, compels employers to hire even those deemed less fit. Although in recent years there may have been some progress, the number of women making use of such opportunities is still small. Obviously, the vast majority is not actively engaged in the strife. As mentioned above, there are some two million women now in their thirties and forties who realize that they have no chance to marry, simply because of lack of men. The self-respect of these women depends primarily on the appreciation of their work by superiors, colleagues and friends. However, even they do not rebel. Rather, they believe that the situation is unalterable. Why should this be so?

Again the answer must be sought mainly in the force of tradition which influences women no less than men. Growing up in a world which directly and even more indirectly tells women that they are unsuited for intellectual and technical work, for executive or other superior jobs, and for political activity, many actually become incapable. They have no chance to develop that kind of self-confidence which is a precondition of success. Further, they fear being considered unfeminine. If political activity, interest in a career, and professional ambition are considered unfeminine, then, of course, many women will behave "femininely" and avoid deviating from the commonly-accepted pattern. Instead of emancipating themselves from the outdated concepts, they adjust. Being afraid of society's criticism, and of becoming outsiders to their reference groups, they surrender, suppressing whatever fighting spirit might once have been in them.

One more cause for the resignation of many German women should be mentioned. Many accept things as they are from sheer physical and psychic exhaustion. The women of this country have for decades known no stability of national life, and hence none in their personal existence. Brought up in the misery of wars, thwarted by the experience of the vast unemployment in the late 1920's, witnesses to a totalitarian dictatorship, intimately acquainted with the horrors of refugee life—no wonder that they are exhausted, drained. Also, too many have lost their husbands, and devoted themselves entirely to bringing up the children without help. How could there be much energy left in them?

There are undoubtedly exceptions. It is on them, their activity, stamina and work performance that the future position of working women in Germany depends, to a considerable extent.

Outlook

Modern society grants many privileges to all its members, male and female alike. It gives them freedom from poverty and from ruinous physical labor; it prolongs the average individual's life; it makes free education available to all. In the democracies, each citizen enjoys a measure of political and personal freedom which was formerly unknown even to the ruling classes.

At the same time, society puts high demands on everyone, above all on women. They must act responsibly, not only in the family but also in the business world. More than ever before, the functioning and efficiency of the productive process depend on their cooperation; but, again more than ever before, also the functioning of the family depends on them. Whether the family will be able to realize its new possibilities: to be a humanizing agency, a haven for the individual where he can relax from, and shake off, the regimentation and discipline of his work, all this, almost entirely, depends on women. It is they who, more than men, will determine the future personalities of their children.

Moreover, women have to fill a third role as well, that of a citizen capable of forming judgments of her own and arriving at rational political decisions. In the political sphere, too, women have become indispensable. Western society, with all the economic well-being and social security it grants its members, is in constant danger not only from threats of war, but from domestic perils. The dangers of rightist or leftist totalitarianisms, with their tendency to transform men into masses, to deprive the individual of his own identity, to dehumanize the human being, threaten women no less than men. Thus, the political fight against them is of concern to both sexes. If women want to preserve their privileges they must become citizens not only formally but in substance.

Thus far, women in Germany are as ill-equipped for these tasks as for securing their rights. They still have a long way to go in order to become mentally and psychologically independent, and able to judge for themselves. Too many of them are still shaped in the traditional image of femininity. What is needed is to abandon the old model and to replace the former virtues of passivity, unconcerned subordination, and adaptation, with the virtues of reflection, critical thinking, and the courage to resist domination.

In Germany there are few historical models for such a change. For many generations the country has idealized the pious woman, subservient to husband, church, and throne. To this, the Nazis added a special note, degrading women to biological machines whose primary function was to give birth to as many children—future soldiers—as possible. Undoubtedly, there is today some awareness that these norms do not suffice, and certainly only a tiny lunatic fringe still pays homage to the Nazi idea. The lack of sensible historical models at least partly explains why the majority of women has no clear idea of what they should be. Nor has the public at large. Both male and female shuttle, so to speak, uneasily between present and past. This insecurity makes itself felt everywhere: in the ambivalent attitude towards working mothers; in taking for granted female labor while excluding women from the higher ranks; in granting them suffrage but discouraging them from political activity; in the overburdening of rural women and housewives; in granting personal freedom, while maintaining the traditional type of femininity as the ideal.

It will take a long time until the majority of German women arrive at a better understanding of their new position and of the new demands. Much depends on education, for which, however, the educators themselves still have to be educated. Some people have begun to formulate progressive programs. The goal is to make female students and teachers alike more intimately acquainted with the society they live in, and, above all, as has been pointed out by Marianne Grewe, to help them "get rid of their own prejudice as regards their inferiority . . . to give them better criteria for the evaluation of men, and for the social order in general."

PART 5

The Nature
of Modern People

Most historians are reluctant to define the central characteristics of the modern outlook, and perhaps the modern outlook is too complex and varied to be described clearly. Yet the modernization process has had a certain direction, and it is important, after having considered some of its major features, to talk about its possible end results or at least about the results to date.

The four selections that follow are written by social scientists, which is almost all they have in common. Different professional training and experience lead to different evaluations of the nature of modernization. Different approaches—the attempt to provide a general model, for example, as against a study of a particular class or region—lead to different evaluations of the extent of the process. Fortunately the student of the modernization process in Europe is not forced simply to weigh one contemporary evaluation against another. He can apply his understanding of key stages in history of society during recent centuries. He can compare current institutions and values to those that antedate modernization. Out of this mix, hopefully, will come some sense of what modern man is like, how new he is, and what his prospects are.

Bibliography

The twentieth-century French peasant has received considerable attention from scholars, who disagree about the extent of traditional behavior in rural society. See Gordon Wright, *Rural Revolution in France: The Peasantry in the Twentieth Century* (Stanford, 1968), and Robert T. and Barbara G. Anderson, *Bus Stop for Paris* (New York, 1966). Lawrence W. Wylie, ed., *Chanzeaux: A Village in Anjou* (Cambridge, Mass., 1966), studies a particularly conservative region. Henri Mendras, *The Vanishing Peasant: Innovation and Change in French Agriculture*, trans. by Jean Lerner (Cambridge, Mass., 1970), is a recent interpretation that posits the end of peasant society in France and elsewhere.

The modernization model has often been applied to studies of non-Western societies; see Ronald P. Dore, ed., *Aspects of Social Change in Japan* (Princeton, 1967), and M. B. Jansen, *Changing Japanese Attitudes Toward Modernization* (Princeton, 1965). Cyril E. Black, *The Dynamics of Modernization: A Study in Comparative History* (New York, 1966), sketches a general history of the subject.

Herbert Marcuse, *One Dimensional Man* (Boston, 1964), is a criticism of modernity somewhat related to Laing's. Fritz R. Stern, *The Politics of Cultural Despair: A Study in the Rise of the Germanic Ideology* (Berkeley, 1961), traces some earlier manifestations of intellectual hostility to modernity.

French Peasants

LAURENCE WYLIE

German National Characteristics

RALF DAHRENDORF

The following two selections raise important questions about the extent of the modernization of European outlook. They remind us of the magnitude of the change required to produce a modern personality, which explains why many people have not yet made a full transition. Facile generalizations about what modern man is like, then, must be qualified. There are variations, and tradition has not been entirely displaced. This same complexity raises problems for the critics of modernization as well. Their approach has also depended on the assumption of great change; but possibly more people have retained a protective cushion of tradition than the critics recognize. And there is another possibility. It may be the incomplete transition that causes the greatest tensions. It may not be the rationalistic, individualistic, secular personality that has the most trouble coping with urban life, but rather the semitraditionalist personality facing the same objective conditions.

The first selection, by an American anthropologist, is a close study of a rural village in southern France. Peasant life, in France and elsewhere, has changed greatly over the past century. Most peasants in southern France have lost their traditional religion. For more than a century they have faced economic change. Since the Second World War they have become increasingly aware of a new technology. They have, then, adapted to important aspects of modern life. But much of their basic character is still traditionalistic, and many modern institutions seem incomprehensible, if not positively hostile, as a result. At the same time, peasants remain an important minority of the European population. And even as their numbers diminish, their outlook may be carried on by immigrants from the countryside to the city. If peasants have resisted the many pressures to convert to a modernized personality—including the educational system and, more recently, mass communications—we cannot assume that city dwellers necessarily surrender their traditions easily.

The second selection has broader implications. It suggests the possibility that a society can industrialize and urbanize with great rapidity while the bulk of the population remains fundamentally unmodern in outlook. Ralf Dahrendorf is a prominent German sociologist. He has a fairly clear set of criteria by which he defines what is modern, and he likes modernity. But he finds most of his countrymen lagging behind, despite the great industrial surge Germany has experienced since the mid-nineteenth century. Dahrendorf sees some signs that traditionalism is breaking down as more Germans become devoted to individual material gain, but these are very recent developments. In the past, much of Germany's distinctive history has been due to the tensions between a modern economy and widespread traditional values. Accepting this approach leads to a sweeping interpretation of the problems of modern Germany. The claim is, of course, that no other country has experienced the same kind of tension. Yet we can grant that the tension was particularly acute in Germany and still ask if it has not existed to some degree in other societies—indeed whether it still exists. The twofold question is how completely traditional values have been shattered, and whether the key strains in modern life are inherent in the modern personality or are the result of the failure of the modern personality to become dominant. And if the modern personality has not yet fully emerged, will it do so finally? Will the definitions offered by critics and supporters alike remain in part abstractions, as modern men refuse to shake off a number of traditional values?

FRENCH PEASANTS

When I think of the individual of Peyrane faced with collective human power, an image immediately occurs to me. I see Alphonse Peretti stoically walking from school up to the church with his messy school theme pinned to his back so that people along the way will make fun of him. Or I see a little girl walking in a circle in the school yard, alone, with her hands on her head, with the sign "thief" pinned to her back, while the other children point at her and mock her. These are extreme and unusual cases, but they point forcefully to the essential disciplinary tools—shame and ridicule—which adults use with children both at home and at school. Children need not fear violence, mutilation, loss of love, separation from parents, threats of damnation or any of the other weapons which people in the world use to secure obedience from children. They are constantly faced, however, with shaming fingers and mocking laughter. To avoid the pain of public shame and ridicule children must learn to conform—on the surface at least. The revenge that is sometimes tolerated is for them to stand at a safe distance and shout insults.

How can a child avoid feeling as he grows up that people are ready to assail him collectively with the force of public scorn whenever he deviates from the behavior that is expected of him? And since no one can live without deviating from an ideal social code—both in action and in thought—almost everyone feels that society has cause to attack him. He is even further

Reprinted by permission of the publishers from Laurence Wylie, *Village in the Vaucluse*, 2nd Edition, Cambridge, Mass.: Harvard University Press, Copyright, 1957, 1964, by the President and Fellows of Harvard College.

convinced that humans collectively are hostile because he assumes that they feel as hostile toward him as he feels toward them.

As the child grows up these personal feelings about collective human power are reinforced by conventional attitudes that have undoubtedly been current in Peyrane since the first individuals settled on the red hill. For there has never been a time since the beginning of Peyrane's history, when contact with organized humanity has meant anything but the exploitation and manipulation of the individual. The wandering hordes, the Romans, the feudal lords—including the neighboring papal rulers, the agents of Provençal counts and French kings, the nineteenth-century régimes set up by Paris, the twentieth-century bureaucracy centralized in Paris—all these form an unbroken past in the vague memory of the village. They all mean domination by a human power beyond the control of the individual. At best the domination has brought unsought modifications in living habits. At worst it has brought disaster. And so it has become conventional to think of human power as a plague to be classed with the plagues of nature: the odious government, the leveling mistral, the flooding Durance. . . .

The feeling of frustration does not paralyze all their activities. . . . When immediate family concerns are at stake there is no such despair. Members of the family participate positively in every aspect of family life. A child learns very young that he must share the problems. One after another, responsibilities are thrust on him, so that he acquires a growing sense of responsibility for the family's welfare. In this sphere he is impelled to act constructively.

But in other spheres of life, corporate responsibility and constructive participation by the individual are not stressed. . . . The school experience tends toward passivity and immobility. Children are not made to feel that the initiative is theirs as it is in the family. Spontaneity is not officially recognized in the educational system as it operates in Peyrane. A child who acts spontaneously risks being punished, and the punishment consists of forced immobilization of the body combined with shame. In formal learning emphasis is placed on deduction: children are not encouraged to "discover" a principle by themselves; it is presented to them as something to accept passively. Even in art class there is no place for free expression; children are asked to reproduce as realistically as possible a flower or a vase that is put before them. Recess play on the playground is unplanned, but children must behave with civilized caution. School experience does not, on the whole, develop an urge to act, to act adventurously to dominate one's own situation, to act coöperatively to improve the situation of the whole group. So far as the average student is concerned responsibility is something to be avoided. It may be recalled why Jacques Leporatti worked hard in school: "So they'll leave me alone!"

GERMAN NATIONAL CHARACTERISTICS

. . . It is precisely this lacking awareness of social inequality that illustrates the peculiarity of the divided society in Germany. The question of how the other half lives is rarely raised in Germany. Existing conditions are accepted without protest; they are as they are, and nobody can do much about them. It is part of the order of the world, and no reason for doubt, that there is a borderline between Above and Below.

This is the point at which our suspended explanation of the flagrant inequalities of educational opportunity in Germany becomes possible. We seen that certain groups—workers, children, children from the country, girls— are heavily underrepresented in German secondary schools and universities. We have moreover seen that they are not formally underprivileged, so that their condition must have reasons other than legal. These form a complex pattern. They range from the financial preconditions of education to the availability of schools, from the mentalities of social strata that are hostile to education—such as the absence of a sense of deferred gratification—to aspects of school and university life that discriminate against certain groups. But there is much to be said for seeking one of the main causes of the inequalities of educational opportunity in Germany in the minds of those hit hardest by them, that is, with workers and peasants and with parents of girls, as well as with their children. Among all these people, an attitude of traditionalism prevails that prevents them from perceiving the chance to shorten and simplify the mountain hike to the peaks of stratification by using the funicular of educational institutions. Part of the same attitude is the failure to recognize any necessity to move more than a few steps from one's place in society. This is a social, not an individual attitude, of course; we are not trying to charge workers with willful neglect of their opportunities, but are merely looking at their motives as an expression of social patterns.

In detail, these motives are complex and involved. So far as workers are concerned, their social consciousness is dominated by a sense of dichotomy and of the distance associated with it: "The people with money, well, they send their children, never mind if they are dim or not. And they get through, too. And not only in school; where good apprenticeships are concerned too. Among the poor there are sure to be good people left, but they do not get through. We have seen that ourselves in my firm. There were sons of rich people too, who got in all right, but they were certainly not as good as others, who had no money. That is why they did not get in. This is how it is in secondary schools too. Just go and look how many children of rich people there are!" This from a forty-three-year-old smith and father of several children of school age, resigned rather than aggressive in his mood.

There is more in such remarks than the mere distinction between poor and rich. The rich and "their" secondary school present themselves as distant and strange. "Strange, threatening, unpleasant, rigid, demanding"—this according to a survey conducted by J. Hitpass, is how the secondary school appears to German workers; and the university seems to them "situated in space, sinister, incomprehensible like Picasso." There is a familiar and there is an alien world. They are separated by an enormous social distance, which means that one has little real knowledge of the alien world and therefore gets along with simple stereotypes, whose objective falsehood does not impair their subjective effectiveness. The distance and the substitution of stereotypes for information holds the other way too, of course. While the geography of societies permits that distance from Below to Above is greater than that from Above to Below, it is questionable whether this is the case in Germany. But on either side of the fence, lack of information and strangeness is easily translated into a feeling of threat. The conclusion drawn from this product of strangeness and anxiety is the conclusion of traditionalism: people refuse to be drawn into the venture of the road to the unknown.

The case of country children and girls resembles that of working-class children in many respects, except that in the former case parents can more easily be held personally responsible for the persistence of traditional ties. If peasants want to keep the one-class school in their village at the risk of blocking the road to the top for their children, they do so also because they fear that the traditional patterns of village life might be endangered if their children received a higher education in distant places. (This is not so different from the concerns of Catholic priests who, worried about the secularization of the faithful, confined their educational zeal to those who promised to become priests themselves.) Parents who remove their talented daughter from school before she takes her degree because they want her to help at home deliberately perpetuate the traditional role of the woman, which is defined by the absence of independence, motivation, and initiative. In all these half-conscious restrictions a traditionalism becomes evident that prefers the conservation of the heritage to the rise into the unknown heights of modernity.

In the long run, traditionalism needs homogeneous social structures in order to thrive. A mentality that rejects novelty and initiative is most easily upheld in groups that are uniform in their ethnic origin and religious affiliation, their regional and occupational attachment, their dialect and their collective memory. H. Peisert has been able to show that motivation for higher education decreases as the social contexts in which people live become more homogeneous, regardless of the basis of such homogeneity: homogeneously Protestant regions are as traditionalist as homogeneously Catholic ones; in all cases, inherited likeness in kind is an obstacle to development. . . .

. . . It would be perfectly plausible to interpret [the figures that indicate that over half of all Germans are living in the place where they grew up] quite differently and point out that there is considerable vertical mobility in

Germany, and that in certain groups, such as state officials, a motivation for upward mobility is systematically inbred. The fact that almost one-half of all people did not grow up in the place where they are living today may be taken, by comparison to strictly traditional conditions, as a sign of remarkable mobility. In other words, the persistence of a basic attitude of traditionalism is not the whole truth of contemporary German society.

This can be put in more dynamic terms. The mixture of modernity and unmodernity, rationality and traditionalism, in the mentality of large social groups once again displays the faults that Imperial Germany and the industrial revolution have bequeathed to German society. Alongside a nearly immobile peasant estate there is alleged modernity in the form of the civil service; next to mobile metropolitan Berliners there are firmly rooted small townspeople unprepared to move at any price. Admittedly, this is one of the respects in which the volcanic surface of German society has been shaking for some time. While state social policy is still trying to chain people to their social places, the dynamics of economic development, the brutal struggle of National Socialism against tradition, as well as more sensitive and courageous measures by farsighted reformers in churches, other institutions, and the state have lowered many of the barriers of traditionalism in Germany. The threshold holding back the assault of modern rationality is therefore no longer very high today. There are examples in the field of educational policy that show how little may suffice to make people who never even considered a higher education for their children change their motives. The traditional attachments of the Germans' social psychology are probably on the whole relics of a passing epoch, striking as their vitality may still appear at some points.

This reminder adds a reservation to our thesis, but does not invalidate it. Nor is the advent of modernity in Germany to be secured solely by the dissolution of traditional motivations with respect to education. Groups that are at a factual disadvantage in the exercise of citizenship rights merely document extreme cases of a far more general pattern. When David Riesman distinguished between three social characters—inner-directed, other-directed, and tradition-directed—he, like others who used similar distinctions, left the notion of "tradition" residual without paying much attention to it. Yet it is far more descriptive of some apparently modern societies, including Germany, than Riesman and others seem to think. The core of traditionalism (and in this it differs from all modern mentalities) is the notion that we cannot do much about things because they have always been as they are. There is a defeatism about traditional attitudes, which can hardly encourage the spread of citizenship, or indeed of civilization. Where people might feel motivated to act and change unsatisfactory conditions, one hears instead in Germany the resigned comment that they are "fate" (Schicksal), accompanied by a helpless shrug of the shoulders. It is in contrast to this defeatism that the notion of modernity (which we are using rather freely and perhaps seemingly indefinitely here) has to be understood.

How about the implication that modernity makes men happier than tradition possibly could? What reason is there to believe that a more modern, active mentality is preferable to a traditional one? The question is remarkably patronizing in the first place: Who can presume the right to decide for others what is good for them and what not? But apart from this matter of taste, the fact remains that modernity is a liberation of men from unquestioned ties, and therefore opens up new avenues of self-expression for people. Such optimism, it is true, creates its own frustrations, whether they result from problems of discrepant status, of rapid mobility, or from other sources. But by making all problems, including these, appear manageable, modernity transcends the subtly paralyzing hopelessness of tradition.

Such hopes are, however, promise rather than analysis. In our context, another version of the question of the price of modernity is more relevant, and may also help us give some sociological substance to the praise of modernity: What are the political consequences of a society that shuns the road to modernity? What were, and are, these consequences in German society, past and present? We are still concerned with restrictions of citizenship by social roles that accompany ascribed social positions. What happens then if people make their political decisions not on the basis of their interests and a rational calculation of the gains and losses involved in various political lines, but allow themselves to be guided by expectations in which they have become entangled without being able to free themselves by their own efforts?

Modern Man

ALEX INKELES

In the following description, modern man seems very new and quite a good fellow, well adjusted to a changing environment. Do these virtues—which sound remarkably like those urged by Enlightenment philosophers and middle-class optimists long ago—really describe the evolution toward a modern outlook? Are they consistent, for example, with changes in family relationships, where dignity and even democracy might be concretely expressed? Do they leave sufficient room for national or class differences in values?

Inkeles' approach makes one thing quite clear: for him, rural tradition must not be idealized; it is full of hardship and confusion. Hence movement to the city is actually an opportunity not only for higher earnings, but for a much more constructive human personality.

Inkeles discusses the variety of causes necessary to produce a modern outlook, most of them going back at least a century in European experience. He leaves room also for a gradual evolution toward modern values, and this is an important qualification to what might otherwise seem a simplistic approach. Urban man is not necessarily modern; pockets of tradition remain, and even when they begin to collapse there may be many stages before full modernization is attained.

This basic approach to defining modern values has been used by a number of social scientists studying the modernization process outside the Western world. Inkeles has applied his criteria of modernity to studies of Russia. Others have used similar characteristics in assessing the extent of modernization in Japan and elsewhere. They might disagree with Inkeles on some specific points (many definitions stress the secularism of the modern outlook, for example, whereas Inkeles tries to integrate religion), but they would agree that modernity is definable and good.

But what is the modern man, and what makes him what he is? The answer to this question is inevitably controversial, and almost no one enters on a discussion of it without arousing a good deal of emotion. The reasons are not hard to find. In the first place, the change from more traditional to more modern qualities in man often means someone must give up ways of thinking and feeling that go back decades, sometimes centuries; and to

From Chapter 10, "The Modernization of Man" by Alex Inkeles in Modernization: The Dynamics of Growth edited by Myron Weiner, © 1966 by Basic Books, Inc., Publishers, New York.

abandon these ways often seems to be abandoning principle itself. For another thing, the qualities that make a man modern often do not appear to be neutral characteristics that any man might have, but instead represent the distinctive traits of the European, the American, or the Westerner that he is bent on imposing on other people so as to make them over in his own image. In the third place, many of the characteristics that are described as modern, and therefore automatically desirable, in fact are not very useful or suitable to the life and conditions of those on whom they are urged or even imposed. These are most serious issues, and we shall return to them briefly after sketching some details of what we mean by modern man.

The characteristic mark of the modern man has two parts: one internal, the other external; one dealing with his environment, the other with his attitudes, values, and feelings.

The change in the external condition of modern man is well known and widely documented, and it need not detain us long. It may be summarized by reference to a series of key terms: urbanization, education, mass communication, industrialization, politicalization. These terms signify that in contrast to his forebears living in the traditional order of his society, the modern man is less likely to work the land as a farmer and is more likely to be employed in a large and complex productive enterprise based on the intensive use of power and advanced technologies. The various economies yielded by the concentration of industry in certain sites and the further demands of those industrial concentrations make it likely that the contemporary man will live in a city or some other form of urban conglomeration. Here, he will experience not only crowding but access to all manner of resource and stimulation characteristic of urban life. Inevitably, one of these stimuli will be the media of mass communication: newspapers, radio, movies, and perhaps even television. His experience of new places and ideas will be augmented by the impact of schooling, if not directly for him, then for his children, who may carry the influence of the school into the home. He is much more likely to have some connection with politics, especially on the national scale, as he is more exposed to mass communication, more mobilized in the surge of urban life, more courted by the competing political movements that seek his support as he may enlist their aid to replace that of the chief, the patron, or the family head whose assistance he would ordinarily have sought in his native village. Indeed, another mark of the contemporary man is that he will no longer live enmeshed in a network of primary kin ties, perhaps supplemented by ties to a small number of fellow villagers, but rather will be drawn into a much more impersonal and bureaucratic milieu in which he is dependent for services and aid in times of distress on persons and agencies with which he has a much more formal and perhaps tenuous relationship.

These are all attributes of his life space that may impinge on the modern man, but in themselves they do not constitute modernity. The densest urban centers may still shelter the most traditional network of human relations: the media of mass communication may mainly disseminate folk tales and traditional wisdom, factories may run on principles not far different from those of the estate or the hacienda, and politics may be conducted like an extension of the village council. Although his exposure to the modern setting may certainly contribute to the transformation of traditional man, and although that setting may in turn require new ways of him, it is only when man has undergone a change in spirit—has acquired certain new ways of thinking, feeling, and acting—that we come to consider him truly modern.

Although there is no single standard definition of the modern man that all accept and use, there is quite good agreement among students of the modernization process as to the characteristics that distinguish the more modern man from the more traditional. To convey my impression of his traits, I have chosen to describe him in terms of a series of attitudes and values that we are testing in a study of the modernization process among workers and peasants in six developing countries. This permits me not only to present the characteristic profile we define as modern but also to indicate some of the questions we are using to study its manifestation in concrete cases. The order in which these characteristics are presented here is not meant to suggest that this is the actual sequence in the process of individual modernization. So far, we are not aware that there is a clear-cut sequence, but rather have the impression that the process develops on a broad front with many changes occurring at once. Neither does the order in which the characteristics are given suggest the relative weight or importance of each characteristic in the total syndrome. Here, again, we have yet, through our scientific work, to assess the relative contribution of each characteristic to the larger complex of attitudes, values, and ways of acting that we consider modern. We do, however, assume that this complex of attitudes and values holds together: that in the statistical sense it constitutes a factor, and a relatively coherent factor. In time, our scientific evidence will show whether or not this is a reasonable assumption.

The first element in our definition of the modern man is his readiness for new experience and his openness to innovation and change. We consider the traditional man to be less disposed to accept new ideas, new ways of feeling and acting. We are speaking, therefore, of something that is itself a state of mind, a psychological disposition, an inner readiness, rather than of the specific techniques or skills a man or a group may possess because of the level of technology they have attained. Thus, in our sense, a man may be more modern in spirit, even though he works with a wooden plow, than someone in another part of the world who already drives a tractor. The readiness for new experience and ways of doing things, furthermore, may express itself in a variety of forms and contexts: in the willingness to adopt a new drug or sanitation method, to accept a new seed or try a different fertilizer, to ride on a new means of transportation or turn to a new source of news, to approve a new form of wedding or new type of schooling for young people.

Individuals and groups may, of course, show more readiness for the new in one area of life than another, but we can also conceive of the readiness to accept innovation as a more pervasive, general characteristic that makes itself felt across a wide variety of human situations. And we consider those who have this readiness to be more modern.

The second in our complex of themes takes us into the realm of opinion. We define a man as more modern if he has a disposition to form or mold opinions over a large number of the problems and issues that arise not only in his immediate environment but also outside of it. Some pioneering work on this dimension has been done by Daniel Lerner, of the Massachusetts Institute of Technology, who found that the individuals within any country, and the populations of different countries, in the Middle East varied greatly in their ability or readiness to imagine themselves in the position of prime minister or comparable government leader and thus to offer advice as to what should be done to resolve the problems facing the country. The more educated the individual and the more advanced the country, the greater was the readiness to offer opinions in response to this challenge. The more traditional man, we believe, takes an interest in fewer things, mainly those that touch him immediately and intimately; and even when he holds opinions on more distant matters, he is more circumspect in expressing them.

We also consider a man to be more modern if his orientation to the opinion realm is more democratic. We mean by this that he shows more awareness of the diversity of attitude and opinion around him, rather than closing himself off in the belief that everyone thinks alike and, indeed, just like him. The modern man is able to acknowledge differences of opinion without needing rigidly to deny differences out of fear that these will upset his own view of the world. He is also less likely to approach opinion in a strictly autocratic or hierarchical way. He does not automatically accept the ideas of those above him in the power hierarchy and reject the opinions of those whose status is markedly lower than his. We test these values by asking people whether it is proper to think differently from the village headman or other traditional leader and, at the other end, by inquiring as to whether the opinions of a man's wife or young son merit serious consideration when important public issues are being discussed. These questions prove to be a sensitive indicator in helping us to distinguish one man from another and, we believe, will be an important element in the final syndrome of modernity we shall delineate.

A third theme we deal with at some length is that of time. We view a man as more modern if he is oriented to the present or the future, rather than to the past. We consider him as more modern if he accepts fixed hours, that is to say, schedules of time, as something sensible and appropriate, or possibly even desirable, as against the man who thinks these fixed rules are something either bad or perhaps a necessity, but unfortunately also a pity. We also define a man as more modern if he is punctual, regular, and orderly in organizing his affairs. These things can be very complicated, and this is a good opportunity to point out that it is a mistake to assume that our measures of modernity differentiate between traditional and nontraditional people as they would ordinarily be defined. For example, the Maya Indians had a better sense of time than their Spanish conquerors and they preserve it to this day. The qualities we define as modern can, in fact, be manifested in a people who seem to be relatively unmodern when you consider the level of technology or the amount of power they have. We are talking about properties of the person, which in turn may be a reflection of the properties of a culture that could emerge in any time or place. Indeed, when I described this list to a friend of mine who is doing an extensive study of Greece, he said, "My goodness, you are talking about the ancient Greeks!" He said there were only two respects in which the Greeks did not fit our model of the modern man. And, of course, the Elizabethan Englishman would also fit the model. So, this concept is not limited to our time. "Modern" does not mean merely contemporary in our approach.

A fourth theme that we include in the definition is planning. The more modern man is oriented toward and involved in planning and organizing and believes in it as a way of handling life.

A fifth, and important, theme we call efficacy. The modern man is the one who believes that man can learn, in substantial degree, to dominate his environment in order to advance his own purposes and goals, rather than being dominated entirely by that environment. For example, a man who believes in efficacy is more likely to respond positively to the question, "Do you believe that some day men may be able to develop ways of controlling floods or preventing destructive storms?" The more efficacious man, even though in fact he has never seen a dam, would say, "Yes, I think that some day man could do that."

Sixth, an element we consider part of the modern complex and include in our set of themes is calculability. By our definition, the modern man is one who has more confidence that his world is calculable, that other people and institutions around him can be relied on to fulfill or meet their obligations and responsibilities. He does not agree that everything is determined either by fate or by the whims of particular qualities and characters of men. In other words, he believes in a reasonably lawful world under human control.

The seventh theme that we stress is dignity. The more modern man, we feel, is one who has more awareness of the dignity of others and more disposition to show respect for them. We feel this comes through very clearly in attitudes toward women and children.

The modern man has more faith in science and technology, even if in a fairly primitive way. This provides our eighth theme.

Ninth, we hold that modern man is a great believer in what we call, for this purpose, distributive justice. That is to say, he believes that rewards should be according to contribution, and not according to either whim or special properties of the person not related to his contribution.

You could easily extend this list; you could also divide some of these items into still others; but I think this will serve to give an idea of the complex of attitudes and values that we consider important in defining the modern man. We have chosen to emphasize these themes because we see them as intimately related to the individual's successful adjustment as a citizen of a modern industrial nation. They are qualities that we feel will contribute to making a man a more productive worker in his factory, a more effective citizen in his community, a more satisfied and satisfying husband and father in his home.

We must of course, acknowledge that the nine themes just described are not the only way to approach the definition of modernity. Although we have stressed certain themes that cut across numerous concrete realms of behavior, some students of the problem prefer to emphasize attitudes and behavior relating mainly to certain important institutional realms, such as birth control or religion. . . . For each of these realms, one can define a position that can be considered more modern and an attitude one can define as more traditional, although at times the process of definition becomes very complex.

There is, for example, a very widespread notion that people lose their religion merely because they leave the countryside and go to the city. As a matter of fact, exactly the contrary is very often the case. There are two forces that bring this about. In the first place, really to practice your religion well, you must be a reasonably well-composed, well-contained individual. The person who is emotionally disturbed neglects his social obligations and involvements. Despite the idyllic image that many people have of the countryside, the great majority of the world's peasants are in a state of culture shock produced not by modernity but by the hard conditions of rural life. When a man goes to the city, and especially if he secures a job in industry, he comes to have much more respect and becomes much more self-controlled. This makes it more feasible for him to practice his religion. He turns to things that he previously neglected in his effort just to hold himself together. He reintegrates himself, if you like, with the formal things around him, one of which is his religion.

The second factor that may contribute to facilitate religious practice in the city is economic. To practice your religion generally costs something. For example, you may have to buy candles. If there is a religious ceremony, usually the religious specialist who performs the ceremony must be given some kind of payment. Something is required of you. If you are living a sufficiently marginal existence as a peasant, this may be one of the costs you forgo. When you get to the city and earn a more stable and steady income, you may be more willing to underwrite these costs. So, on this issue we are actually taking a rather unorthodox position and predicting that our city workers are going to be more rather than less religious, if not in spirit at least in terms of performing their formal religious obligations.

So much for our conception of the qualities that make a man modern. What can we say about the forces that produce such a man, that most rapidly and effectively inculcate in a population those attitudes, values, needs, and ways of acting that better fit him for life in a modern society? Just as modernity seems to be defined not by any one characteristic, but by a complex of traits, so we find that no one social force, but rather a whole complex of influences, contributes to the transformation from traditional to modern man.

Within this complex of forces, however, one certainly assumes pre-eminence: namely, education. Almost all serious scientific investigations of the question have shown the individual's degree of modernity to rise with increases in the amount of education he has received. Some reservations must be introduced, of course, to qualify this statement. In many countries, the weakness of the nation's resources permits schooling to be only of very poor quality, and the pressures on the poorer people force the children to be quite irregular in their attendance. In a number of countries, it has been observed that if children can obtain only two or three years of schooling, and especially if they do so under conditions where their environment does not particularly reinforce or support the school, there the effects of education on modernization will be very modest indeed. Similarly, the degree of traditionalism of the school itself plays some role. Little or no change toward modernity is evident in the more traditional schools that devote themselves mainly to passing on religious practices or inculcating and preserving traditional lore and skills. This is a characteristic of schools not only at the primary level; it may apply to those offering nominally advanced education. The "finishing" schools for young ladies from polite society in the United States may be taken as an example. Allowing for reservations of this sort, we may still say that education, especially in schools emphasizing the more modern type of curriculum, seems to be the most powerful factor in developing a population more modern in its attitudes and values. This effect depends in part on the direct instruction provided, but we assume as well that the school as a social organization serves as a model of rationality, of the importance of technical competence, of the rule of objective standards of performance, and of the principle of distributive justice reflected in the grading system. All these models can contribute to shaping young people in the image of the modern man as we have described him.

There is little agreement as to the rank order of influences other than education that we see affecting the degree of modernization of individuals. Many analysts of the problem propose the urban environment as the next most important input. The city is itself a powerful new experience. It encourages, and indeed to some degree obliges, the individual to adopt many new ways of life. By exposing men to a variety of ways of living, a wide range of opinions and ideas, increased mobility, more complex resources of all kinds, it accelerates the process of change. At the same time, in the city the

prospect is greater that the individual will be relatively free from the obligations and constraints placed on him in the village by his extended kinship
ties, the village elders, and the tight community of his neighbors. These
structural differences free the individual to change; but, of course, they do
not in themselves guarantee that he will change in ways that make him more
modern. In many cities, there are powerful examples of rationality, of the use
of technology to master the physical demands of life, of rewards adjusted to
technical skill and competence, of the value of education, and of the guarantee of human dignity under law. But many great cities also provide powerful
lessons that run counter to these modernizing influences on every score. If
they breed a new type of man, they hardly make him in the image we have
called modern. In addition, under conditions of very rapid growth, the city is
often unable to absorb and integrate all the in-migrants, so that on the outer
edges or in the older districts of the city, huge slum communities may develop
in which people are in the city but not of it, cut off from many of its benefits
and from the modernizing influence of urban life.

One source of modernization which generally accompanies urbanization
but is also an independent influence is mass communication. Almost all studies
of the growth of individual modernization show that those who are more exposed to the media of mass communication have more modern attitudes. Since
such exposure, especially in the case of the newspaper, depends on literacy and
education, it is important to stress that the modernization effects of the mass
media can be shown to exert their influence within groups at almost any educational level. Of course, there remains the possibility that it is the man with modern attitudes who seeks out the mass media, rather than that the media make the
man modern, but there seems little reason to doubt that influence is at least
mutual. These media greatly enlarge the range of human experienec with which
the individual can have contact, even if only vicarious. They constantly present
and illustrate new tools, items of consumption, means of transportation, and
a myriad of new ways of doing things. They show examples of efficacious behavior of the most powerful kind in the building of dams, the taming of
floods, the irrigation of deserts, and even the conquest of space. They also
provide models of new values and standards of behavior, some of which are
far beyond the reach of most men, but many of which can be copied and do
influence behavior directly. As in the case of urban influences, we must
acknowledge that the media of communication can and often do carry mes-
sages that mainly reaffirm traditional values, beliefs, and ways of acting or
disseminate a concept of the new that is nevertheless not congruent with the
model of the modern man here described.

Another source of modernizing influence is the development of the
national state and its associated apparatus of government bureaucracy, political
parties and campaigns, military and paramilitary units, and the like. The more
mobilized the society, the more dedicated the government to economic development and spreading the ideology of progress, the more rapidly and widely
may we expect the attitudes and values of modernity to expand. Some of the

agencies of the state—in particular, the army—may play an especially important role in introducing men to the modern world, both in the direct instruction they offer and indirectly in the model of routine, scheduling, technical skill, and efficacy that inheres in many of their operations. Here again, however, we must acknowledge that the power of the state may also be used to reinforce more traditional values: politics may be conducted in a way that hardly sets an example of modern behavior, and armies may be run so as scarcely to induce a man to exert himself, to practice initiative, or to respect the dignity of others.

One last source of modernizing influence that we may cite . . . is the factory or other modern productive and administrative enterprise. Certain features of the modern factory are relatively invariant, and they communicate the same message, no matter what the cultural setting in which they may be installed. In them there is always an intense concentration of physical and mechanical power brought to bear on the transformation of raw materials; orderly and routine procedures to govern the flow of work are essential; time is a powerful influence in guiding the work process; power and authority generally rest on technical competence; and, as a rule, rewards are in rough proportion to performance. In addition, a factory guided by modern management and personnel policies will set its workers an example of rational behavior, emotional balance, open communication, and respect for the opinions, the feelings, and the dignity of the worker which can be a powerful example of the principles and practice of modern living.

In modern times we are experiencing a process of change affecting everything, yet controlled by no one. It is, in a sense, strictly spontaneous; yet it is in some ways the most strictly determined process history has yet known. Since no one can escape it, no one may be unconcerned with it. Man himself is being transformed. Many evils are being erased, but no end of new forms of corruption and wickedness may be loosed in the world. Some people in backward countries are ready to believe that any change is for the good. Others feel that much they now have is superior to what is being offered, and they are deeply convinced that many of the changes the contemporary world is introducing into their lives are no improvement, while others are positively disastrous. I have pointed to a set of qualities of mind that I call modern, which I believe have much to recommend them. They are not compatible in all respects with qualities that are widespread in traditional cultures, but I believe they are qualities men can adopt without coming into conflict, in most cases, with what is best in their cultural tradition and spiritual heritage. I believe they represent some of the best things in the modernization process. But whether we view them as positive or negative, we must recognize these qualities that are fostered by modern institutions, qualities that in many ways are required of the citizens of modern societies. We must, therefore, come to recognize them, to understand them, and to evaluate them as important issues in contemporary life.

The Horror of Modernization

R. D. LAING

Early in the modernization process, important intellectual criticism developed. Conservative intellectuals criticized excessive rationalism and individualism, which they believed endangered public order. By the later nineteenth century, attacks on modern values came even from intellectuals who were not politically conservative, but who thought that society was deteriorating as it moved away from traditional values. It was probably inevitable that many intellectuals would resent a society that placed so much emphasis on material achievement. The intellectuals' uncertainty about their own role in such a society encouraged criticism.

So intellectual attacks on modernity have a considerable history. They result in part from the impact of the modernization process on an articulate social group, which does not necessarily mean that they are biased or wrong.

R. D. Laing is a British psychoanalyst with a particular interest in schizophrenia. His training thus differs considerably from that of the sociologist Inkeles. Yet his list of the characteristics of modern man is by no means completely different. He agrees that modern man is new, that modern man claims rationality, and so on. But he views these attributes from a completely different perspective. It is possible, of course, that he is talking only about *some* modern people, not *all*, or about people only at certain times or in certain moods. But Laing does not think so. Like Inkeles, he finds it possible to describe modern man, period.

Laing places the development of modern education and family structure in the forefront of his attack. Above all, he contrasts modern values with those of the past, even though he does not describe the past in detail. Premodern man had faith and dreams. He could accept a creative madness. He was not alienated.

So in a sense we come full circle. Laing invites us to evaluate premodern as well as modern people. And if he is right that modern society has deteriorated, is this a cause for hope or despair? Are there values from the past that we should try to recover, and, given the enormous impact of modernization, do we have any hope of success if we do try?

Few books today are forgivable. Black on the canvas, silence on the screen, an empty white sheet of paper, are perhaps feasible. There is little conjunction of truth and social "reality." Around us are pseudo-events, to

From R. D. Laing, *The Politics of Experience* (London: Penguin Books, Ltd., 1967), pp. xi–xii, 15–26, 49–51, 53–55. © R. D. Laing, 1967. Reprinted by permission of Penguin Books Ltd.

which we adjust with a false consciousness adapted to see these events as true and real, and even as beautiful. In the society of men the truth resides now less in what things are than in what they are not. Our social realities are so ugly if seen in the light of exiled truth, and beauty is almost no longer possible if it is not a lie.

We live in a moment of history where change is so speeded up that we begin to see the present only when it is already disappearing.

It is difficult for modern man not to see the present in terms of the past. The white European and North American, in particular, commonly has a sense, not of renewal, but of being at an end: of being only half alive in the fibrillating heartland of a senescent civilization. Sometimes it seems that it is not possible to do more than reflect the decay around and within us, than sing sad and bitter songs of disillusion and defeat.

Yet that mood is already dated, at least insofar as it is not a perennial possibility of the human spirit. It entails a sense of time, which is already being dissolved in the instantaneous, stochastic, abrupt, discontinuous electronic cosmos, the dynamic mosaic of the electromagnetic field.

Nevertheless, the requirement of the present, the failure of the past, is the same: to provide a thoroughly self-conscious and self-critical human account of man.

No one can begin to think, feel or act now except from the starting point of his or her own alienation. We shall examine some of its forms in the following pages.

We are all murderers and prostitutes—no matter to what culture, society, class, nation, we belong, no matter how normal, moral, or mature we take ourselves to be.

Humanity is estranged from its authentic possibilities. This basic vision prevents us from taking any unequivocal view of the sanity of common sense, or of the madness of the so-called madman. However, what is required is more than a passionate outcry of outraged humanity.

Our alienation goes to the roots. The realization of this is the essential springboard for any serious reflection on any aspect of present interhuman life. Viewed from different perspectives, construed in different ways and expressed in different idioms, this realization unites men as diverse as Marx, Kierkegaard, Nietzsche, Freud, Heidegger, Tillich and Sartre.

More recent voices in the United States continue to document different facets of our fragmentation and alienation, whether it is the exposure of sham, the spatialization and quantification of experience or the massive economic irrationality of the whole system.

All such description is forced to describe what is, in the light of different modulations of what is not. What has been, what might have been, what should be or might be. Can we describe the present in terms of its becoming what it is not-yet—a term of Ernest Block's, so frightening, so ominous, so cataclysmic, that it is sometimes easier to see the present already darkened by the shadow of a thermonuclear apocalypse, than either to envisage further declensions from that from which our nostalgia absents us, or to see a redemptive dialectic immanent in the vortex of accelerating change.

At all events, we are bemused and crazed creatures, strangers to our true selves, to one another, and to the spiritual and material world—mad, even, from an ideal standpoint we can glimpse but not adopt.

We are born into a world where alienation awaits us. We are potentially men, but are in an alienated state, and this state is not simply a natural system. Alienation as our present destiny is achieved only by outrageous violence perpetrated by human beings on human beings. . . .

Even facts become fictions without adequate ways of seeing "the facts." We do not need theories so much as the experience that is the source of the theory. We are not satisfied with faith, in the sense of an implausible hypothesis irrationally held: we demand to experience the "evidence."

We can see other people's behavior, but not their experience. This has led some people to insist that psychology has nothing to do with the other person's experience, but only with his behavior.

The other person's behavior is an experience of mine. My behavior is an experience of the other. The task of social phenomenology is to relate my experience of the other's behavior to the other's experience of my behavior. Its study is the relation between experience and experience: its true field is *interexperience*.

I see you, and you see me. I experience you, and you experience me. I see your behavior. You see my behavior. But I do not and never have and never will see your *experience* of me. Just as you cannot "see" my experience of you. My experience of you is not "inside" me. It is simply you, as I experience you. And I do not experience you as inside me. Similarly, I take it that you do not experience me as inside you.

"My experience of you" is just another form of words for "you-as-I-experience-you," and "your experience of me" equals "me-as-you-experience-me." Your experience of me is not inside you and my experience of you is not inside me, but *your experience of me is invisible to me and my experience of you is invisible to you.*

I cannot experience your experience. You cannot experience my experience. We are both invisible men. All men are invisible to one another. Experience is man's invisibility to man. Experience used to be called the Soul. Experience as invisibility of man to man is at the same time more evident than anything. *Only* experience is evident. Experience is the *only* evidence. Psychology is the logos of experience. Psychology is the structure of the *evidence*, and hence psychology is the science of sciences.

If, however, experience is evidence, how can one ever study the experience *of the other?* For the experience *of the other* is not evident to me, as it is not and never can be an experience of mine.

I cannot avoid trying to understand your experience, because although I do not experience your experience, which is invisible to me (and nontastable, nontouchable, nonsmellable, and inaudible), yet I experience you as *experiencing*.

I do not experience your experience. But I experience you as experiencing. I experience myself as experienced by you. And I experience you as experiencing yourself as experienced by me. And so on.

The study of the experience of others is based on inferences I make, from my experience of you experiencing me, about how you are experiencing me experiencing you experiencing me. . . .

Social phenomenology is the science of my own and of others' experience. It is concerned with the relation between my experience of you and your experience of me. That is, with *interexperience*. It is concerned with your behavior and my behavior *as I experience it*, and your and my behavior *as you experience it*.

Since your and their experience is invisible to me as mine is to you and them, I seek to make evident to the others, through their experience of my behavior, what I infer of your experience, through my experience of your behavior.

This is the crux of social phenomenology.

Natural science is concerned only with the observer's experience of things. Never with the way things *experience us*. That is not to say that things do not react to us, and to each other.

Natural science knows nothing of the relation between behavior and experience. The nature of this relation is mysterious—in Marcel's sense. That is to say, it is not an objective problem. There is no traditional logic to express it. There is no developed method of understanding its nature. But this relation is the copula of our science—if science means *a form of knowledge adequate to its subject*. The relation between experience and behavior is the stone that the builders will reject at their peril. Without it the whole structure of our theory and practice must collapse.

Experience is invisible to the other. But experience is not "subjective" rather than "objective," not "inner" rather than "outer," not process rather than praxis, not input rather than output, not psychic rather than somatic, not some doubtful data dredged up from introspection rather than extrospection. Least of all is experience "intrapsychic process." Such transactions, object relations, interpersonal relations, transference, countertransference, as we suppose to go on between people are not the interplay merely of two objects in space, each equipped with ongoing intrapsychic processes.

This distinction between outer and inner usually refers to the distinction between behavior and experience; but sometimes it refers to some experiences that are supposed to be "inner" in contrast to others that are "outer." More accurately this is a distinction between different modalities of experience, namely, perception (as outer) in contrast to imagination, etc. (as inner). But perception, imagination, fantasy, reverie, dreams, memory, are simply different *modalities of experience*, none more "inner" or "outer" than any other.

Yet this way of talking does reflect a split in our experience. We seem to live in two worlds, and many people are aware only of the "outer" rump. As long as we remember that the "inner" world is not some space "inside" the body or the mind, this way of talking can serve our purpose. (It was good enough for William Blake.) The "inner," then, is our personal idiom of experiencing our bodies, other people, the animate and inanimate world: imagination, dreams, fantasy, and beyond that to ever further reaches of experience.

Bertrand Russell once remarked that the stars are in one's brain.

The stars as I perceive them are no more or less in my brain than the stars as I imagine them. I do not imagine them to be in my head, any more than I see them in my head.

The relation of experience to behavior is not that of inner to outer. My experience is not inside my head. My experience of this room is out there in the room.

To say that my experience is intrapsychic is to presuppose that there is a psyche that my experience is in. My psyche is my experience, my experience is my psyche.

Many people used to believe that angels moved the stars. It now appears that they do not. As a result of this and like revelations, many people do not now believe in angels.

Many people used to believe that the "seat" of the soul was somewhere in the brain. Since brains began to be opened up frequently, no one has seen "the soul." As a result of this and like revelations, many people do not now believe in the soul.

Who could suppose that angels move the stars, or be so superstitious as to suppose that because one cannot see one's soul at the end of a microscope it does not exist?

Interpersonal Experience and Behavior

Our task is both to experience and to conceive the concrete, that is to say, reality in its fullness and wholeness.

But this is quite impossible, immediately. Experientially and conceptually, we have fragments.

We begin from concepts of the single person, from the relations between two or more persons, from groups or from society at large; or from the material world, and conceive of individuals as secondary. We can derive the main determinants of our individual and social behavior from external exigencies. All these views are partial vistas and partial concepts. Theoretically we need a spiral of expanding and contracting schemata that enable us to move freely and without discontinuity from varying degrees of abstraction to greater or lesser degrees of concreteness. Theory is the articulated vision of experience. . . .

Can human beings be persons today? Can a man be his actual self with another man or woman? Before we can ask such an optimistic question as, "What is a personal relationship?," we have to ask if a personal relationship is possible, or, are persons possible in our present situation? We are concerned with the possibility of man. This question can be asked only through its facets. Is love possible? Is freedom possible?

Whether or not all, or some, or no human beings are persons, I wish to define a person in a twofold way: in terms of experience, as a center of orientation of the objective universe; and in terms of behavior, as the origin of actions. Personal experience transforms a given field into a field of intention and action: only through action can our experience be transformed. It is tempting and facile to regard "persons" as only separate objects in space, who can be studied as any other natural objects can be studied. But just as Kierkegaard remarked that one will never find consciousness by looking down a microscope at brain cells or anything else, so one will never find persons by studying persons as though they were only objects. A person is the me or you, he or she, whereby an object is experienced. Are these centers of experience and origins of actions living in entirely unrelated worlds of their own composition? Everyone must refer here to their own experience. My own experience as a center of experience and origin of action tells me that this is not so. My experience and my action occur in a social field of reciprocal influence and interaction. I experience myself, identifiable as Ronald Laing by myself and others, as experienced by and acted upon by others, who refer to that person I call "me" as "you" or "him," or grouped together as "one of us" or "one of them" or "one of you."

This feature of personal relations does not arise in the correlation of the behavior of nonpersonal objects. Many social scientists deal with their embarrassment by denying its occasion. Nevertheless, the natural scientific world is complicated by the presence of certain identifiable entities, re-identifiable reliably over periods of years, whose behavior is either the manifestation or a concealment of a view of the world equivalent in ontological status to that of the scientist.

People may be observed to sleep, eat, walk, talk, etc. in relatively predictable ways. We must not be content with observation of this kind alone. Observation of behavior must be extended by inference to attributions about experience. Only when we can begin to do this can we really construct the experiential-behavior system that is the human species.

It is quite possible to study the visible, audible, smellable effulgences of human bodies, and much study of human behavior has been in those terms. One can lump together very large numbers of units of behavior and regard them as a statistical population, in no way different from the multiplicity constituting a system of nonhuman objects. But one will not be studying persons. In a science of persons, I shall state as axiomatic that: behavior is a function of experience; and both experience and behavior are always in relation to someone or something other than self.

When two (or more) persons are in relation, the behavior of each towards the other is mediated by the experience by each of the other, and the experience of each is mediated by the behavior of each. There is no contiguity between the behavior of one person and that of the other. Much human behavior can be seen as a unilateral or bilateral *attempt* to eliminate experience. A person may treat another *as though* he were not a person, and he may act himself *as though* he were not a person. There is no contiguity between one person's experience and another's. My experience of you is always mediated through your *behavior*. Behavior that is the direct consequence of impact, as of one billiard ball hitting another, or experience directly transmitted to experience, as in the possible cases of extrasensory perception, is not personal.

Normal Alienation from Experience

The relevance of Freud to our time is largely his insight and, to a very considerable extent, his *demonstration* that the *ordinary* person is a shriveled, desiccated fragment of what a person can be.

As adults, we have forgotten most of our childhood, not only its contents but its flavor; as men of the world, we hardly know of the existence of the inner world: we barely remember our dreams, and make little sense of them when we do; as for our bodies, we retain just sufficient proprioceptive sensations to coordinate our movements and to ensure the minimal requirements for biosocial survival—to register fatigue, signals for food, sex, defecation, sleep; beyond that, little or nothing. Our capacity to think, except in the service of what we are dangerously deluded in supposing is our self-interest and in conformity with common sense, is pitifully limited: our capacity even to see, hear, touch, taste and smell is so shrouded in veils of mystification that an intensive discipline of unlearning is necessary for *anyone* before one can begin to experience the world afresh, with innocence, truth and love.

And immediate experience of, in contrast to belief or faith in, a spiritual realm of demons, spirits, Powers, Dominions, Principalities, Seraphim and Cherubim, the Light, is even more remote. As domains of experience become more alien to us, we need greater and greater open-mindedness even to conceive of their existence.

Many of us do not know, or even believe, that every night we enter zones of reality in which we forget our waking life as regularly as we forget our dreams when we awake. Not all psychologists know of fantasy as a modality of experience, and the, as it were, contrapuntal interweaving of different experiential modes. Many who are aware of fantasy believe that fantasy is the farthest that experience goes under "normal" circumstances. Beyond that are simply "pathological" zones of hallucinations, phantasmagoric mirages, delusions.

This state of affairs represents an almost unbelievable devastation of our experience. Then there is empty chatter about maturity, love, joy, peace.

This is itself a consequence of and further occasion for the divorce of our experience, such as is left of it, from our behavior.

What we call "normal" is a product of repression, denial, splitting, projection, introjection and other forms of destructive action on experience (see below). It is radically estranged from the structure of being.

The more one sees this, the more senseless it is to continue with generalized descriptions of supposedly specifically schizoid, schizophrenic, hysterical "mechanisms."

There are forms of alienation that are relatively strange to statistically "normal" forms of alienation. The "normally" alienated person, by reason of the fact that he acts more or less like everyone else, is taken to be sane. Other forms of alienation that are out of step with the prevailing state of alienation are those that are labeled by the "normal" majority as bad or mad.

The condition of alienation, of being asleep, of being unconscious, of being out of one's mind, is the condition of the normal man.

Society highly values its normal man. It educates children to lose themselves and to become absurd, and thus to be normal.

Normal men have killed perhaps 100,000,000 of their fellow normal men in the last fifty years.

Our behavior is a function of our experience. We act according to the way we see things.

If our experience is destroyed, our behavior will be destructive.

If our experience is destroyed, we have lost our own selves.

How much human *behavior*, whether the interactions between persons themselves or between groups and groups, is intelligible in terms of human *experience?* Either our interhuman behavior is unintelligible, in that we are simply the passive vehicles of inhuman processes whose ends are as obscure as they are at present outside our control, or our own behavior towards each other is a function of our own experience and our own intentions, however alienated we are from them. In the latter case, we must take final responsibility for what we make of what we are made of.

We will find no intelligibility in behavior if we see it as an inessential phase in an essentially inhuman process. We have had accounts of men as animals, men as machines, men as biochemical complexes with certain ways of their own, but there remains the greatest difficulty in achieving a human understanding of man in human terms.

Men at all times have been subject, as they believed or experienced, to forces from the stars, from the gods, or to forces that now blow through society itself, appearing as the stars once did to determine human fate.

Men have, however, always been weighed down not only by their sense of subordination to fate and chance, to ordained external necessities or contingencies, but by a sense that their very own thoughts and feelings, in their most intimate interstices, are the outcome, the resultant, of processes which they undergo.

A man can estrange himself from himself by mystifying himself and others. He can also have what he does stolen from him by the agency of others.

If we are stripped of experience, we are stripped of our deeds; and if our deeds are, so to speak, taken out of our hands like toys from the hands of children, we are bereft of our humanity. We cannot be deceived. Men can and do destroy the humanity of other men, and the condition of this possibility is that we are interdependent. We are not self-contained monads producing no effects on each other except our reflections. We are both acted upon, changed for good or ill, by other men; and we are agents who act upon others to affect them in different ways. Each of us is the other to the others. Man is a patient-agent, agent-patient, interexperiencing and interacting with his fellows.

It is quite certain that unless we can regulate our behavior much more satisfactorily than at present, then we are going to exterminate ourselves. But as we experience the world, so we act, and this principle holds even when action conceals rather than discloses our experience.

We are not able even to *think* adequately about the behavior that is at the annihilating edge. But what we think is less than what we know; what we know is less than what we love; what we love is so much less than what there is. And to that precise extent we are so much less than what we are.

Yet if nothing else, each time a new baby is born there is a possibility of reprieve. Each child is a new being, a potential prophet, a new spiritual prince, a new spark of light precipitated into the outer darkness. Who are we to decide that it is hopeless? . . .

It is not enough to destroy one's own and other people's experience. One must overlay this devastation by a false consciousness inured, as Marcuse puts it, to its own falsity.

Exploitation must not be seen as such. It must be seen as benevolence. Persecution preferably should not need to be invalidated as the figment of a paranoid imagination; it should be experienced as kindness. Marx described mystification and showed its function in his day. Orwell's time is already with us. The colonists not only mystify the natives, in the ways that Fanon so clearly shows, they have to mystify themselves. We in Europe and North America are the colonists, and in order to sustain our amazing images of ourselves as God's gift to the vast majority of the starving human species, we have to interiorize our violence upon ourselves and our children and to employ the rhetoric of morality to describe this process.

In order to rationalize our industrial-military complex, we have to destroy our capacity to see clearly any more what is in front of, and to imagine what is beyond, our noses. Long before a thermonuclear war can come about, we have had to lay waste our own sanity. We begin with the children. It is imperative to catch them in time. Without the most thorough and rapid brainwashing their dirty minds would see through our dirty tricks. Children are not yet fools, but we shall turn them into imbeciles like ourselves, with high I.Q.s if possible.

From the moment of birth, when the Stone Age baby confronts the twentieth-century mother, the baby is subjected to these forces of violence, called love, as its mother and father, and their parents and their parents before them, have been. These forces are mainly concerned with destroying most of its potentialities, and on the whole this enterprise is successful. By the time the new human being is fifteen or so, we are left with a being like ourselves, a half-crazed creature more or less adjusted to a mad world. This is normality in our present age.

Love and violence, properly speaking, are polar opposites. Love lets the other be, but with affection and concern. Violence attempts to constrain the other's freedom, to force him to act in the way we desire, but with ultimate lack of concern, with indifference to the other's own existence or destiny.

We are effectively destroying ourselves by violence masquerading as love.

I am a specialist, God help me, in events in inner space and time, in experiences called thoughts, images, reveries, dreams, visions, hallucinations, dreams of memories, memories of dreams, memories of visions, dreams of hallucinations, refractions of refractions of refractions of that original Alpha and Omega of experience and reality, that Reality on whose repression, denial, splitting, projection, falsification, and general desecration and profanation our civilization as much as on anything is based.

We live equally out of our bodies and out of our minds.

Concerned as I am with this inner world, observing day in and day out its devastation, I ask why this has happened?

One component of an answer . . . is that we can *act* on our *experience* of ourselves, others and the world, as well as take action on the world through behavior itself. Specifically this devastation is largely the work of *violence* that has been perpetrated on each of us, and by each of us on ourselves. The usual name that much of this violence goes under is *love*.

We act on our experience at the behest of the others, just as we learn how to behave in compliance with them. We are taught what to experience and what not to experience, as we are taught what movements to make and what sounds to emit. A child of two is already a moral mover and moral talker and moral experiencer. He already moves the "right" way, makes the "right" noises, and knows what he should feel and what he should not feel. His movements have become stereometric types, enabling the specialist anthropologist to identify, through his rhythm and style, his national, even his regional, characteristics. As he is taught to move in specific ways out of the whole range of possible movements, so he is taught to experience out of the whole range of possible experience. . . .

If human beings are not studied as human beings, then this once more is violence and mystification.

In much contemporary writing on the individual and the family there is assumed some not-too-unhappy confluence, not to say pre-established harmony, between nature and nurture. Some adjustments may have to be made on both sides, but all things work together for good to those who want only security and identity.

Gone is any sense of possible tragedy, of passion. Gone is any language of joy, delight, passion, sex, violence. The language is that of a boardroom. No more primal scenes, but parental coalitions; no more repression of sexual ties to parents, but the child "rescinds" its Oedipal wishes. For instance:

> The mother can properly invest her energies in the care of the young child when economic support, status, and protection of the family are provided by the father. She can also better limit her cathexis of the child to maternal feelings when her wifely needs are satisfied by her husband.

Here is no nasty talk of sexual intercourse or even "primal scene." The economic metaphor is aptly employed. The mother "invests" in her child. What is most revealing is the husband's function. The provision of economic support, status and protection, in that order.

There is frequent reference to security, the esteem of others. What one is supposed to want, to live for, is "gaining pleasure from the esteem and affection of others." If not, one is a psychopath.

Such statements are in a sense true. They describe the frightened, cowed, abject creature that we are admonished to be, if we are to be normal— offering each other mutual protection from our own violence. The family as a "protection racket."

Behind this language lurks the terror that is behind all this mutual back-scratching, this esteem-, status-, support-, protection-, security-giving and getting. Through its bland urbanity the cracks still show.

In our world we are "victims burning at the stake, signaling through the flames," but for some, things go blandly on. "Contemporary life requires adaptability." We require also to "utilize intellect," and we require "an emotional equilibrium that permits a person to be malleable, to adjust himself to others without fear of loss of identity with change. It requires a basic trust in others, and a confidence in the integrity of the self."

Sometimes there is a glimpse of more honesty. For instance, when we "consider society rather than the individual, each society has a vital interest in the *indoctrination* of the infants who form its new *recruits*."

What these authors say may be written ironically, but there is no evidence that it is.

Adaptation to what? To society? To a world gone mad?

The family's function is to repress Eros; to induce a false consciousness of security; to deny death by avoiding life; to cut off transcendence; to believe in God, not to experience the Void; to create, in short, one-dimensional man; to promote respect, conformity, obedience; to con children out of play; to induce a fear of failure; to promote a respect for work; to promote a respect for "respectability."